THE POLITICS OF HUNGER

The Politics of Hunger

The Global Food System

JOHN W. WARNOCK

METHUEN
Toronto   New York   London   Sydney   Auckland

Canadian Cataloguing in Publication Data

Warnock, John W., 1933–
  The politics of hunger

Includes index.
ISBN 0-458-80630-7

1. Food supply.   2.   Hunger.   3. Agriculture and
politics.   I. Title.

HD 9000.5.W37 1987   338.1'9   C86-094368-2

Library of Congress Cataloguing-in-Publication Data

Warnock, John W., 1933–
  The politics of hunger

Includes index.
1. Food supply—Developing countries.   2.   Agriculture
—Economic aspects—Developing countries.   3.   Hunger
I. Title

HD 9018.D44W37   1987   363.8'09172'4   87-1659

ISBN 0-458-80630-7 (PBK.)

British Library Cataloguing in Publication Data

Warnock, John W.
  The politics of hunger: the global food system
  1. Food supply—Political aspects
  I. Title.
  338.1'9   HD9000.6

ISBN 0-458-80630-7

COVER DESIGN: Fortunato Aglialoro
TEXT DESIGN: Brant Cowie/Artplus
COVER PHOTOGRAPH: CARE Photo by Rudolph von Bernuth

Printed and bound in Canada

1 2 3 4   87   91 90 89 88

To the memory of John Wilson Warnock and his family and the other victims of the Great Famine who fled Ireland for the New World, and of those who were not so fortunate.

Contents

Preface

The world re-discovered hunger in the mid-1980s. Hardly a week went by without the media dramatically reporting a major crisis in one country or another.

In Brazil in 1983 and 1984 there were numerous food riots, and the looting of supermarkets and government food warehouses became a regular affair. In Chile the demonstrations against the Pinochet dictatorship increasingly stressed the need for food for the growing numbers of unemployed and hungry people. Peru's United Left (IU) coalition shocked western governments, in October 1983, by electing the mayor of Lima on a platform that attacked the national administration's "policy of hunger" and promised one million breakfasts daily to Lima's poor children.

In April 1984 troops battled rioters for two days in the Dominican Republic protesting price increases of up to 50% on basic foods. One month later, in Haiti, troops had to be called out to halt rioting after it was revealed that essential CARE foods were being diverted from the poor to the black market. Bolivian trade unions called a 72-hour general strike in May to protest a 75% devaluation of the peso and large increases in food prices. In the fall of 1984 political unrest in Jamaica forced Prime Minister Edward Seaga to promise a food stamp and school lunch program to feed the estimated one-half of the island's population that was suffering from food shortages and hunger.

In January 1984 around 100 people were killed and 3,000 were arrested in Tunisia during seven days of rioting and protest over the government's decision to double the price of bread. The price was rolled back. Next door, in Morocco, more than 100 people were killed in riots, after rumours were spread that King Hassan planned similar sharp increases in food prices. The King changed his mind. After one day of rioting in October, the government of Egypt rolled back price increases for macaroni and cooking oil and promised to restore the size of the standard subsidized loaf of bread, the staple food item for the poor majority.

By the end of 1984 many people began to refer to the new "urban famine" in both the poor and the middle-income underdeveloped countries.

In many cases the increase in food prices was due to austerity programs imposed by western banks trying to collect interest on their loans. The terms for renegotiation of foreign debts were often set by the International Monetary Fund, and the riots were often referred to as the "IMF riots."

While the debt crisis dominated the attention of the media throughout 1982, by the beginning of 1983 the drought and famine in Africa began to attract notice. The devaluation of local currencies, caused primarily by the debt crisis, raised the price of food for a population already suffering from chronic undernutrition. In June 1983 the director of relief for the Food and Agricultural Organization of the United Nations (FAO) reported that famine threatened eighteen African countries. The following October, representatives of twenty-two African countries met with the FAO to detail their food assistance needs for the upcoming year.

The tenth session of the World Food Council (WFC) met in Addis Ababa, Ethiopia, in June 1984, and concentrated on the African famine. The Director of the WFC called on member countries to increase their food aid pledges to $1 billion to meet the growing crisis. But this was opposed by the delegates from the United States, Canada, West Germany, and Japan who argued that the donor countries had not even met their existing levels of commitment. Representatives from the recipient countries concluded that, while food aid was essential in times of crisis, the real solution would have to come from increased food self-sufficiency. In contrast, the delegate from the United States reiterated the Reagan Administration's opposition to food self-sufficiency and continued commitment to the principle of producing food for the international market.

The representatives of African governments held a meeting in July at Harare, Zimbabwe, to deal with the food crisis. They chose to reject the policy position of the U.S. government, the International Monetary Fund (IMF), and the World Bank, who insisted that African states concentrate on producing agricultural crops for export. Thirty countries signed a declaration pledging themselves to put a higher priority on producing their own food. But there was no magic cure for the growing famine.

Suddenly, in the late fall of 1984, television (and therefore the world) "discovered" that there were hundreds of thousands of people actually dying of starvation in Africa. Although it was widely known that the famine was serious in at least twenty-four countries, media and public attention was focused on one country, Ethiopia. Hunger was back on the political agenda.

But hunger is not just a Third World problem. In December 1982 the United States Conference of Mayors reported that, of 55 American cities surveyed, the majority identified food as "the emergency service most in demand." A follow-up survey of eight of the largest U.S. cities in June 1983 concluded that, although there were several emergency problems facing urban centres, hunger was "probably the most prevalent and the most insidious." In a special report prepared for the U.S. Conference of City Human Services Officials in October 1983, the mayors argued that, despite "extraordinary efforts" to feed the needy, "the gap between the demand for assistance and local public and private resources available to meet that demand continued to widen."

While world public attention began to focus on famine, food shortages and widespread hunger, the U.S. government introduced a major program to pay farmers not to grow grain. The Canadian Grains Council likewise warned farmers that prices for wheat would continue to be low because of the "glut" on the world market. Meanwhile, the European Economic Community (EEC) was facing a crisis trying to decide what to do with its food surpluses. Obviously, there is something fundamentally wrong with the world's system of production and distribution of food.

On a world-wide basis we know that there is no food shortage. In 1985 world grain reserve stocks were at a peak of 190 million metric tonnes. Total world grain production in the 1983/4 crop year was estimated at 1,612 million metric tonnes. That alone was more than enough to provide every man, woman, and child in the world with 3,000 calories and 65 grams of protein per day. Over the past forty years, world food supplies have been steadily increasing at a rate of around 2.5% per annum. Furthermore, this period has seen a steady decline in real food prices. On the other hand, the amount of arable land available on a per-capita basis shrank by about 35%. The result is greater dependence on energy-based inputs in agricultural and fishery production. At the same time, the number of countries depending on food imports has greatly increased.

The reader will note that I have dedicated this book to the memory of my great-great-grandfather, John Wilson Warnock, who, with his family, fled Ireland during the Great Famine in the spring of 1846. They had little to lose. They were tenant farmers at Dunfanaghy, County Donegal, on land owned by A.J. Stewart of Ards, growing flax. The land was part of the Ulster Plantation, taken from the Irish in the early part of the 17th century. The western counties of Donegal, Mayo, and Kerry were hardest hit by the potato blight, and the tenant farmers there were the most dependent on the potato for food.

The issues raised by the Irish famine are the same issues that are raised today. The potato was introduced into Ireland around 1588. As it required less land and labour than grains, it appeared to be a defence against famine. But Ireland was not an independent country; it was England's first colony. Under British rule, by the early 18th century all farmland had been confiscated from the Irish and had been granted to Protestant landlords, 70% of whom were non-resident. In the 19th century, Ireland was a major exporter of food to Great Britain: wheat, barley, oats, flour, cattle, pork, bacon, ham, eggs, poultry, etc. The landlord's rent, paid in kind, was high, taking all of the commercial crops; the tenant farmers were allocated a small parcel of land on which they grew potatoes for survival.

At the time of the first major famine (1739), the population of Ireland was just over 2 million; around 300,000 died. The census of 1841 recorded over 8 million people, of whom 5.5 million (69%) were totally dependent on agriculture. Farms were very small; 48% were under one acre, and another 45% were between one and five acres. The tenant farmers cultivated the potato out of sheer necessity. Given their small subsistence plots, no other food could get them through the year.

The blight first appeared in the autumn of 1845; the harvest of 1846 was a disaster. There were crop failures in Europe as well; the governments there prohibited the export of food. In contrast, all during the Irish famine enormous amounts of food were shipped in British vessels to the imperial country—under heavy military guard. The starving farmers and their families continued to allocate all of their cash crops to the landlords; to "eat the rent" would mean eviction from the land and almost certain death by starvation.

The results are well known. Within ten years 2 million people starved to death and another two million emigrated. Labour became Ireland's major export, and its population today is still only around one-half of what it was in 1841.

Some who have studied the Great Famine blame the tragedy on reliance on one variety of potato, which was susceptible to disease. In the Andes, the Incas grew over fifty varieties of potato, and carefully selected disease-resistant varieties from their stockpile of wild resources. Agrologists have told me that the Irish famine could not occur today, because the use of fungicides would control the blight. Ecologists blame it on the high population that exceeded the carrying capacity of the land. But today's mainstream economists point out that the population of Japan greatly exceeds the carrying capacity of the islands and argue that Ireland's problem in 1846 was the lack of economic development that could have provided alternative employment and the ability to purchase adequate food from abroad. Some insist that if the landlord system had been abolished, farm families would have been able to consume the food that they were actually producing. But this assumes that, if Ireland had been an independent country, the Irish system of landlord-tenant farming would have been either abolished or very different. It is for good reason that the Irish have traditionally blamed the Great Famine on British colonial policy. The imperial country was to be the industrial power, the colonies were to feed it and keep it supplied with raw material.

But the Irish famine was also a major test of Adam Smith's theory of laissez-faire, or the free market. As Cecil Woodham-Smith points out in her classic study of the famine, almost every politician at that time, Whig or Tory, embraced this classical economic theory with religious fervour:

individuals should be allowed to pursue their own self interests; private property in the means of production was sacred; the landlord must be free to charge the rent the market would bear. In this instance, the British government was not to interfere in the legitimate commerce of selling Irish food and agricultural products to the highest bidders.

Under political pressure to do something about the famine, Robert Peel bought some Indian corn (maize) from the United States. This was justified on the ground that there was no existing market or trade in maize, as it was not valued by either the Irish or the English. But instead of using the maize to replace the blighted potato crop, Peel kept it in reserve, releasing part of it on the market from time to time to keep grain prices down. Some of the taxes collected in Ireland were allocated by the British government for public works in Ireland. But they could not be used to bring additional "waste" land into production; the law decreed that these funds could only be used for projects having to do with the infrastructure, roads, bridges, piers, etc., deemed to be "unproductive," and so not in competition with private enterprise. Sir Charles Trevelyan, Lord of the Treasury, reflecting the prevailing ideology of the day, insisted that trade and legitimate profit would be "paralyzed" if the government were to provide free food for the starving peoples of Ireland.

This book examines the major questions raised by the Irish famine. Why do hunger and poverty persist in a world of plenty? What are the prospects for more egalitarian development? I have not attempted to review the history of development and industrialization in general; instead, I have tried to focus on the role played by the food and agricultural sector in the process. Yet it is impractical to try to separate agriculture from development in general, because agriculture is the first economy of any nation.

Why is there such a gap in standards of living between the low income countries and the industrialized world, both capitalist and state socialist? Inevitably, the question arises as to the relation of colonialism to "late development" in former colonies. Did imperialism really end with the dismantling of colonialism in the period after World War II? Does "free trade" really benefit all countries equally, as David Ricardo said and his followers insist?

Most studies on the world food question either concentrate on production and distribution or on ecological issues. I have addressed the problem of hunger from both perspectives. While at the present time the world is primarily concerned with the question of more equitable distribution, there is growing concern about the sustainability of the food production system in the long run. As we become more dependent on fossil fuel subsidies in agricultural production, we must also confront the reality of the unequal distribution and control of such key resources. These issues are raised in Chapters 7 through 9. It is hoped that this book will help bridge the ideological gap between the two basic schools of thought.

One of the most dominant characteristics of the world is the uneven level of development: between continents, nation states, and regions. In the past the former colonies were described as "backward areas." In the more recent past they were lumped together as part of the "Third World," as distinguished from the first world, the industrialized capitalist countries, and the second world, the industrialized state socialist countries. International agencies use the terms "developing" and "less developed." Most recently the term "Fourth World" has been used to describe the thirty-five countries classified as "low income" by the World Bank. For the most part I have adopted the use of the term "underdeveloped," despite the controversy over its use in development theory. It seems to be the best term available. Underdevelopment does not indicate lack of development. Nor does it necessarily connote immiseration. Like the concept of poverty, it expresses a comparative phenomenon. Underdevelopment exists only in relation to more advanced development.

The other controversial concept is the term "development" itself. For the most part, economists equate this with economic growth, usually measured in per capita gross national product. For many writers and political activists working in this area, however, development is seen as something more than just economic growth. For development to be occurring, there must be an expansion of those things which are required for survival, such as food, clothing, shelter, health, and education. But from this *moral perspective*, development must also include full employment, greater equality, and the full range of 20th century political rights.

I might illustrate the complexities of the question of development and underdevelopment by referring again to Ireland and the comments of those keen observers of the time, Karl Marx and Frederick Engels. Marx and Engels were very conscious of Ireland and the Irish question. They saw that racism against Irish immigrants was splitting the British working class, and that the British government and ruling classes were using nationalism to denigrate the Irish and to rally support for their own oppressive policies. In 1867 Marx noted that "every time Ireland was just about to develop herself industrially, she was 'smashed down' and forced back into a mere 'agricultural country'." He documented the outflow of capital to the British landlords and the treasury. In 1870 he wrote of the problems of underdevelopment in Ireland, which he attributed to the "domination of England over Ireland." He counselled that what the Irish needed to begin development was (1) independence from Britain; (2) an agrarian revolution; and (3) protective tariffs against English industrial goods. Engels started to write a history of Ireland, but never finished the work. He wrote to Marx in 1869, concluding that "Irish history shows one what a misfortune it is for a nation to have subjugated another nation." Later he wrote that "the more I study the subject the clearer it is to me that Ireland has been stunted in its development by the English invasion and thrown centuries back." Those themes are explored in Chapters 3 through 5 of this book, where I examine the role of agriculture in economic development and the impact of mercantilism and colonialism on the "backward" areas of Latin America, Africa, and Asia. In Chapters 10 and 11 I examine the more recent experiences of "growth with equity" in newly industrializing capitalist countries and post-revolutionary socialist countries.

The approach I have used in this work is that of political economy, commonly identified as interdisciplinary social science. Scientific political economy originated with Adam Smith and David Ricardo. However, in the 19th century, following industrial capitalism's rise to power in Great Britain, political economy degenerated into apologetics, rationalizing and defending the existing order. In this form it was harshly criticized by Marx and Engels. More recently, political economy has become associated with radical social science as it once again addresses the questions of the accumulation of capital; the role of labour in production; the class, gender, and racial divisions in society; the role of government and political movements; and imperialism. In contrast to orthodox economics and social science in general, it recognizes the evolution of societies and the historic specificity of theories like "free trade." In dealing with complex issues like hunger and development, it is also necessary to be familiar with basic scientific and ecological concepts. Marx and Engels revived that tradition.

The research and writing of this book has been greatly aided by many friends and colleagues. I would especially like to thank those who have read and commented on all or part of the manuscript: Betty Andrews, Harold Bronson, Bill Carroll, John Garson, Phyllis Hopkinson, Frances Moore Lappé, John McConnell, Don Mitchell, Terry Padgam, and Bob Stirling. Of course, I am fully responsible for the text as it appears. I would also like to thank the staff at the libraries at the University of Victoria, the University of British Columbia, and Simon Fraser University, for their very helpful support. Finally, I would like to thank the Boag Foundation of Vancouver for the grant that permitted me to use a word processor while preparing the manuscript. Recognition should go to freelance editor Lorraine Fairley and to Kate Forster, Anita Miecznikowski, and Peter Milroy at Methuen, all of whom gave important editorial assistance in the preparation of the manuscript.

John W. Warnock
Victoria, May 15, 1986

CHAPTER ONE

The Persistence
of Hunger

Malnutrition is found in all societies. Most commonly it is identified with the poor in underdeveloped countries. In the early 1980s, the mass media dramatically brought us the picture of hunger from Africa—starving children, skin and bone, with their bloated bellies, too weak to even stand up. People in the industrialized western countries responded with an outpouring of funds for famine relief. But the persistent malnutrition experienced by people living in poverty in other areas of the world was largely ignored.

Malnutrition is not limited to those who are forced to exist on inadequate diets; it is also found among those who suffer from excessive consumption. (Eckholm and Record, 1976). The diet of the advanced industrialized countries brings an increase of cancer and heart disease. (Burkitt, 1976; Ackerman, 1972; Prior, 1971.) As Malcolm Caldwell has argued, this is a problem of "overdevelopment," and it is not limited to the rich or the advanced capitalist states, but is also found in the industrialized state socialist countries. But, for these people, malnutrition is a matter of lifestyle and poses a less serious problem. (Caldwell, 1977:98-138) Our concern must be with the persistence of malnutrition among those who are unable to get enough to eat.

In its early years the Food and Agricultural Organization of the United Nations (FAO) used the term "undernutrition" to indicate an inadequate intake of calories. The term "malnutrition" was used to describe the lack or deficiency of other basic requirements, particularly protein, vitamins, or minerals. (Poleman, 1983:47) When speaking of nutrition in underdeveloped countries, it is common to concentrate on lack of calories. But Coluther Gopolan, Director of the Nutrition Foundation of India, insists that deficiencies in major nutrients contribute very significantly to undernutrition, and warns that political concentration on the number of calories leads to the assumption that "malnutrition" is of minor concern. (Gopolan, 1983a:591) For the purposes of this study, I have used the term "undernutrition" to describe a deficient diet, whether it derives from a shortage of calories, protein, or other nutrients.

The most common problem in underdeveloped countries today is marasmus, severe chronic undernutrition in children and infants caused by a deficiency in energy. Children of undernourished mothers normally are born with less weight than is normal, and need more than normal nutrition. The most serious effect of early marasmus is impaired growth, particularly brain growth. Marasmus in children results in a reduced number of brain cells and overall brain size.

The other major problem is kwashiorkor, the deficiency of certain amino acids found in protein. This form of malnutrition is often found in areas of the world where the staple foods of the poorer people are either starchy roots or plantains. Where the staple food is a cereal, and adequate intake is available, there is rarely a problem of protein deficiency. However, kwashiorkor can be found where cereals are the staple but where consumption is inadequate. In this case the body consumes the needed protein as energy.

Protein is essential for the growth and development of all body tissues. During digestion, proteins are broken down into amino acids. The body requires 22 amino acids; all but eight of these are produced by the body itself. Thus the eight "essential amino acids" must be supplied by the diet. However, for protein synthesis to occur, all eight must be present at the same time and in the proper proportions. Here Liebig's Law of the Minimum applies: the amino acids present will be utilized for body development only to the level of the lowest one present; the surplus will be burned as energy or excreted from the body. Most of the staple foods we consume are deficient in at least one amino acid, referred to as "the limiting amino acid" (LAA). Nutritionists refer to "net protein utilization" (or NPU) in classifying certain sources of protein, based on the balance of amino acids.

The term "higher quality" protein is also commonly used. This refers to the fact that certain protein sources have a high level of amino acids, in a good balance, and thus have a high NPU rating. Some of these include eggs, dairy products, and fish, which have an NPU rating of 75% or above. Because red meats and poultry concentrate nutrients, they supply a high percentage of limiting amino acids. In contrast, cereals are often described as "low quality proteins," because they all are relatively deficient in one or more of the essential amino acids. For example, wheat is low in lysine and theonine, rice in methionine, and maize in lysine and tryptophan.

Where fish, meat, or dairy products are in short supply or too expensive to buy, it is essential to supplement the staple grain with other food sources that balance the amino acids. For example, in Latin America maize and rice are balanced with beans, in the Caribbean rice is balanced with peas, in China rice is balanced with soya, in India wheat and rice are balanced with pulses, and in the Middle East wheat is eaten with cheese.

The B vitamins are essential to human development, and it is widely recognized that they should be consumed together. Most of them are present in adequate amounts in whole grain cereals. However, vitamin B12 is only available in meats, eggs, and dairy products; it is not present in plant foods. Nutritionists agree that this vitamin is necessary in small amounts for proper body growth.

Poor people generally have limited diets. Often they do not have access to high quality proteins. If they are also denied a mix of foods to provide all the essential amino acids, to acquire adequate protein they must consume additional amounts of the staple cereal. Yet very often this is not possible.

Undernutrition is not limited to insufficient protein or calories. The lack of key vitamins and minerals in a diet can lead to common diseases. Lack of vitamin A, or carotene, can lead to blindness; it is a serious problem where lower income classes have only limited access to fresh vegetables, or to fish liver oil or dairy products, its major sources. Where vitamin D is lacking, it can lead to rickets among infants and children. It is found in high altitudes and in urban slums where exposure to sunlight is limited. Lack of milk or eggs is also a common cause.

Scurvy (lack of vitamin C) is found where a diet is deficient in fruits and vegetables. Among infants it can occur in those under one year of age who have not been breast fed. Niacin is very important for the body when diets are heavy in sugar and starches. Pellagra (niacin deficiency) is found in societies where there is heavy reliance on maize, sorghum, or millet as a staple food, all of which are low in the amino acid, tryptophan. Milk consumption has been the traditional cure for pellagra.

Lack of thiamin (Vitamin B1) can result in beri-beri, which was once known as the "scourge of the East." Though it is found in the husks of cereals, it is removed in milling and refining. Thus, cultures that are dependent on polished rice have had a history of beri-beri. Thiamin is essential for the normal metabolism of refined sugar and starches.

A common problem in underdeveloped countries is iron-deficiency anemia, in which the amount of hemoglobin in red blood cells is reduced. Iron is found in eggs, meat, pulses, and whole grains. In tropical countries, anemia is also produced through blood loss caused by intestinal parasites, or where certain vegetables are eaten that interfere with iron availability. Other common problems of undernutrition include vitamin K deficiency in infants, riboflavin deficiency, and endemic goitre. (Last, 1980:1474-1484; Scrimshaw and Young, 1976; Kirschmann, 1975; Pyke, 1970:110-127)

There is a close relationship between undernutrition and health problems, particularly infectious diseases. There is a decrease in intestinal absorption of nutrients when diarrheal diseases are present. The body's stress response to infectious diseases results in an increase in the excretion of nitrogen, vitamin A, vitamin C, zinc, and other nutrients. Thus, a sick person needs additional nutrition over and above what is required by a normal healthy person. It is not surprising to find that infectious diseases are often accompanied by nutritional anemia.

In low-income areas, once the protective effect of breast milk diminishes, a child is often exposed to infectious diseases like measles, chicken pox, and whooping cough which, combined with a low nutrient intake, can result in poor health and development. If diarrhea develops, growth is even more stunted, and death can occur.

The human body fights infectious diseases by the formation of antibodies. It is now well known that deficiencies in protein, vitamin A, vitamin C, thiamine, riboflavin, pyridoxine, folic acid, vitamin B12, and iron interfere with normal antibody formation. The immune system acts through the development of T-cells and B-cells whose production varies according to the availability of essential nutrients. The reduction of these cells has been linked to decreased resistance to infection among those suffering from mild to moderate undernutrition. (Last, 1980:1484-1490)

It is well established that in the underdeveloped countries there is a close and even synergistic relationship between undernutrition and infectious diseases. (See Gopolan and Rao, 1984; Delgado et al, 1983; Chossudovsky, 1983; Escudero, 1978; Field and Levinson, 1974) While governments are often willing to spend considerable sums curing infectious diseases, they are much more reluctant to finance the major preventative measure—the reduction of undernutrition. From a political perspective, it is much easier for governments in capitalist countries to expand in the area of medical services. Getting involved in the area of distribution of food is much more difficult, because it requires a move into the economic area and may infringe upon the accumulation of private capital.

The effects of undernutrition on human beings are well known. The Institute of Nutrition of Central America and Panama (INCAP) points out that male agricultural workers in tropical developing areas are known for "their small size, leanness, slow working pace, and, in the lowlands, often their pallor." They are often described as "lazy, inefficient workers" who find it extremely difficult to participate in normal after-work activities; but this is due to lack of food energy and to chronic iron-deficiency anemia. (Viteri, 1974:87)

Coluther Gopolan, Director of the Nutrition Foundation of India, describes chronic undernutrition in his country: "there is a broad twilight zone of morbidity, functional impairment of various kinds, apathy, lack of sense of well-being, poor physical stamina and low productivity." (Claiborne, 1983) While the lack of mental development is a known characteristic, we are only just beginning to comprehend the behavioural changes that come with prolonged undernutrition. (Gopolan and Rao, 1984:9)

The effects on children are of particular concern. The impact is described by Field and Levinson (1974:100):

> Early malnutrition not only leads to physical limitations, but also affects learning and behaviour. Inadequate nutrition during the period of most rapid brain growth may be manifest in neurological damage. Perhaps more important, malnutrition and its accompanying apathy

and listlessness may limit the child's social and emotional interaction with his family and environment.

Setting Nutritional Standards

Over the years there has been continued controversy over the standards set for the normal consumption of calories and protein. The early standards set by the committee of the Food and Agriculture Organization (FAO) and the World Health Organization (WHO) were based on achievement levels in the western industrialized countries. They were widely criticized for setting consumption levels unattainable in the underdeveloped countries. By the 1970s many were arguing that consumption standards in the industrialized countries were excessive, and were contributing to new forms of malnutrition associated with overconsumption. Furthermore, western standards did not take into account the reduced physical activity of people now in more sedentary jobs. As a result, a major revision was made in 1973 to try to take into account age, weight, activity level, and environment. The standard "reference man" is now set at between 20 and 39 years of age, weighs 65 kg, has 8 hours of moderate activity per day, 8 hours of rest, and 8 hours of light housekeeping and recreational activities. The standard "reference woman" has a weight of 55 kg and is considered moderately active. The environment is set at an average of 10 degrees Celcius. (Mehta, 1982:1332, 1339)

One prominent critic (Poleman, 1983:42-47) notes that the trend since 1953 has been continued downward modification of the standards. For example, most recently the number of kilocalories (kcal) set for the standard U.S. "reference man," now considered to be "not very active," is 2700 per day, down 500 kcal from the 1953 level. This is based on the 1973 FAO/ WHO recommendations for daily consumption: 50 kcal per kilogram of body weight for an adult living midway between moderate and very active levels of activity. Prior to the 1974 World Food Conference, the FAO/WHO adopted a different standard for use in the underdeveloped countries: setting minimal energy requirements at 1.5 times the basal metabolic rate (1.5 BMR) allowing for a +/- 20% standard deviation. Many have suggested that this new standard is too low. In 1971 the FAO/WHO-recommended daily protein consumption for adults was reduced from 61 grams to 40 grams.

Since the days of the League of Nations, international and national public health authorities have been setting recommended daily allowances (RDAs) of basic nutrients. These averages, based on sampling, assume that individual variations are distributed on a bell-shaped curve around the mean requirement. Those set in the United States, and most commonly cited, are intended to cover only healthy people, and are often inadequate for people suffering from acute or chronic diseases. (Scrimshaw and Young, 1976:60-62)

The Indian Council of Medical Research sets its standards on the assumption that the average basal metabolic rate (BMR) of the population plus two standard deviations would cover the needs of 97% of the population. This worked out to a daily per capita average of 2150 kcal and 45.2 grams of protein, roughly a third lower than the U.S. standard. The differences were accounted for by the adjustments for a younger population, with people of small stature, in a country with a hot climate. (Achaya, 1983:587-588)

Standards for average calorie consumption have been used to estimate the number of undernourished people in the world. (See Reutlinger and Selowsky, 1976; Reutlinger and Alderman, 1980) Different approaches have also led to a wide range of opinion on minimal energy requirements. For example, Knudsen and Scandizzo (1982) of the World Bank attempted to determine the average daily calorie needs of individuals in six low-income underdeveloped countries. Following FAO/WHO guidelines, their recommended levels ranged from a low of 1910 kcal for India to a high of 2276 kcal for Morocco. At the other end of the scale, the Institute of Nutrition of Central America and Panama (INCAP) concludes that an agricultural worker in Guatemala who wishes to remain normally active after work requires 3590 calories per day. (Viteri, 1974:94)

Political considerations play an important role in the setting of standards. For example, in 1980 the average Cuban consumed 2860 calories per day, substantially above the official FAO/WHO standard set at 2500. The government planned to raise the average individual consumption of calories to 3155 by 1985. Cuban officials believe that the FAO/WHO standards for calorie consumption are set artificially low as a concession to the governments of underdeveloped capitalist countries who are trying to avoid criticism for having a large percentage of their populations existing on diets judged to be below minimum standards. (Benjamin et al, 1984:108)

Another example of the political problems associated with setting standards for nutrition is cited by Achaya (1983:588). Vitamin B12 is derived only from animal foods, and in India they are in short supply, very expensive, and out of reach for the majority. In the United States in 1980, government recommendations for the consumption of vitamin B-12 were raised five-fold for older infants and doubled for infants. Not only was no similar action taken by the Indian Council of Medical Research, which sets RDAs for India, but, in contrast with its policy regarding other nutrients, it departed from the standard of optimum intake and set the RDA at the level of minimum requirement.

The setting of goals or standards is closely tied to the conventional understanding of nutrition, often referred to as the "genetic potential model." It assumes that health is a positive condition of personal fulfilment, not just the absence of disease or illness. According to this view, human beings, given the opportunity to obtain adequate nutrition, can develop to their full potential. Physical growth and intellectual development are associated with good nutrition and are considered to be proper goals. Individuals differ in their needs simply because of their genetic constitutions. In considering differences in stature, it is noted that Europeans were also small in stature before there was an agricultural and industrial revolution that permitted them to fully develop. (See Payne and Cutler, 1984)

The purpose of nutritional standards is set forth by the Institute of Nutrition of Central America and Panama (INCAP):

> In public health practice, the definition of a standard should be based on other criteria than that dictated by paediatric practice. The usual notion of a growth standard is one showing the potential upper limit of mean growth for the population (not for the individual). The use of such a standard permits one then to judge the timing and strength of environmental factors detrimental to growth. (Habicht et al, 1974:614)

Thus INCAP, in a landmark survey, attempted to determine whether genetic differences in growth *potential* could be estimated and, if so, whether differences warranted the establishment of local height and weight standards for preschool children. Their review of anthropometric surveys from both developed and underdeveloped countries found that environmental (socio-economic) factors influenced growth much more than genetic factors. There were very small differences noted between children of higher income groups, regardless of genetic background or geographical region. Thus they concluded that height and weight data from any well-to-do group of children could be used as a standard for potential growth achievement. (Habicht et al, 1974:611-614)

Determining the Existence of Undernutrition

There are numerous techniques for determining the existence of undernutrition and classifying or grading it. All have their limitations. The surveys and their standards are used primarily for social reasons, and are of particular interest to public health officers and other government officials. They are of much less utility to medical practitioners dealing with individual cases of malnutrition. The methods most commonly used involve measuring the human body and its parts and functional capacities; these are known as "anthropometric measurements". However, nutritional investigations have also used household consumption surveys, clinical assessments, socioeconomic and environmental status assessments, biochemical tests, and epidemiological surveys (such as those inquiring into the cause of death).

The most widely used anthropometric technique for measuring growth retardation is weight-for-age, commonly referred to as the Gomez Standard. A second technique, usually employed with the first, is weight-for-height, often referred to as the Waterlow Standard. A third technique is height-for-age. Sometimes the three are combined as an average.

Other techniques include measurements of the arm, chest, and head. Many believe that chest and head measurements do not adequately reveal the degree of an individual's undernutrition. Some investigators have used a measurement of skinfold thickness of the triceps. Again, it is claimed that this technique is unreliable, but it does show lack of body fat. It is widely believed that weight and arm circumference are the key variables. (Jelliffe, 1966)

The Gomez Standard includes arbitrary classifications of undernutrition: 90% of standard is considered "mild", 75% "moderate", and 60% "severe." The Waterlow Standard also tries to differentiate between "stunting" and "wasting" as categories of severity. In many surveys, these categories have been used to make rather precise conclusions as to the degree of undernutrition, although it seems that all the authors intended was that the technique should provide a broad indication of the problem.

Economists and statisticians working in the field of measuring malnutrition seem exclusively to use figures related to average, per capita, daily consumption of calories. Gopolan (1983a:591-592) argues that, although measuring household calorie intake may be a useful tool for estimating poverty, it tends to underestimate undernutrition. A much better standard, he believes, is the hemoglobin test for iron-deficiency anemia. Nevertheless, because of the very inexact nature of nutrition as a science, he advocates the use of a comprehensive battery of tests.

In practice, these surveys have served to identify groups for nutrition intervention programs. Often these programs are limited to those people identified as experiencing "severe" undernutrition. Gopolan and Rao (1984:8) are concerned, because this leads to complacency regarding "mild" and "moderate" degrees of growth retardation. They stress that children in these categories are clearly at risk and also deserve attention from public authorities. For instance, it is widely recognized that kwashiorkor represents a severe form of undernutrition, yet it is found in children who show less severe degrees of growth retardation. In recent years the standards for anthropometric measurements for undernutrition have come under criticism. Those most commonly used are the Harvard Reference Standard and the standard set by the U.S. National Center for Health Statistics. It has been argued that lower standards are needed for the underdeveloped countries. (e.g., Srinivasan, 1983a)

One example will illustrate the technical and political problems associated with setting and using standards. Seth and his colleagues at the All-India Institute of Medical Sciences have pointed out that the reference standards set by the Indian Council of Medical Research (1972) indicate that even those in the class 1 socio-economic status are "much below" the Harvard Reference Standards. But they also argue that it would be "unrealistic" to use the high socio-economic classes in India as reference standards, because the vast majority of Indian people are not in this classification. Thus, in their survey of pre-school children from the urban slums of Delhi, they chose as their standard the upper 25% of the group surveyed. (Seth et al, 1979:37-38)

Who is Undernourished and Why?

The academic and official literature on hunger concentrates on statistics related to per capita consumption of calories and protein. Normally, such studies compare national averages, country by country. Not surprisingly, such aggregate figures ignore the status of particular classes of people in any society.

For example, in 1970 the average consumption of calories and protein for Trinidad was listed at 119% and 127% of the current standards set by WHO/FAO. On the basis of these data one could conclude that there was no problem for Trinidad with either food or nutrition. Yet a survey by the Caribbean Food and Nutrition Institute found 39% and 31% of households deficient in calories and protein. (Gupta, 1981)

Sri Lanka is often cited as an example of what can be accomplished by a Basic Human Needs program. For a low-income country, the figures for physical quality of life are quite good. Yet a very extensive nutritional survey in 1975 concluded that "a problem of undernutrition of an impressive magnitude exists in the rural Sri Lanka pre-school population." Chronic undernutrition was found among 62.4% of the children of plantation (estate) workers and among 30.8% of village children. In contrast, the survey included a special group of children attending a private school in Colombo: only 2.7% were found to be suffering from chronic undernutrition. (Brink et al, 1978)

As one would expect, undernutrition is found to be rather widespread in countries whose per capita gross national product places them within the World Bank's category of "low income" or "poor" countries. The key factors widely reported are socio-economic: the poorer classes of people, and the less educated, have the highest levels of undernutrition. This is reported in nutritional surveys for Haiti (Smith et al, 1983); El Salvador (Valverde et al, 1980); Guatemala (Delgado et al, 1983; Valverde et al, 1981); Bangladesh (Chen et al, 1980); Sri Lanka (Brink et al, 1978); Pakistan (Khan, 1982; Nagra et al, 1984); and four states in West Africa. (Siddique and Abengowe, 1984)

Nutritional marasmus is also evident among children in middle-income and "newly rich" oil exporting states. Again, the key variables are socio-economic, with those classes of people in the lowest per capita income situation, urban or rural, experiencing the highest levels of undernutrition. This has been reported for Iraq (Pellett, 1977; 1981); Libya (Mamarbachi et al, 1980); Saudi Arabia (Abdullah et al, 1982; Abaheseen et al, 1981); Iran (Salimpour, 1982; Froozani et al, 1980); Barbados, Trinidad/Tobago, and Guyana (Gupta, 1981) and St. Vincent (Greiner and Latham, 1981).

One interesting study in Israel attempted to determine the effect on personal household consumption of the rise in food costs due to inflation. Like the surveys previously cited, it found lower caloric, protein, and iron intakes among the poorer social classes. But during the period of increased inflation (1976-1980) the impact on household consumption was mitigated by the indexing of wages to the rate of inflation and by the extension of the National Security payment to families with only one or two children. (Palti et al, 1983). It would be interesting to see what changes occurred after the Israeli government reduced subsidies for staple foods and began to de-index wages.

Numerous studies reveal that where food is in short supply it is not distributed on an equitable basis within the family. The nutritionally vulnerable are most often young children (particularly females), pregnant women, and the nursing mother. The low nutritional status of women is common to patriarchical societies where this is reinforced by institutionalized religion. (Fleuret and Fleuret, 1980; Dewey, 1979; Berg, 1973)

It is also widely believed that undernutrition is primarily a rural phenomenon. (Srinivasan, 1983a; World Bank, 1982) In the poorer underdeveloped countries, the majority of the people still live in rural areas and depend on agriculture for sustenance. However, Fleuret and Fleuret (1980:254) argue that in underdeveloped countries low nutritional status "has been most evident in urban areas, where low wage rates, lack of access to well-understood traditional foods, the need to prepare quick, fuel-efficient meals, and nutritionally inefficient cash expenditure may separately or together undermine the nutritional status of the poor majority."

This conclusion is supported by Sanders and Lynam (1981:18) who found that surveys in India, Sri Lanka, and Brazil reveal "a consistently lower calorific availability to the urban poor." The importance of subsidized food (often imported) for the urban poor was demonstrated when there was starvation in Dacca in 1975, not because there was no rice available, but because the poor could not afford it. (Rider, 1983:29)

There appears to be widespread agreement with the World Bank that undernutrition is largely a reflection of poverty: people do not have enough income for food. (World Bank, 1980:59) This is true regardless of the level of economic development of the country. For example, at a conference in Budapest in 1979, Buzina reported that undernutrition in western Europe was mainly due to vitamin and mineral deficiencies; those most affected were in the "poorer population strata." (Rojke, 1979)

Sheeler (1975:211) and Berg (1973:47-48) point out that those who suffer from undernutrition are poor, have experienced social deprivation, are the children of the unemployed, the families of the low paid worker, the unmarried and unsupported mother, or the farmer at the margin of subsistence.

Adapting to Undernutrition

In recent years, a challenge has been presented to the long-established genetic potential position on nutrition and undernutrition. A vigorous debate has ensued, centred in India, appearing primarily in the *Economic and Political Weekly*. The most influential dissenter has been P.V. Sukhatme, a statistician formerly with the FAO and now with the Association for the Cultivation of Science. With Professor Sheldon Margen of the University of California, he published the landmark article in 1978. Their new approach to the key issues surrounding undernutrition is often referred to as the "individual adaptability model." (See Payne and Cutler, 1984)

The central thesis of this school is that the nutritional standards for calorie and protein consumption set by traditional nutritionists are too high. There is considerable intra-individual variation of energy needs; that fact has been widely recognized. However, Sukhatme and his followers go much farther and assert that "our body has reversible mechanisms to bring about for itself a change it needs over time for maintaining health and activity, by slowing down or speeding up rates of metabolism to preserve homeostasis." (Sukhatme, 1982:2012) A few studies are commonly cited suggesting that a low intake of energy (calories) "may not necessarily be a handicap in the so-called malnourished individuals in all cases." (2013) Therefore, it has to be concluded that "the energy expenditure on well-defined desired activities is not fixed (as assumed in current nutrition literature) but varies from person to person and over time in the same person." Because of this, nutritional measurements like the Gomez standard for mild or moderate undernutrition "must be considered to have little or no meaning." (2014) In its popularized form, the Sukhatme argument is that many people with low food intakes have experienced "long-term genetic adaptation" to this situation, and their bodies' basal metabolic rate has adjusted: they don't need as much food. The individual adaptability school has also argued that the primary cause of growth retardation is the persistence of infectious diseases—not the lack of adequate food. (Srinivasan, 1983a:25; 1983b:81)

In contrast to the genetic potential approach, the concerns of the individual adaptability group are confined to (1) those people whose state of nutrition or food supply puts them directly at risk of death or debility and (2) those whose limited access to food makes it impossible for them to secure work that could improve their economic position. (Sukhatme, 1982:2014-2015)

Beyond this point the statisticians take over, and the debate appears to be a numbers game. In India, the National Nutrition Monitoring Bureau (NNMB) sets acceptable levels of calorie intake on the basis of household surveys. The NNMB has been doing household consumption surveys since 1972. The 1980 cut-off levels (minimums) are established as the recommended calorie consumption (mean of 2700 kcal) minus twice the standard deviation (400 kcal). This works out to a minimum cut-off of 1900 kcal per day per capita for an individual. When averaged on a household basis of four people, including children, the adult average minimum cut-off reaches 2300 kcal. Using this criterion, the NNMB concluded in 1981 that 46.5% of the Indian population was undernourished (Dandekar, 1982:203-204)

Maintaining his position on individual variation in needs, Sukhatme (1982:2000) argues that acceptable levels of calorie intake set by the NNMB are too high; the standard deviation must be raised to 450 kcal (mean, less two standard deviations, or mean-2 SD). Thus, under his guidelines, a sedentary Indian man needs only 1850 kcal per day and a moderately active man 2200. Sukhatme has been widely quoted as saying that Indian children are only undernourished if their weight-age deficits are more than 40% of the norm. Using calorie consumption as a guide to poverty, Sukhatme has argued that only about 20% of the Indian rural population could be considered poor. (Claiborne, 1983; Dandekar, 1982:203)

There are, of course, numerous critics of the individual adaptability school. Achaya (1983:589) notes that the studies cited by Sukhatme (which found that basal metabolic rates of people on low food intakes were twice those on high intakes doing the same work) were of too short a duration to be meaningful. Mehta (1982:1334) argues that Sukhatme's position fails to distinguish between energy intakes and requirements, and thus contradicts the First Law of Thermodynamics. In the human body, the addition or removal of energy will lead to an increase or decrease in body weight. Furthermore, output in the form of useful body functions can never balance intake, as we know from the Second Law of Thermodynamics. Mehta insists that poor people in the underdeveloped countries are smaller in height and weight "not because of any genetic differences, but simply because they eat less." (1336) That many agricultural workers and marginal farmers in India survive on lower calorie intakes is likely due to their leading relatively sedentary lives, unemployed as they are for most of the year. (1337)

The chief critic of the individual adaptability school has been Coluther Gopolan, Director of the Nutrition Foundation of India. First, he points out that calorie intake is only one factor in nutrition, and that Sukhatme and his followers have ignored the reality of other nutritional deficiencies, which are many. For example, one survey found that 63% of Indian children under five years of age suffered from iron-deficiency anemia. Secondly, even using Sukhatme's standard of m-2 SD, where SD=450 rather than 400, a 1979 survey found more than 50% of India's children suffering from a calorie deficit. Of children under five, surviving at Sukhatme's calorie level (m-2

SD), only 65% could meet their daily protein requirement. (Gopolan, 1983a: 591-592; 1983b:2164) Thus Gopolan concludes that the adaptation to a poor diet represents not a normal stage but one of "strategic metabolic and functional retreat" in response to stress. This may ward off death, but it will not help the individual to lead a productive life. The calorie levels advocated by Sukhatme are no more than "a survival ration" and are rejected by "those interested in building a strong vigorous nation, of healthy productive adults, and of active children. . . ." Small may be beautiful, he adds, but the parents of Indian children do not think so. (Gopolan, 1983a:593)

The new individual adaptability theory conveniently emerged during the rise of monetarist ideology in the industrialized west and the international lending institutions. It was quickly taken up by supporters of expanding the free market and reducing government expenditures on social services. Sukhatme and his followers, like T.N. Srinivasan, an economist at the Yale School of Development, have advocated the elimination of food supplement programs for the poor and greater reliance on public health and education measures. (Sukhatme, 1984:2015; Srinivasan, 1983a:25)

Mehta (1982:1338-1339) fears that greatly lowering the estimates of the undernourished in India will lead to cut-backs in supplementary feeding programs and possible lowering of targets for food production. By classifying the nutritionally vulnerable section of society as "perfectly normal," one is in danger of condemning them to accept a lower standard of living permanently. Gopolan (1983b:2175) points out the contradiction that, while poverty remains constant in India, the government is trying to grapple with the formidable problem of how to store millions of tonnes of surplus grain.

In addition to the individual adaptability school, there are other views occasionally advanced to explain the persistence of undernutrition. It is sometimes argued that there are "cultural blocks" that could explain why certain peoples are "trapped" in patterns of undernutrition. Others point to household consumption surveys showing that poor people in large urban centres often choose to spend their limited incomes on commodities other than food, resulting in continued undernutrition.

Certainly, "cultural blocks" to good dietary practice are to be found. But even where these "food habits" are strongly evident, the wealthiest segments of the population do not seem to be suffering from undernutrition. (Fleuret and Fleuret, 1980:254) To anyone who continued with the questions, Why don't poor people spend more on nutritious food? Why do they choose to "waste" their money on other consumption goods? it would have to be pointed out that poor people generally have a wide range of unmet needs that compete for their limited income. The persistence of undernutrition is directly linked to the persistence of poverty and inequality.

Poverty and Inequality

Economic growth rates in low-income underdeveloped countries averaged around 4.4% per year throughout the 1960s; the middle-income states averaged 5.9%. Over the decade of the 1970s, the economic growth rates were almost as high. Generally, these rates were above the historic growth rates of the industrialized western countries. Supporters of the orthodox theory of economic development were pleased. (World Bank, 1982)

In spite of the steady increase in gross domestic product (GDP) over the 1960s, a number of studies revealed that inequalities of income were not only persisting but in many cases were actually increasing. (Oshima, 1962, 1970; Kuznets, 1963; Kravis, 1960). The contradiction did not go unnoticed. In 1969 the International Labour Organization began promoting its World Employment Program, which had as its stated objective full, productive employment along with high rates of economic growth. Soon afterwards the World Bank began to study the problem of the "forgotten poor," the "bottom 40%" of the population in the underdeveloped countries. Subsequent independent studies confirmed the phenomenon of high economic growth and rising inequality. (Griffin, 1981; International Labour Office, 1977; Arndt, 1975; Wells, 1974; Adelman and Morris, 1973; Fishlow, 1972; Weiskoff, 1970). These seemed to be supported by several World Bank studies. (Jain, 1975; Chenery et al, 1974) While the reliability of much of the income distribution data for underdeveloped countries was challenged (Kuznets, 1976:4), many began to question whether the orthodox "trickle down" approach to economic growth was working.

In response to rising criticism, a new theory was advanced. Kuznets (1963) and Paukert (1973) argued that increases in inequality appeared to be inevitable as the poorer underdeveloped countries began the process of modernization within the system of the market economy. Citing evidence from a selected group of countries, they argued that, as per capita GDP increased, inequalities were lowered. This is now commonly referred to as the "U-hypothesis." While the natural course of economic growth was unfolding, the interim policy answer was to identify the poor and apply traditional social welfare programs. By the mid-1970s this model became the orthodox liberal/social democratic approach to the problems of the underdeveloped world. Later, the U-hypothesis was questioned both on the basis of its statistics and its methodology. (Saith, 1983)

Nevertheless, the model posed some problems for government and international planners. For example, Jain's random survey revealed that the lowest quintile in the industrialized capitalist states received, on average, only 5% of the country's total income, a percentage *no different from that in the capitalist underdeveloped countries*. Secondly, compared to Kuznet's earlier data, Jain's much wider survey revealed that in most underdeveloped countries *the share of national income going to the poorest 60% of the population was declining*. How could a country have a welfare program with such a large target group? Thirdly, the most unequal societies in terms of income distribution were the *middle-income* capitalist countries like those in Latin America. What did this hold out for the many low-income under-developed countries? Decades of continued poverty, inequality, and persistent undernutrition?

All the same, in order to advance welfare programs, the policy orientation of development experts shifted to identifying those living in poverty. First it was necessary to define what was meant by the term "poverty." The World Bank, the Institute of Development Studies at Sussex University, and others supporting the "trickle down" approach to economic growth, centred on "absolute poverty." Robert McNamara, then President of the World Bank, defined this as "a condition of life so limited by malnutrition, illiteracy, disease, high infant mortality and low life expectancy as to be below any rational definition of human decency." At this level of poverty physical survival was extremely difficult. (World Bank, 1980:32-35)

The more widely accepted standard is "relative poverty." This is a recognition that one's position is related to that of others in one's own society. Adam Smith advanced this definition in 1776, when he described the necessities of life as including not only what is indispensable to support life but also "whatever the custom of the country renders it indecent for creditable people, even of the lowest order, to be without." (Griffin, 1978: 154-155; Seers, 1972:22-25)

Townsend (1970:42) describes the poor as those who are "unable to participate in the activities and have the living conditions and amenities which are customary in that society." This view of poverty as social deprivation means that poverty standards will rise as living conditions improve, but poverty will continue to exist unless there is social change that eliminates the inequalities of income and wealth.

Advocates of both concepts of poverty agree that poverty is culturally specific to each country. It is not possible to create any universal "poverty line." For example, in 1984 a family of four could live quite well in Mexico on an annual income of $10,000 per year. But the same income would condemn a family of four in Vancouver, British Columbia, to severe poverty.

The concept of relative poverty can be illustrated by looking at a few examples. The first two are Mexico and Brazil, defined as upper middle-income countries by the World Bank. Both of them had high levels of economic growth in the 1960s and the 1970s and are in the top five of the most industrialized underdeveloped countries. The third example is Canada, a high-income industrialized capitalist state.

Hunger in Mexico

Mexico was one of the shining stars of the middle-income underdeveloped countries. In 1980, its per capita GNP was $2090, well above the average for middle-income countries. Between 1960 and 1980 industry and manu-

facturing experienced growth rates twice as high as those of the industrialized market economies. With Mexico as a major source of petroleum,
foreign investors concluded that the future looked good. (World Bank,
1982)

The Green Revolution in agriculture had its initial success in Mexico in
the 1960s. Following the orthodox economic development strategy, the
government favoured incentives to commercial operators, free play of the
market, and production for the world market. However, in the 1970s per
capita production of food began to decline. Production shifted away from
staples of the Mexican diet—corn and beans. While Mexico increased
production of bananas, coffee, tomatoes, strawberries, meat, and cocoa for
export, it became more and more dependent on staple cereal imports. A
large trade deficit emerged. (Heimpel, 1981; Sanders, 1979)

Mexico's aggregate figures on economic growth masked one of the most
inegalitarian societies in the world. The most widely used measure of
equality is the Gini coefficient; derived from the Lorenz curve, it shows
cumulative percentages of income received for the society as a whole. (e.g.,
see Todaro, 1985:144-147) Between 1950 and 1975 the Gini index of
income distribution worsened for Mexico. The share of total income of the
bottom 60% of the population declined. The bottom quintile suffered an
absolute decline in real income. (Felix, 1982a:267)

In 1979 the Mexican Nutrition Institute published their major survey of
undernutrition. They concluded that 52% of the population existed on diets
which did not meet the minimum standard of 2750 calories (kcal)
established by the Institute as necessary for normal life in Mexico. The
average Mexican only consumed about one-third of the recommended
protein level, set at 80 grams per day. They estimated that 28% of the
population (or 19 million) suffered from "serious malnutrition." The
Institute concluded that, with careful planning, an average-sized family
could survive on the minimum wage and just barely maintain acceptable
nutritional levels. (Horn, 1983:26; Hardy, 1982:503; Link, 1981:10)

The 1980 census reported that only 50% of the labour force was regularly
employed. More than 60% of the employed did not earn the official
minimum wage. The bottom 40% of the population existed on US$300 per
year or less, below the official poverty line. The bottom 20% were judged to
be living at a subsistence level. (Harris, 1982:3; Horn, 1983:27)

Given the structure of Mexican society, the recession and debt crisis of
1980-4 was a disaster. In 1982 the annual inflation rate was 98%; it
declined slightly to 80% in 1983, and then to 65% in 1984. In contrast, the
minimum wage was only raised by 55% and stood at about US$4 per day at
the end of 1984. In 1984 the Congreso de Trabajadores accepted wage
increases of 20%, well below the increase in inflation. The peso was
devalued several times, and the real standard of living declined dramatically. In January 1985 the average real income of the Mexican wage earner

was 34.8% below the level of January 1982. The Mexican Employers' Confederation estimated in early 1985 that 10 million workers were unemployed and another 10 million were underemployed, defined as working at menial jobs which earned them less than the daily minimum wage, US$3.60. (Beene, 1985)

In the meantime, Mexico's foreign debt approached $85 billion. Demands by the International Monetary Fund and the foreign banks led to massive cuts in government social services. In August 1982 the government doubled the price of bread and tortillas. Again, in 1984, the price of bread was raised by 50% and tortillas by 40%. A household consumption survey taken by the National Consumer Institute in early 1985 reported that the majority of the population had significantly cut back on vegetables, and 60% were no longer eating meat. (Beene, 1985) *The New York Times* (June 29, 1983) concluded that Mexico's international financial position had strengthened because of the policies undertaken by its government. Yet it noted that the improvements were largely due to "a dramatic plunge in the standard of living of its workers."

The Brazilian Economic Miracle

The "economic miracle" in Brazil is well known. Economic growth was phenomenal in the period following the seizure of power by the military in 1964. Industry and manufacturing grew at annual rates close to 10%. Like Mexico, Brazil was considered one of the new Third World industrial giants. (World Bank, 1981:70)

Brazil has one of the highest ratios of good arable land to population in the world. As in Mexico, the military government chose the orthodox economic development strategy. The rapid expansion of production of soybeans for export for animal consumption is viewed by the World Bank as "a dramatic agricultural success story" for the economic theory of international comparative advantage. (World Bank, 1982:50) However, the shift to soybean production and cattle ranching brought increased rural unemployment and a more rapid migration to the urban slums. The *boias frias*, those only occasionally employed, grew to represent half of the agricultural labour force. (Almeyra, 1984:29, 32)

As is so often the case, aggregate per capita figures distort the reality of Brazil. Between 1960 and 1980 real wages actually fell by 30%. (Hewlett, 1982:321; Fishlow, 1972:71) By 1983 only 20% of those employed were earning the official minimum wage. (Almeyra, 1984:30) Infant mortality rates increased, even in the urban areas, and life expectancy rates fell. (Felix, 1982b:168; Wood, 1977:61) Between 1960 and 1976 inequality of income increased significantly. In 1976 the top 1% of the population received a greater share of the national income than the whole of the bottom 50%! (Hewlett, 1982:320-321)

The gross inequalities in Brazil were reflected in statistics on undernutrition. The 1974-5 National Household Expenditure Study found that 68% of Brazilians consumed less than the FAO/WHO minimum daily caloric requirement for normal physical activity. It found that first-degree (mild) malnutrition affected 37% of all children through age 17, while 20% were judged to be suffering from second-degree (severe) malnutrition. (Felix, 1982b:146; Hewlett, 1982:322)

Then came the world capitalist "recession" of the 1980s. In 1982 the inflation rate rose to 104%; in 1983 it reached 220%. Brazil's foreign debt topped $100 billion, and the IMF and foreign banks increased their demands. Social spending was cut. Unemployment rose dramatically. The government decreed limitations on wages for those lucky enough to have a job; wages and salaries were reviewed every six months, but could not be increased by more than 80% of the inflation rate. The real standard of living of the majority continued to decline. Social strife escalated.

In order to help pay for Brazil's enormous foreign debt, incentives were introduced to expand production of coffee, sugar, oranges, and soya for export. As a result, staple food products came to be in short supply. In one year the price of beans rose 619%, the price of rice 217%, and the price of beef 325%. Rice and kidney beans virtually disappeared from the worker's table. Though per capita consumption of beef reached 27.4 kg per capita in 1979, it dropped to 15.2 kg in 1983. Just as in Mexico, the government's policy of debt management, imposed by the international banks and the International Monetary Fund, led to an increase in hunger and undernutrition. (Almeyra, 1984:30-31; Berman, 1984:12; Horvitch, 1983)

In 1978, the World Bank listed the per capita gross national product of Mexico at $1090 and Brazil at $1140. They ranked near the top of the 95 underdeveloped countries surveyed, 76th and 77th. By 1982, Mexico's had risen to $2270 and Brazil's to $2240. Yet, during this period of continued economic growth, poverty and hunger increased for the majority of the population.

Undernutrition in Canada

Canada is one of the wealthiest countries in the world. In 1982 the gross national product (GNP) per capita for Canada was $11,320, slightly above the average for the nineteen industrialized capitalist states, 2.4 times the average of the east European state socialist societies, and 7.5 times the average of the sixty-two middle-income underdeveloped countries like Argentina, Turkey, Iran, Brazil, South Africa, etc. (World Bank, 1982:Table 1)

Between 1970 and 1980, industry and manufacturing in Canada grew at a rate higher than the average for the industrialized capitalist states. Growth in agriculture was twice that of these countries. Canada ranked first in the world in per capita energy consumption, a key measure of economic development.

Canada ranked near the top in key quality-of-life indexes in 1982. Life expectancy at birth was 75 and adult literacy was 99%, the average for the industrialized capitalist countries. Infant mortality rates were 10 per 1000 live births, the average of the industrialized capitalist countries and one-seventh that of the middle-income capitalist countries. (World Bank, 1982:Tables 1, 23)

On the other hand, unemployment rose to very high levels during the 1982-4 mini-depression. There was a proliferation of food banks run by private charities all across Canada. They could not meet the demand. Lineups increased at churches and other charities giving hot meals to those in need. Could hunger actually exist in one of the richest countries in the world?

What is the nutritional status of Canadians? In 1970 the federal and provincial governments undertook a national nutrition survey that took two years to complete. (Nutrition Canada, 1973) The individual provincial reports found that a significant number of Canadians were "at risk" of being malnourished. Much of the data revealed problems of overconsumption and poor diet; the most common problems were gross obesity and high blood cholesterol. But the other major problems were inadequate iron, calcium (mainly among children and teenagers), and vitamin C.

The national survey also carried out separate studies of the health status of Indians and Inuit. (Nutrition Canada, 1975) Finally, Health and Welfare Canada conducted a special study of the relationship between nutrition and income. (Canada, 1975) These studies, plus some independent research, reveal a consistent link between poverty and inadequate diet.

Myres and Kroetsch (1978) reported that nutrient deficiency was most likely to be found in lower-income groups. The poorest diets among adults were found among women and the elderly. A study of teenagers in rural Nova Scotia did not look directly at the link between income and nutrition, but found that the lower the level of educational attainment by the parents, the poorer the diet of the children. (Haley et al, 1977)

A number of studies have found that a high percentage of the elderly in Canada suffer from inadequate diets. A Health and Welfare Canada survey of elders in eight centres between 1956 and 1963 found that only 9% of the subjects had good diets. A survey of low-income elders in Winnipeg in 1963 found that only 15% were consuming diets that met the Canadian Dietary Standards (CDS). A survey of 50 elderly citizens in a southern Ontario city found that the mean caloric intake was 1593 kcal and that a fairly high percentage of the elders had dietary intakes below two-thirds of the CDS. Those with greater financial resources had "nutritionally superior diets." (Reid and Miles, 1977)

The native populations of Canada (Indian and Inuit) have physical quality of life statistics significantly worse than those of white Canadians. (Last, 1982) Accompanying the problems of poverty, the impact of the culture of advanced capitalism has had a devastating effect on the health of native peoples. (Schaefer et al, 1980)

Poverty and undernutrition have been closely linked to health problems. A federal study revealed in 1981 that people on low incomes do not live as long as other people; native people only live to an average age of 44 years. The Canadian Health Survey of 1982 revealed that people in lower income brackets experienced a much higher incidence of mental disorders, diabetes, anemia, sight problems, hearing disorders, hypertension, heart disease, bronchitis, asthma, and ulcers. (*Financial Post*, April 14, 1984) In December 1983 the Canadian Mental Health Association reported to the Macdonald Royal Commission on Economic Union that increased unemployment led to higher rates of alcoholism, drug abuse, and suicides. (*The Globe and Mail* [Toronto], December 16, 1983)

The persistence of hunger in Canada is linked to the persistence of poverty. There are three poverty lines widely cited: those by Statistics Canada, the Senate Committee on poverty, and the Canadian Council on Social Development. With slight variations, they all construct a budget of "items of basic needs" that comes close to equalling 50% of the average Canadian family income. For 1982, the estimates of those living in poverty in Canada ranged from 17% (Statistics Canada) to 25% (Canadian Council on Social Development). (Ross, 1983)

Ken Battle, Director of the National Council on Welfare, (established in 1969 as the federal government's advisory board on social policy) has noted that people in Canada seem to be obsessed with the accuracy of the poverty lines themselves, and overlook the fact that the incomes of the poor in Canada are substantially below any recognized poverty line. (*Times-Colonist* [Victoria], July 17, 1984) The Canadian Council on Social Development reported in 1984 that the poor family in Canada had an income on average $4000 below the established poverty lines. (*Times-Colonist* [Victoria], June 30, 1984) Most people living in poverty were receiving social assistance, and in 1984 these income levels were between 30% and 60% below the most conservative poverty line, that set by Statistics Canada. (*The Globe and Mail* [Toronto], November 7, 1984) During the mini-depression of the early 1980s, the number of families living below the poverty line set by the National Council on Welfare increased significantly. By 1985 20% of Canada's children were living in families categorized as low income. (*The Globe and Mail* [Toronto], March 28, 1985)

There are several major reasons for continuing poverty (and thus hunger) in Canada. The first is the existence of gross inequalities in income. Between 1951 and 1978 the share of national income going to the lowest quintile (20%) of the population actually declined from 4.4% to 3.9%; the share going to the top quintile of the population increased slightly to 42.8%. (Hunter, 1981:56-57; Osberg, 1981:11; Johnson, 1979:163-165)

Secondly, the distribution of wealth is even more unequal. In 1976, only one income earner in 15 (7%) received any income from ownership in corporate stocks or bonds. The dividend income received by the top 1698 recipients was roughly equal to that received by the bottom 60% of all income earners! When one looks at ownership and control of productive assets, there are few signs that Canada has become a "people's capitalism." (Knight, 1982; Hunter, 1981:64-70; Osberg, 1981:35-40)

The persistence of inequality of income and wealth is assisted by government policy. The share of taxes paid by corporations has steadily declined over the years. Taxes on the rich have been progressively reduced. For the past 25 years, Canadian governments have consistently followed a policy of "trickle down" economic development. This has meant a wide variety of tax loopholes for the rich and incentives to private investment. (Brooks, 1981; Gillespie, 1980:164-173)

Conclusion

Hunger, poverty, ill health, and inequality are persistent problems in the world today. They are very closely linked. While the major concern is with the large numbers of disadvantaged peoples in the low-income underdeveloped countries, it is clear that the problems are common to capitalist countries with high rates of growth, high levels of gross national product, and very high levels of economic development.

References

Abaheseen, Monira et al (1981). "Nutritional Status of Saudi Arab Preschool Children in the Eastern Province." *Ecology of Food and Nutrition*, X, No. 3, pp. 163-168.

Abdullah, M.A. et al (1982). "Nutritional Status of Preschool Children in Central Saudi Arabia." *Ecology of Food and Nutrition*, XII, No. 2, pp. 103-107.

Achaya, K.T. (1983). "RDAs: Their Limitations and Application." *Economic and Political Weekly*, XVIII, No. 15, April 9, pp. 587-590.

Ackerman, L.V. (1972). "Some Thoughts on Food and Cancer." *Nutrition Today*, VII, No. 1, pp. 2-9.

Adelman, Irma and Cynthia Taft Morris (1973). *Economic Growth and Social Equity in Developing Countries*. Stanford, Stanford University Press.

Almeyra, Guillermo (1984). "Brazil: Counting the Costs of the Abandoned Countryside." *Ceres*, XVII, No. 3, May-June, pp. 29-33.

Arndt, H.W. (1975). "Development and Equality: The Indonesian Case." *World Development*, III, Nos. 2 & 3, February/March, pp. 77-90.

Benjamin, Medea et al (1984). *No Free Lunch; Food & Revolution in Cuba Today*. San Francisco: Institute for Food and Development Policy.

Berg, Alan (1973). *The Nutrition Factor: Its Role in National Development*. Washington, D.C.: The Brookings Institute.

Berman, Daniel (1984). "The $100 Billion Question: Can Brazil's New Democratization Survive the IMF?" *Multinational Monitor*, V, No. 2, February, pp. 10-15.

Brink, E.W. et al (1978). "Sri Lanka Nutrition Status Survey, 1975." *International Journal of Epidemiology*, VII, No. 1, March, pp. 41-47.

Brooks, Neil (1981). "Making Rich People Richer." *Saturday Night*, XCVI, No. 11, July, pp. 30-35.

Burkitt, D.P. (1976). "Economic Development—not all bonus." *Nutrition Today*, XI, No. 4, January/February, pp. 6-13.

Caldwell, Malcolm (1977). *The Wealth of Some Nations*. London: Zed Press.

Canada. Department of National Health and Welfare. Health Protection Branch. Bureau of Nutritional Sciences (1975). *Report on the Relationship between Income and Nutrition*. Ottawa: Department of National Health and Welfare.

Canada: Nutrition Canada (1975). Survey Reports on Indians and Eskimos. Ottawa: Information Canada.

Canada. Nutrition Canada (1973). Nutrition: A National Priority. Ottawa: Information Canada.

Chen, Lincoln D. et al (1980). "Epidemiology and Causes of Death among Children in a Rural Area of Bangladesh." *International Journal of Epidemiology* IX, No. 1, March, pp. 25-33.

Chenery, Hollis et al (1974). *Redistribution with Growth*. London: Oxford University Press.

Chossudovsky, Michel (1983). "Underdevelopment and the Political Economy of Malnutrition and Ill Health". *International Journal of Health Services*, XIII, No. 1, pp. 69-83.

Claiborne, William (1983). "Nutritionist Sounds Alarm Bell in India". *Times-Colonist* (Victoria), February 15, A-5.

Cockroft, James D. (1983). "Immiseration, Not Marginalization: The Case of

Mexico." *Latin American Perspectives*, X, Nos. 2 & 3, Spring/Summer, pp. 86-107.

Crawford, M.A. and J.P.W. Rivers (1975). "The Protein Myth." In F. Steele and Arthur Bourne, eds. *The Man/Food Equation*. London: Academic Press, pp. 235-245.

Dandekar, V.M. (1982). "On Measurement of Undernutrition." *Economic and Political Weekly*, XVII, No. 6, February 6, pp. 203-212.

Delgado, Hernan L. et al (1983). "Diarrheal Diseases, Nutritional Status and Health Care: Analysis of their Interrelationships." *Ecology of Food and Nutrition*, XII, No. 4, pp. 229-234.

Dewey, Kathryn G. (1979). "Agricultural Development, Diet and Nutrition." *Ecology of Food and Nutrition*, VIII, No. 4, pp. 265-272.

Eckholm, Erik and Frank Record (1976). "The Two Faces of Malnutrition." *Worldwatch Paper*. Washington, D.C., The Worldwatch Institute, Report No. 9, December.

Escudero, Jose Carlos (1978). "The Magnitude of Malnutrition in Latin America." *International Journal of Health Services*, VIII, No. 3, pp. 465-490.

Felix, David (1982). "Interrelations between Consumption, Economic Growth and Income Distribution in Latin America since 1800: A Comparative Perspective." In Henri Baudet and Henk vander Meulen, eds. *Consumer Behaviour and Economic Growth in the Modern Economy*. London: Croom Helm, pp. 133-177.

Field, John Osgood and F. James Levinson (1974). "Nutrition and Development: The Dynamics of Commitment." In Nevin S. Scrimshaw and Moises Behar, eds. *Nutrition and Agricultural Development*. New York, Plenum Press, pp. 99-111.

Fishlow, Albert (1972). "Brazilian Size Distribution of Income." *American Economic Review*, LXII, No. 2, May, pp. 341-402.

Fleuret, Patrick and Anne Fleuret (1980). "Nutrition, Consumption and Agricultural Change." *Human Organization*, XXXIX, No. 3, pp. 250-260.

Foxley, Alejandro, ed (1976). *Income Distribution in Latin America*. Cambridge: Cambridge University Press.

Froozani, Mino D. et al (1980). "Growth of a Group of Low Income Infants in the First Year of Life." *Journal of Tropical Pediatrics*, XXVI, No. 3, June, pp. 96-98.

Gillespie, W. Irwin (1980). *The Redistribution of Income in Canada*. Toronto: Gage Publishing Ltd.

Gopolan, Coluther (1983a). "Measurement of Undernutrition." *Economic and Political Weekly*, XVIII, No. 15, April 9, pp. 591-595.

Gopolan, Coluther (1983b). "Development and Deprivation; The Indian Experience." *Economic and Political Weekly*, XVIII, No. 51, December 17, pp. 2163-2168.

Gopolan, Coluther and Kamala S. Jaya Rao (1984). "Classification of Undernutrition—their Limitations and Fallacies." *Journal of Tropical Pediatrics*, XXX, February, pp. 7-10.

Greiner, T. and M.C. Latham (1981). "Factors Associated with Nutritional Status among Young Children in St. Vincent." *Ecology of Food and Nutrition*, X, No. 3, pp. 135-141.

Griffin, Keith (1981). *Land Concentration and Rural Poverty*. Hong Kong: Macmillan.

Griffin, Keith (1978). *International Inequality and National Poverty*. London: Macmillan.

Gupta, P.N. Sen (1981). "Comparative Studies on Food Consumption and Nutrition in Three Caribbean Countries: Barbados, Trinidad and Tobago and Guyana." *Ecology of Food and Nutrition*, XI, No. 3, pp. 177-189.

Habicht, Jean-Pierre et al (1974). "Height and Weight Standards for Preschool Children." *The Lancet*, No. 7858, Volume I for 1974, April 6, pp. 611-615.

Haley, Maudie et al (1977). "A Comparative Study of Food Habits: Influence of Age, Sex, and Selected Family Characteristics." *Canadian Journal of Public Health*, LXVIII, No.4, July/August, pp. 301-306.

Hardy, Chandra (1982). "Mexico's Development Strategy for the 1980s." *World Development*, X, No. 6, June, pp. 501-512.

Harris, Richard L. (1982). "The Political Economy of Mexico in the Eighties." *Latin American Perspectives*, IX, No. 1, Winter, pp. 2-19.

Heimpel, Gretchen (1981). "Trade Boom with Mexico Creates Problems and Opportunities." *Foreign Agriculture*, XIX, No. 11, November, pp. 5-7.

Hewlett, Sylvia Ann and Richard S. Weinert, eds. (1982). *Brazil and Mexico: Patterns in Late Development*. Philadelphia: Institute for the Study of Human Issues.

Horn, James J. (1983). "The Mexican Revolution and Health Care, or the Health of the Mexican Revolution." *Latin American Perspectives*, X, No. 4, Fall, pp. 24-39.

Horvitch, Sonita (1983). "Brazil's Financial Woes Just Keep Piling Up." *The Financial Post*, September 10, p. 11.

Hunter, Alfred A. (1981). *Class Tells: On Social Inequality in Canada*. Toronto: Butterworth.

International Labour Office (1977). *Poverty and Landlessness in Rural Asia*. Geneva: ILO for the World Employment Programme.

Jain, S. (1975). "Size Distribution of Income: Compilation of Data." Washington, D.C.: World Bank.

Jelliffe, D.B. (1966). *The Assessment of the Nutritional Status of the Community*. Geneva: World Health Organization. Monograph Series No. 53.

Johnson, Leo (1979). "The Capitalist Labour Market and Income Inequality in Canada." In John Allen Fry, ed. *Economy, Class and Social Reality*. Toronto: Butterworths, pp. 153-168.

Khan, Shaukat Raza (1982). "State of Children's Health in Pakistan—1979." *Journal of Tropical Pediatrics*, XXVIII, No. 4, August, pp. 175-179.

Kirschmann, John D. (1975). *Nutrition Almanac*. New York: McGraw-Hill for Nutrition Search, Inc.

Knight, Graham (1982). "Property, Stratification and the Wage-form." *Canadian Journal of Sociology*, VIII, No. 1, Winter, pp. 1-17.

Knudsen, Odin K. and Pasquale L. Scandizzo (1982). "The Demand for Calories in Developing Countries." *American Journal of Agricultural Economics*, LXIV, No. 1, February, pp. 80-86.

Kravis, Irving B. (1960). "International Differences in the Distribution of Income." *Review of Economics and Statistics*, XLII, No. 4, November, pp. 408-416.

Kuznets, Simon (1976). "Demographic Aspects of the Size Distribution of Income: An Exploratory Essay." *Economic Development and Cultural Change*, XXV, No. 1, October, pp. 1-94.

Kuznets, Simon (1963). "Quantitative Aspects of the Economic Growth of Nations: Distribution of Income by Size." *Economic Development and Cultural Change*, II, No. 2, January, pp. 1-80.

Last, John M. (1982). "Health of Native Canadians—Its Relevance to World Health." *Canadian Journal of Public Health*, LXXIII, No. 5, September/October, pp. 297-298.

Last, John M., ed. (1980) *Macey-Rosenau's Public Health and Preventative Medicine*. 11th edition. N.Y.: Appleton-Century-Crofts.

Link, John E. (1981). "Mexico Aims Self-Sufficiency in Basic Foods, Reduced Imports." *Foreign Agriculture*, XIX, No. 1, January, pp. 9-11.

Mamarbachi, D. et al (1980). "Observations on Nutritional Marasmus in a Newly Rich Nation." *Ecology of Food and Nutrition*, IX, No. 1, pp. 43-54.

Mehta, Jaya (1982). "Nutritional Norms and Measurement of Malnourishment and Poverty." *Economic and Political Weekly*, XVII, No. 33, August 14, pp. 1332-1340.

Myres, A.W. and Daniele Kroetsch (1978). "The Influence of Family Income on Food Consumption Patterns and Nutrient Intake in Canada." *Canadian Journal of Public Health*, LXIX, No. 3, May/June, pp. 208-221.

Nagra, Saeed A. et al (1984). "A Longitudinal Study in Body Weight of Pakistani Infants as Influenced by Socioeconomic Status." *Journal of Tropical Pediatrics*, XXX, No. 4, August, pp. 217-221.

Osberg, Lars (1981). *Economic Inequality in Canada*. Toronto: Butterworths.

Oshima, Harry T. (1970). "Income Inequality and Economic Growth: The Postwar Experience of Asian Countries." *Malayan Economic Review*, XV, No. 2, October, pp. 7-41.

Oshima, Harry T. (1962). "The International Comparison of Size Distribution of Family Incomes with Special Reference to Asia." *Review of Economics and Statistics*, XLIV, No. 4, November, 439-445.

Palti, H. et al (1983). "The Effect of Rises in Food Costs on Food Intake of Three Year Olds in Jerusalem." *International Journal of Epidemiology*, XII, No. 4, pp. 426-432.

Paukert, Felix (1973). "Income Distribution at Different Levels of Development: A Survey of the Evidence." *International Labour Review*, CVIII, Nos. 2 & 3, August/September, 97-125.

Payne, Philip and Peter Cutler (1984). "Measuring Malnutrition; Technical Problems and Ideological Perspectives." *Economic and Political Weekly*, XIX, No. 34, August 25, pp. 1485-1496.

Pellett, Peter L. (1981). "Malnutrition, Wealth and Development." *Food and Nutrition Bulletin*, III, No. 1, January, pp. 17-19.

Pellett, Peter L. (1977). "Marasmus in a Newly Rich, Urbanized Society." *Ecology of Food and Nutrition*, VI, No. 1, pp. 53-56.

Poleman, Thomas T. (1983). "World Hunger: Extent, Causes, and Cures." In D. Gale Johnson and G. Edward Schuh, eds. *The Role of Markets in the World Food Economy*. Boulder: Westview Press, pp. 41-75.

Prior, I. (1971). "The Price of Civilization." *Nutrition Today*, VI, No. 4, pp. 2-11.

Pyke, Magnus (1974). *Man and Food*. New York: McGraw-Hill.

Reid, Dianne L. and J. Elizabeth Miles (1977). "Food Habits and Nutrient Intakes of Non-institutionalized Senior Citizens." *Canadian Journal of Public Health*, LXVIII, No. 2, March/April, pp. 154-158.

Reutlinger, Shlomo and Harold Alderman (1980). "The Prevalence of Calorie-Deficient Diets in Developing Countries." *World Development*, VIII, pp. 399-411.

Reutlinger, Shlomo and Marcelo Selowsky (1976). *Malnutrition and Poverty;*

Magnitude and Policy Options. Baltimore: The Johns Hopkins Press for the World Bank.

Rider, Leslie (1983). "Determinants of the Nutritional Impact of Cash Cropping." In Georgio R. Solimano and Sally A. Lederman, eds. *Controversial Nutrition Policy Issues.* Springfield, Ill.: Charles C. Thomas, pp. 27-50.

Rojke, Sandor, ed. (1979). *Workshop on Food and Nutrition.* Budapest: Akademial Kiado.

Ross, David P. (1983). *The Canadian Fact Book on Poverty—1983.* Toronto: James Lorimer & Co.

Saith, Ashwani (1983). "Development and Distribution; A Critique of the Cross-Country U-Hypothesis." *Journal of Development Economics,* XIII, pp. 367-382.

Salimpour, R. (1982). "Some Aspects of Malnutrition in Tehran." *Journal of Tropical Pediatrics,* XXVIII, No. 1, February, pp. 29-34.

Sanders, J. H. and J. K. Lynam (1981). "New Agricultural Technology and Small Farmers in Latin America." *Food Policy,* VIII, No. 1, February, pp. 11-18.

Sanders, Thomas G. (1979). "The Plight of Mexican Agriculture." In Barbara Huddleston and Jon McLin, eds. *Political Investment in Food Production.* Bloomington: Indiana University Press, pp. 19-40.

Schaefer, O. et al (1980). "General and Nutritional Health in Two Eskimo Populations at Different Stages of Acculturation." *Canadian Journal of Public Health,* LXXI, No. 6, November/December, pp. 397-405.

Scrimshaw, Nevin S. and Vernon R. Young (1976). "The Requirements of Human Nutrition." *Scientific American,* CCXXXV, No. 3, September, pp. 51-64.

Seers, Dudley (1972). "What Are We Trying to Measure?" In Nancy Baster, ed. *Measuring Development: The Role and Adequacy of Development Indicators.* London: Frank Cass, pp. 21-36.

Seth Vimlesh et al. (1979). "Growth Reference Standards for Developing Countries." *Journal of Tropical Pediatrics,* XXV, No. 1, February, pp. 37-41.

Sheeler, Erica F. (1975). "Nutrient Requirements." In F. Steele and Arthur Bourne, eds. *The Man/Food Equation.* London, Academic Press, pp. 207-213.

Siddique, A.K. and C.U. Abengowe (1984). "Protein-Energy Malnutrition in Nigerian Children in Savanna Belt." *Journal of Tropical Pediatrics,* XXX, No. 1, February, pp. 45-47.

Smith, Meredith F. et al (1983). "Socioeconomic, Education and Health Factors Influencing Growth of Rural Haitian Children." *Ecology of Food and Nutrition,* XIII, No. 2, pp. 99-108.

Srinivasan, T.N. (1983a). "Measuring Malnutrition." *Ceres,* XVI, No. 2, March-April, pp. 23-27.

Srinivasan, T.N. (1983b). "Hunger: Defining It, Estimating its Global Incidence, and Alleviating It." In D. Gale Johnson and G. Edward Schuh, eds. *The Role of Markets in the World Food Economy,* Boulder: Westview Press, pp. 77-108.

Sukhatme, P.V. (1982)."Measurement of Undernutrition." *Economic and Political Weekly,* XVII, No. 50, December 11, pp. 2000-2016.

Sukhatme, P.V. (1975). "Human Protein Needs and the Relative Role of Energy in Meeting Them." In Arthur Bourne and F. Steele, eds. *The Man/Food Equation.* London: Academic Press, pp. 53-75.

Sukhatme, P. V. and Sheldon Margen (1982). "Auto-regulatory Homeostatic Nature of Energy Balance." *American Journal of Clinical Nutrition,* XXXV, pp. 355-365.

Todaro, Michael P. (1985). *Economic Development in the Third World*. London: Longman, 3rd Edition.

Townsend, Peter ed. (1970). *The Concept of Poverty*. London: Heinemann.

Valverde, Victor et al (1981). "Income and Growth Retardation in Poor Families with Similar Living Conditions in Rural Guatemala." *Ecology of Food and Nutrition*, X, No. 4, pp. 241-248.

Valverde, Victor et al (1980). "Life Styles and Nutritional Status of Children from Different Ecological Areas of El Salvador." *Ecology of Food and Nutrition*, IX, No. 3, pp. 167-177.

Viteri, Fernando E. (1974). "Definition of the Nutrition Problem in the Labor Force." In Nevin S. Scrimshaw and Moises Behar, eds. *Nutrition and Agricultural Development*. New York, Plenum Press, pp. 87-98.

Weiskoff, Richard (1970). "Income Distribution and Economic Growth in Puerto Rico, Argentina and Mexico." *Review of Income and Wealth*, XVI, No. 4, December, 303-332.

Wells, John R. (1974). "Distribution of Earnings, Growth, and the Structure of Demand in Brazil during the 1960s." *World Development*, II, No. 1, January, pp. 259-279.

Wood, Charles H. (1977). "Infant Mortality Trends and Capitalist Development in Brazil: The case of Sao Paulo and Belo Horizonte." *Latin American Perspectives*, IV, No. 4, Fall, pp. 56-65.

World Bank. (1982; 1981; 1980). *World Development Report*. Washington, D.C.

CHAPTER TWO

Ideological Approaches to World Hunger

The problem of persistent hunger is certainly not new to the world. In recent years, public awareness of the issue has increased following the cereal shortfall in 1973, the rapid increases in oil prices beginning in 1973, the famines in Bangladesh and the Sahel region of Africa in 1973 and 1974, the World Population Conference at Bucharest in 1974, the World Food Conference in Rome in 1974, and the drought and depression of the 1980s.

While the primary focus had been on poverty as the cause of hunger, there was a growing concern over the impact of modern industrialization and technology on the environment. In the 1960s and early 1970s the environmental movement expanded in the industrialized countries, spurred on by the publication of a number of popular studies that focused on growing populations and the increase in environmental degradation. Once again, the old Malthusian questions were raised. Can the world continue to support a steady increase in population? Are there enough natural resources available to eliminate poverty and extend the "age of mass high consumption" to all areas of the world? Are there enough foodlands and other resources to feed the world a western diet? Are there enough energy resources available? Even if the resources are available, wouldn't their full utilization place an unbearable burden of pollution on the world's ecosystem? These key questions could no longer be quickly dismissed. For one, the visible degradation of agricultural foodlands made many realize that the question of hunger was not just one of production and distribution, but was closely linked to the issue of global sustainability.

In 1798 the English political economist Thomas Malthus first published his famous *Essay on the Principle of Population*. His central argument was that "population, when unchecked, increases in a geometrical ratio. Subsistence increases only in an arithmetical ratio." The assumptions of this view were that resources were limited (land was finite); the lower classes would always produce many children; and food was necessary for human survival. It followed that, if the natural checks on population were removed by human intervention, eventually the time would come when the world's resources would not be able to provide enough food. In Malthus's time the world's population was less than one billion people, but throughout Europe there was widespread poverty, disease, and hunger.

Malthus was not concerned with what caused poverty and hunger. At the time, governments supported the notion of large populations for geopolitical reasons, and the rising capitalist class wanted a large pool of cheap labour. Malthus opposed birth control, emigration, and any governmental intervention to support the poor, as these would interfere with the free market and individualism. He concluded that England's Poor Laws would only encourage the underclasses to have more children. He opposed trade unions for the same reason. Most important to Malthus was the right of individuals to private property in the means of production and to have a government that would protect this right. This made him most vulnerable to attack from the socialist left. (Catton, 1982:126-129; Michaelson, 1981:14-16; O'Riordan, 1976:42-44; Malthus et al, 1960:13-59)

The Malthusian view of population growth carried over to the law of diminishing returns, most commonly identified with the English political economist, David Ricardo. With respect to food production, population increases and demand for food would lead farmers to increase inputs (like labour) onto a fixed piece of land; eventually a point would be reached where the output would no longer justify the added costs of the inputs. Ricardo argued that, as population increased, it would be necessary to produce food on more marginal or less fertile land, resulting in greater costs of production. This could lead to (relative) costs increasing to a point where a society would have to make sacrifices in other areas to increase the production of food. (Perelman, 1978:212-219; Perelman, 1975:701-704; Samuelson and Scott, 1971:21-33)

The major critique of Malthus came from Karl Marx and Frederick Engels. They argued that there was no law of population; the organization of any society for production created its own laws of population. Thus capitalism created the surplus population of the unemployed; this was not due to resource scarcity. Scarcity was not a natural phenomenon but a creation of the capitalist mode of production. There were no food shortages. The problem was the capitalist system of production and distribution. Marxists have traditionally argued that science and technology would enable humans to overcome relatively scarce resources. (Sandbach, 1978:26-28; Perelman, 1975:701-704) Very few have dissented from his position, the most important being Malcolm Caldwell (1977).

The intervening 150 years seemed to prove Malthus wrong. The opening of the New World to European settlement eased population pressures and resulted in a significant increase in food production. The other major development was the tapping of fossil fuel reserves that were quickly adapted to the production of food. (Luten [1980] points out that today's population is only 4.5 times that of 1800, while food production has increased 7 fold.) This has led to the dominant view that there is a basic difference between human ecology and the ecology of lower organisms. As the highest form of life, humans are able to create their own habitat.

However, the relationship of land to population was not the only question raised by Malthus. In 1820 he argued that disaster would come if humans were able to create an unlimited facility to produce food in a limited space. The question was not Can we produce more food? but What are the ecological consequences of doing so? Malthus feared that greatly increased ability to produce food would simply allow a larger population to run into other limits, such as air and water. This question of the carrying capacity of the earth is stressed by contemporary neo-Malthusians. (Daly, 1977:11)

A new war of assumptions about populations and food production was instigated by the publication of several books on "human overpopulation." Following William and Paul Paddock (1967), Paul Ehrlich, in *The Population Bomb* (1968), argued that no food aid should be given to underdeveloped countries unless they established a comprehensive program for birth control. It was his view that hundreds of millions of people were going to starve in the 1970s, because of an inadequate food supply. *The Population Bomb* was a trade book, destined for the general public, and so had less of an impact on the "growth" establishment than a scholarly book would have had. But then a second book, this time a collaboration between Paul and Anne Ehrlich, gave warning on its publication in 1970 that the neo-Malthusian challenge was indeed serious.

In their much more sophisticated *Population, Resources, Environment; Issues in Human Ecology (1970)*, the Erhlichs further advanced the argument that "human overpopulation" was the central problem facing the world. The underdeveloped countries would be "unable to escape from poverty and misery" unless their populations were controlled.

The growth of population in the underdeveloped countries was contributing to international tensions. The Ehrlichs (36-37) found that "Russia, India and other neighbours of grossly overpopulated China guard their frontiers nervously." The continued growth of population in China would leave her "little long-range choice but to expand or starve."

What about science, technology, and industrialization? The Ehrlichs argued that the underdeveloped countries "could quite accurately be called 'never-to-be-developed'." (2) There were limits to the available energy resources, and also real limits to the availability of industrial raw materials. Finally, the world environment could simply not survive the elevation of the underdeveloped countries to the American standard of living.

But the Ehrlichs also pointed to the unequal distribution of the world's resources. The United States, with only 6% of the world's population, was consuming as high as 50% of the world's raw materials. U.S. energy consumption per capita was eight times the average of the rest of the "free world." To help solve this problem, they proposed the "de-development" of the United States and a shift in investment to the underdeveloped countries. (60-61; 323) It was this proposal that aroused the most hostility from those committed to high growth rates and "the consumer society."

In 1965 George Borgstrom, Professor of Food Science and Geography at Michigan State University, had published *The Hungry Planet: The Modern World at the Edge of Famine*. It was widely read, and as Borgstrom was widely recognized as one of the world's leading authorities on the fisheries resource; his stature had lent considerable weight to the neo-Malthusian position.

Borgstrom stressed the fragile nature of the world's food-producing systems. Most of the underdeveloped areas were already farming their productive land; adding marginal resources to production would not only be costly but ecologically risky. Many of the industrialized countries were exhausting their food resource base. Some, like the Soviet Union, faced drought and frost conditions that greatly limited expansion of agriculture.

In judging the success of the food system in any country, Borgstrom insisted that trade in food must be included. The carrying capacity of certain countries could be expanded by drawing on the resources of others. To judge national food self-sufficiency, he devised a standard of "ghost acreage," based on the tilled land that would be necessary to replace the protein accounted for by (1) a nation's share of the world's ocean fisheries and (2) the net balance of food imports over food exports. An additional factor, the net importation of fertilizers, was recognized but not included. Using this calculation, Borgstrom concluded that Japan was only 17% self-sufficient in food and The Netherlands only 37%. The power of the industrialized countries enabled them to capture most of the world's fisheries and to buy the additional food they needed from the few net food exporters in the developed countries and the many net exporters in the underdeveloped countries. (Borgstrom, 1972:75-81)

These books by Paul and Anne Ehrlich and Georg Borgstrom inspired a growing interest in ecology and the debate on hunger. But the battle with the growth optimists did not begin in earnest until the publication of *The Limits to Growth* in 1972.

The Club of Rome

In April 1968 a group of thirty individuals met in Rome on the initiative of Dr. Aurelio Peccei, an industrial manager with Fiat and Olivetti. The group, since expanded, includes what must be termed "establishment" figures from a number of advanced capitalist states. The Club of Rome, as it came to be called, embarked on the Project of the Predicament of Mankind to examine "poverty in the midst of plenty; degradation of the environment; loss of faith in institutions; uncontrolled urban spread; insecurity of employment; alienation of youth; rejection of traditional values; and inflation and other monetary and economic disruptions." (Meadows et al, 1972:9-12)

The initial phase of their project was a joint effort centred at the Massachusetts Institute of Technology, where Professor Jay Forrester had created a global computer model. Seventeen specialists, headed by Professor Dennis Meadows, supported by a grant from the Volkswagen Foundation, set out to examine five major factors that could limit growth on the planet: population, agricultural production, natural resources, industrial production, and pollution. The result was the very influential *The Limits to Growth.*

In a stunning conclusion, the authors argued that, if world trends continued, the limits to growth on this planet would be reached sometime within the next one hundred years. The most probable result would be "a rather sudden and uncontrollable decline in both population and industrial capacity." The report was a warning. There was, however, an alternative: to establish "a condition of ecological and economic stability that is sustainable far into the future." This "state of global equilibrium" could be designed "so that the basic material needs of each person on earth are satisfied and each person has an equal opportunity to realize his [sic] individual human potential." (Meadows et al, 1972:24; 126)

The Club of Rome study repeated the Malthusian concern over exponential growth of population and the fixed nature of the earth's resources. The richest, most accessible, land was already under cultivation; the cost of bringing the remaining marginal land into production would be high in both capital and energy. Their computer projected that, even with the most optimistic assumptions of land utilization, there would still be a "desperate land shortage" before the year 2000 *if* population growth rates remained as they were and food production continued to require the same level of land per capita. (51)

Given the world's system of distribution of food (the market system, or ability to pay), they projected that food prices would rise so high that some people would starve and others would be forced to decrease their consumption and change their basic diet. Following Ricardo, the Club of Rome noted the "law of increasing costs" in world food production: the use of inputs was growing faster than output, so total factor productivity was declining. (52-53)

The hostile reaction that came from the "optimists" on both the political right and left was astonishing. Business interests and their ideological supporters had traditionally argued that population and economic growth were necessary for the survival of capitalism. The position of the Club of Rome betrayed the presence of dissent within the ranks. The Marxist left was quick to denounce the report in classic terms as petit bourgeois nonsense.

The group venting the most outrage were the orthodox economists. Their critiques of the *The Limits to Growth* bordered on hysteria. (e.g., see the summaries in Luten, 1980:140-144; Riordan, 1976:52-65) The Club of Rome's methodology was attacked. Their use of computers was attacked.

Their model was found to be biased to achieve the desired results. They had ignored science and technology. And they had overlooked the equilibrium effects of the pricing system. But what upset the economists most was the proposal for a steady-state or "no growth" model for the industrialized countries.

The second report of the Club of Rome, *Mankind at the Turning Point*, included more traditional academic analysis. (Mesarovic and Pestel, 1975) It stressed the growing gap between the rich and the poor and the impact of higher oil prices. But the solutions advocated for the "world food situation" were the usual liberal reforms that again stressed "an effective population policy." The report called for a "new global ethic." The likelihood of a potential disaster in the food area could be lessened "if the eating habits in the affluent part of the world would change, becoming less wasteful." (127)

In a special report, *Beyond the Age of Waste* (Gabor et al, 1978), the Club of Rome attempted to deal with the most widely cited criticism of its world model: there was no examination of the role of science and technology and how these might prevent, or at least delay, the "approach to the material limits." This report stressed the problems of energy, materials, and food production. After a long survey of energy supplies, the report emphasized that the underdeveloped countries are constrained from growth by the fact that the developed countries (with 30% of the population) consume 85% of the world's energy.

To meet another criticism of *The Limits to Growth*, the authors presented a breakdown of materials, identifying those in short physical supply. They concluded that under existing economic and technology conditions, raw materials were "adequate only for the short term," and some were in critical supply. (108-109) But, in contrast to their approach to the energy question, there was no discussion of geographical distribution or use.

The authors found that per capita food production in the underdeveloped countries had been "rather static" in the 1970s, despite the adoption of Green Revolution technology. There continued to be a wide disparity between rich and poor countries, in the quality of food consumed. They projected that the number of malnourished people would rise to 750 million by 1985. (151-152) In addition to the distribution issue, the report detailed the constraints to increasing production in the more tropical climates.

Contemporary Neo-Malthusianism

The neo-Malthusian position on the food issue has been greatly advanced by the development of ecology as a scientific discipline. It has also been a major inspiration for much of the popular environmental movement. One of the most influential recent books among environmentalists has been William R. Catton's *Overshoot* (1982). His emphasis is on the carrying capacity of the earth: for humans, living in a given manner, this means the number of people a given environment can support indefinitely. While the popularization of Malthus has led to a concentration on the question of the amount of food the earth can produce, Catton instead stresses Liebig's Law of the Minimum: any substance or circumstance that is a necessity sets the carrying capacity of the earth. (3-4; 158)

Catton, like most ecologists, argues that Malthus's law was postponed by two factors, the discovery of the New World outside Europe, which could absorb surplus population, and the tapping of fossil fuels and materials for food production and development. These discoveries, plus the development of science and technology, created a myth of limitlessness that now dominates capitalist and socialist ideology. They have permitted us to exceed the carrying capacity of the earth (this excess is termed "overshoot"). Our civilizations are now "drawing down" our non-renewable resources, granting a temporary extension to overshoot. This is not a "crisis" yet, but to someone like Catton it is a serious "predicament."

On the whole, science and technology have made possible the high-energy way of life; in the process, however, *Homo sapiens* became a detritovore, *Homo colossus*. Thus, while the political establishment in the industrialized countries anguishes about excessive population growth in China and India, each American uses 60 times as much of the world's resources as do the Chinese or Indians, with all the adverse effects that accompany this consumption. It is because of this that most of the underdeveloped countries are "destined never to become developed." (170-175)

In recent years the neo-Malthusian theory of the food crisis has been widely publicized by the Worldwatch Institute in Washington, D.C. Since its formation in 1975 it has produced a series of influential Worldwatch Papers and books on various aspects of the food issue and environmental concerns.

The key people with the Institute have been Lester R. Brown and Erik P. Eckholm. They authored *By Bread Alone*, published by the U.S. Overseas Development Council just before the World Food Conference in Rome in 1974. The study emphasized the population argument, but devoted considerable attention to the environmental threats to food production: loss of farmland to other uses, degradation of water supplies, questions of energy supply, increasing dependence on manufactured fertilizers, and depletion of the ocean's fisheries. As critics pointed out, it stressed "demand-side causes of food problems". (Taylor, 1975:829) The basic concerns of the authors are summarized as follows:

If, for purposes of discussion, we accept the U.N. medium projection of a population of 6.5 billion by the end of the century, and if we assume an average global food-consumption level approximating that currently prevailing in Western Europe (nearly a half ton of grain per person each year), we can project a need for almost 3 billion tons of grain annually, or roughly 2.5 times current output, by the year 2000. (44)

This theme was expanded upon in the special papers published by the Institute, and two of their more influential books, Eckholm's *Losing Ground: Environmental Stress and World Food Prospects* (1976) and Brown's *Building a Sustainable Society* (1981). Eckholm's book expanded on environmental constraints associated with increasing food production in the underdeveloped countries: deforestation, desertification, salting and silting of irrigations systems, soil erosion in mountain areas, the problems of introducing temperate agricultural techniques into the humid tropics, and the effects of pollution on the estuaries that provide the basis for the world's ocean fisheries.

Brown stressed that the world's basic biological systems were under mounting pressure: per-capita production of wood (from forests), fish and beef, mutton and wool (from grasslands), had peaked in the 1970s and were now in decline. The key to increasing grain production is the additional use of fertilizers; but, since the 1950s, the yield response to fertilizer had been steadily declining. Of great concern to Brown was the increasing dependence of underdeveloped countries on cereal exports from North America.

But, in contrast to earlier works, the major thrust of Brown's effort was to outline a possible road to a sustainable society which, among other things, required family planning, conservation of resources, a shift to renewable energy resources, and a reduction of conspicuous consumption in the industrialized countries to enable the poor to meet their fundamental needs. Since 1984 the Worldwatch Institute has been annually publishing the *State of the World*, which continues these themes. (Brown et al, 1985)

In 1978 U.S. President Jimmy Carter directed the Council on Environmental Quality and the Department of State to study the "probable changes in the world's population, natural resources and environment through the end of the century" in order to facilitate planning by the American government. It was a major research effort, involving fourteen U.S. government agencies, and included detailed reports from every country in the world. The three-volume, 1200 page study, *Global 2000 Report to the President*, was released in mid-1980. (Barney, 1980)

To no one's surprise it also concentrated on the production side of the issue of hunger and food. Using the sophisticated computer model established by the U.S. Census Bureau, its "most likely" projection was that the world's population would increase at an average rate of 1.8% per year, reaching 6.3 billion by the year 2000. (109; 141)

Given the trends from the recent past, it projected that average world per capita consumption of food would rise by 15% by the year 2000. But, as for the underdeveloped countries, no improvement was expected in South Asia, North Africa, or the Middle East. For Africa south of the Sahara, a decline in per capita food consumption was projected. In East Asia and Latin

America, per capita consumption was expected to improve. The report was prepared at a time of high inflation and before the world economic crisis of the early 1980s; thus the pessimistic forecast was in part attributed to the projected real (uninflated) rise in incomes and demand for food which, they believed, would result in increased prices for food. Given this framework, they projected a 95% increase in the real price of food by the year 2000. (116-118; 141-143)

The *Global 2000 Report* gave additional support to the Malthusian position. Their surveys reported widespread concern over environmental degradation and its effects on food production. (161-169) Increasing agricultural production in the underdeveloped countries would require large inputs of fossil fuel energy. Yet these needs are constrained by a number of factors. (182-183) While many had dismissed *The Limits to Growth* as an oversimplified study, the *Global 2000 Report* appeared to be a much more serious effort.

The conclusions of the *Global 2000 Report* on the possibilities for increased agricultural production in the underdeveloped countries were much less optimistic than the subsequent report by the Food and Agriculture Organization of the United Nations, *Agriculture: Toward 2000* (1981). the FAO noted the decline in arable land: "in the early 1970s one hectare of arable land supported an average of 2.6 persons; by 2000 one hectare will have to support 4 persons." They foresaw only a 4% increase in arable land between 1975 and 2000. This was because of the "absolute constraints" on land resources. In Western Europe, Eastern Europe, Japan, South Asia, China, North Africa, the Middle East, and parts of Central America and East Asia the area of arable land would quite likely begin to contract before the year 2000. Yet the FAO projected that agricultural production would increase by 2.2% per year as a result of increased energy-based inputs on existing arable land. For example, fertilizer was expected to increase by 180% over the 25-year period. (60-61; 63; 67; 73-74)

Growing public concern over environmental degradation led to the Stockholm Conference of 1972 and the creation by the General Assembly of the United Nations Environment Programme in December of that year. While the operating theme of UNEP was "ecodevelopment," or economically sound development, the studies and reports of the agency further popularized the neo-Malthusian position. For example, on the tenth anniversary of the Stockholm conference, the UNEP released a major study, *The World Environment: 1972-1982*. It recorded a continuing degradation of the earth's environment.

The UNEP noted that the average annual increase in population had decreased from 1.94% in the first five years of the decade to 1.72% in the last five years. But if the population growth in the underdeveloped countries continued at a rate of 2.2% per year, a 4% annual increase in food production would be required to meet FAO standards for minimum food consumption. (UNEP, 1982:29-33)

In the area of "bioproductive systems," the UNEP recorded large losses of good arable land in the underdeveloped countries to other uses, soil degradation, desertification and deforestation, airborne pollution, and growing pesticide and fertilizer pollution. It was argued that the key problem was not only the lack of adequate funds but that the subject "was not given sufficient priority by the governments concerned." The challenges for the next decade remained the same as they had been many years earlier. (37-41)

The Steady State and Entropy

The contemporary neo-Malthusian position has been strongly supported by ecologists like Eugene P. Odum (1971) and Howard T. Odum (1971) and a group of dissenting economists who have stressed the need for a steady-state economy. The most prominent economists include Kenneth Boulding (1970), Herman E. Daly (1977), and William Ophuls (1977).

The key to the steady-state economy is a stationary human population and an attempt to hold constant all the earth's capital stock. Instead of an emphasis on the exponential increase in the quantity of goods, there must be a shift to the quality of life. A steady-state economy means maintaining all life at some desired, sufficient level by production; but at the same time there must be the lowest feasible flows of matter and energy. Daly (1961:23) sets forth the argument:

> Modern man is the only species to have broken the solar-income budget restraint, and this has thrown him out of ecological equilibrium with the rest of the biosphere. Natural cycles have become overloaded, and new materials have been produced for which no natural cycles exist. Not only is geological capital being depleted but the basic life-support services of nature are impaired in their functioning by too large a throughput from the human sector.

These writers stress that the modern food production system is heavily dependent on a continuous subsidy of nonrenewable fossil fuels, chemicals, and fertilizers. Eugene Odum (1971:411-413) argues that, as a general rule, doubling the output of staple crops requires increasing the energy subsidy tenfold. Many orthodox economists point to the Japanese example to prove that food self-sufficiency is not required. But Odum points out that to make Indian agriculture as intensive and productive as Japan's would require around 100 times the current input of energy.

The extension of monoculture in industrial agriculture is not only contrary to the natural order but dangerous, because of the increase in genetic vulnerability. The high-response·cereal varieties of the Green Revolution are no solution, as they are heavily dependent on fossil fuel subsidies. (Berndt, 1978:78; Wade, 1975:448; Daly, 1971:11) As Daly

(122) argues, labour, the fertility of the soil, and the sun are renewable resources; minerals and fossil fuels are not. "Elementary economic logic tells us that we should maximize the efficiency of the scarcest factor."

The neo-Malthusian argument leads inevitably to the question of entropy. Here the most important work has been done by Nicholas Georgescu-Roegen, for many years Professor of Economics at Vanderbilt University. His central thesis is that the advocates of exponential growth, both the orthodox economists and the Marxists, have ignored the laws of thermodynamics. (Georgescu-Roegen, 1979b; 1977; 1971)

The First Law of Thermodynamics says that energy is neither created nor destroyed, but only transformed from one form to another. The Second Law of Thermodynamics, or the entropy law, states that, as energy is transformed from one state to another, there is a certain loss in the total amount available to perform some kind of work. This is entropy, the steady decrease in the amount of energy available for work, commonly called "waste" or "pollution." (See also Umana and Daly, 1981:5-20)

The key here is that the earth's environment (including the sun) is a closed subsystem; the earth exchanges energy only with its environment. Therefore, available matter and energy are continuously being degraded into an unavailable state. Recycling may help conserve important matter, but it cannot overcome the entropy law. (Georgescu-Roegen, 1977:266-270)

Both orthodox and Marxist economists ignore the laws of thermodynamics. The standard production-consumption models are equilibrium models, and they assume an endless supply of energy and matter. Both theoretical approaches assume that exponential growth can continue with no end in sight. For the orthodox economists, the market system and pricing automatically solve all questions of relative (or Ricardian) scarcity.

In the Soviet Union many natural resources have been treated historically as "free goods" in accordance with the Marxist labour theory of value. There have been changes since the 1960s, and the system of cost-benefit analysis has been adopted from orthodox economics. However, the orthodox economists in the west have already found it impossible to put a price on the services we get from nature: photosynthesis, the water, oxygen, nitrogen and carbon dioxide cycles, decay, stability, etc. The market system simply cannot deal with these areas. (See Ayres, 1978)

For Georgescu-Roegen (1979a; 1979b) this is only one problem with the market system. If we are going to use the market to make judgements, then all users of the resource must bid. And, he argues, that must include not only all present potential users but future ones, as well. Orthodox resource economists today rarely use a discount rate of more than 50 years, implying that the value of events beyond that time-frame is nil. Thus Georgescu-Roegen concludes that the solution lies in the area of ethics rather than economics. For the group of dissenting economists this poses no problem. Daly (1977:7) points out that both "ecology" and "economics" have the same Greek root (aikos) which means "management of the household," most appropriate for our larger household, the planet. Values were central to the discipline in the past, when it was called "political economy."

Once one accepts the ethical standard of "love thy species as thyself," the present generation turns to "minimizing future regrets." If the human species is to continue on earth for endless generations, then a population level has to be established that can be fed by organic agriculture alone. (Georgescu-Roegen, 1979a:99-100; 1977:270)

When asked to comment on Georgescu-Roegen's theories of economics and the laws of thermodynamics, the noted economist Paul Samuelson professed incompetence to judge. However, he added that his tennis partner, a scientist, told him that they were essentially sound. (Wade, 1975:450) Another economist is impressed by the argument, but concludes that, like Malthus's argument, the timing of the prediction may be off by several hundred years. In the meantime, other problems seem to be more binding. (Berndt, 1978:78-79)

The Marxist Critique

Marxists and most radical political economists still adamantly oppose the neo-Malthusian position on hunger. They argue that there is adequate food today in the world to provide everyone with a healthy diet. The problem, according to this view, is the capitalist mode of production and its inevitable results: poverty, unemployment, and inequality. There is no overpopulation. There is no real scarcity. Even critics of Marxism recognize that the existing socialist countries of the Soviet Union and eastern Europe have solved the hunger problem for their citizens by providing full employment with social production.

The underdeveloped countries are trapped, according to the Marxists, because of the legacy of colonialism and the existing world capitalist system of production and trade. Food production is for profit and export and not for local need. The countries suffering most from food production problems lack capital, science, and technology. The industrialized capitalist states have billions for arms but precious little for the needs of the underdeveloped countries. The governments of the poorer countries (usually dictatorships) are controlled by local ruling classes and are closely linked to the power of foreign capital and the governments of the advanced capitalist states.

Marxists agree that, in certain countries and certain regions of underdeveloped countries, population pressure contributes to scarcities. But the problem is the level of economic development. Marxists insist that high birth rates in the underdeveloped countries are due to underdevelopment and poverty. With full employment, assured food supplies, health care, and education, population growth rates would decline. (Redclift, 1984:7-19; Wisner et al, 1982:9-12; Ceresto, 1977:34-39)

Contemporary Marxists have maintained a very optimistic view of the potential to increase food production. For example, Ivan Frolov of the USSR Academy of Sciences, expressing the official Soviet view of the world food situation, concluded in 1978 that only 11% of potential world foodland resources were being used for that purpose, and only 41% of the land suitable for cropping was being worked. Using modern methods, about 10.5 billion hectares of land could be farmed, enough to feed additional billions of people. Technology could be used in a drive against deserts, salty soils, and permafrost, and to harvest the flora and fauna of the oceans. Where the law of diminishing returns exists, he considered it a result of plunderous farming based on private-property relations. Professor Frolov argued that farming yielded only 3-4 per cent of the volume it could yield with efficient use of modern science and technology in all countries. (Frolov, 1978) The position of Marxists in non-Soviet countries is essentially the same.

In his *Dialectics of Nature* Frederick Engels noted that from the beginning humans had shaped nature to meet their own needs. Many of the laws of nature were revealed in Charles Darwin's work. Through science we can come to understand how nature works, how humans have affected its laws, and how to react to what we have done. (Engels, 1970:66-75) In his essay, "The Part Played by Labour in the Transition from Ape to Man," Engels displayed a remarkable grasp of the science of ecology, whose origin is generally identified with Ernst Haeckel in 1870. While noting the environmental destruction caused by humans through farming, overgrazing, and deforestation, he remained optimistic about our ability to learn from these experiences and eventually to gain full mastery over nature.

The mastery of nature is also central to Marx's writings. Capitalism is praised for transforming the raw materials of nature into products of human industry. (see Lee, 1980) In the third volume of *Capital* Marx describes the destruction of the soil in farming. He attributes this to capitalist production, the drive to maximize returns. There is a basic contradiction in this social form of agriculture, according to Marx. The necessity of preserving the soil for future generations "is confronted everywhere with insurmountable barriers stemming from private property." (Marx, 1967) But, for Marx and Engels, the ecological issues are really only mentioned in passing. These issues were not pre-eminent in their time, nor were they central to their research.

Marxists have generally been contemptuous of the current ecology movement. For example, in 1981 the Soviet Union sponsored a symposium at Prague that served as a platform for members of Communist parties from around the world to denounce the "eco-socialism" movement emerging in western Europe. The advocates of the new movement were castigated for their middle-class background, their petit bourgeois ideologies, their pro-capitalist message, the advocacy of "no-growth" strategies, and, in general, their anti-communism. (Zaradov, 1981) The same arguments were used by

Hans-Magnus Enzenberger in his widely cited critique of the environmental movement in *New Left Review* (1974).

Environmental degradation appears to be a necessary byproduct of the development of certain forces of production themselves. Some of these are obvious, such as the widespread use of pesticides and chemical fertilizers. But Marxists insist that these problems can only be overcome by further developing science and technology. However, they would not concede that the problems of pollution can be solved within the capitalist system of production, ruled as it is by the profit motive. In contrast, the socialist mode of production would offer the possibility of solving these problems. (Tolman, 1981)

Marxists insist that modern neo-Malthusians who are concerned about the persistence of hunger have failed to come to grips with the class nature of capitalist society and the existence of imperialism. Very seldom do they talk about distribution. Because they avoid the central issue of power in society, their proposed solutions remain utopian.

Lowe and Worboys (1978) describe popular ecology as arguing that the world crisis is such that it transcends the left-right conflicts dominating contemporary politics. Its "holistic character" transcends conflict; indeed, political differences are seen as an impediment to solving the major world crisis. As a result, therefore, the environmental movement has been largely apolitical and naive, offering few real solutions, and easily co-opted by governments. As such, popular ecology is "a deeply conservative response" to the crisis of authority in capitalist societies.

Paehlke (1985) notes that environmentalists have been joining forces with the socialist left on many issues in recent years, and concludes that Enzenberger's description of them is incorrect. Yet Paehlke argues (145-146) that, while socialists see class as the moving force in history, environmentalists see energy use as the central organizing concept. For the environmentalist, limiting energy and material throughputs "is more profound than any of the distributive questions" that most Marxist critics recognize.

Marxists have yet to try to integrate their analysis of the socio-political system with the laws of thermodynamics. As many neo-Malthusians have pointed out, the Marxist economic model is a closed system, similar to that of orthodox economics. It is assumed that reproduction can go on indefinitely; the existence of a material basis is given. Furthermore, the labour theory of value does not lend itself to energy analysis. Alier and Naredo (1982) argue that Marx and Engels, like orthodox economists, maintained that physics and economics are separate. When confronted by the early attempts of Sergei Podolinsky to reconcile Marxism with thermodynamics, Engels was "uninterested," and chose to ignore the problem. Alier and Naredo (219) conclude that "Marxism, by refusing to tackle energy problems, has been able to keep alive a vision of future unlimited abundance."

Economists as Cornucopians

Orthodox economists have long believed that food scarcities and hunger are isolated problems of relative scarcity that can be corrected by economic incentives provided by the pricing system and free market allocation. Like the Marxists, their models assume an equilibrium between production and consumption and the existence of adequate resources. Emphasis has always been on the production side of the equation.

Colin Clark (1970:157-160), one of the deans of the profession, argues that the efficient use of existing technology on the resource base could provide for very high standards of food consumption for around 35 billion people. Roger Revelle (1974:167-168) has argued that, with the use of mechanical energy from fossil fuels and with further use of science and technology, we could provide a diet of between 4000 and 5000 calories per day to between 38 and 48 billion people. Clark (48) states the case for orthodox economics:

> We can now see that the "Malthusians" have got things upside down. It is not an improvement in agricultural productivity which promotes population growth. It is population growth which promotes improvements in agricultural (and industrial) productivity.

The logic of the liberal view of economic man is clear. People pursue their own immediate self-interest. The goal is to maximize personal well being, right now, today. There can be no concern for future generations. As Robert Heilbroner (1977:485) points out, given this view of life "no argument based on reason will lead me to care for posterity or to lift a finger in its behalf. Indeed, by every rational consideration, precisely the opposite answer is thrust upon us with irresistible force." And he cites several distinguished orthodox economists who argue this point of view.

Those who do not have adequate food are the poor, those with inadequate income. The solution to hunger is to increase agricultural production and productivity, thus increasing incomes and providing additional food, either through domestic production or trade. (Johnson, 1981:549) The larger economic pie will allow the poor to escape from absolute poverty. In his critique of the neo-Malthusian position, Lance Taylor (1975:837) concludes that "truth still abides in the old Structuralist axiom that increasing income inequality is the key to maintenance of aggregate demand under conditions of elastic supply of all products (including food)."

The key is to make agriculture profitable. The argument is put forward by the eminent economist from the University of Chicago, D. Gale Johnson (1981:555):

> If the research is undertaken, if policies are adopted that provide reasonable incentives for farmers and other rural people, if access to necessary supplies at reasonable prices is obtained, and if products are

permitted to be sold at the best possible prices, the incomes of the world's poorest people will grow and malnutrition will be largely eliminated.

But one of the prerequisites to solving the problem is to get governments out of the business of food and to rely on the free market. (Johnson, 1983:2)

The view of the orthodox economists is reflected in the research done by the World Bank (Thomas and Bhattasali, 1982). It is the central theme in the Bank's major policy statement on Africa, the area of greatest concern for food production and famine. *Accelerated Development in sub-Saharan Africa* (1981) recommends: (1) less state activity, in particular, food subsidies for the poor; (2) freeing of the market, with the exception of support for private entrepreneurs; (3) using price incentives in agriculture, stressing the "comparative advantage" of cash crops for export; (4) reduced emphasis on food self-sufficiency; and (5) a reduction in state spending on basic human needs. Following the monetarist trend at the time, they even recommend the privatization of education and health or at least the introduction of user fees.

On a world-wide basis, orthodox economists believe we need only a minimum program for hunger. This would include a system of food reserves, the continuation of foreign aid to underdeveloped countries, and incentive to farmers. In some cases of extreme poverty, concessional aid might be needed. Finally, emergency food aid would be required when there were famines.

The neo-Malthusians insist that the world's mineral, energy, and foodland resources are limited, and can only support so many people at the level of industrial society. This view is staunchly opposed by orthodox economists. (see Aage, 1984) One of the classic statements of this position is H. J. Barnett and C. Morse, *Scarcity and Growth* (1963). When their book was published, the authors were economists at Resources for the Future, based in Washington, D.C., which is often referred to as the "Pollyanna Institute." Like most economists, they project trends from the past into the future. There are no general shortages of resources; pricing and the market system efficiently allocate their use. Science and technology create substitutes for the few materials that come into short supply. The possibility of fossil fuel energy shortages will be overcome through the use of nuclear energy.

Economists do not see the possibility of a shortage of foodland resources. (Crosson, 1982a) Philip M. Raup (1982:271), a prominent American agricultural economist, insists that the central error of the neo-Malthusians "springs from the use of a physical concept of supply to measure the availability of resources that can only be defined in economic terms." For example, land deemed marginal for cropping is only a reflection of current market conditions. If needed for production at some future date, the use of capital, energy, science, and technology would make that land productive. Taylor (1975:830), in a critique of the approach of the Worldwatch

Institute, argues that at present "the question is how new techniques can be found and brought to the land."

Johnson (1981:554-555) argues that natural resources "have a relatively minor role in the determination of the wealth of nations." Like many economists, he cites the example of Japan to demonstrate that countries can become rich and well fed with very limited natural resources, particularly in the food and energy area.

Thus, this argument goes, we should not worry about preserving highly productive arable land. At the present much good farmland is found adjacent to urbanized areas where it has a market value much higher when used for other purposes. To block such other uses by zoning methods results in foregone income for the present owner. Pierre Crosson (1982b:9) argues that there is no solid evidence for overriding the market in the utilization of agricultural land. William Fischel (1982:256-257) claims that pressure to preserve prime agricultural land through zoning comes from local "anti-development interests" and from other outside communities that are often wealthy. Such zoning is wrong, because it constitutes the "taking" of private property from existing owners without just compensation.

Both the orthodox economists and the Marxists can be seen to have an unshakable faith in the ability of science and technology to overcome problems. (Aage, 1984:108-109) Crosson (1982b:9) argues that, in the past, the U.S. has eased growing pressures on its resources by developing technological substitutes, and that this "yielded spectacularly successful results in reducing the demand for cropland," and "it can be done again if we will increase the resources devoted for development of higher-yielding, less-erosive technologies." Raup (1982:272) adds that "those who object that this point of view reflects a blind faith in a continuing 'technological fix' are themselves trapped in a belief in a fixed technology." Johnson (1981:550) points to the success of the Green Revolution in new high-response seeds, and insists that what we need now is a "stream of revolutions."

The optimistic views of Marxists and orthodox economists have been influenced by the historical record of the Soviet Union and the United States, two of the most resource-rich countries in the world. Marshall Goldman (1972) and Boris Komarov (1980) both stress that in the USSR the official view is that the resources of the nation are "unlimited" and "inexhaustible." Emery Castle (1982:811) believes that agricultural economists in the United States are uniformly in the "camp of the Cornucopians," because their main concern since the 1920s has been "managing abundance."

Very close to the orthodox economists are the "Think Tanks," created and financed by big business. They advance the optimistic view in a more polemical manner. For example, Herman Kahn (1976) and the Hudson Institute insist that "overcrowding, famine, resource scarcity, pollution, and poverty . . . should be seen as temporary or regional phenomena that society must deal with rather than as the inevitable fate of man." (8) In the area of food, "the world is likely to be better fed 100 years from now than it is today; after 200 years current American standards, or even better, could very well be the norm." (111) This is possible because of science and technology and the fact that "long-term energy prospects—resting on sources that are inexhaustible—are very good." (214) In a later book, *The Coming Boom* (1982:17-19), Kahn attacks the pessimism of *The Limits to Growth* and the *Global 2000 Report* while praising the Reagan Administration, Milton Friedman and the Chicago School of Economics and the New Right.

In 1984 Herman Kahn and Julian Simon published *The Resourceful Earth*, sponsored by President Reagan's Environmental Protection Agency and financed by the right-wing Heritage Foundation, most noted for its assault on the United Nations. (*The Globe and Mail*, May 30, 1983) The contributors to the report found a bright future everywhere: world birth rates were falling, life expectancy was increasing; food production was rising, the pollution situation was improving, supplies of water were adequate and its quality improving, the climate continued to be stable, forest resources were increasing, there was more than adequate agricultural land, soil erosion was being reduced, world fisheries could easily be increased, seed banks and recombinant DNA permitted us to actually expand the earth's genetic resources, the free market was still guaranteeing adequate mineral supplies, and nuclear power was proving to be a better and cheaper fuel than coal or oil.

The report (originally titled "Global 2000 Revised") took a strong stand against government regulation of the economy, even to protect the environment; however, economic incentives for private firms were often needed to stimulate investment. They insisted that there should be no more government funding of research on population, resources, and the environment. Julian Simon, an economics professor at the University of Illinois but then working for the Heritage Foundation, reported that the Reagan Administration had not officially adopted their report as policy but found it more acceptable than the report commissioned by President Carter. (*The Globe and Mail* [Toronto], June 5, 1983)

Scientists and Resource Scarcity

At the centre of the debate between the neo-Malthusians and the optimists is the question of the availability of resources. If there are, indeed, limits to materials, energy, and good arable land, then a strong argument can be made to conserve them, not only for possible future generations but also to provide a more equitable distribution among the current world population. We have seen that, in general, the Marxists and the orthodox economists deny that there are physical limits that cannot be overcome by science and technology. At this point it is useful to review the position of the scientists working in this area.

One of the most important factors is the high degree of concentration of mineral reserves. M. H. Govett and G. J. S. Govett, geologists who have written extensively on this subject, point out that five countries (the United States, USSR, Canada, Australia, and South Africa) supply most of the basic 20 minerals that account for more than 90% of the minerals consumed in the world. These countries also have a very high percentage of the world's known reserves. The Soviet Union has significant deposits of all 20 minerals, and her share of the world's reserves is very high. (Govett and Govett, 1978:109; Govett, 1975:357-361)

Unfortunately, these significant inequalities are not just a reflection of differences in the exploration effort. Cook (1976:677) points out that the formation of ores and mineral fuels required rather unusual geological conditions, and the deposits are unevenly deposited in space and time. They are concentrated in the earth's crustal plates. For example, well over 50% of the world's known conventional crude oil deposits are found in the middle east; five countries produce 65% of the world's copper; and coal deposits are concentrated in the temperate belt of the Northern Hemisphere. Govett (1975:361, 368) cites the U.S. Geological Survey, which concludes that any radical change in the distribution of the world's mineral supplies will likely come from non-conventional sources of minerals and the exploitation of existing, known, low-grade deposits, rather than from any major new discoveries.

Of more importance is the fact that North America, western Europe, the Soviet Union, and Japan consume the majority of the world's minerals. The United States and western Europe alone consume more than two-thirds of the world's petroleum. (Govett, 1975:365) K.J. Walker (1979:252) points out that between 1951 and 1975 the world demand for materials increased more rapidly than did population. If the Third World moves towards industrialization, it is logical to expect that there will be an even more rapid increase in demand, and difficulties in supply would seem probable over the next 50 years.

The position of most of the physical scientists is summarized by Govett and Govett (1978:112): while there are ultimate limits to the supply of nonrenewable minerals, the actual supply at any one time is a factor of economics, political constraints, and the utilization of energy. In contrast to the orthodox economists, physical and natural scientists regularly question whether the system of free market pricing can overcome physical scarcities; they are much more skeptical of the possibility of mining low-grade ore deposits, are much more aware of the energy problem in resource extraction, and are willing to recognize the environmental consequences of extracting low-grade mineral deposits.

Earl Cook (1976:677), Dean of Geosciences at Texas A & M University, summarizes the common view of scientists on the limits on resources. First, there is the limit of "net energy profit (or work savings)" as it is applied to energy resources themselves. This is the "energetic limit." Energy is the key to recovery of other materials; as this cost increases, there is some point at which society will conclude that the sacrifices required for continued extraction are too high, and there will be "no more resources" of that material. (See also Costanza, 1980; Walker, 1979; Hayes, 1976)

Secondly, if a cheaper substitute is available, a material or form of energy will cease to be a resource used by society. Substitution, made possible by science and technology, is the hopeful option cited by orthodox economists and Marxists.

Finally, there is the possibility that a society will decide that it is unwilling to pay the cost of the exploitation of a resource, even if there is a net energy saving. The most commonly cited contemporary example is the change to plutonium energy, using the nuclear fast breeder reactor.

Are there any limits to substitution? This question was addressed by H. E. Goeller and Alvin M. Weinberg (1976:683) of the Oak Ridge National Laboratory in a widely cited article. The authors see human history in three stages: (1) dependence on fossil fuel energy (mainly oil), which should last for another 30 to 50 years; (2) a period (perhaps "several hundred years") when we will depend primarily on coal and more highly priced fossil fuels (e.g., tar sands and shale); and (3) the Age of Substitutability, when fossil fuels will be exhausted and we will depend on the "free energy" of the breeder reactor (and possibly solar energy).

According to the authors, the only basic elements we need to sustain our industrial society that are not essentially "inexhaustible" are phosphorus and a few trace minerals needed for agriculture. (684) We will have to exploit lower-grade mineral resources. But this will be possible "provided man finds an inexhaustible, nonpolluting source of energy." (688) That is the key, and the authors, not surprisingly, believe this to be the fast breeder reactor. (686)

There is widespread agreement that as we utilize more of the readily available minerals, continued development and exploitation become more costly in terms of both energy use and the environmental disruption and pollution caused by use of low-grade ores and mineral fuels. Hayes (1976:662) reminds us that the extraction, conversion, and transportation of energy itself is the most energy-consuming sector in the American economy. And while U.S. mineral production rose 50% over the past 50 years, energy consumption increased by 600% over the past 25 years.

Neo-Malthusians are quick to argue that the cornucopian scenario conveniently dodges the question of environmental pollution and ignores the Second Law of Thermodynamics, the entropy factor. For example, Nicholas Georgescu-Roegen (1979:1031) considers the quest for the "inexhaustible, non-polluting source of energy" an example of the search for a perpetual motion machine and a technique for converting lead into gold.

There are limitations to the use of energy and materials (both in problems of extraction and abuse to the environment) that lead many scientists to support efforts at conservation. Walker (1979:253) notes that the fossil fuel revolution has resulted in a substitution of inorganic for organic resources. If we are to move on to Stage 3 of the Goeller/Weinberg scenario, this implies a greater need for land and other organic resources that may no longer be available.

Thus it is not uncommon to find a wide variety of scientists who are in favour of conserving prime arable land. For example, the U.S. National Resource Council of the U.S. National Academy of Sciences (1974:12-14) supports the use of zoning legislation to "preserve land for food and fibre production" where soil and climate favour higher yields and less costly production. In order to prevent further land degradation, they also support identification and preservation of fragile areas for less intensive uses such as grazing, wildlife preservation, and recreation.

Distributive Justice

There is another broad ideological approach to the issue of world hunger that does not fit neatly into the above categories. I have called this the "distributive justice" approach. Following the declarations adopted at the 1974 World Food Conference in Rome, it is argued that freedom from hunger and malnutrition is an inalienable human right. There is agreement that adequate food is now being produced in the world; therefore, the central issue is distribution. The supporters of this position on the cause of world hunger generally reject the neo-Malthusian position either by design or by avoiding the issues raised.

This general approach follows the consensus position adopted at the World Conference on Population at Bucharest in 1974. There is a rejection of the U.S. government's policy of emphasizing family planning in low-income underdeveloped countries. But at the same time there is a rejection of the traditional Marxist position that population growth is important to development and does not pose a problem in a socialist society. The Bucharest position argues that population growth in underdeveloped countries is not the cause of hunger but is the result of persistent poverty and inequality, and the lack of education, health services, social security, and employment. (Dyck, 1977:274-276; Carder and Park, 1975:17-19)

Within the broad category of distributive justice, there are two general tendencies. The first emphasizes an ethical or moral approach; in the industrialized capitalist countries, these groups and individuals are very often connected with traditional Christian institutions. The second group presents a more radical political perspective, often populist in its analysis and proposals for solutions.

The position of the first group is summarized by Suzanne C. Toten (1982:63), writing for Orbis Books, the publisher of the Catholic Foreign Mission Society of America (Maryknoll):

> Hunger is a moral problem. The policies and practices of nations reflect not only political and economic choices but moral choices as well. They reflect the choice of certain goods or values over others. The choice by the First World to structure the world economic order to its own advantage, despite the poverty and hunger that this decision produces in the Third World, is a moral choice.

While the emphasis is clearly on distribution of food and other resources among present generations, and in particular on overconsumption by the rich, concern is also expressed about how our present "habits and technologies" will affect generations of people who are yet unborn.

Ronald Green (1977:260-264) of the Department of Religion at Dartmouth College argues that (1) we are bound by ties of justice to real future persons; (2) the lives of future persons ought to be at least no worse than our own; and (3) sacrifices for future generations must be distributed equitably among those presently living. Green stresses that "just regard for the future is inseparable from just policies at the present." (Malthus, an aristocrat and anti-democrat, showed little concern for the plight of the disadvantaged; that attitude is reflected by many of his contemporary followers.)

Several of the more prominent organizations in the United States reflecting the "distributive justice" or "moral" approach to the world food issue include Bread for the World, the Institute for World Order, the Interreligious Taskforce on U.S. Food Policy, Clergy and Laity Concerned, the National Catholic Coalition for Responsible Investment, and the Interfaith Center on Corporate Responsibility. In Canada, groups include Gatt-Fly, the Canadian Council for International Co-operation, and the Inter-Church Committee for World Development Education.

One of the most active organizations in this category is Bread for the World, a Christian citizens' group in the United States. Their position is that, for Christians, the issue of hunger is no longer a matter of charity but rather an issue of justice. The major problem is overconsumption by the rich. Investment desperately needed by the poorer nations is not available, largely because of massive spending on arms by the rich countries. The continued poverty of the underdeveloped countries is due also to the legacy of colonialism and the unequal patterns of trade that persist to this day. Hunger is a moral question, and it is up to individuals to change their own values and put pressure on governments to redirect their policies. (See the essays in Byron, 1982.)

Liberation theology and Christian radicalism, particularly within the Roman Catholic Church, has been an important development within this ideological approach to world hunger. The Second Vatican Council (1962-65) opened the door for new approaches to the problems of poverty; it also recognized that major attention should be directed to Latin America. There was widespread dissatisfaction among activists in the Church with the reality of the Christian Democratic parties. Instead of becoming a "third force" between capitalism and socialism, they became just another party defending capitalism. Following Vatican II the worker-priest experiment and Basic Christian Communities (BCCs) developed in Latin America. When the Colombian priest and noted sociologist, Camillo Torres, broke with the hierarchy of the Church, joined the revolutionary movement, and was killed in battle, shock waves reverberated through Latin America and the Roman Catholic Church. Latin American bishops met at Medellin, Colombia, in 1968, and the result was a call for sweeping social and economic changes and the integration of Christian theology with the everyday struggles of the poor. In 1972 Christians for Socialism held their first international meeting at Santiago, Chile. (Berryman, 1984:32-33; Dodson, 1979:205-208)

Central to the position of liberation theology is "dependency theory" as it developed in Latin America. The orthodox liberal model of development had not worked in the underdeveloped areas of the world, because there were significantly different circumstances. Poverty and hunger for the poor majority were the result of colonialism, neo-colonialism, and gross inequalities of wealth, income, and power. The priests working with the poor were radicalized as they struggled with the overt oppression of the local ruling classes, their dictatorial governments, the military, and the death squads. The success of the Sandinista revolution in Nicaragua in overthrowing an oppressive dictatorship long supported by the U.S. government was a triumph of the movement. Many believed it would be the first experiment in Catholic socialism. (See also Toten, 1982; Nelson, 1980; Goulet, 1971)

The difficulties facing the supporters of liberation theology were soon evident. In March 1983 Pope John Paul II visited Nicaragua, criticized the local clergy for supporting the Sandinista government, supported the local Archbishop who had backed the Somoza dictatorship, refused to criticize the U.S. government for attacks on Nicaragua, and refused to recognize any of the real achievements of the Sandinista government. (*The Globe and Mail* [Toronto], March 7, 1983)

Six months later the Vatican's Congregation for the Doctrine of the Faith issued a formal report, endorsed by the Pope, attacking liberation theology. The Reverend Leonardo Boff, a Franciscan priest in Brazil, was called to the Vatican to officially defend his influential book, *Church: Charisma and Power*, which criticized the Church for its failure to take a strong stand on human rights. The Reverend Boff was a leading supporter of liberation theology and the BCC movement in Brazil. (*The Globe and Mail* [Toronto], September 10, 1984)

When the Pope visited Latin America again in January 1985 his public pronouncements warned against liberation theology. Roman Catholics were to reject class hatred and not resort to violence to change their station in life. Speaking in poverty-stricken Lima, Peru, where the people had just elected a Communist as Mayor, Pope John Paul took the position that the "preferential option for the poor" also included "so many rich men who are terribly poor in spirit." The visit was followed by orders from the Vatican that the four Roman Catholic priests who held cabinet positions in the Nicaraguan government must either resign their positions or be suspended from the priesthood. (*The Globe and Mail*, February 2, 1985; January 27, 1985)

While working closely with religious movements on food and development issues, the second tendency in my broad category of those supporting "distributive justice" generally offers a more radical analysis. The prominent voices include the Transnational Institute (Almeida et al, 1974), the Institute for Policy Studies (George, 1979; Barnet and Muller, 1974) the Institute for Food and Development Policy (Lappé and Collins, 1977), and the British publication *New Internationalist.*

There is general agreement among this group as to the cause of hunger. It is due to (1) the existence of gross inequalities in wealth, income, and power; (2) the unequal levels of national economic development that result in exploitation of the poorer countries through trade, investment, and foreign aid; and (3) the links between the governments of the western states and local regimes in the underdeveloped world. The poor in the Third World, therefore, are unable to feed themselves, because they do not have access to their own resources. There is a strong conviction that technological solutions imported from the industrialized countries, like the Green Revolution, will not solve the hunger problem.

Common to this ideological approach is the identification of the transnational corporation as a major problem. For example, Barnett and Muller (1974:182-183) argue that these global corporations have compounded the world hunger problem by (1) concentrating income and eliminating jobs; (2) controlling the use of arable land; and (3) through advertising, establishing food tastes to suit their interests. The theme of modern transnational corporations as the current form of imperialism is forcefully presented in the study by Earth Resources Research, *Agribusiness in Africa.* (Dinham and Hines, 1983)

This radical approach to the problem of hunger concentrates on the need for social change. It either rejects the neo-Malthusian critique or ignores it. For example, in *Food First* Frances Moore Lappé and Joseph Collins dismiss the fear of the "crisis environmentalists" that overpopulation is the cause of hunger and famine and poses a threat to civilization. (8, 34) While soil erosion, desertification, deforestation, and overgrazing are serious problems, they argue that these are the result of colonial patterns of resource exploitation and existing social relations of agricultural production. (38)

The energy problem has not been one of shortages but of corporate control over the resource. (219) The emphasis is clearly on the need to deal with social injustice today.

There are some basic differences between the distributive justice approach to hunger and that advanced by the Marxists, neo-Marxists, and radical political economists. This analysis of hunger and underdevelopment tends to be populist and social democratic. There is an underlying belief that the governments in the industrialized countries are pursuing the wrong policies, but there is disagreement on how to change these policies. It is generally recognized that basic social change is necessary. But social revolution usually brings hardship, suffering, and death to innocent people. Problems are identified, but they are often seen as the malfunctioning of the capitalist system. For many in this category (particularly those in the United States) hunger and underdevelopment are not seen as a normal part of the functioning of the capitalist mode of production at this stage of history.

Conclusion

It should be clear by now that there is wide disagreement over what causes hunger and what should be done to correct the situation. Furthermore, the issue is not one that fits into traditional left-right political categories.

The neo-Malthusians often refer to the inequities in wealth, income, and power in the world. But issues of distribution are clearly secondary for them. As a group they have been unwilling to make a real commitment to social change.

The Marxists and those concerned with distributive justice emphasize the need for social change. But they have not really faced the long-run issues raised by finite resources, environmental pollution, and the laws of thermodynamics.

While there are differences among orthodox economists (e.g., between neoclassicists, monetarists, and Keynesians), as a general rule they do not believe in egalitarianism or distributive justice. There is a basic faith in the market system and individual pursuit of self-interest. Reflecting the dominant ideology of capitalism, they believe this is best accomplished through a competitive society based on inequalities.

In his review of the debate over *The Limits to Growth*, Luten (1980:142-145) concludes that the conflict is primarily between social scientists and natural scientists. The differences seem to be in their models or paradigms. But he is pessimistic over the debate itself: "I have no evidence that anyone has been won over from the one side to the other, whether by reason, by weight of numbers, or by volumes in print." Indeed, when one reads *The Resourceful Earth* and then *State of the World* one wonders if they are describing the same planet.

O'Riordan (1976:11-14) sees the debate primarily between a technocentric approach and an ecological approach. The technocentric mode is anthropocentric, whose ideological roots go back to the biblical exhortation to "be fruitful and multiply and replenish the earth and subdue it. . . ." (*Genesis*, chapter 1, v.28) Technocentrism has a faith in professionalism, what O'Riordan calls a tribal ideology; only the group is capable of informed decision making, and other, parochial, interests must be brushed aside.

Marxists and radical political economists have their own form of tribalism. Only a tiny minority have ever dealt at any length with the issues raised by the ecologists. They conform tightly to Marx's mid-19th century critique of Malthus.

One of the tasks of this book is to see if there is any common ground between those who view hunger and development as a social problem and those who are primarily concerned about the long-term impact of economic growth on the ecosystem.

References

Aage, Hans (1984). "Economic Arguments on the Sufficiency of Natural Resources." *Cambridge Journal of Economics*, VIII, No. 1, March, pp. 105-113.

Alier, J. Martinez and J.M. Naredo (1982). "A Marxist Precursor of Energy Economics: Podolinsky." *Journal of Peasant Studies*, IX, No. 2, January, pp. 207-224.

Almeida, Silvio et al (1974). *World Hunger; Causes and Remedies.* Washington: Transnational Institute.

Ayres, Robert U. (1978). *Resources, Environment, and Economics: Applications of the Materials/Energy Balance Principle.* New York: John Wiley & Sons.

Barnet, Richard J. and Ronald E. Muller (1974). *Global Reach: The Power of the Multinational Corporations.* New York: Simon and Schuster.

Barnett, H.J. and C. Morse (1963). *Scarcity and Growth.* Baltimore: Johns Hopkins Press for Resources for the Future.

Barney, G.O., ed. (1980). *Global 2000 Report to the President.* Washington, D.C.: U.S. Government Printing Office.

Berndt, Ernst R. (1978). "Review of Nicholas Georgescu-Roegen." *Canadian Journal of Agricultural Economics*, XXVI, No. 3, November, pp. 76-79.

Berryman, Philip (1984). "Basic Christian Communities and the Future of Latin America." *Monthly Review*, XXXVI, No. 3, July-August, pp. 27-40.

Borgstrom, Georg (1972). *The Hungry Planet: The Modern World at the Edge of Famine.* New York: Macmillan.

Boulding, Kenneth E. (1970). *Beyond Economics: Essays on Society, Religion and Ethics.* Ann Arbor: University of Michigan Press.

Brown, Lester et al (1985). *State of the World, 1985.* Washington: W. W. Norton for the Worldwatch Institute.

Brown, Lester R. (1981). *Building a Sustainable Society.* New York: W. W. Norton & Company.

Brown, Lester R. and Erik P. Eckholm (1974). *By Bread Alone.* New York: Praeger Publishers.

Byron, William (1982). *The Causes of World Hunger.* New York: Paulist Press.

Caldwell, Malcolm (1977). *The Wealth of Some Nations.* London: Zed Books.

Carder, Michael and Bob Park (1975). "Bombast in Bucharest: Report on the World Population Conference." *Science for the People*, VII, No. 1, January, pp. 17-19.

Castle, Emery N. (1982). "Agriculture and Natural Resource Adequacy." *American Journal of Agricultural Economics*, Proceedings Issue, LXIV, No. 5, December, pp. 811-820.

Catton, William R. Jr. (1982). *Overshoot: The Ecological Basis of Revolutionary Change.* Chicago: University of Illinois Press.

Ceresto, Shirley (1977). "On the Causes and Solution to the Problem of World Hunger and Starvation: Evidence from China, India and other Places." *The Insurgent Sociologist*, VII, No. 3, Summer, pp. 33-52.

Chonchol, Jacques et al (1974). *World Hunger: Causes and Remedies.* Washington, D.C.: The Transnational Institute.

Clark, Colin (1970). *Starvation or Plenty?* New York: Taplinger Publishing Co.

Cook, Earl (1976). "Limits to Exploitation of Nonrenewable Resources." *Science*, CXCI, No. 4227, February 20, pp. 677-682.

Costanza, Robert (1980). "Embodied Energy and Economic Valuation." *Science,* CCX, No. 4475, December 12, pp. 1219-1224.

Crosson, Pierre (1982a). *The Cropland Crisis: Myth or Reality?* Baltimore: Johns Hopkins Press for Resources for the Future.

Crosson, Pierre (1982b). "A Shortage of Agricultural Land?" *Resources,* No. 69, March, pp. 7-9.

Daly, Herman E. (1977). *Steady-State Economics.* San Francisco: W. H. Freeman and Company.

Dansmann, Raymond F. et al (1973). *Ecological Principles for Economic Development.* Toronto: John Wiley & Sons for the International Union for Conservation of Nature and the Conservation Foundation.

Dinham, Barbara and Colin Hines (1983). *Agribusiness in Africa.* London: Earth Resources Research Ltd.

Dodson, Michael (1979). "Liberation Theology and Christian Radicalism in Contemporary Latin America." *Journal of Latin American Studies,* II, No. 1, May, pp. 203-222.

Dunham, Kingsley (1978). "World Supply of Non-Fuel Minerals; the Geological Constraints." *Resources Policy,* IV, No. 2, June, pp. 92-99.

Dyck, Arthur J. (1977). "Alternative Views of Moral Priorities in Population Policy." *Bioscience,* XXVII, No. 2, April, pp. 272-276.

Eckholm, Erik P. (1976). *Losing Ground: Environmental Stress and World Food Prospects.* New York: W.W. Norton & Company.

Ehrlich, Paul (1968). *The Population Bomb.* New York: Ballantine.

Ehrlich, Paul and Anne H. Ehrlich (1970). *Population, Resources, Environment; Issues in Human Ecology.* San Francisco: W. H. Freeman and Company.

Engels, Frederick (1970). *Dialectics of Nature.* Moscow: Progress Publishers.

Enzenberger, Hans-Magnus (1974). "A Critique of Political Ecology." *New Left Review,* No. 84, March-April, pp. 10-25.

Fischel, William A. (1982). "The Urbanization of Agricultural Land: A Review of the National Agricultural Lands Study." *Land Economics,* LVIII, No. 2, May, pp. 236-259.

Food and Agriculture Organization of the United Nations (1981). *Agriculture: Toward 2000.* Rome: FAO.

Frolov, Ivan (1978). "The Agrarian Question and the Peasantry's Role in Developing Countries." *World Marxist Review,* XXI, No. 12, December, pp. 79-83.

Gabor, Dennis et al (1978). *Beyond the Age of Waste.* New York: Pergamon Press.

George, Susan (1979). *Feeding the Few: Corporate Control of Food.* Washington, D.C.: Institute for Policy Studies.

Georgescu-Roegen, Nicholas (1979a). "Comments on the Papers by Daley and Stiglitz." In V. Kerry Smith, ed. *Scarcity and Growth Reconsidered.* Baltimore: Johns Hopkins Press for Resources for the Future, pp. 95-105.

Georgescu-Roegen, Nicholas (1979b). "Energy Analysis and Economic Valuation." *Southern Economic Journal,* XLV, No. 4, April, pp. 1023-1058.

Georgescu-Roegen, Nicholas (1977). "The Steady State and Economic Salvation: A Thermodynamic Analysis." *BioScience,* XXII, No. 4, April, pp. 266-270.

Georgescu-Roegen, Nicholas (1971). *The Entropy Law and the Economic Process.* Cambridge: Harvard University Press.

Goeller, H.E. and Alvin M. Weinberg (1976). "The Age of Substitutability."

Science, CXCI, No. 4227, February 20, pp. 683-689.

Goldman, Marshall I. (1972). *The Spoils of Progress: Environmental Pollution in the Soviet Union*. Cambridge: MIT Press.

Goulet, Denis (1971). *The Cruel Choice: A New Concept in the Theory of Development*. New York: Atheneum.

Govett, M.H. (1975). "The Geographic Concentration of World Mineral Supplies." *Resources Policy*, I, No. 6, December, pp. 357-370.

Govett, M.H. and G.J.S. Govett (1978). "Geological Supply and Economic Demand." *Resources Policy*, IV, No. 2, June, pp. 106-114.

Green, Ronald M. (1977). "Intergenerational Distributive Justice and Environmental Responsibility." *BioScience*, XXVII, No. 4, April, pp. 260-265.

Hayes, Earl T. (1976). "Energy Implications of Materials Processing." *Science*, CXCI, No. 4227, February 20, pp. 661-665.

Heilbroner, Robert L. (1977). "What Has Posterity Ever Done for Me?" In Thomas C. Emmel, ed. *Global Perspectives on Ecology*. Palo Alto: Mayfield Publishing Co., pp. 484-489.

Johnson, D. Gale (1983). "The World Food Situation: Recent and Prospective Developments." In D. Gale Johnson and G. Edward Schuh, eds. *The Role of Markets in the World Food Economy*. Boulder, Col.: Westview Press, pp. 1-33.

Johnson, D. Gale (1981). "The World's Poor: Can They Hope for a Better Future?" *Social Service Review*, LV, No. 4, December, pp. 544-556.

Kahn, Herman (1982). *The Coming Boom*. New York: Simon and Schuster.

Kahn, Herman et al (1976). *The Next 200 Years; A Scenario for America and the World*. New York: William Morrow & Co. for the Hudson Institute.

Kahn, Herman and Julian Simon, eds. (1984). *The Resourceful Earth*. Oxford: Blackwell.

Komarov, Boris (1980). *The Destruction of Nature in the Soviet Union*. New York: M.E. Sharpe Inc.

Lappé, Frances Moore and Joseph Collins (1977). *Food First: Beyond the Myth of Scarcity*. Boston: Houghton Mifflin Company.

Lee, Donald C. (1980). "On the Marxian View of the Relationship between Man and Nature." *Environmental Ethics*, II, No. 1, Spring, pp. 3-16.

Lowe, Philip and Michael Worboys (1978). "Ecology and the End of Ideology." *Antipode*, X, No. 2, July, pp. 12-21.

Luten, Daniel B. (1980). "Ecological Optimism in the Social Sciences." *American Behavioral Scientist*, XXIV, No. 1, September-October, pp. 125-151.

Malthus, Thomas et al (1960). *Three Essays on Population*. New York: Mentor Books.

Marx, Karl (1967). *Capital*. New York: International Publishers.

Meadows, Donella H. et al (1972). *The Limits to Growth*. New York: Universe Books.

Mesarovic, Mihajlo and Eduard Pestel (1975). *Mankind at the Turning Point*. London: Hutchinson and Company.

Michaelson, Karen L., ed. (1981). *And the Poor Get Children*. New York: Monthly Review.

Nelson, Jack A. (1980). *Hunger for Justice: The Politics of Food and Faith*. Maryknoll, N.Y.: Orbis Books.

Odum, Eugene P. (1971). *Fundamentals of Ecology*. Philadelphia: Saunders.

Odum, Howard T. (1971). *Environment, Power and Society.* New York: John Wiley & Sons.

Ophuls, William (1977). *Ecology and the Politics of Scarcity.* San Francisco: W. H. Freeman and Company.

O'Riordan, Timothy (1976). *Environmentalism.* London: Pion.

Paddock, William and Paul Paddock (1967). *Famine--1975.* Boston: Little, Brown & Co.

Paehlke, Robert (1985). "Environmentalism and the Left in North America." *Studies in Political Economy,* No. 16, Spring, pp. 143-151.

Perelman, Michael (1978). *Farming for Profit in a Hungry World.* Montclair, N.J.: Allenheld, Osmun & Co.

Perelman, Michael (1975). "Natural Resources and Agriculture under Capitalism: Marx's Economic Model." *American Journal of Agricultural Economics,* LVII, No. 4, November, pp. 701-704.

Raup, Philip M. (1982). "An Agricultural Critique of the National Agricultural Lands Study." *Land Economics,* LVIII, No. 2, May, pp. 260-274.

Redclift, Michael (1984). *Development and the Environmental Crisis.* London: Methuen.

Revelle, Roger (1974). "Food and Population." *Scientific American,* CCIV, No. 3, September, pp. 160-171.

Samuelson, Paul A. and Anthony Scott (1971). *Economics.* Toronto: McGraw-Hill.

Sandbach, Francis (1978). "Ecology and the 'Limits to Growth' Debate." *Antipode,* No. 2, July, pp. 22-32.

Taylor, Lance (1975). "The Misconstrued Crisis: Lester Brown and World Food." *World Development,* III, Nos. 11 & 12, pp. 827-837.

Thomas, Vinod and Deepak Bhattasali (1982). "Price Intervention Analysis in Agriculture." *World Bank Research News,* III, No. 3, Fall/Winter, pp. 3-15.

Tolman, Charles (1981). "Karl Marx, Alienation and the Mastery of Nature." *Environmental Ethics,* III, No. 1, Spring, pp. 63-74.

Toten, Suzanne C. (1982). *World Hunger: The Responsibility of Christian Education.* Maryknoll, N.Y.: Orbis Books.

Umana, Alvaro F. and Herman E. Daly, eds. (1981). *Energy, Economics and the Environment.* Boulder, Col.: Westview Press.

United Nations Environment Programme (1982). *The World Environment: 1972-1982.* Report of the Executive Director. Dublin: Tycooly International.

United Nations Environment Programme (1982). *The State of the World Environment, 1972-1982; Report of the Executive Director.* Nairobi: UNEP.

United States National Resource Council (1974). *Productive Agriculture and a Quality Environment.* Washington, D.C.: U.S. National Academy of Sciences.

Wade, Nicholas (1975). "Nicholas Georgescu-Roegen: Entropy the Measure of Economic Man." *Science,* CXC, No. 4213, October 31, pp. 447-450.

Walker, K.J. (1979). "Materials Consumption Implications of a Fully Industrialized World." *Resources Policy,* V, No. 4, December, pp. 242-259.

Wisner, Ben et al (1982). "Hunger: A Polemical Review." *Antipode,* XIV, No. 3, December, pp. 1-16.

World Bank (1981). *Accelerated Development in sub-Saharan Africa.* Washington, D.C.: World Bank.

Zarwadov, Konstantin (1981). "Mass Ecological Protest in the Class Struggle." *World Marxist Review,* XXIV, No. 4, May, pp. 60-70.

CHAPTER THREE

Agriculture and
Economic Development

It is widely recognized that agriculture, the first industry in any economy, played a key role in the development of the present industrialized countries. It is also very clear that if hunger and poverty are to be overcome in the underdeveloped countries, agriculture must make a major contribution. Most of the development models put forth by economists in the post- World War II period have reflected the experience of the industrialized western countries. They all assume the existence of the capitalist mode of production, a capitalist world market, and close ties to the industrialized capitalist countries via trade and investment. Before examining the appropriateness of these models to the underdeveloped world, it is useful to examine their general principles and the actual experience of the major industrialized countries.

Most of the models for development agree on certain basic points. First, the level of production in agriculture must steadily increase in order to improve the general welfare of the rural population engaged in it.

Second, the absolute level of food production must rise to create a surplus that can be used to feed those in the non-agricultural sectors of the society. In addition, it is widely recognized that total-factor productivity (or at least labour productivity) must increase as well. To stimulate development in the urban areas, falling real food prices are needed to release urban demand for other consumer goods. If agricultural productivity is not rising at the same time, falling urban food prices will likely lead to falling prices for agricultural producers, resulting in lower standards of living and stagnation in the rural areas.

Third, the agricultural sector must provide labour for the urban sector. Increased labour productivity or higher birth rates are required. Historically, the percentage of population engaged in agriculture has declined with economic development; in the industrialized countries, the absolute number of people in agriculture and the rural areas has declined as well.

Fourth, rising rural incomes create a demand for both consumer and producer goods provided by the urban sectors. In the language of development economics, the agricultural sector creates backward and forward linkages with the manufacturing sector. The experience of the industrialized countries suggests that economic growth should be roughly balanced between agriculture and manufacturing, and that, within the manufacturing sector, there should be growth of both the consumer goods and the capital goods sectors.

Fifth, the agricultural sector can provide capital for investment in the non-agricultural sector. However, capital investment in agriculture is necessary if productivity is to be increased. But the experience of the presently industrialized countries is that agriculture can provide a surplus in capital for investment in the manufacturing sector. The challenge here is to extract the surplus without depressing the standard of living of those in agriculture.

Closely related to this is the role of the agricultural sector in providing entrepreneurs for the non-agricultural sector. The earliest manufacturing was very closely related to agricultural production. The precedent here comes from the United Kingdom, where entrepreneurs in manufacturing were more likely to come from the agricultural and rural sector than from capitalists who were merchants or financiers.

Finally, agriculture can make a contribution to the accumulation of foreign exchange. This is more important today for the underdeveloped countries than it has been for most of the industrialized countries.

Among the development economists, opinion varies widely on the role of the government in stimulating this process. As a minimum, there is agreement that governments have a key role to play in the development of infrastructure (particularly transportation), support for basic research and development, education and training, and the "social modernization" of the rural population. There is much more disagreement in other key areas of government intervention, including marketing agricultural products and developing policies on pricing and distribution of farm inputs, levels and forms of taxation, and land tenure. (See Williams and Young, 1981; Johnston and Kilby, 1975; Bairoch, 1969; Hayami and Ruttan, 1971; Hirschmann, 1971; Mellor, 1966; and Nicholls, 1964)

The principles that form the general theory of the role of agriculture in economic development are drawn primarily from the western European experience, and in particular that of the United Kingdom. Other notable examples widely cited include the United States and Japan. Finally, there is the special case of industrialization and agricultural development under state socialism in the USSR. The following sections will look briefly at these specific cases.

The Western European Experience

The first agricultural revolution is widely associated with the United Kingdom. There are differences as to when it began, but the evidence seems to point to the early 17th century. (Mathias, 1969:14-15; Jones, 1967:3) The industrial revolution is generally identified with the introduction of the flying shuttle and the spinning jenny in the textile industry, between 1760 and 1770. Thus Bairoch (1969:13-18) concludes that expansion of agricultural production and innovation preceded the industrial revolution in the United Kingdom by 30 to 50 years. The general opinion is that, by 1750, the standard of living in the United Kingdom was significantly higher than on continental Europe. (Deane, 1979:48-50; Landers, 1969:13)

In 1600 the population of Europe was around 75 million people, of whom only around 3.5 million lived in the "large cities." Average life expectancy was around 23 to 25 years. Between 25% and 40% of all children died at birth. (Mols, 1972:30,59) Cereals were the staple diet and, while the rich ate bread, the poor majority survived on coarse soups, gruels, and porridges usually made of the cheaper grains: millet, buckwheat, and oats. (Braudel, 1967:92-95)

Farming productivity was low, with surplus production beyond farm family use only around 20% to 30%. Yields were low, around 4 to 1 in good years. In many areas of Europe, they actually declined between the 13th and 17th centuries. (Duby, 1969:29-30; Braudel, 1967:81-83) Calorie consumption was low; Bairoch (12-13) estimates that it must have been around 1800 kcal per day on average in 1650 in the United Kingdom. Furthermore, calories were derived almost exclusively from vegetable sources; inadequate fodder greatly limited animal production, and few animals could be carried over the winter. Meat was for the rich. People were of small stature, similar to those who exist on similar diets in South Asia today.

Poverty was widespread. Gregory King's social survey of 1688 concluded that over half the total population of the United Kingdom could not earn enough to support themselves and had to rely on charity and poor relief. (Mathias, 1969:24-26) Crop failures meant "social massacres"; famine, usually followed by epidemics of plague, smallpox, typhus, scurvy, and pellagra. Towns were surrounded by armies of the poor. Before the 17th century the United Kingdom experienced, on average, 12 famines every century. This declined to four in the 17th, five in the 18th, and only one (in 1812) in the 19th. France had 13 famines in the 16th century, 11 in the 17th and 16 in the 18th. In 1696-97, a famine in Finland killed between one-fourth and one-third of the population. (Bairoch, 1969:11; Braudel, 1967-38-43).

In the medieval period European farmers used the three-year rotation system. As the population increased, farmers were forced to cultivate their fields for two out of the three years, and there was a definite drop in productivity. Because of the lack of manure, total crop production often declined. Arable land lacked fertilization, was overworked, and under-rested. (Duby, 1969:29-33)

Changes in farming began to appear by the 17th century, particularly in the United Kingdom. The techniques used involved the addition of manure, resting the soil through fallowing, widespread pasturing (mainly for sheep), and the three-field rotation of wheat, barley or oats, and fallow. By 1700 production was increasing. Bairoch (1969:13) points out that cereal exports from the United Kingdom reached 200,000 metric tonnes in 1750, or 30 kg per person. Assuming that average per capita consumption had risen to 2500 kcal, that would have amounted to 13% of the total cereal requirements. Still, throughout Europe, between 75% and 80% of the population was engaged in agriculture.

Innovations in agriculture came from Flanders, and had been known for some time. Dunman (1975:25) points out that Barnaby Googe's book on husbandry, dealing with farming in the Low Countries, was published in 1577. But the main impetus for the widespread adoption of the new techniques came with those who returned from Flanders after the restoration in 1689. By 1730 the United Kingdom was leading Europe in agricultural technology.

The key to change was the Norfolk four-field rotation: wheat, turnips, barley or oats, and clover. The new rotation improved the quality of the soil and permitted the abandonment of fallowing. The introduction of winter roots (turnips, beetroot, and swedes) and fodder crops (clover and rye) dramatically stimulated the production of livestock and its important byproduct, manure. Caldwell (1977:28-29) places high emphasis on the introduction of "Dutch clover," which fixed nitrogen, permitting the introduction of additional protein into the food system. Breeding improved livestock, and the practice became more widespread. Seed selection improved. Land planted to cereals declined, but productivity rose; more land was planted to fodder crops. The new crop rotation permitted the cultivation of the Lowland Zone light soils that for centuries had been limited to pasture for sheep. (Deane, 1979:38-42; Johnston and Kilby, 1975:184; Hobsbawm and Rude, 1969:31; Jones, 1967:7-10; Birnie, 1964:14-15)

The widespread adoption of new farm implements using iron and steel was important, in particular the iron plough, scythe, and sower, and the horseshoe. The use of horses in place of oxen involved a 50% increase in labour productivity in many farm operations. (Bairoch, 1969:20-21)

But there were other factors contributing to the agricultural revolution in the United Kingdom. The most spectacular was the flight from the land. Bairoch (1969:24-25) notes that agriculture still occupied 75% of the population in 1688. Between 1801 and 1851 the absolute size of the agricultural labour force rose from 1.7 million to 2.1 million. But the percentage of the labour force in agriculture dropped from 36% to 22%. From the earliest census figures available, it is evident that, in terms of labour productivity, the United Kingdom was well ahead of any of the other countries in Europe.

Much of this shift out of agriculture can be attributed to the parliamentary enclosures of common and waste land that accelerated after the middle of the 18th century. It had a disastrous effect on small peasant farmers. But both Hobsbawm (1968:80-82) and Deane (1979:42-46) conclude that this factor has been overemphasized. Equally important were the power of the market system that squeezed out yeoman farmers and the determination of the rich in England to buy farmland and become part of the rural gentry.

By the beginning of the 19th century the social structure of farming in Great Britain was unique in Europe. There was a landlord class that owned around three-quarters of the cultivated land. But they did not work; their farms were operated by tenant farmers. These in turn relied on the rural proletariat, hired farm workers. Finally, there remained the small, independent commodity producers. British farming was capitalist farming. By 1851, around 70% of those working in agriculture were hired labourers. (Lis and Soly, 1979:55-57; De Vries, 1976;75-78; Johnston and Kilby, 1975:187-188; Jones, 1967:12; Birnie, 1964;19)

The result was the accumulation of large agricultural holdings. Whereas, on the continent, middle peasants were farming between 10 and 12 acres, in the United Kingdom farms of 100 acres were very common, sometimes considered small. In 1851 a national survey reported 225,000 farms, about half of them between 100 and 300 acres, with the all-farm average at 110 acres. (Hobsbawm and Rude, 1969:24; Hobsbawm, 1968:82)

Others attribute the success of British farming to the significant capital investment made in agriculture at that time, primarily to develop the newly fenced lands and drain the "waste" lands. Deane (1979:46-52) stresses the entrepreneurial and innovative outlook of British landlords and tenant farmers. Capital came from outside agriculture, from the wealthy merchants. (Jones, 1967:16) It had two major sources: (1) the very profitable trade in slaves and (2) the high returns from plunder and mercantile trading with the "backward countries." After 1757 much of it came from the tribute extracted from India. In contrast, outside investment in Dutch agriculture collapsed at the end of the seventeenth century. (See De Vries, 1976; Williams, 1966; Dobb, 1963; Mannix, 1962; Davidson, 1961; and Strachey, 1959). Investment in English farms was also stimulated when the rates of interest on farm mortgages fell from 10% before 1625 to around 5% after 1680. (Mathias, 1969:71-75)

The population of the United Kingdom doubled between 1750 and 1820. Yet food production increased even faster. Some grain was imported, when crops failed, but even then this was marginal. Hobsbawm (1968:77) stresses that transport costs and technology did not permit major imports. In addition, the Corn Laws (1815-1846) offered protection to British farmers. In the 1830s home production accounted for 98% of British grain consumption. Even after the repeal of the Corn Laws (1846), British farmers remained isolated from international competition until the late 1870s. (Deane, 1979:49-50; Hobsbawm and Rude, 1969:27, 30)

A second level of innovation was established around the middle of the 19th century. First, there was the introduction of the Deanston system of draining fields by the use of clay tiles. The new system greatly improved the condition of the soil. (Birnie, 1964:16) Second, Liebig's book on plant nutrition (published in 1840) led to the introduction of artificial fertilizers. Phosphates were extracted from slag; potash was imported from Germany; and nitrates (guano) were shipped from Chile. Third, the introduction of the stationary steam engine around 1850 facilitated the threshing of grain and the draining of fields. (Deane, 1979:40-42; Johnston and Kilby, 1975:185-186)

Ester Boserop (1981:116-117) argues that this second agricultural revolution owed less to improved agricultural techniques and much more to the development of ocean transport, refrigeration, and the railway network, particularly in the "new" countries overseas. The 1870s saw the real beginning of the international market in food and agricultural products.

By the time the Corn Laws were repealed in 1846, only 25% of the labour force was left in the agricultural sector. Those forced to leave the land because of restructuring were either absorbed into industry, migrated overseas, or were pauperized. Between 1821 and 1924, around 55 million Europeans migrated overseas, 19 million from the British Isles. (Milward and Saul, 1973:146) The United Kingdom was clearly the leading industrial and military state. As Britain began to import cereals from overseas, the farming sector began the shift to livestock agriculture and other higher quality foods produced for a growing middle class. (Hayami and Ruttan, 1971:15; Bairoch, 1969:35-37)

While the agrarian revolution ended widespread famines, it was extremely harsh on the majority of the population. Relatively, the poor grew poorer. The smaller, poorer farmers were driven off the land in the second wave of Parliamentary enclosures, between 1760 and 1820. (Hobsbawm, 1968:80-81; Dobb, 1963:226-7) Not only was there proletarianization, there was widespread pauperization. The percentage of people receiving relief rose considerably. Absolute poverty was widespread. After the 1790s the Poor Laws were essential for mere survival. Not only did per capita consumption of food decline, the quality of the diet also deteriorated, as the poor majority were forced to shift from grains to potatoes. Between 1816 and 1830, the rural proletariat, made desperate by poverty and unemployment, resorted to riots and sabotage. (See Lis and Soly, 1979: Hobsbawm and Rude, 1969)

The agricultural revolution was first successful in the United Kingdom, but eventually it spread to the rest of Europe and America. Bairoch (1969:15) sets the approximate dates for the onset as follows: France, 1750-60; the United States, 1760-70; Switzerland, 1780-90; Germany and Denmark, 1790-1800; Austria, Italy, and Sweden, 1820-30; and Russia and Spain, 1860-70.

In all these cases, industrialization followed the agricultural revolution by between 20 and 50 years. At the onset of change roughly 80% of the population was in agriculture. The key was improvement in agricultural productivity. Bairoch (1969:29-31) has created an index for eleven European countries, measuring calories produced per agricultural worker. He compares this with a second index of industrial production. For the period between 1840 and 1900 he finds a very high degree of correlation between industrial development and increased labour productivity in agriculture. Perhaps it is not a "cause-and-effect link," as Bairoch concludes, but there seems little doubt that the increase in agricultural productivity has proven to be an important factor in industrialization.

The late development of modern agriculture (and industrialization) in eastern and southern Europe has been attributed to a farming system polarized between mini-holdings and large estates. Peasants were transformed from "free colonists to enserfed labourers on huge grain estates." (De Vries, 1976:55-57) The main problem in the early period was a shortage of labour; the local aristocracy pursued a policy of oppression of the peasants that further undermined the remaining free peasants. (Milward and Saul, 1973:53-68) Soviet economists refer to this as the Prussian or "Junker" approach to agriculture, a system of large private landholdings not very different from feudalism. This is in contrast to the petit bourgeois system of individual landholders that came to dominate western Europe and the new countries abroad. (Morozov, 1977:24-25)

While the agricultural revolution provided the basis for the industrial revolution in the United Kingdom, it was not the primary source of capital for investment. Deane (1979:51-52) points out that agricultural and land taxes provided nearly 60% of state revenues in the early 19th century. She concludes that had commerce and industry paid their "fair share" of the costs of the Napoleonic wars, "it is likely that the industrial revolution, then in its early stages, would have suffered a severe setback." But the industrial revolution in the United Kingdom was primarily financed by international commerce. (Deane, 1979:53-71)

Hoffman (1958:28-31) lists three sources of capital for the first industrial revolution: (1) profits from overseas trade in the 17th and 18th centuries; (2) profits (which were large) from the early textile factories; and (3) domestic credit and savings, which were considerable, compared to continental Europe. Hobsbawm (1968:33-36) emphasizes (1) the stimulation to industry by the maritime war economy, particularly in shipbuilding and iron-works; (2) the rise of a market for overseas products, with the trade controlled by the United Kingdom; (3) the development of production overseas of these new products and with it the profitable slave trade; (4) the addition of profitable new colonies, particularly India; and (5) government support through protection, incentives, and the use of the power of the state. Mandel (1968:443-445) argues that between 1760 and 1780 "the profits from India and the West Indies alone *more than doubled* the accumulated money available for rising industry." During this crucial period around 70%

of Britain's exports were to its colonies.

While most people identify Britain with free trade, this policy was not adopted until between 1846 and 1849, when Britain was clearly the world's first ranking industrial power. Protection of British industry was not limited to high tariffs. For example, by 1700 British manufacturers secured the *complete prohibition* of Indian cotton imports. The importation of Indian textiles, essential to the East India Company, was limited to goods that were re-exported. It is also widely recognized that the British were major technological innovators in the iron and steel industry. Yet high tariffs provided protection to this industry until 1825. (Hobsbawm, 1968:33, 41-42; Hoffmann, 1958:44)

Agriculture in the United States

The United States began as a number of colonies of the western European imperial powers. Before the 19th century immigration was limited, and settlement was mainly east of the Appalachian mountains. Adam Smith pointed out that the northern areas were characterized by a harsh climate; ecological conditions were not very different from Europe, and the immigrants brought with them knowledge and experience of the new farming techniques. To a large extent, however, agriculture was semi-subsistence.

The economic potential for agriculture in the southern colonies was much greater. The climate was more favourable, the land was rich, and of course it was virtually free. With a supply of labour, capital could be accumulated, and the importation of slaves from Africa solved the problem. Plantations were introduced, growing rice, sugar, and tobacco for export. As Frank (1979:30, 58) points out, the Protestant ethic, often identified with the yeoman farmer tradition, was even stronger in the American south than in New England. However, the material conditions made plantation agriculture based on slavery more profitable. The slave economy was not just a product of British colonialism; it was maintained by the new liberal country for eighty years after independence from Great Britain. (Hadwiger and Talbot, 1979:22-23; Gray, 1958, II:43-57)

That part of the North American continent which is now the United States unquestionably contains the best environment for agriculture in the world. Climate and rainfall are ideal. Carter and Dale (1974:221) stress that when the European settlers came they found two-thirds of the country covered with "magnificent forests or lush grass." The fertility of the soil was striking to the new immigrants who practised continuous cropping without fertilization or the British system of crop rotation. After ten or twenty years, fertility and yields declined. Between 1840 and 1860 serious declines in yields were reported. (Hayami and Ruttan, 1971:140)

The alternative was to move west. Fortunately for the new state, there were only around one million native inhabitants, non-whites, who were easily pushed off the valuable land by military force. The U.S. government seized the land and presented it to corporations and individuals. As the plantations depleted the soils in the old South, the move began to the Southwest. Farmers on depleted lands in New England moved to the virgin lands of the Middle West. In general, the expansion across the continent was well under way. Between 1790 and 1850, the territory of the United States grew from less than one million to more than three million square miles. In the early 1820s around 7000 new immigrants were arriving each year; by the 1850s this had risen to over 300,000. Half of them were still becoming farmers. (North, 1961;98-99)

In the New England colonies the market created by independent farmers was limited. If the urban-based economy was to grow, exports were required. The British Navigation Act of 1661 stimulated trade with the more southerly colonies, and manufacturing centred on the shipbuilding industry. Gradually, the New England merchants expanded their trade with the West Indies. By the middle of the 18th century they had carved out a profitable share of the triangular trade of rum, slaves, and molasses. Provisions shipped from New England supplied the slave plantations in the South and the Caribbean. (Frank, 1979:61-66; Mannix, 1962:153-170)

At Independence in 1790, the total population of the United States was less than 4 million, of whom 700,000 were slaves. Only 200,000 people lived in urban areas, and no city was larger than 50,000. British protectionist policies excluded American merchants from the Caribbean trade. The demand for staple exports like rice, wheat, and tobacco was weak. However, this bleak situation was saved by the British wars with France from 1793 to 1815. As a neutral, the United States benefitted greatly from the carrying trade. (North, 1961:17-25)

Tariffs were imposed as early as 1798, and trade was directed to U.S. ships. From the very beginning the U.S. government rejected the ideology of free trade and granted protection to manufacturing. The United States experienced a favourable balance of exports over imports. In the 19th century, cotton, tobacco, cereals, meat, and other agricultural products sent to the European markets accounted for around 80% of total American exports. But while overseas markets were important, the main markets were developing within the United States. (Dunman, 1975:61-66; North, 1961:166-167)

The growth of agriculture in the United States followed the expansion of cultivation and animal husbandry across the continent. The United States absorbed millions of immigrants from Europe in the 19th century. The labour force in agriculture continued to rise in absolute size until 1910. But the peak year is usually given as 1880, marking the point where the farm labour force ceased to grow as fast as the total labour force. This was the "end of the frontier" as described by the U.S. historian, Frederick Jackson Turner. In 1850 the agricultural labour force accounted for 55% of the total;

this declined only to 51% by 1880 and then to 31% by 1910. Over most of the 19th century the labour force in the United States grew at an annual rate of around 3%. (Johnston and Kilby, 1975:196-198)

Labour productivity in agriculture was increased through the introduction of new technology and mechanization. As in the United Kingdom, local inventions were developed in conjunction with farmers. The developments of the 19th century are often referred to as "horse mechanization." There were continuous improvements in the design and adoption of tillage, seeding, and harvesting equipment. A major innovation was wire fencing, which permitted the enclosure of western lands for cultivation. (Hayami and Ruttan, 1971:139-141)

There was a steady decline in the price of farm machinery relative to labour. Due to the abundance of land, improvement in yields was not important until the 1930s. Agricultural research stations were very late developing. Indeed, the extensiveness of the land provided little incentive to control soil erosion. (Johnston and Kilby, 1975:223-224)

While agriculture was rapidly expanding, so was the industrial sector of the economy. Capital came from agriculture but also from significant foreign investment in the form of bonds for specific projects. There was an abundance of mineral resources and cheap energy in the form of coal and oil. Non-farm employment grew at the most rapid rate recorded in history. The rail and transportation system required by agriculture was a major stimulus to growth. Industrialization was oriented to the domestic rather than to foreign markets. In spite of a high natural increase in population and a very significant level of immigration in the 19th century, there was no concern about labour absorption, because manufacturing technologies were still relatively labour-intensive. Agriculture was the key to rapid American development. (Johnston and Kilby, 1975:198-200)

In New England, a capital market developed from the profits gained in the triangular trade and the control of cotton exports. The textile industry developed in Massachusetts in the 19th century, relying on cheap labour from Ireland. The iron and steel industry developed in Philadelphia, and was spurred on by railroad construction. In both cases backward and forward linkages expanded the manufacturing sector of the economy. Furthermore, with a shortage of labour, and relatively high costs, technological innovation was high. In the rapidly developing Middle West, the high cost of imports isolated the communities from foreign and outside competition, and local manufacturing developed, linked to the expansion of commercial agriculture. In contrast, the South increasingly depended on a plantation-slavery system producing cotton for export. It remained relatively backward; slavery and the poverty of white farmers greatly limited the market, and little manufacturing was developed. (North, 1961:122-134; 156-176)

The development of agriculture and industry in the United States differed somewhat from the European experience. The plantation system in the

South, based on slavery, provided major cash crops for export. While agriculture in the New England area mainly served the local market, the expansion to the west opened up additional export potential. The abundance of excellent land for agriculture and an almost ideal climate greatly lowered the cost of production. While immigration provided labour for farms and factories, the general shortage of cheap labour stimulated mechanization and increased productivity.

The U.S. civil war not only ended slavery, it signalled the domination of industrial capital. Behind high tariff barriers, American enterprise grew and prospered, depending primarily on the domestic market. There were costs, of course. Native Americans were driven from their land and virtually exterminated. The African-Americans, freed from slavery, continued to live in abject poverty. The European settlers faced many hardships trying to survive as independent farmers in a hostile capitalist system. And the new non-British factory workers were grossly exploited and forced to live in urban slums. But for most of the new immigrants, life was better than it had been in Europe.

The Japanese Model

In Japan the feudal system of the Tokugawa period ended in 1868 with the Meiji Restoration. The "enlightened rule" of this period brought widespread reforms. In agriculture, the new Meiji government first tried British and American technology, but quickly abandoned it as inappropriate. Good arable land was in short supply. Instead, emphasis was placed on German research in fertilizer and plant development. With strong support from the state in research and development, the "Meiji technology" stressed a seed-fertilizer revolution designed to increase output and productivity per hectare of land under cultivation. In 1880, 75% of the labour force was still in agriculture.

Agricultural research concentrated on improving techniques for cultivation, land improvements (mainly water control) and the development of simple machinery including the rotary cultivator-weeder, the rotary foot-pedal thresher, and the short-soled plow. Agricultural schools and research institutes concentrated on developing high yielding, fertilizer-responsive plant varieties. (Johnston and Kilby, 1975:208-210; Hayami and Ruttan, 1971:154-155; Smith, 1959:108-141)

The strategy depended on expansion of fertilizer as an input. With the development of the steamship, herring meal was imported from Hokkaido and soybean cake from Manchuria. The Tagi Fertilizer Company expanded to become a major supplier of superphosphates and mixed fertilizers. (Hayami and Ruttan, 1971:159-160)

The Japanese experience of agricultural development is often cited as an appropriate model for Asian underdeveloped countries. There was a very low ratio of arable land to population. The expansion of production was based on the existing system of small farms with labour-intensive technologies. In 1917 70% of the farm households had less than one hectare. Productivity was increased with a minimum demand on capital and foreign exchange. Agriculture also served as the major source of capital for the non-agricultural sector: there was a major new outflow of capital from agriculture, primarily via the state tax. Growth in agriculture was concurrent with growth in industry. Finally, the government not only played a major role in promoting agricultural research and development but also in capital investment. Between 1887 and 1936 investment by the state amounted to around 30% of fixed capital formation, and this excludes military investment. In both agriculture and industry, modern Japanese governments placed a high priority on independent development. (Johnston and Kilby, 1975:212-213; Ohkawa and Rosovsky, 1964:46-50)

Foreign exchange was required to purchase capital goods that were not produced in Japan. In the early period of "modernization," these necessary imports were largely financed through the expansion of sericulture. Between 1870 and 1920 production of silk increased tenfold, to account for 15% of total agricultural production. The expansion of cotton textiles for export was rejected, as it would have required major importation of cotton and produced less foreign exchange. Between 1868 and 1930 silk products accounted for 42% of total exports. (Hayami and Ruttan, 1971:300-302)

While the revolution in "appropriate technology" formed the basis for the beginning of industrialization in Japan, problems developed rather quickly. By 1893 farmers could no longer supply the domestic market. In the 1910s the rate of increase in rice yields began to decline. The expansion of urbanization and industrialization brought increased demand for food. Food shortages led to price increases that exceeded wage increases; the conflict peaked with the Rice Riots of 1918.

The response of the government was to greatly increase imports of rice and fertilizers from its overseas colonies. Following the war of 1894-95, China had ceded the province of Taiwan to Japan. At the end of the war of 1904-05, Russia had recognized Japanese primacy in Korea. Through military force, Japan had reduced Korea to a protectorate; in 1910 it was formally annexed and put under military rule. The price of rice imports was low because the standard of living in the colonies was greatly depressed. With major imports from the colonies, the domestic price of rice declined. However, Japanese agriculture experienced reduced income and a decline in incentives to produce. (Johnston and Kilby, 1975:213-215; Hayami and Ruttan, 1971:161; Ohkawa and Rosovsky, 1964:57-59)

In the interwar period, Japan continued to rely on imports of rice, fertilizers, and raw materials from the colonies. Low prices for rice were essential in order to keep industrial wages low. By this time, the non-agricultural sector of the labour force was as large as the agricultural sector. The return on capital was high, and there was rapid industrial expansion and investment. At the same time, there was no major drain on foreign exchange; necessary raw materials were obtained from the colonies. Data covering the period from 1890 to 1940 reveal the heavy contribution of agriculture to state revenue (compared to income, business, and customs taxes); in turn, government revenues were used to finance social overhead, manufacturing, and armaments.

The government put a very high priority on the country's own political independence and sovereignty. They did not want to become another China, dominated by Western imperialism. Industrial development was protected by the government. Low prices for manufactured goods permitted Japan to compete in international markets, and necessary capital goods could be imported. Thus, while agriculture initially spurred industrialization during the period of economic transformation, it became a depressed sector of the economy. (Johnston and Kilby, 1975:215; Ohkawa and Rosovsky, 1964:61-64)

Hayami and Ruttan (1971:228) argue that the agricultural sector remained depressed, not only because of cheap food imports from the colonies, but also because of the state industrialization policy which emphasized increased productivity through labour-saving, capital-intensive methods of production. The Zaibatsu conglomerates were closely linked to finance and the government. Their preferential status increased the financial strain on the more labour-intensive manufacturing sectors. In addition, depressed wages in the industrial sector restricted demand for consumer goods and a more diversified diet of "higher quality" foods.

Japanese peasants certainly paid a high price for industrialization. For them, little was changed by the Meiji restoration. When the feudal land system was abolished in 1871, the peasants were promised all state lands, but these were taken, instead, by the new class of landlords. Furthermore, there was no reduction in the land tax. The new Land Tax of 1873 was a fixed money tax, collected from landowners, based on the assessed productive value of the land. Lockwood (1968:98) reports that in 1873 it amounted to around 33% of the total crop. The landlords took between 50% and 60% of the crop from their tenants. On top of this there were usurious debt charges.

The amount of land controlled by absentee landlords rose. By 1915 46% of the land was tilled by tenants. Of the tenants, 28% had no land at all. But there was no class of landless wage labourers. Peasants had no political rights under the new bourgeois regime; voting rights were limited to less than 1% of the population, those with substantial property holdings.

The result was widespread peasant discontent that peaked in 1873 when the new regime introduced military conscription. During the first decade of the Meiji period there were 200 peasant uprisings. Other major revolts occurred in 1884-1885 and after World War I. (Ohkawa and Rosovsky, 1964:50-51; Moore, 1966:255-258; 270-272)

The heavy tax on farmers was paid primarily by their tenants. Between 1888 and 1892, this tax provided 85% of the government's revenues. The major imports of rice from the colonies greatly depressed prices and the standard of living of the agricultural sector. While the terms of trade between agricultural and non-agricultural commodities were even and stable between 1878-1917, the relative standard of living of the peasant steadily declined, and poverty intensified after 1928. (Ohkawa and Rosovsky, 1964:49, 57-59)

The Japanese road to industrialization is widely praised by mainstream economists. Few recount the heavy price that peasants and workers paid in this process. Even fewer consider the role played by the colonized peoples in Taiwan, Korea, and Manchuria.

Agriculture and Development under State Socialism: the USSR

In 1875 Russia was the most backward economy among the major countries in Europe. Some industrialization had been carried out under Peter the Great (1700-1725) in order to increase the power of the state. But during most of the 19th century the Imperial government, with its support concentrated in the landed aristocracy, showed little interest in further development. Before the emancipation of the serfs in 1861, manufacturing was primarily limited to consumer goods, with textiles and sugar being the primary commodities.

There was, however, one area of significant development: the construction of railroads between 1840 and 1880. In the 1870s the railroads played a key role in the export of grain. Historians note two periods of acceleration of economic development before the Bolshevik revolution: 1885 to 1900, and 1907 to 1913.

The key to economic growth during these two periods was the role of the state. First, the state had built most of the railroads. Second, high tariffs were introduced between 1877 and 1891. Third, foreign capital was encouraged through government profit guarantees, tax reductions, tax exemptions, and the easing of laws and regulations. Foreign investment became very important in iron and steel, coal mining, petroleum extraction, additional railroad construction, and banking. Fourth, capital was protected by the regular use of the police and the military to control strikes and labour disputes. (Grossman, 1971:5-20; Gerschenkron, 1963:426-436)

But as Grossman notes (1971:6, 9), these were "islands of economic strength and modernity" within a "vast sea of poverty and backwardness." In 1913 Russia was listed as the fifth largest industrial power in the world, but on a per capita basis it ranked much lower; at best, it was one-tenth as industrialized as United States. In per capita income it was one of the lowest in Europe.

What industrialization had occurred had been at the expense of the peasants. Gerschenkron (1963:429-431) stresses that during this period they "had been eking out a miserable existence from a barbarously primitive agriculture." The peasants not only owed landlords heavy rents and usurious interest rates, grain was extracted from them for export to pay for foreign investment and imports of capital goods. When the peasants revolted against their oppression, they were repressed by the military.

Russia was well known for its famines. Between 1880 and 1910, when famines were unknown in western Europe, there were numerous local famines. In 1911-12 there was a major famine which struck 60 regions of the country. Yet, during that year, Russian grain merchants exported 13.5 million metric tonnes of grain, one-fifth of the country's production. Russia was one of the "breadbaskets of Europe," accounting for almost 25% of the grain sold on the world market. (Voskresensky, 1981:24)

Between 1860 and 1913 the population of Russia grew from 74 to 164 million. Agricultural production grew at a slightly higher rate, based on increased use of labour and land. But the technological level of agriculture was very low by European standards; the three-field rotation system still dominated, and mechanization had hardly begun. At the outbreak of World War I, over 80% of the economically active population was still on the farm. Workers in mining and manufacturing accounted for less than 2%. (Grossman, 1971:11-16)

A major factor contributing to the persistence of famine is the ecology of agriculture in the Soviet Union, described by M. Gardner Clark (1977:4) as "a colossal mismatch between soil and moisture." Only about 1 percent of Soviet farmland receives 70 centimetres of rain per year. The best soils, the chernozem or black earth zones, only receive between 20 and 40 centimetres per year. The high population areas are in the podzolic soil zones, characterized by conifer forests, acidity, and leaching, with adequate rainfall, but needing drainage. Most of European Russia, the centre of population, is above 52 degrees north, well above the settled areas of Canada; the short cool summers greatly limit the types of crops that can be grown. Much of the land in the warmer areas can be cultivated only when irrigation is possible. Thus modern productive agriculture requires substantial investment, technology, and a heavy subsidy of fossil fuel energy. The immense size of the country also creates special problems of storage, preservation, and transportation of food. (See Lydolph, 1977)

But the political and economic system in Russia was also a major contributing factor in repeated famines. The government was an anachronism, the absolute Tsar supported by a feudal aristocracy. The serfs were "liberated" from feudalism in 1861, but as peasants they were compelled to work for or rent land from the large landlords, their previous masters. Their "freedom" was purchased through large debts that they could not pay. The annual distribution of the peasants' land was controlled by the village Mir, and holdings were in widely scattered strips, as in the Middle Ages. After 1861 the landlords consolidated their control over the land, and peasants continued to revolt.

The second major agricultural reform followed the wave of peasant revolts against landlords and the state. In 1906 the "Stolypin Plan" was decreed by the Tsar; it was a liberal program designed to replace the communal Mir with individual ownership of land. Peasants were to be allowed to buy land through a new system of mortgages. The kulak class was quick to exploit these reforms, buying up the land of small-holders whom they converted into hired hands. Peasant revolts continued until World War I. (Morozov, 1977:24-27; Dunman, 1975:90-93; Volin, 1970:94-107)

The successful Bolshevik revolution created the first "workers' state" in a backward society only beginning to really develop capitalism. According to Marx and Engels, the socialist revolution was to emerge out of the contradictions of advanced capitalism. The capitalist system would provide the material pre-conditions for socialism: a highly industrialized society, the dominance of industry over agriculture, the advanced state of science, technology, and the productive forces, and a politically organized, highly skilled working class. But none of these conditions existed in the Soviet Union. And there were no models of socialist states to follow. Building socialism meant first of all building the productive base for the society, and this could only be done through trial and error.

The first acts of the Soviet government were designed to solidify support among the peasants, the overwhelming majority of the population. The Decree of 1917 confiscated all property of landlords without compensation, nationalized all land and resources, and limited farming to those who cultivated the land without hired help. All rent was abolished. Peasants' debts to the Land Bank were written off, and they were given the landlord's farm implements. The Decree of 1918 permitted the government to establish collective farms "for the purpose of a transition to a socialist economy," and co-operative farms were to be given preferential treatment in the allotment of land confiscated from the landlords. However, the actual distribution of land was done on the local level by peasants themselves, along the lines of the communal mir; only a very small percentage of confiscated land was used to create collective and state farms. "Dwarf agriculture" persisted: in 1917, 70% of the households in agriculture had less than 5 ha of land; after redistribution in 1919, 80% had less than 5 ha. (Wadekin, 1982: 10-12; Stanis, 1976:45-46; Volin, 1970:128-130)

The World War, the civil war that followed, and foreign interventions brought massive destruction to agriculture. The period between 1918 and 1921 is referred to as "War Communism," as the infant socialist state struggled to survive. Mandel (1968:549) points out that economic activity during this period was more a system of rationing than development, with production greatly restricted by the war situation. In agriculture the surplus-appropriation system, established by the Provisional Government in 1917, was enforced by the local Communist Party and the Committees of the Poor; grain was extracted to feed the army and the urban sector. The low prices fixed by the state grain monopoly offered no incentive to produce or deliver. The large estate that had produced marketable grain in the past no longer existed. Inflation was rampant. What goods were distributed came from the state, as all trade was nationalized. Barter was the norm, and work was often paid in kind. Grain deliveries to urban centres declined dramatically. In 1921 there was famine.

Following the victory in the civil war, the revolutionary government introduced the New Economic Policy (NEP) in an effort to recover the basic productive forces of the country. A tax in kind was imposed on farmers, less than that imposed by the appropriation system, a free market was established for agricultural production above the tax, and various measures were introduced to encourage the development of co-operatives. By 1924 agricultural production had recovered to 80% of the 1913 level. (Mozorov, 1977:32-33; Stanis, 1976:62-68; Volin, 1970:161-188)

During the 1920s there was a major, open debate in the Soviet Union on the role of agriculture in the accumulation of surplus for investment. Industrialization was a top priority with the Communist Party. It was also seen as a solution to agrarian overpopulation and as necessary to expand the socialist sector of the economy. Rapid development was deemed necessary to stave off another intervention by the capitalist powers. Where was the source of investment? There were no colonies to exploit. The Soviet government had repudiated the Tsar's foreign debts, and outside investment was not available; furthermore, the Party wanted to avoid "enslaving loans from abroad." The only major alternative was to extract surplus from industrial and agricultural labour.

Preobrazhensky argued for the extraction of a surplus from agriculture by the system of non-equivalent exchange. Under capitalism, surplus is extracted from farmers by the cost-price squeeze: prices to farmers lag behind the prices for necessary farm inputs. The surplus is accumulated by merchant and finance capital. Under "original socialist accumulation," the same extraction process could occur, but with the state imposing the unfavourable terms of trade as buyer of farm products and as the seller of farm inputs. This position was supported by the "leftist" faction of the Party around Trotsky.

The other faction in the Party was led by Bukharin, who argued that if the new socialist state wanted the peasants to increase production, there had to be financial incentives. Whereas the left argued that class warfare between the kulaks and the poor peasants was inevitable and necessary to promote socialism in the rural areas, in 1925 Bukharin urged that accumulation be more indirect and traditional, through taxation and the banking system.

(Khan and Ghai, 1980:21; Ellman, 1979:93-94; Dunman, 1975:121-123; Volin, 1970:190-194)

In December 1926, the Central Committee urged the intensification of the organization of collective and state farms. The collective-farm movement was endorsed by the Party's 15th Congress in December 1927. As Mandel (1968:553) argues, the decision was forced by the kulaks in the winter of 1927-1928 when they organized a veritable strike against supplying food for the towns. At the July 1928 Plenum of the Central Committee Stalin endorsed the process of "internal accumulations" via the working class and the peasantry. The Soviet state was "compelled to levy for the time being" the agricultural "tribute" or "supertax" in the form of unequal exchange, in order to finance industrialization. (Ellman, 1979:84-85; Volin, 1970:196-202)

By 1928 industrialization had begun to exceed pre-war levels. But the marketable surplus of grain was only 37% of the pre-war level. One of the major reasons was the dramatic increase in the number of farms, from 16 million in 1913 to 25 million in 1928. The peasants lived better, consumed more, but had less to sell to the market. Most of the marketable surplus was controlled by the three million kulaks. But the kulaks were not a large segment of the farming population, and they did not control an excessive amount of land. The vast majority of peasants (70%) had less than two hectares of land. At the same time, the ability of the collective and state farms to produce a marketable surplus, and to guarantee delivery, had been demonstrated; their percentage of the crop marketed far exceeded that of the small and middle peasants. The Party concluded that the NEP system and the proliferation of small subsistence peasant farms were not serving the needs of the socialist state. (Perlo, 1977:111; Stanis, 1976:87-89; Volin, 1970:209-212; Mandel, 1968:551-553)

At the end of 1929 the Party launched its policies of collectivization and dekulakization of agriculture. Peasants were given contracts to deliver grain, and local committees forcefully collected the "surplus." Individual farmers were prohibited from hiring farmhands. Land leases were abolished. New machinery was directed to collective farms. Kulaks were prohibited from joining collective farms. Property confiscated from kulaks and other peasants was turned over to collective farms organized by local peasants and agricultural workers. By 1932 61% of all farm households were on collective or state farms; by 1937, 93%.

The cost was great. Coercion was necessary, since the peasants as a class resisted socialization. There was a mass slaughter of livestock. Resistance by the kulaks and other peasants was widespread; workers sent to collect the grain were tortured and murdered. Workers on the collective farms were attacked by groups of angry peasants. In some places there were peasant insurrections. Some of the most vociferous opponents fled the country; a great many kulaks were transported to other regions. The persecution and scattering of the most progressive and efficient farmers was a blow to agricultural production. The rural standard of living declined. But, as Ellman notes, (1979:94) the marketable supply of grain, potatoes, and vegetables increased between 1929 and 1931; it then fell off during the drought of 1931-1933. Yet, to meet urban needs, the state increased grain procurement. But in the countryside, a famine resulted. (Wadekin, 1982:15-21; Laird, 1979:7-9; Stanis, 1976:88-91; Volin, 1970:216-222; Mandel, 1968:554-555)

The goals of collectivization were clear: (1) the socialization of the rural areas and the elimination of political opposition from the petit bourgeois class; (2) the rational use of land and farm mechanization to increase agricultural productivity, permitting low purchase prices; (3) an increase in the marketable surplus of agricultural products needed by the urban and industrial sector; (4) an increase in the surplus available for investment in the economy as a whole; and (5) a more rational use of labour in order to release workers for the expanding industrial labour force.

The policy, while very harsh, achieved its goals. Between 1929 and 1940 industrialization rapidly increased. The Soviet Union was able to survive the Nazi invasion. But agriculture was badly neglected, under-equipped, and had a low level of labour productivity. In 1952 the state procurement prices for grain and meat were only one-seventh that of the international price. The standard of living in the rural areas remained very low. Major investments in agriculture did not begin until the 1960s. (Khan and Ghai, 1980:25; Ellman, 1979:96-97; Shaffer, 1977:60-63; Clark, 1977:1-3; Perlo, 1977:111)

The critics of primitive socialist accumulation are many. Those on the political right (e.g., Volin) would have found fault with the Soviet experiment no matter what policy had been implemented. Wadekin (1982:21) emphasizes the forced nature of the collectivization as a repudiation of Lenin's admonition to win over the peasants gradually through the example of the state and collective farms and through co-operatives. Ellman (1979:92-98) argues that the "coercive model" led to high costs and low productivity in agriculture, sabotage by the peasants, and the loss of rural markets for industrial goods. Following the Soviet economist Barsov (1974), he concludes that the unequal exchange under socialism was not as effective in extracting a surplus from the agricultural sector as was the capitalist market economy in Russia in 1913. Increasingly, the surplus for investment came from the working class itself, through low wages and a low standard of living.

This last point is stressed by one critic from the left, Mandel (1968:553-554). There was a "terrible tribute" extracted from the Soviet people in order to finance rapid industrialization. Mandel argues that the burden would not have been so great if the 5- to 7-year planning periods had been stretched over 10 to 12 years, and if the annual rates of increased production had been reduced from the very high 20% to 23% levels. This was a clear option. But given the world political and economic situation, Stalin chose rapid industrialization at the expense of agriculture.

The radical change in social relations in the rural area, and the sabotage by those who resisted collectivization, took a heavy toll. By 1940 grain production was only 32% above the 1909-13 average. Meat and milk production had just barely reached the pre-war levels. (Voskresensky, 1981:63; Volin, 1970:248-261)

The impact of World War II was devastating. Twenty million people were killed and another 30 million were injured, leaving the farming sector with a severe labour shortage. The Nazi armies occupied the most fertile lands. Villages, state and collective farms were plundered and looted; all machinery disappeared. Buildings were destroyed, and orchards and vineyards were levelled. By 1945 grain production had fallen below 1913 levels. Livestock in the occupied areas were slaughtered or transferred to Germany. Gross food production was down 55% from 1940 levels. (Shaffer, 1977:62; Morozov, 1977: 42; Volin, 1970:294-300)

The Soviet Union was weak at the end of the war. Reconstruction required heavy capital investment. The onset of the Cold War again led Stalin and the Party to stress rapid industrialization. Farm procurement prices were kept at their 1937 levels, and investment was primarily directed to industry and transportation, Again, Soviet farm workers were called on to serve the goals of the state. General improvement in the standard of living had to wait until the 1960s. (Shaffer, 1977:63)

Conclusion

This chapter's introduction summarized the orthodox model of economic development and the special role of agriculture. Seven contributions were singled out as general principles. They are regularly cited when development economists give advice to governments of underdeveloped countries. In the brief review of the history of the major advanced industrialized countries these factors were identified as important. But in each case there were also other very important contributing factors.

In the primary example, the United Kingdom, there was substantial investment in agriculture from the outside; this has been widely attributed to merchant capital accumulated from overseas plunder, colonialism, and slavery. For the United Kingdom and the rest of western Europe, the problem of "overpopulation" in rural areas during increases in agricultural productivity was eased by substantial overseas migration. Japanese development also benefitted from exploitation of overseas colonies at a crucial period of industrialization, but this had a depressing effect on the agricultural sector.

The United States is the primary example of development in the "new areas" overseas. Obviously, this option is closed to the present underdeveloped countries. The North American continent, well suited for agriculture, was only sparsely settled. The local inhabitants were forcibly removed from the prime settlement areas, victims of American expansion across the continent. In the South, slavery was the key to agricultural development. At a key period of expansion, major markets in Europe were opened to agricultural exports. While the westward march was aided by portfolio investment in railroads, most capital accumulation was from domestic sources. The agricultural sector of the economy grew along with the industrial sector, and the consumer goods industry developed in balance with the capital goods industry.

Bairoch (1969:39) stresses that after the industrialization of the United Kingdom and a few other European states by the end of the 19th century, the list of additional countries achieving agricultural and industrial development was cut short for 40 or 50 years. Japan and the Soviet Union remain the primary examples of "late development."

In the underdeveloped countries, there is considerable interest in the Soviet experience. At the time of the Bolshevik revolution, Russia was overwhelmingly a peasant society. Without outside capital, the Soviet Union managed to industrialize in spite of the massive destruction brought on by two world wars, the civil war, and the disruption that resulted from agricultural collectivization. But the development of agriculture was held back, and the standard of living of the rural people remained relatively low until the 1960s. But, even here, there were special conditions denied to most of the present underdeveloped countries. In spite of its poor climatic conditions, the USSR has a very high ratio of arable land to population and very extensive natural resources, including abundant and relatively inexpensive energy sources.

In all four cases of high industrialization, the working people in both agriculture and industry experienced a great deal of suffering and hardship. In the later-developing economies, Japan and the Soviet Union, there was extreme exploitation of the peasants to provide much of the surplus for investment.

It is also important to note that all of the major industrialized states used protection from foreign competition at key times during industrialization. And as Gerschenkron (1963) stresses, the backward states or late developers all relied heavily on state intervention in the economy. Free trade and free enterprise were the policies of those who were already highly developed.

References

Bairoch, Paul (1969). *Agriculture and the Industrial Revolution*. London: Fontana Books.

Birnie, Arthur (1964). *An Economic History of Europe, 1760-1939*. London: Methuen.

Boserup, Ester (1981). *Population and Technological Change*. Chicago: University of Chicago Press.

Braudel, Fernand (1967). *Capitalism and Material Life, 1400-1800*. London: Weidenfeld and Nicolson.

Caldwell, Malcolm (1977). *The Wealth of Some Nations*. London: Zed Press.

Carter, Vernon Gill and Tom Dale (1974). *Topsoil and Civilization*. Norman: University of Oklahoma Press.

Clark, M. Gardner (1977). "Soviet Agricultural Policy." In Harry G. Shaffer, ed. *Soviet Agriculture; An Assessment of its Contributions to Economic Development*. New York: Praeger, pp. 1-47.

Davidson, Basil (1961). *Black Mother*. London: Gollancz.

Deane, Phyllis (1979). *The First Industrial Revolution*. London: Cambridge University Press.

De Vries, Jan (1976). *Economy of Europe in the Age of Crisis, 1600-1750*. Cambridge: Cambridge University Press.

Dobb, Maurice (1963). *Studies in the Development of Capitalism*. New York: International Publishers.

Duby, Georges (1969). *Medieval Agriculture, 900-1500*. London: Fontana Books.

Dunman, Jack (1975). *Agriculture: Capitalist and Socialist*. London: Lawrence and Wishart.

Ellman, Michael (1979). *Socialist Planning*. Cambridge: Cambridge University Press.

Frank, André Gunder (1979). *Dependent Accumulation and Underdevelopment*. New York: Monthly Review Press.

Gerschenkron, Alexander (1963). "The Early Phases of Industrialization in Russia and Their Relationship to the Historical Study of Economic Growth." In Barry E. Supple, ed. *The Experience of Economic Growth*. New York: Random House, pp. 426-444.

Gray, Lewis C. (1958). *History of Agriculture in the Southern United States to 1860*. II vols. Gloucester, Mass.: Peter Smith.

Grossman, Gregory (1971). *The Industrialization of Russia and the Soviet Union*. London: The Fontana Library.

Hadwiger, Don F. and Ross B. Talbot (1979). "The United States: A Unique Development Model." In Raymond F. Hopkins et al, eds. *Food, Politics, and Agricultural Development*. Boulder: Westview Press, pp. 21-43.

Hayami, Yujiro and Vernon W. Ruttan (1971). *Agricultural Development: An International Perspective*. Baltimore: The Johns Hopkins Press.

Hirschmann, Albert (1958). *Strategies of Economic Development*. New Haven: Yale University Press.

Hobsbawm, Eric J. (1968). *Industry and Empire*. London: Weidenfeld and Nicolson.

Hobsbawm, Eric J. and George Rude (1969). *Captain Swing*. London: Lawrence and Wishart.

Hoffmann, Walter G. (1958). *The Growth of Industrial Economies.* Manchester: Manchester University Press.

Johnston, Bruce F. and Peter Kilby (1975). *Agriculture and Structural Transformation.* London: Oxford University Press.

Jones, E. L., ed. (1967). *Agriculture and Economic Growth in England 1650-1815.* London: Methuen.

Khan, Azizhur Rahman and Dharam Ghai (1980). *Collective Agriculture and Rural Development in Soviet Central Asia.* New York: St. Martin's Press.

Laird, Roy D. (1979). "The Plusses and Minuses of State Agriculture in the USSR." In Ronald A. Francisco et al, eds. *The Political Economy of Collectivized Agriculture.* New York: Pergamon Press, pp. 3-20.

Landes, David S. (1969). *The Unbound Prometheus.* London: Oxford.

Lis, Catharina and Hugo Soly (1979). *Poverty and the Capitalism in Pre-Industrial Europe.* Sussex: Harvester Press.

Lockwood, William W. (1954). *Japan's Emergence as a Modern State.* Princeton, N.J.: Princeton University Press.

Lydolph, Paul E. (1977). *Geography of the USSR.* Toronto: John Wiley & Sons.

Mandel, Ernest (1968). *Marxist Economic Theory.* Volume II. London: Merlin Press.

Mannix, Daniel P. (1962). *Black Cargoes.* New York: The Viking Press.

Mathias, Peter (1969). *The First Industrial Nation.* London: Methuen.

Mellor, John W. (1966). *The Economics of Agricultural Development.* Ithaca: Cornell University Press.

Milward, Alan S. and S. B. Saul (1973). *The Economic Development of Continental Europe, 1780-1879.* London: George Allen & Unwin.

Mols, Roger (1972). *Population in Europe, 1500-1700.* London: Fontana Books.

Moore, Barrington, Jr. (1966). *Social Origins of Dictatorship and Democracy.* Boston: Beacon Press.

Morozov, V. (1977). *Soviet Agriculture.* Moscow: Progress Publishers.

Nicholls, William H. (1964). "The Place of Agriculture in Economic Development." In Carl Eicher and Lawrence Witt, eds. *Agriculture in Economic Development.* New York: McGraw-Hill, pp. 11-44.

North, Douglas C. (1961). *The Economic Growth of the United States, 1790-1860.* Englewood Cliffs, N.J.: Prentice Hall.

Ohkawa, Kazushi and Henry Rosovsky (1964). "The Role of Agriculture in Modern Japanese Economic Development." In Carl Eicher and Lawrence Witt, eds. *Agriculture in Economic Development.* New York: McGraw Hill, pp. 45-69.

Perlo, Victor (1977). "How Agriculture is Becoming an Advanced Section of Socialist Society." In Harry G. Shaffer, ed. *Soviet Agriculture: An Assessment of Its Contributions to Economic Development.* New York: Praeger, pp. 109-143.

Shaffer, Harry G. (1977). "Soviet Agriculture: Success or Failure?" In Harry G. Shaffer, *Soviet Agriculture: An Assessment of its Contributions to Economic Development.* New York: Praeger, pp. 58-98.

Smith, Thomas C. (1959). *Agrarian Origins of Modern Japan.* Palo Alto: Stanford University Press.

Stanis, Vladimir (1976). *The Socialist Transformation of Agriculture.* Moscow: Progress Publishers.

Strachey, John (1959). *The End of Empire.* London: Gollancz.

Volin, Lazar (1970). *A Century of Russian Agriculture.* Cambridge: Harvard

University Press.

Voskresensky, Lev (1981). *Farming; The Soviet Union Today and Tomorrow.* Moscow: Novosti Press Publishing House.

Wadekin, Karl-Eugen (1982). *Agrarian Policies in Communist Europe; A Critical Introduction.* Towota: Allenheld, Osmun.

Williams, Eric (1966). *Capitalism and Slavery.* New York: Capricorn Books.

Williams, Douglas and Roger Young (1981). *Taking Stock: World Food Security in the Eighties.* Ottawa: The North-South Institute.

CHAPTER FOUR

Agriculture and
Late Development:
Latin America and Africa

One of the most striking characteristics of the world today is the uneven level of economic development: between continents, nation states, and regions. Even though it can be shown that, in an economic sense, all human societies are progressing, differences in the level of development are enormous. For example, 1982 data provided by the World Bank (1984:Table 1) reveal that the average per capita gross national product of the "low-income economies," representing 50% of the world's population, was only $280; the average for the industrialized market economies, with just 17% of the population, was $11,070, or roughly 40 times as great.

The issue of food production and the persistence of hunger is closely intertwined with the issue of general economic development. When European states began to expand their influence around the globe in the 16th century, the differences in standard of living were less apparent. Indeed, in the 16th century, China was more highly developed than Europe. Why was it that Europe rushed ahead while economic development in the rest of the world stagnated? This is the key question addressed in Chapters IV and V. But the concern here is primarily with the impact of the European intrusion of local production and distribution of food and other agricultural products.

The expansion of European militarism and colonialism had a tremendous impact on the rest of the world. By the 18th century European colonialism was introducing capitalism to the other continents. Most orthodox social scientists, as well as many Marxists, stress that capitalist intrusion was a progressive force: it destroyed the old feudal system and began the process of modernization. Nevertheless, the process of development under conditions of colonialism was quite different from that in the independent industrialized states in Europe, the United States, and Japan.

First, there was no national direction by an indigenous capitalist class. Power was exercised by foreign rulers, and their priorities were quite different from those of the local peoples. National cultures themselves were fragmented, as the borders of nations were changed at will. Colonized peoples had no political power or civil rights, and they were universally subjected to racial discrimination. The imperial powers regularly used force and coercion to implement policies and to suppress rebellion. Social support was generally limited to modest improvements in hygiene required by an implanted European community. The ideology of colonialism and white supremacy was re-inforced by Christian missionaries.

Second, economic development was dictated by the principles of mercantile colonialism. Tariffs and other protectionist measures directed trade to the mother country. Natural trading relationships, both internal and regional, were disrupted. European firms were given monopoly rights and concessions. Indigenous handicraft industries, textiles, and other infant industries were destroyed by imperial policies and by competition from more technologically advanced European firms. Capital investment was directed to the most profitable areas and was invariably foreign-owned. While the local population increased, employment opportunities in manufacturing were greatly limited, resulting in the rapid expansion of the service sector of the urban economy. The destruction of the infant manufacturing sector disrupted village and town life and "agrarianized" societies: people were forced back into agriculture.

Industrialization was advancing rapidly in Europe. However, the colonial powers did not transfer their technology or industrial capital to their colonies. Thus, while Europe, the United States, and Japan were shifting to industrial capitalism in the 19th and 20th centuries, the colonized areas remained captives of merchant capitalism. In the industrializing countries, development was a complementary process between agriculture and manufacturing, and between the consumer goods industry and the capital goods industry. This was simply not the case in any of the colonized areas.

The chief characteristics of the colonial political economy were (1) concentration on the production of agricultural crops and minerals for export; (2) the imposition of a variety of local taxes to finance colonialism and to force food producers into the cash economy; (3) theft of land from the indigenous peoples and its bestowal on foreign interests or sale to local landlords; (4) compulsory labour on infrastructure and other colonial projects; and (5) the extraction of economic surplus from colonial producers (mainly farmers and farm labourers) and its transfer to the metropolitan country through the circulation process of merchant capitalism.

Therefore, even merchant capitalism had a profound effect on many underdeveloped countries. Village self-sufficiency was dissolved, and local producers were forced into a larger market. Land ceased to be communally owned, and became a commodity to be bought and sold in the market. For agriculturalists crop production was not only more market-oriented, it was directed towards production for a world market. But these developments, generally viewed by European social scientists as progressive, must be weighed against the fact that, in the underdeveloped countries, the colonial powers aligned themselves politically with the old, pre-capitalist ruling classes: absolutist royalty, the traditional aristocracy, and the landlords. The new classes that developed were the comprador merchant class and the colonial middle class (primarily in the state bureaucracy), both of which were closely linked to the imperial system.

But it was the peasant economy that was most affected by mercantile colonialism. The best land was often stolen and granted to corporations or white settlers. The plantation system brought slavery and then semi-slavery in the form of indentured labour; peasants were shipped all over the globe to labour and die for capitalist agriculture. In order to pay their colonial taxes, peasants were forced to grow cash crops for export, most of which had no value as food. Over the years, the merchant capitalists found that they could often make even higher profits by the indirect exploitation of peasants through the market system; direct production on plantations was not necessary. Thus simple commodity production of cash crops by individual farm families became the dominant form of agricultural production in these countries in the 20th century.

The result everywhere was the neglect of food crops. Technological innovations were almost entirely orientated to cash crops for export. In direct contrast to what was happening in the industrialized countries, the productivity of food crops declined while the rural population increased. Peasants were forced onto more marginal lands. As the ratio of rural population to cultivated land worsened, peasants became more impoverished.

In fragile ecological areas, shifting agriculture was progressively replaced by sedentary agriculture, leading to serious problems of erosion. Many of the export crops themselves (e.g., groundnuts, coffee, tobacco, sugar, and cotton) were destructive of the soil. As the land farmed by plantations deteriorated, it was abandoned to subsistence peasant agriculture; the preferred crops were moved on to deplete new lands.

As Alavi (1980:392) stresses, the shift from food to export crop production under the political conditions of colonialism was a process of "internal disarticulation and external integration." But the question that arises, even in the 19th century, is whether this process of distorted development is limited to the colonial system. The evidence from Africa (Liberia and Ethiopia), Latin America, and Asia (the Philippines and Thailand) indicates that the structure of agriculture and development was not very different under conditions of "free trade" and political independence. Where there are profound differences in political and military power, and very unequal levels of development, the "free market" turns out to be just another form of exploitation. This chapter and the following one on Asia briefly describe the historical impact of imperialism and colonialism on the rest of the world, with particular reference to the production and distribution of food and agricultural products.

Latin American Agricultural Civilizations

When Columbus and the other Spanish explorers reached the American continents, they thought they had reached Paradise or Utopia. Indeed, one Spanish lawyer wrote a two-volume work arguing that the Garden of Eden was in South America. (Galeano, 1973:24; Wolf, 1959:159-160)

While the American continents were vast in territory, they were certainly not uninhabited. The Circum-Caribbean peoples, the tribes of the Amazon basin, and the peoples of eastern Brazil, the Gran Chaco, the Pampa, Patagonia, and Tierra del Fuego lived primarily on hunting, fishing, and gathering wild foods, and occasionally practising shifting (slash-and-burn) agriculture. At the same time, there were highly developed civilizations: the Aztecs and Maya of Mexico and Central America and the Inca of the Andes. (Sanders and Price, 1968:80-88; Herring, 1961:28-29)

Anthropologists and historians disagree on the size of the indigenous population. Sanders and Price (1968:84) cite estimates that range between a low of 8 to 9 million to a high of 90 to 112 million. The early explorers and missionaries put rather high figures on the native populations. The Inca empire along the Andes mountains in South America stretched over 3000 miles from north to south. Those who first made contact estimated the population at between 3 and 33 million. More recently, anthropologists put the figure between 4.5 and 7.5 million. When the Incas launched a war on Quito, they marched with an army of 300,000. (Sanders and Price, 1968:76; Herring, 1961:47; Von Hagen, 1961:158, 198). Wolf (1959:31) notes that population estimates for the Mexican region range between 11 and 15 million. More recent studies put the figure as high as 25 million. (Stein and Stein, 1970:34; Braudel, 1967:5) Population figures for the Maya civilization vary widely, but Weaver (1981:274) concludes that, in the lowland alone, the overall population "must have been in the millions."

The Spaniards were awed by the size and beauty of the cities they found. Teotihuacan, the religious centre twenty-five miles northeast of Tenochtitlan (now Mexico City), had a population of between 50,000 and 120,000 at the time of conquest. (Wolf, 1959:74, 93) Tenochtitlan had between 150,000 and 200,000 people, was much larger than Madrid, and more than twice the size of Seville, Spain's largest city. The total population of the Basin of Mexico was around 1.2 million in 1519. (Adams, 1977:26; Galeano, 1973:27) Estimates for Tikal, one of the oldest of the Mayan cities, are around 100,000 at A.D. 600. (Wolf, 1959:98) The smaller of the Mayan city states contained between 6000 and 18,000 people; the population around Dzibilchaltun has been estimated at 250,000. (Adams, 1977:142-143; Herring, 1961:33) The Spanish King's Inspector reported that Cuzco, the centre of the Inca Empire, contained 100,000 houses. While this was an exaggeration, it reflected the size of the population. (Von Hagen, 1961:128)

To put this into perspective, in 1700 the total population of Europe was around 50 million. The largest country, France, had a population of less than 20 million. The United Kingdom and Spain, the next largest, had populations of around 6 million. The total population of the Lowlands was 2.5 million and that of Portugal did not exceed 1 million. (Williams, 1966:49-50)

The political, legal, social, and economic systems of the three American civilizations were well developed. Mining, metallurgy, weaving, and handicraft production were advanced. The Spanish were amazed at the massive architectural centres and the engineering achievements of the indigenous peoples. Their highly productive agricultural systems were developed without draft animals or the wheel.

In Mexico a diversified agricultural system permitted high levels of population. This was accomplished by slash-and-burn agriculture in the high areas, dryland farming, two-field cultivation, elaborate systems of terracing, irrigation with dams and canals, and the *chinampas*, or floating gardens, with its complex of dikes. (Weaver, 1981:451-2; Adams, 1977:27-29; Wolf, 1959:74-78) The Maya faced a continuous drought problem; in response, their engineers designed and built complex systems of cisterns and reservoirs. (Von Hagen, 1960:25, 67) The engineering achievements of the Incas were even more astonishing to the Spanish: vast terracing of the highland slopes, immense water reservoirs, complicated irrigation systems, with canals and straightened rivers. Roads and bridges were built to connect the several parts of the empire and to provide access to varied foods. (Bankes, 1977:74-79; Baudin, 1961:220-221; Von Hagen 1961:66-67)

These highly productive agricultural systems made possible the establishment of elaborate cities, temples, handicrafts, and class societies. The key was the staple grain, maize. Yields were very high, compared to cereal production in Europe. Braudel (1967:110-111) reports that in dry areas one sown grain would yield between 70 and 80 grains: in intense irrigated areas, it could yield as high as 800 grains. In the warmer areas (like Mexico) it was possible to obtain two crops in one year.

In most of Mexico the production of food required less than two months of intermittent work, releasing labour for other projects and leisure. While the *chinampas* gardens were very productive, the Aztec civilization in Tenochtitlan, with over 80,000 non-farmers, depended on substantial tribute in food from subordinate states. The valley of Mexico was very fertile and maize production was well suited to the area. This staple was supplemented by amaranth, beans, squashes, tomatoes, onions, peppers and fruit; meat was limited to the domesticated dog, turkey and duck, and fish. Crops grown specifically for the market and trade included cocoa, tobacco, rubber, cotton, and henequen (sisal). There is evidence, however, that the lower class of peasants lived in relative poverty, undoubtedly because the ruling classes lived in splendour. (Weaver, 1981:453-459; Adams, 1977:26-29; Peterson, 1959:31-34, 168-169; Wolf, 1959, 53-54, 63-66).

The staple crop for the Maya was also maize. Where shifting cultivation was employed, food production could take as much as six months' labour.

But this was not the norm. The ramon (breadnut) tree, planted in groves, was of equal importance; the nut was highly nutritious, required no cultivation after planting, was easily harvested, and could be stored for up to eighteen months. These foods were supplemented by a wide variety of fruits and vegetables including beans, squash, peppers, sweet potatoes, manioc, melons, papayas, and avocados. Cocoa and cotton were grown for a trading market. The Maya were seafarers and maritime traders, and fish was an important food item. In addition to domesticated turkey and ducks, deer meat was readily available. In general, dependence on maize and ramon nuts left a great deal of labour time for building elaborate cities and religious temples. (Weaver, 1981:275-277; Coe, 1980:143-145; Adams, 1977:140-142; Sanders and Price, 168:92-93)

The basic diet of the Inca people included maize and chili peppers, sun-dried llama meat, potatoes, quinoa, and oca. Fishing was practised on the Pacific coast and around Lake Titicaca. Staples were supplemented with fruits and vegetables grown in the lower elevations of the empire: tomatoes, beans, squashes, papaya, avocado, and guavas. In the upper Amazon regions the Incas cultivated peanuts, cocoa, manioc, and pineapples. Cotton was grown for the textile industry. Plant breeding, seed selection, and hybridizing were well developed; cultivated fields were fertilized with guano. While the people were primarily farmers, the highly productive agricultural system provided a significant amount of time for labour on extensive and elaborate communal projects that maintained the empire. (Bankes, 1977:73-81; Baudin, 1961:221-228; Von Hagen, 1961:58-63; Herring, 1961:200-201) In all three civilizations, land was communally owned, and citizens' obligations to the community and the state were paid as labour-time or in kind.

Thus the food requirements of the peoples of these classic civilizations were adequately supplied; but, as their population grew, they became vulnerable to natural disasters. The average diet was of a high quality as well, with adequate calories, protein, vitamins and minerals. Contemporary standards might suggest that they were short of meat and animal products: the Spanish and Portuguese introduced horses, cattle, sheep, goats, pigs, and chickens. But protein was available to all from maize, pulses, potatoes, and yams, supplemented by fish and local meats. Where poverty was found, as among the poor peasants in the Aztec empire, it was due to the hierarchical and exploitative class system. One reason the Spanish believed they had found Paradise was the bounty of the food system. In Europe at this time the average person regularly suffered from food deprivation, particularly over the winter months, and famine was a recurring fact of life. (Braudel, 1967:38-42)

Of the three areas of the underdeveloped world, none was more dramatically affected by European colonialism than the Americas. The decimation of the indigenous population has rightly been called "the first great holocaust." The native Americans had no immunity to the diseases imported from Europe, and there were widespread epidemics, the most serious of which were smallpox, typhoid fever, and measles. Malaria and yellow fever were apparently imported from Africa in the slave ships. The first contacts with the Aztecs brought a smallpox epidemic that destroyed entire communities and killed so many adults that fields went untilled and local famines resulted. The first contact between the Mayan people and the Spanish in 1516 brought a smallpox epidemic that killed untold thousands; other waves of diseases further decimated the population. Between 1519 and 1650, six-sevenths of the indigenous population of Middle America was wiped out. (Furtado, 1970:5; Herring, 1961:131; Von Hagen, 1960:210; Wolf, 1959:195-197)

Columbus's second voyage to the Americas set the imperial tone for European rule. The people native to the Caribbean islands, the Arawaks and the Caribs, objected to slavery and the seizure of their women; when they resisted, they were slaughtered. These Caribbean people were virtually obliterated. (Galeano, 1973:22-23; Herring, 1961:29, 123-124)

Between 1515 and 1520, Cortez, in alliance with tributary states, conducted his military campaign against the Aztecs. In 1520 he began the total destruction of Tenochtitlan, which he called "the most beautiful city in the world." (Herring, 1961:129-133) Soon after, a military campaign was launched against the Mayan civilization. The Spanish celebrated a major victory in 1546; those who resisted the "peace" were slaughtered, and 500,000 were sold into peonage. But those who survived resisted, moving to the higher country of El Peten. There they avoided the Spanish until they were finally conquered in 1697. The Mayan civilization of 3700 years had been brought to an end (Von Hagen, 1960:209-212)

Pizzaro's final assault on the Incas began in 1530. His success was greatly aided by the turmoil that remained after three years of civil war over the succession to the last great Inca ruler, Huayna Capac. Cuzco fell in 1533; by 1535, the Spanish were in control of most of the empire. However, the native people continued to resist. The military conquest of Chile and the subjugation of the remaining native civilizations took even longer, well into the 1550s. (Herring, 1961:136-145)

The European Impact on Latin America

The Spanish came to the Americas in the search for precious metals. Mercantile capitalism at this time was little more than pillage. To assist the enterprise, the Spanish state established the *encomienda*: a group of native people were made wards of the commanders of the military orders, supposedly for the purpose of conversion to Christianity. As part of this system, the native people owed economic tribute and personal services. In operation, it became a right to labour exploitation and land.

The native people were required to perform forced labour in placer mining. Between 1543 and 1569, a series of large and deep silver mines was opened in Mexico. The famous silver deposit at Potosi was discovered in 1545, in what is now Bolivia, 13,000 feet above sea level. Natives were sold as slaves to work these mines; others were forced to perform *mita*, or compulsory labour service. The work was made much more hazardous with the adoption of the mercury amalgam process whose effects destroyed the strongest workers in less than four years. Deaths in the mines were astronomical. Galeano (1973:50-1) claims that, over a 300 year period, the Potosi mine "consumed 8 million lives." Herring (1961:191) quotes contemporary observers describing the mass of dead bodies that surrounded the mines in Mexico.

The native people lost control of their most productive land in confiscation by the Spanish system. Agriculture was organized to serve the mining communities and the towns and cities that grew up around them. For example, agriculture in Chile was re-oriented to serve the silver mines around Potosi; the regions of northern Argentina provided textiles and draught animals. On the Mexican Pacific coast, the Spanish destroyed enormous areas of intense cultivation, and other prime areas died out for lack of farmers. Also lost were the floating gardens in the lake surrounding Mexico City. With the decimation of the Inca civilization, large tracts of irrigated land became deserts. (Galeano, 1973:53-57; Furtado, 1970:13-14; Stein and Stein, 1970:37-38)

In 1493, Pope Alexander VI issued the famous bull, *Inter Caetera*, which divided the new world into areas of exploration between Spain and Portugal. Thus what is now Brazil fell within the Portuguese sphere of interest. At the beginning of the 16th century, Portugal was a relatively small, weak, imperial power, primarily interested in trade with the Far East. Brazil was populated by more primitive indigenous peoples; there were no great urban civilizations, and the people had not developed gold or silver. The Portuguese government encouraged settlement by granting large tracts of land to "captains," but immigration did not increase until after the establishment of the Inquisition in 1536. The first major commercial development was the sugar industry on the coastal land where fertility and rainfall was adequate. However, expansion was limited by lack of labour. Despite the best efforts of the *bandeirantes*, the native population could not provide nearly enough slaves. After the destruction and dispersal of the indigenous population, the sugar industry turned to slaves from Africa.

The Brazilian sugar plantation, the *engenho*, became the model for the plantation system of agriculture as it developed in the Americas. Limited to tropical or sub-tropical zones, it specialized in the production of a single crop for export to the colonial power. Food and other necessities for production were imported from other areas; in Brazil, the northeast sugar plantations were supplied mainly by *hacienda* agriculture in the south, dependent on Indian labour. While the plantation was based on slavery, it was a part of the mercantile capitalist system. As an economic form of agriculture, it was reproduced in areas of the Caribbean and the American colonies by the French, Dutch, Spanish, English, and American entrepreneurs.

During the first half of the seventeenth century, Brazil was the world's major supplier of sugar. But by 1650 plantation production was expanding in the Caribbean, and Brazil's industry began to decline. In 1893 gold was discovered in Minas Gerais, and slaves were driven to the mines. Later, other mines were developed in Matogrosso and Goiaz, and in 1728 diamonds were discovered. In agriculture, there was a shift to plantation production of cotton; during the 18th century Brazil became Europe's largest single source, only to lose this position to the plantations of the American south. Brazilian agriculture maintained its export orientation, however, with diversification into tobacco, cocoa, coffee, rice, vanilla, spices, and indigo. (Galeano, 1973:67, 73-75; Stein and Stein, 1970:41-43; Furtado, 1970:15-16; Herring, 1961:220-235)

In the Caribbean the native peoples were eliminated, and agriculture developed under the plantation/slavery system, serving Europe. Sugar became the major tropical crop promoted by all the colonial powers. The famous Triangular Trade was very profitable for the merchants of England, the Netherlands, and the New England colonies: slaves were brought from Africa, cotton and sugar went to Europe, and foodstuffs, timber, and other supplies went to the plantations. The "Sugar Islands" were completely transformed and integrated into the world market economy. (Galeano, 1973:91-91; Williams, 1966:51-60)

Between 1500 and 1650 well over two thirds of the indigenous peoples in Latin America had been killed by disease, slaughter, or forced labour. Local agricultural systems were radically changed, and social patterns emerged that persisted for over 300 years.

First, there was the development of plantation agriculture, a system of crop specialization for export to the metropolitan centres. The plantation was organized by European capitalists. While originally based on slavery, it not only persisted after the introduction of wage labour but continued to expand. (See Beckford, 1972; Gray, 1958)

With the beginning of the mining economy, the *encomienda* system changed to that of the *hacienda*, the large landed estate with direct ownership of the land, purchased from the Crown. Having lost their land to the imperial invaders, the survivors were now invited to settle on the *hacienda* permanently, as peons. The landlord would pay their tribute to the Crown in return for labour time. The landlord also advanced credit to buy supplies from the *hacienda* storehouse; the peons paid for this in labour time. In addition, the *hacienda* allocated small plots of poorer land to the peons for subsistence agriculture.

The landlords constantly acquired more land, not for the purpose of increasing production, but to force the native people to become dependent on the *hacienda* for land and employment. With the decline in the mining economy, markets shrank; the *hacienda* responded by reducing production and maintaining self sufficiency. Only the best land was farmed; much was left undeveloped. Where the climate was suitable, large pastoral estates were created. There was no effort to increase productivity. It was a unique system. While some have described it as "feudal," the peon had no rights and was often sold like a commodity. Throughout Latin America, the settler-landlords became the dominant local ruling class. (Furtado, 1970:16-18; Wolf, 1959:203-206)

The third form of agriculture was attempted by the indigenous peoples who survived the holocaust and were outside the *hacienda* system. They fled to the hills and the forests to avoid the Christians, relying on subsistence agriculture on the poorest lands. As commercial agriculture expanded in the 19th and 20th centuries, they were systematically driven off the better lands.

Most of Spanish and Portuguese Latin America achieved political independence between 1810 and 1825. While formal colonialism was ended, economic development in the new countries did not follow the pattern of the European model. There were two factors which explain the difference. First, there was the widespread adoption of the ideology and policy of free trade, the "major export" of the United Kingdom. Second, the ruling classes in Latin America at this time consisted of the agricultural and livestock exporters, the mining interests, and the major merchant houses specializing in imports. They were mercantile in outlook, pursuing their own self-interest. Politically, they captured state power as liberal reformers. Any opposition to their support of free trade was denounced as backward feudalism. They steadily acquired ownership of the lands of the Church and the Indians. (Frank, 1979:164-167)

Independence and free trade were pushed by British interests. Between 1800 and 1850 British merchants came to dominate Latin American trade; a flood of imports from Britain crushed most of the local industries. In the latter part of the 19th century, the British dominated Latin American capital markets, mining, and industry. In agriculture, Latin America continued as a source of "colonial staples" for the metropolitan markets. (Pregger-Roman, 1984:416-420; Galeano, 1973:191-224; Stein and Stein, 1970:124-155; Semmel, 1970)

But British commercial interests did not rest solely on free trade ideology. In the 1840s the populist dictator of Argentina, Juan Manuel de Rosas, imposed tariffs on British imports and sought to expand his influence throughout the pampas. Pressed by British bankers, traders, and industrialists, in 1845 the British and the French used gunboat diplomacy to restore laissez faire. (Galeano, 1973:200-206; Herring, 1961:628-640)

Of more significance was the experience of Paraguay. A land-locked country, after independence in 1813 it developed under the paternalism of three exceptional leaders. In a strong alliance with the masses, and by using the state, they pursued a national development strategy that excluded foreign capital and utilized protectionism. British commerce was concerned about this dangerous example. The British government responded, and their diplomats helped organize the War of the Triple Alliance. Between 1864 and 1870 the Brazilian and Argentine military exterminated around four-fifths of the population of Paraguay, and free trade was restored. (Galeano, 1973:2067-212; Herring, 1961:712-714)

European colonialism had a devastating impact on the indigenous peoples of Latin America. Those who survived the holocaust and forced labour were relegated to subsistence farming on dwarf holdings or became peons on the *hacienda*. Plantation agriculture brought slavery and large-scale importation of Africans. Commercial crop production was oriented to tropical crops for export. Well-developed handicraft industries were destroyed, and replaced by imported commodities.

The local ruling classes were drawn from the *latifundia*, the large estates, and merchant capital. Thus, after the end of formal colonialism in the early 19th century, the patterns of mercantile colonialism persisted as the Latin American governments adopted the ideology of free trade and continued subservience to European capital.

Pre-colonial Africa

Traditionally, western histories of Africa begin in 1415, the year the Portuguese captured and occupied Ceuta on the north coast of Africa. This opened exploration down the west coast of Africa, triggered by the search for gold and a new route to the spice islands. Madeira was occupied in 1418, and Portuguese settlers established orchards, vineyards, and the first sugar plantations. By 1445 they reached the Senegal River. The Papal bull of 1454 allocated Africa and its route to the East Indies to Portugal. By the end of the 15th century the Portuguese had established sugar plantations on São Tomé using African slave labour. Slaves from Africa were shipped to the Caribbean on Columbus's second voyage, staged their first major revolt on Hispaniola in 1522, were widely used in Mexico in 1530, and were the foundation of the sugar plantation economy in northeast Brazil after 1538.

In the 16th century Africa was different from Asia or the Americas. First, population was very low in relation to the land base. There are no records, and population estimates range considerably. Rodney (1974:97) cites a figure of 100 million for the year 1650. Wickins (1981:54) notes that estimates for the 18th century vary between 50 and 150 million. Munro (1976:20-23) uses estimates for 1750 ranging between 54 and 135 million, putting population density between four and ten people per square kilo-metre. At the same time, population density in Europe (excluding Russia) was between thirty-five and forty per square kilometre.

Population was held down by famines induced by droughts in steppe-savanna areas. There were epidemic diseases such as cholera, smallpox, and the plague. In the tropical areas, malaria, yellow fever, meningitis, dengue, blackwater fever, and sleeping sickness (caused by trypanosomiasis) persisted. Parasites were common, including Guinea worms and hookworm. Other serious problems were yaws, elephantiasis, and leprosy. Infant mortality rates were high.

With an abundance of land, hunting, gathering and nomadism were easy methods of sustaining life. Where agriculture was practised, it was usually slash-and-burn (or shifting) cultivation, the logical approach where the soil was fragile and relatively infertile. (Levi and Havinden, 1982:9-10) There was little incentive to adopt a more intensive form of agriculture. Munro (1976:25) stresses that pioneering colonization by African cultivators "seldom outgrew the supply of land exploitable by the existing technology."

Fishing was an important source of food and traditionally was combined with some form of agriculture. Native cereals cultivated included sorghum, bulrush millet, and finger millet, all of which can be grown on relatively infertile soil with minimal rainfall. Wild rice was cultivated in west Africa, particularly in the Niger delta. The Guinea forest yam, along with the oil palm, were major staple foods. A variety of vegetables was grown, balanced with the cowpea. On the east coast of Africa additional food crops had been introduced around 200 A.D., presumably from Indonesia; the important ones included bananas, coconuts, colocasia, yams, and taro. Muslim traders brought Asian rice, citrus fruits, sugar, and various vegetables.

Different breeds of cattle had been introduced to Africa; the first was the longhorn humpless, which came via the Nile valley around 5000 B.C. Horses had come across the Sahara from the Mediterranean area. The distribution of cattle and horses was limited by the tsetse fly.

Many of the American foods brought to Europe by the Spanish and Portuguese were also introduced into Africa. The most important were maize and cassava, which became staple foods; groundnuts, cocoa, and tobacco became cash crops for export. (Levi and Havinden, 1982:28-32; Gann and Duignan, 1972:167-173)

In the early 16th century handicraft development in Africa was not much different from that of Europe. The working of iron was discovered at an early period, formed the basis of the Meroe civilization in Sudan around 500 B.C., and from there was widely dispersed throughout Africa. Cloth made of bark and palm fibre was of a high quality, and cotton cloth was widely manufactured before the arrival of the Europeans. Pottery, basketry, woodwork, and leather work were all of a very high quality. But the technology for manufacture was less advanced than in Europe. Large canoes were built for river transportation, and in east Africa boats of up to 50 tons with sails of palm matting were constructed for coastal trade. The difference in the level of development of the handicraft industries between

Europe and Africa at this time was primarily scale of production. (Wickins, 1981:84-114; Munro, 1976:23-28; Rodney, 1974:41-43)

Social development also reflected the high ratio of land to population; communalism, based on lineage, was the norm. A number of societies existed with social stratification and state structures, but languages were varied, and territorial boundaries were constantly changing. The ruling classes (a small minority based on royalty) were much weaker than they were in Asia or the American civilizations. Transportation was difficult, and trade was mainly in key products such as salt and iron. Land was owned in common, although individually farmed. Politically, the Africans were living in relatively small communities, divided by language; they were no match for the arrival of the Europeans, backed by the modern nation-state and its military apparatus. (Gann and Duignan, 1972:202-245)

The success of Portugal in Africa rested on superiority in weaponry and ocean-going ships plus sailing and fighting skills. The trade that this small country developed was clearly based on military force. The search for gold led to the fort of Elmina on the Gold Coast (1481) and the domination of what is now Angola and Mozambique. In east Africa the fort at Sofala was used to export gold from what is now Zimbabwe. Later, Angola and East Africa were major sources of slaves sent to Brazil.

The new lands and plantations in America required labour, and Africa proved to be the best available source at the time. Slaves began pouring into Brazil in the 1530s. By 1540 over 10,000 slaves per year were arriving in the West Indies. Great Britain entered the slave trade in 1564, backed by the Crown; they built a fort at James Island, at the Gambia River, in 1608. The Dutch West Indies Company was formed in 1621 for the express purpose of exploiting the slave trade. In 1626 the French took the island of St. Louis, off Senegal. Finally, by 1645 shipping interests in New England also entered the trade. While there was continual conflict between trading nations throughout the 17th century, the slave trade boomed after the Treaty of Utrecht in 1713.

The famous triangular trade between Europe, Africa, and America had begun by 1530. That Africans were drawn into this notorious trade indicates the power of mercantile capitalism even at this early date. The Europeans supplied the Africans with guns and ammunition, woolens, linen, metal-wares, calicoes from India, and silk from China. The Africans had little to trade except palm oil, ivory, and some gold. The export of slaves was necessary to pay for the trade deficit. (Freund, 1984:46-55; Munro, 1976:33-35; Gann and Guignan, 1972:314-318)

At an early date, the Europeans found raiding for slaves to be too costly, and instead developed a system based on African suppliers. Slaves were primarily acquired through raiding wars and kidnapping. But as Mannix (1962:90-103) points out, many kings sold their own people after sentencing them for some pretended crime. Slaving was by no means limited to class states; raiding and selling was also practiced by egalitarian societies. The demand for slaves exceeded the supply along the coast, and the trade spread deep into the interior of Africa.

While some writers have concluded that the slave trade had the beneficial effect of promoting the exchange economy (Gann and Duignan, 1972:352; Freund, 1984:51), its effects on African development were devastating. First, it lasted for over 400 years and was the central focus of the African economy for at least 200 years. How many slaves actually arrived in the Americas is not known, but estimates range from eight to twelve million. It is widely agreed that another 15% or so died on the "middle passage." Countless others were killed in the wars and forced marches. The African labour force was decimated by the loss of the most able-bodied young men and women. Widespread kidnapping caused social chaos. Rodney (1974:97) stresses that between 1650 and 1900 the population of Africa grew by only 20%, whereas the population of Europe quadrupled and that of Asia more than tripled.

The commerce in slaves had a major impact on African production. Emphasis was on war, not on economic activity, and development stagnated. The kingdom of Dahomey went from being an exporter of agricultural products to a state of famine in the 19th century. (Rodney, 1974:99) The Kongo shifted to the gathering of people rather than producing food. (Freund, 1984:46) The Krumen, skilled fishermen and boaters, all but gave up production for the business of transporting slaves. (Mannix, 1962:48)

Commodities imported by the Europeans destroyed the local handicraft industry in contact areas. Furthermore, none of the technology that was being developed in Europe was introduced into Africa. There was almost no European investment of capital. (Munro, 1976:38, 62; Rodney, 1974:105-106)

The trade in slaves was banned in Great Britain in 1807, in the United States in 1808, in Holland in 1814 and in France in 1815. The British organized fleets of warships to enforce the ban. However, the demand for slaves remained high in Cuba, Brazil, and the southern United States, and profits remained high. In 1805 a slave could be bought in Africa for $25 to $50 and sold in Cuba or the United States for $500 to $650. By 1860 the price of a "prime field hand" in the United States had risen to $1800, reflecting the rise in the price of cotton. There, the local production of slaves was an essential "intermediate good." But the high price for slaves, and the enormous profits to be gained, greatly increased the contraband trade.

The evidence suggests that the trade in slaves did not decline until 1850, but the source shifted from west Africa to Angola and east Africa. Indeed, the east African trade peaked between 1810 and 1860. Even after 1870 there was a slave trade between east Africa, the Arab countries, and Asia. However, the long era of slavery was finally ending and the time had come for "legitimate commerce." (Munro, 1976:43-63; Mannix, 1962:194-199)

To a significant degree, African diseases kept white settlers and colonialists out of most of Africa for four centuries. The "white man's graveyard" was well known in Europe. Seamen hired for the slave trade had a high mortality rate; for example, it reached 21% for Liverpool and Bristol ships in the late 18th century. (Mannix, 1962:151) The Portuguese successfully introduced sugar and cocoa plantations with slave labour on the islands of Saõ Tomé and Fernando Po. They tried with less success to develop export crops in the Kongo kingdom. Danes introduced coffee plantations in west Africa in the late 18th century. (Gann and Duignan; 1972:339)

The initial major export crops from European plantations in Africa were vegetable oils used in Europe for the manufacture of candles and soap. Palm oil was first gathered in west Africa and then cultivated on plantations. In Senegal the French encouraged the commercial production of groundnuts. The early slave plantations on Zanzibar produced cloves, copra, and sesame seed for Europe. (Freund, 1984:62; Munro, 1976:45; Wickins, 270-271)

The price for vegetable oil began to fall in the 1860s; it dropped dramatically after the opening of the Suez Canal in 1869. Europeans began experimenting with other crops. Cotton and coffee were grown in Angola during the U.S. Civil War. Coffee was introduced to the Gold Coast around 1870, but cocoa proved to be a more suitable crop. In the latter part of the 19th century rubber production expanded, first by foraging wild plants and then by the introduction of plantations. The growing wealth in industrializing western Europe greatly increased the demand for tropical agricultural products.

The other major development in agriculture during this period was the white settler economy in South Africa. In 1652 the Dutch established the first colony in Africa at the Cape. While South Africa serviced the Asian trade, the mediterranean climate and absence of tropical diseases permitted European settlement. The Bushmen and Hottentots were driven off their land, which was then given to freehold farmers. Crops were grown to supply the ships in port, but staples, like wheat and grapes, were also grown for export. In the dryer regions cattle ranching was introduced.

In 1806 the British defeated the Dutch and transformed the Cape into a Crown Colony. The Boers migrated inland and established the Orange Free State and the Transvaal, in order to escape British rule. The merino sheep was introduced in the mid-1840s, and wool became the staple export to England's woollen industries. Sugar plantations were introduced in Natal; when slave trading was abolished, contract labourers from India were imported. (Freund, 1984:55-57, 76-81; Munro, 1976:55-63)

During the first half of the nineteenth century, barter terms of trade favoured the primary producers in the international economy. The development of manufacturing in Europe reduced the price of textiles and metal manufactures. Free trade in Africa was destroying handicraft and infant manufacturing industries in the coastal areas. In north Africa, exports of cotton textiles virtually ceased; instead there was concentration on the production of cotton for export, less emphasis on the production of food, and growing dependence on food imports. (Wickins, 1981:186-287; Rodney, 1974:103-105)

During the first four hundred years of contact with Europe, the emerging African business class was totally preoccupied with the slave trade. To use the Asian term, it was a comprador class, completely dependent on trade with the Europeans. The merchant middlemen did not change with the shift to "legitimate commerce"; they remained agents of foreign powers. (Freund, 1984:64-67)

Agriculture and Development in Colonial Africa

It is impossible here to recount the history of the European annexation of Africa (1870-1896) or to examine all the theories that have been advanced to explain it. But there were some major factors that greatly affected agriculture and development in general.

First, by 1870 the industrial predominance of Great Britain had been successfully challenged by Germany, France, and the United States. These industrial giants rejected the British ideology of free trade and built their economic power behind protectionist barriers. Austria, Spain, Italy, Belgium, and Switzerland were adopting the same course. Their success expanded world manufacturing capacity, drove down prices, and increased competition for all markets, including those in Africa. The rise of production of raw materials and foodstuffs in the Americas and Asia led to a decline in the prices of many primary products after 1870. In Europe the standard of living of the still large farming community was threatened. These trends culminated in the Great Depression of 1873-1896. (Munro, 1976:64-66)

As a result of the depression, there was a revival of mercantilist policies, particularly in relation to the underdeveloped areas. Where overseas colonies and protectorates existed, tariff barriers were instituted. Governments began to charter companies again, and grant them monopoly powers. Business interests in Europe feared that the doors to profits in Africa would be closed. They orchestrated a campaign to "open up" Africa to trade and investment. Industrial leaders sought new raw materials and were sure they would be found in Africa. Sanderson (1975:42-44) reminds us that in Europe at this time the traditional conservative advocates of colonial expansion gained the support of the middle class who embraced the ideologies of imperialism and social Darwinism.

Other factors made a policy of formal colonialism more practicable. By the 1830s quinine was in full production, and expeditions to the African interior could be made without fear of death from malaria. The steamship had not only regularized trade and transportation between Africa and

Europe, it facilitated navigation on African rivers. Freund (1984:75) stresses that the costs of imperial conquest were lowered by greatly improved armaments and the availability of cheaply-paid African mercenaries.

In European eyes, Africa at this time was relatively backward, lacking modern political development, capital for investment, technical expertise, and a modern infrastructure. Therefore, it was argued, colonialism was a necessary prerequisite to profitable development. (Freund, 1984:86-87; Munro, 1976:84-5)

By the early 19th century Africa was integrated into the world capitalist economy. But between the 1880s and World War I the colonial powers had to use military force to defeat the major African states and to put down local rebellions. Political power was centralized in the hands of the European rulers. For a period of around seventy years (1890-1960) the direction of development was completely outside the control of Africans. It was precisely during this period that the world experienced a high level of industrial and technological development, both in the capitalist and state socialist countries. As Rodney (1974:224) concludes, "It is against those decisive changes that events in Africa have to be measured."

The policies of the European governments towards sub-Saharan Africa were consistent: colonies were to assist in the development of the metropolitan country. Colonial authorities repressed and limited movements for local autonomy. Intra-African trade was blocked. Infrastructure like ports, railroads, and roads were built only when necessary and designed to serve the needs of imperial capital. When mining was being developed, the colonial state used force and coercion plus heavy poll taxes to recruit the necessary labour. Local industrialization was greatly restricted; Africa became dependent on the import of consumer goods from the metropolitan country. (See Freund, 1984; Ake, 1981; Munro, 1976; Rodney, 1974)

Between 1896 and 1914 there was a boom in the world economy that greatly increased the demand and price for primary products produced or mined in Africa. However, from the beginning of World War I down to the onset of the Depression in 1929, Africa's exports grew at a much slower pace. Furthermore, during the war and in the following period, the terms of trade turned against primary products exported from Africa. Independent countries might have reacted by introducing import-substitution policies, but this option was not available for colonial Africa. (Munro, 1976:87-88; 122-125; 144)

The trend towards the production of agricultural cash crops for export continued under direct European rule. The metropolitan governments allocated very little to state spending on agriculture in Africa, and priority was given to the development of crops like cotton, needed in Europe. While subsistence agriculture still dominated, three forms of commercial agriculture were carried on: peasant production for the market, white settler production, and capitalist plantations. The latter two forms relied on peasant labour. Poll and hut taxes were used to force peasants out of predominantly subsistence farming. Taxes could be paid in kind with foraged products like ivory or wild rubber. The colonial state took control of land and allocated it on a concessionary basis to white settlers or large corporations. There were, of course, significant regional differences.

In west Africa, emphasis was placed on small-scale production. Plantations were tried in several colonies (for bananas, coffee, and rubber), but they had limited success; only in the German colonies of Togo and the Cameroons were they the dominant form of agriculture. In the British areas, cocoa was promoted as the dominant crop. In Senegal, the production of groundnuts was emphasized to such an extent that the colony became Africa's first food-deficit area, dependent on the importation of rice from Asia.

In west central Africa, peasant agriculture persisted. Private corporations were given large land concessions with monopoly powers, but emphasis was on foraged products: timber, ivory, and wild rubber. Force was used to try to get Africans to grow cotton. Plantations were introduced in the Belgian Congo, but only after 1912; the emphasis was on palm oil.

In the southern part of Africa, commercial agriculture was primarily oriented to serving the rapidly growing mining community; growing cash crops for export was secondary. In these areas the colonial governments gave large monopoly concessions of land to joint-stock companies for exploitation and development. The higher lands were reserved for the development of white settler agriculture. The latter produced primarily maize and livestock for the mining communities. Indeed, the mining corporations co-operated with the white farmers to try to limit the development of this form of cash-cropping by African peasants. (Munro, 1976:111) White settlers also established coffee, tea, and tobacco estates, dependent on African farm labour.

In East Africa, Sudan exported livestock and cotton. In the areas controlled by Great Britain and Germany, all three forms of agriculture existed. There was peasant cash cropping, mainly of coffee and cotton. The white settlers in the higher lands produced food grains and dairy products. And there were also plantations, particularly coffee, rubber, tea, and sisal. (Freund, 1984:111-142; Ake, 1981:43-67; Tosh, 1980:79-94; Munro, 1976:86-118; Rodney, 1974:149-201; Grigg, 1974:235-240)

The development of South Africa was significantly different. The autonomy granted by the British allowed the colony to begin its own industrial revolution. The Langden Commission, appointed by Lord Alfred Milner in 1902, supported segregation by race, including land in agriculture. Union of the states was achieved by the Constitution of 1910; the Land Act of 1913 re-enforced the system of segregation along racial lines.

White settler agriculture was promoted by state policies; it contrasted with the rest of sub-Sahara Africa in that it was increasingly based on

European technology. In addition to the export market for staple products, there was a growing domestic market for foodstuffs created by the rapidly expanding mining industry. (Freund, 1984:170-190)

Before colonialism, most agricultural production was intended for local use within the family, the village, or the region. Under colonialism, a much larger area of Africa was opened to production for the world market. Some local processing was done, largely to reduce the bulk for export. As Barker (1984:21-22) stresses, "in all cases, the crop left the continent in a relatively raw state: the industrial transformation of the product, and its distribution and retail sale, took place in Europe."

A major factor in the development of a cash-crop-for-export economy was the large, foreign-owned merchant firm with state-supported monopoly power. In west Africa these firms served predominantly as middle men, capturing most of the downstream profits. In central and east Africa they were also vertically integrated back into plantation production. In some cases the commercial corporations directed the overall economic development of the colony. (Halfani and Barker, 1984:39-42; Ake, 1981:47-51; Munro, 1976:98; Rodney, 1974:154-164)

Following the neo-mercantilist practices of the period, the large monopoly firms also facilitated the importation of consumer goods manufactured in Europe. The spur to railroad development came primarily from European industrialists looking for new markets for their products: iron and steel, machinery, and railroad equipment. (Munro, 1976:92-95; Rodney, 1974:212-215)

The emphasis on cash crops for export has traditionally been endorsed as making the most of international comparative advantage. Africa could produce tropical crops "comparatively cheaply" and benefit from importing temperate zone commodities (particularly manufactured goods) not produced in Africa. This exchange would be even more significant if the barter terms of trade were in favour of primary products. During the colonial period the export of tropical crops greatly increased; furthermore, the share of African exports accounted for by countries other than South Africa dramatically increased. (Levi and Havinden, 1982:32-39)

A contrasting view is advanced by Ake (1981:50-59). During the colonial period the sub-Saharan states grew to depend on the export of a very narrow range of primary products. Agriculture in colonies like Ghana, Senegal, and Gambia was directed to a single major agricultural crop. They became very vulnerable to international price fluctuations. Trade was overwhelmingly with the metropolitan country. The monetary system, reserves, and currency were manipulated by the colonial state for the advantage of foreign capital and the metropolitan state. Shipping, banking services, and investment were controlled by metropolitan capital and the colonial state. The African colonies became almost totally dependent on imported technology. The development of an indigenous capitalist class was blocked. The colonial state practiced overt racism; normally race and class were coextensive, as capital was white and foreign while labour was African. The formal policy of restricting education left Africa with an unskilled labour force. The pattern of development established under mercantile colonialism created artificial African proto-states in a dependent relationship with the international system and an internal structure that greatly inhibited autocentric development.

Rodney (1974:205-281) is even more critical of the impact of colonialism on Africa. While the African handicraft industries had survived the long period of slave hunting, they had not advanced in technology and were destroyed by colonial policies. The natural, historic, pan-African trading patterns were completely disrupted. Economic development was limited to agriculture, timber, and mineral extraction. Even a local petty capitalist class was impeded by the arrival of Lebanese, Syrian, Greek, and Indian businessmen who enjoyed preferential status.

The colonial state helped exploit African farmers through the creation of marketing boards with monopoly over the purchase of non-food cash crops. By imposing the head tax, they forced Africans to grow crops or gather products for the merchant corporations and to provide free labour time for a wide variety of "public works," including housing for colonial administrators.

Most of the cash crops encouraged by the colonial system and the European market were for industrial use (cotton, sisal, and oil-bearing nuts) or discretionary consumption items with virtually no food value (coffee, tea, and cocoa). Some, like groundnuts and cotton, were very demanding on the soil; where they were substituted for shifting cultivation they led to soil erosion and, in some areas, to desertification. They also competed with food crops for both land and labour time, increasing the nutritional vulnerability of African farmers. (Tosh, 1980:79-94)

Rodney (236) argues that colonialism "created conditions which led not just to periodic famine but to chronic undernourishment, malnutrition, and deterioration in the physique of the African people." He points out (219) that "the vast majority of Africans went into colonialism with a hoe and came out with a hoe." While some plantations and white settlers used imported agricultural technology, the hoe remained "the overwhelmingly dominant agricultural implement" for African farmers. While capitalism was able to revolutionize agriculture in Europe, it did not do the same for colonized Africa.

An economic surplus was extracted from the African peasant and farm worker during the colonial period. However, this surplus was largely siphoned off by large monopoly corporations that transferred it to Europe. Agricultural production increased, but there was no evidence that it improved the general welfare of the rural population. Indeed, a very good case can be made that the average nutritional standing of Africans declined.

The surplus of agricultural production was exported, but the profits went largely to foreign monopoly corporations. The agricultural sector provided labour for the development of mining, but there was little employment in manufacturing. The poverty of the rural sector provided only a limited market for manufactured goods, and these were mainly imported from Europe.

As Ake (1981:43) points out, the African colonial economy was "disarticulated." The backward and forward links in the production chain were not developed locally. This was not only true of the food and agriculture sector, but was evident also in the other major areas of investment, infrastructure, and mining. Development was greatly distorted.

Formal European colonialism existed in Africa for around seventy years, roughly between 1890 and 1960. During that period industry and technology grew at an unprecedented rate in Europe, the Soviet Union, Japan, the United States, Canada, Australia, and New Zealand. But Africa remained almost exclusively a pre-industrial society, with its local economies orientated to serving the interests of the metropolitan powers, exporting primary products, and importing manufactured goods. Whereas industrial capital was in full command in the more developed countries, merchant capital continued to dominate in Africa.

Conclusion

Prior to the arrival of the Europeans, agriculture and food production were highly developed in the Americas, particularly among the three high civilizations of the Aztecs, the Mayans, and the Incas. By 1650 over 80% of the indigenous peoples had been wiped out by disease, colonial wars, and forced labour. European capitalism brought the plantation economy based on the importation of slaves from Africa. The best agricultural lands were seized by the European settlers and their descendants, who established the *latifundia*; the surviving native population was largely forced into subsistence agriculture.

In Latin America the colonial pattern of agricultural production for export was continued after independence was achieved in the early 19th century. The local ruling classes, linked to the mercantile economy, perpetuated their subservience to European capital through their adherence to the ideology of "free trade."

Most African societies were still primarily based on hunting and gathering, but agriculture, the raising of cattle, and fishing were developed in many areas. The handicraft industries were not that far behind Europe when the ships arrived in the 16th century. Under the impact of European imperialism, for over three hundred years slavery was the primary economic activity in Africa, with devastating long-term effects.

By the mid-19th century slavery had been largely outlawed, and the

Europeans shifted to the development of agricultural cash crops in Africa. White settlers arrived and were granted the best lands. With the formal colonization of Africa in the latter part of the 19th century, any hope for autonomous development disappeared. Mercantile patterns of development and trade persisted; Africa was to remain a supplier of raw materials and an importer of manufactured products from the colonial masters. Local trading patterns were destroyed. In agriculture, priority was given to the production of cash crops for export, most of which had no food value. Production of food for local consumption deteriorated, and the nutritional level of the Africans declined. Under colonialism, formal policies of racism blocked the advance of Africans. While Europe marched ahead with industrial capitalism and Soviet state socialism, both Latin America and Africa were held back by colonialism and "free trade" imperialism.

References

Adams, Richard E.W. (1977). *Prehistorica Mesoamerica*. Boston: Little, Brown & Co.

Ake, Claude (1981). *A Political Economy of Africa*. Essex: Longman.

Alavi, Hamza (1980). "India: Transition from Feudalism to Colonial Capitalism." *Journal of Contemporary Asia*, X, No. 4, pp. 359-399.

Bankes, George (1977). *Peru Before Pizarro*. Phaidon: Oxford.

Barker, Jonathan (1984). "Politics and Production." In Jonathan Barker, ed. *The Politics of Agriculture in Tropical Africa*. Beverly Hills: Sage Publications, pp. 11-31.

Baudin, Louis (1961). *Daily Life in Peru Under the Last Incas*. New York: Macmillan.

Beckford, George L. (1972). *Persistent Poverty*. New York: Oxford University Press.

Braudel, Fernand (1967). *Capitalism and Material Life, 1400-1800*. London: Weidenfeld and Nicolson.

Coe, Michael D. (1980). *The Maya*. London: Thomas and Hudson.

Frank, André Gunder (1979). *Dependent Accumulation and Underdevelopment*. New York: Monthly Review Press.

Freund, Bill (1984). *The Making of Contemporary Africa*. Bloomington: Indiana University Press.

Furtado, Celso (1970). *Economic Development of Latin America*. Cambridge: Cambridge University Press.

Galeano, Eduardo (1973). *Open Veins in Latin America*. New York: Monthly Review Press.

Gann, Lewis H. and Peter Duignan (1972). *Africa and the World*. San Francisco: Chandler Publishing Co.

Gray, Lewis C. (1958). *The History of Agriculture in the Southern United States to 1860*. Gloucester, Mass.: Peter Smith.

Grigg, David B. (1974). *The Agricultural Systems of the World: An Evolutionary Approach*. Cambridge: Cambridge University Press.

Halfani, Mohamed S. and Jonathan Barker (1984). "Agribusiness and Agrarian Change." In Jonathan Barker, ed. *The Politics of Agriculture in Tropical Africa*. Beverly Hills: Sage Publications, pp. 35-63.

Herring, Hubert (1961). *A History of Latin America*. New York: Alfred A. Knopf.

Levi, John and Michael Navinden (1982). *Economics of African Agriculture*. Essex: Longman.

Mannix, Daniel P. (1962). *Black Cargoes: A History of the Atlantic Slave Trade*. New York: The Viking Press.

Munro, J. Forbes (1976). *Africa and the International Economy, 1800-1960*. London: J. M. Dent & Sons.

North, Douglass C. (1961). *The Economic Growth of the United States, 1790-1860.* Englewood Cliffs, N.J.: Prentice-Hall.

Parry, J.H. (1966). *The Establishment of the European Hegemony: 1415-1715.* New York: Harper & Row.

Peterson, Frederick (1959). *Ancient Mexico.* New York: Capricorn Books.

Pregger-Roman, Charles G. (1984). "Dependence, Underdevelopment, and Imperialism in Latin America: A Reappraisal." *Science and Society*, XLVII, No, 4, Winter, pp. 406-426.

Rodney, Walter (1974). *How Europe Underdeveloped Africa.* Washington, D.C.: Howard University Press.

Sanders, William T. and Barbara J. Price (1968). *Mesoamerica: The Evolution of a Civilization.* New York: Random House.

Sanderson, G.N. (1975). "The European Partition of Africa: Coincidence or Conjuncture?" In Ernest F. Penrose, ed. *European Imperialism and the Partition of Africa.* London: Frank Cass, pp. 1-54.

Semmel, Bernard (1970). *The Rise of Free Trade Imperialism.* Cambridge: Cambridge University Press.

Stein, Stanley J. and Barbara H. Stein (1970). *The Colonial Heritage of Latin America.* New York: Oxford.

Tosh, John (1980). "The Cash-crop Revolution in Tropical Africa: An Agricultural Reappraisal." *African Affairs*, VXXIX, No. 314, January, pp. 79-94.

Von Hagen, Victor W. (1961). *Realm of the Incas.* New York: Mentor Books.

Von Hagen, Victor W. (1960). *World of the Maya.* New York: Mentor Books.

Weaver, Muriel Porter (1981). *The Aztecs, Maya and their Predecessors.* New York: Academic Press.

Wickins, P.L. (1981). *An Economic History of Africa from Earliest Times to Partition.* Cape Town: Oxford University Press.

Williams, Glyndwr (1966). *The Expansion of Europe in the Eighteenth Century.* London: Blendford Press.

Wolf, Eric (1959). *Sons of the Shaking Earth.* Chicago: University of Chicago Press.

World Bank (1984). *World Development Report.* Washington, D.C.: World Bank.

CHAPTER FIVE

The European Impact on Asia

Before the agricultural revolution in Europe in the 17th and 18th centuries, there was a shortage of feed for cattle; this meant extensive slaughtering every fall. The meat was preserved by salting and pickling. Other than salt, the preservatives were all spices from the East Indies: pepper, cinnamon, nutmeg, mace, ginger, and cloves. They came to Europe via the Middle East and were controlled by Muslim traders and Venetian merchants who charged monopoly prices. The Spanish and Portuguese explorers of the 15th century were not only looking for gold, they were also searching for a new route to the East Indies to bypass this monopoly trade.

In the early part of the fifteenth century the Portuguese, backed by experienced seamen from Genoa, began explorations along the African coast. Their claim to the African route to Asia was set forth by the Pope in 1454, confirmed by the Treaty of Alcacovas in 1479, and reiterated by the Papal bull of 1494. In 1487 Bartholomeu Dias sailed around the Cape of Good Hope, and in 1497 Vasco da Gama completed the voyage, crossing the Indian Ocean and landing at Calicut. On his second voyage to the Indies de Gama bombarded the town of Calicut, a free trade port for 2000 years, and defeated a local fleet backed by the Malabar Arabs.

There was freedom of the seas and free trade in Asia. Because of the much higher level of development in Asia, the Europeans could not compete with the Arabs in a free market. Thus the Portuguese introduced state piracy, plunder, and "trade" backed by the sword. Superior ocean ships, seamanship, and gunnery won them the spice trade. The terror and brutality brought by the Europeans was rationalized by the Christian church: accepted codes of good behaviour did not apply to heathen cultures. This became the general standard characteristic of western colonialism.

Down to 1580 the Portuguese dominated the trade with the Indies. Henceforth, the Dutch and British Protestants rejected the Pope's declarations and entered the lucrative Asian market. Over the 17th century the British and Dutch competed for influence in the East Indies. The English Navigation Acts of 1651 and 1660, the Staple Act of 1663, and the

Plantations Duties Act of 1673 were all mercantile protectionist measures designed to win the trade war with the Dutch. After years of conflict, the British decided to consolidate their interests in India, while the Dutch settled for the islands now known as Indonesia. (See Parry, 1966; Panikkar, 1965)

Indian Development under British Rule

For almost 250 years Europeans traded on the fringes of India, having little impact on internal development. Beginning in 1600 British trade was monopolized by the East India Company. However, around 1750, Mogul authority began to break down; there were numerous local civil wars, power became more decentralized, and a new phase of the relationship began with Clive's military defeat of the Bengali forces at Plassey in 1757. The period of direct colonial rule began, and British power was consolidated after sixty years of war and repression.

As in almost all societies at this time, governments in India rested on a system of extraction of revenue from peasants. However, tenancy and taxation varied widely, as one would expect in a country as large and diverse as India. But some generalizations are possible. First, there was a relative abundance of land in relation to population. If landlords were overly oppressive, the peasants would simply flee to another area. Thus, from the standpoint of the rulers, the intermediate tax collectors, and the landlords, the central problem was how to make the peasants cultivate the land. The Mogul administration stressed the "duty" of cultivation. Second, probably because of the relative abundance of land, agricultural technology was primitive and changed very little. Third, the Mogul and Hindu taxation systems involved the collection of a proportion of the crop. This form of surplus extraction did little to encourage peasants to increase production. It stands in contrast to the land tax in Meiji Japan, which was a fixed amount. (Moore, 1966:317-334)

In his early writings on India, Marx described this as the Asiatic Mode of Production. (Frank, 1978:138-144; Marx and Engels, 1965) The key characteristics of this pre-capitalist system appeared to be (1) the absence of private property in land; (2) government control of irrigation; (3) a self-perpetuating village economy and society; (4) the customary exchange of agricultural produce for handicrafts; and (5) military repression of village communities. However, Ghosh (1984) argues that this early assessment was based on inaccurate and incomplete information available at the time. While the village administered the taxation system, in general the possession of land was not common but individual; furthermore, land revenue was normally paid in cash. As a result, one third to one half of agricultural produce was in the form of commodities. In addition, many crops (including quality foods, cotton, silk, indigo, and tobacco) were grown strictly for the market. Many of the textiles produced in the villages were also destined for a larger market. Ghosh (44) points out that, in his later works (e.g., *Capital*, Volume III), Marx no longer used the term, "Asiatic Mode of Production," but referred to "pre-capitalistic, national modes of production" in describing India and China. In any case, the key to capital accumulation in India at this time was the extraction of an economic surplus from the peasants.

In 1765, after the beginning of direct British rule, the East India Company obtained a charter from the Mogul emperor to collect the land revenues of Bengal. Under the Permanent Settlement the British took nine-tenths of the revenue collected by the intermediaries, the *zamindar*. In order to try to maintain their own existence, the *zamindar* in turn raised the taxes to roughly double what they had been under the reign of Akbar. This was a crushing burden on the peasants, and over the period 1769-71 there was a severe famine; the population of Bengal declined by one-third. (Bagchi, 1982:79-80; Frank, 1978:154-156; Moore, 1966:345-346)

British land policy in India was driven by both the zeal to collect funds and an ideological commitment to the British structure of agriculture: gentry proprietorship. Thus, in the south and west, they supported the *ryotwari* or peasant tenure system and, in the Punjab, the Northwest Provinces, and Oudh they supported the *mahalwari* system by which land was owned privately by cultivators but taxes were collected communally by the village. Changes the British made to land revenue policies caused a major disruption, leading to significant changes in land ownership and a rural depression. (Charlesworth, 1982:17-20)

Most of India is classified as a wet and dry tropical country, with a long dry season and year-round temperatures ranging from warm to hot. The principal source of rain comes with summer and winter monsoon winds that provide around 90% of the total moisture. Historically, the immediate cause of local famine was either a drought or unseasonably heavy rains that ruined crops and caused flooding. In the pre-British period a major famine occurred on average once every 50 years. Bhatia (1967:7-8) records that between 1765 and 1858 India experienced twelve famines and four "severe scarcities." Between 1860 and 1908 there were 20 famines or severe scarcities.

Why did famines increase under British rule? Bhatia (1967:14-26) cites several contributing factors. (1) There was the disruption caused by changes in the land tenure and taxation systems. (2) The destruction of the handicraft industries depopulated villages and urban areas and forced more people back into farming. (3) There was a rise in the number of landless rural agricultural labourers existing at a subsistence level. (4) The introduction of the British landlord system added a new class of moneylenders that further exploited the peasants. (5) Agricultural productivity stagnated, because peasants had less to invest in agricultural improvements. (6) The Home Charges and Revenue requirements for the Imperial wars against Burma and Afghanistan were financed primarily by the peasants through the land revenue, excise taxes, salt tax, and stamps. (7) After 1860 Indian exports were primarily agricultural products, and there was an increasing reliance on food grains. (8) The price of food grains increased, while wages and opportunities for employment outside agriculture stagnated. Poverty and vulnerability to famine increased substantially among three sections of the rural population: agricultural labourers, tenant farmers, and weavers.

The amount of land cultivated in India increased steadily throughout the 19th century, although it seems likely that the "waste" land was of poorer quality and less productive. The addition appears to have matched increases in population, estimated at about 0.4% per annum. In the 19th century India became a major exporter of raw cotton, rice, wheat, tea, jute, and opium; this trade in primary products increased with the opening of the Suez Canal and the introduction of the steamship. By 1890 these six crops accounted for 60% of India's exports by value. Plantation agriculture was limited to coastal areas, and cotton and sugar replaced food grains on better quality land. (Charlesworth, 1982:20-28)

The statistics available on Indian agricultural production suggest a decline in per capita output from the 1911-12 period to Independence in 1948. The census figures between 1871 and 1931 show a rise in the percentage of the population engaged in agriculture and a decline in the percentage in manufacturing. However, the reliability of these figures has been challenged. (Thorner and Thorner, 1962:70-81) But the best alternative data suggest that the share of the labour force in manufacturing remained fairly constant at 9% between 1911 and 1951. (Charlesworth, 1982:32-33)

At the time of their arrival in Asia Europeans lagged far behind in industrial production. Traders eagerly sought Asian silk, cotton, textiles, jewelry, sugar, and spices. Europeans produced almost nothing that Asians wanted or needed, with the possible exception of guns. For a very long period of time European purchases in Asia were paid for with gold and silver extracted from Latin America. After 1757 the East India Company was able to finance the export of textiles from revenues raised in India, and there was no further bullion drain from the mother country.

India's cotton textiles (calicoes and muslins) were the finest in the world. Merchants financed their production through a "cash advance" system. Production was expanded in urban areas (like Dacca) to meet the new European demand. The East India Company, anxious to maximize the profitable trade, introduced a system of direct coercion of weavers. The markup was three or four times the cost of purchase in India. (Alavi, 1980:378-383)

In the period between 1741-1750 the total value of exports of calicoes alone averaged £1.2 million per year; by 1832 this had declined to £100,000. As Alavi (1980:383-387) argues, Great Britain implemented the first import-substitution policy for industrial development. The initial tariff on Indian textile imports was enacted in 1685, a 10% duty. In 1690 it was doubled. Reacting to mounting pressures by British manufacturers, it was raised to 50% by 1760; by 1813 it was up to 85%. It wasn't until the 1780s that the Crompton mule allowed British manufacturers to produce fine muslin that could compete with Indian quality.

Most of the fine Indian textiles that were shipped to England were re-exported by British merchants. After 1757 cotton goods produced in India were assigned higher excise taxes than cotton goods imported from England. (Frank, 1979:18-19; Bhatia, 1967:16-17; Pannikar, 1965:74-81)

Restrictions on exports to Great Britain were devastating to the Indian industry. In addition, Britain's new technology and its colonial policy allowed it to capture the Indian market. Dutt (1949:114-119) reported that between 1815 and 1832 the population of Dacca, the "Manchester of India" and the home of world-famous muslins, fell from 150,000 to 30,000. The value of British cotton exports to India rose from £110,000 in 1813 to £6.3 million in 1856. British agents reported that by the 1830s the majority of Indians were wearing clothing manufactured in England. British manu-factures had penetrated the Indian market well before the development of the railroad. (Banerji, 1982:9-49; Frank, 1978:163-164; Bhatia, 1967:16-17; Moore, 1966:347-348)

Thus, in India under British rule, agriculture did not play an important role in the development of industry. India did not follow the western European, American, or Japanese road to industrialization. Why was the experience so different?

Moore (1966:316, 344-346, 353) concludes that industrialization was blocked by the existence of a parasitic landlord class, re-inforced by its political alliance with the British colonial government. The peasants created an economic surplus that could have been used for investment; however, it was siphoned off by the British conquerors, the local landlords, and the new class of moneylenders. What was not sent abroad tended to be invested in non-productive areas. Moore argues that the crushing of the Sepoy Mutiny in 1857 destroyed the last chance India had to develop along the lines of Japan.

Indian nationalists have always stressed the drain of capital from India during the period of British colonialism. Bagchi (1982:81) estimates that the drain from Bengal was 5% to 6% of its resources, compared to the investment rate of 7% to 8% in England at the same time of the Industrial Revolution. Alavi (1980, 387-391) estimates that the transfer to Great Britain was around £2 million per year; for the years 1790-1793, this would make it equal to about one-eighth of all gross capital formation. Frank (1978:162-166) argues that the debate over figures tends to overlook the very large personal fortunes made by individuals during their tour of duty in India. In a recent study, Banerji (1982) has demonstrated the difficulty in trying to quantify the imperial drain.

Another major factor in the lack of industrial development was the system of "free trade" imposed by British authorities. All the most developed countries instituted tariff barriers to protect their industry until it was well established. At a time when Indian manufacturing would have been shifting from a high level of handicraft production to industrial production, it was prevented by lack of new technology, the absence of protection, and high excise taxes. What tariffs existed were for revenue purposes only. While some industrial development began in the late 19th century (e.g., cotton and jute textiles), it was confined to regional enclaves, and there was no development of chemicals or heavy electricals. (Banerji, 1982:9-49; Charlesworth, 1982:32-39)

Banaji (1972:2501) concludes that colonialism blocked industrialization in India. The results were (1) the draining away of capital; (2) local investment in non-productive areas; (3) domination of the economy by foreign imports; and (4) the precarious reliance on the export of primary commodities, particularly agricultural products.

There were other major differences, as compared with industrialized countries. Investment in railroads did not spur an industrial "takeoff" as Marx had predicted; there were no backward and forward links to local industries. In 1914 around 75% of total investment in industry and business was foreign-owned and -controlled. British interests controlled shipping, insurance, and banking. There were no stock exchanges in India until 1890. There was no central bank until 1935. All of these factors helped to stifle the development of Indian industry and manufacturing. (Charlesworth, 1982:44-65; Banerji, 1982:vii-8)

England was the most highly developed industrial nation in the world in the 19th century; her industry utilized the most advanced technology. Why was India denied significant capital investment and technology? Colonial capitalism was mercantile; at this time it was not interested in industrialization in the overseas markets. In the latter part of the 19th century, with the rise of industrial capitalism in the United States and western Europe, the British became more and more dependent on India as an export market. After 1870 India became Britain's major export market. By 1910-11 imports of cotton piece goods from England were double the total output of piece goods by Indian mills. India was there to serve the interests of the colonial power. (Charlesworth, 1982:38,50; Bagchi, 1982:83-90; Banerji, 1982:9-24)

Indonesia: Agriculture under Mercantile Colonialism

The Portuguese were the first to arrive at the Spice Islands, seizing Malacca in 1511, the key to trade between the Far East and Europe. They introduced what Sievers (1974:51) calls "the European plague": Christian arrogance, treachery, ruthless rapacity, mass murder, and cruel exploitation. For eighty-five years the Portuguese struggled to control the spice trade, but they were too small and weak a nation to sustain their position. In 1595, the first Dutch fleet sailed for India; three years later they were in the Moluccas, concluding commercial treaties. They won a decisive naval battle with the Portuguese in 1601.

During the 17th century the Dutch and the British were in competition for the Asian trade. In 1602 the four major Dutch trading firms formed the United East India Company, commonly known as the VOC. By 1623 the VOC had consolidated its position in what is now Indonesia, and the British were content to solidify their position in South Asia.

From 1600 through the end of the Napoleonic Wars the VOC struggled to gain mercantile colonial control over the East Indies. It was a very difficult task, calling on all the genius of Calvinism. For example, when the people of Banda resisted the Dutch monopoly over spices by engaging in smuggling, the VOC responded by massacring most of the people and replacing them with slave labour. By 1705 the Dutch consolidated their control over the key island of Java and most of the commercially important outlying centres.

Profits were high, particularly for country trade in Asia. But there were strong forces opposing Dutch rule. The VOC faced constant rebellions and disorders. After one major rebellion in 1741, the VOC massacred all the Chinese and burned their quarters. Elsewhere, the Dutch experienced severe losses while backing the American colonies during their Revolutionary War. During the Napoleonic wars (1793-1816), the British occupied Java and the French occupied The Netherlands. By the turn of the century the VOC was on the verge of bankruptcy. (Ricklefs, 1981:20-104; Sievers, 1974:50-76; Parry, 1966:80-92; Furnivall, 1944:20-52)

The Portuguese and Dutch faced enormous costs in their efforts to establish colonialism, because the Indonesian people were anything but a backward people. Three great empires had developed in the classical period (ca. 700-1200). Melayu and Shri Vijaya were maritime powers based on Sumatra. Madjapahit was a major agrarian state in the interior of Java. While they were not bureaucratic empires in the Roman tradition, they were of the suzerain-client system so typical of Asia. The kingdoms regularly used force in order to collect tribute. They had large naval fleets, experienced seamen, and firearms and cannons gained in their trade with China. Even during the classical period the kingdoms were characterized by extensive trade and commerce, wealth, and cultural creativity. In the early 15th century Islam began to spread throughout the area, eventually embracing all the major islands except Bali. (Ricklefs, 1981:3-19; Sievers, 1974:38-44)

European commentators of the 16th century reported that there was no sign of poverty in the islands. The people were in very good health and had a highly developed system of medical practice; and there was no evidence of hunger or famine due to crop failures. There was a very favourable ratio of people to arable land, adequate rainfall, and steady crop production. The merchant class and the rulers lived in splendour. In 1500, Malacca was estimated to have a population of 100,000, equalling Paris and Naples, while a number of Indonesian cities were over 50,000. The Islamic system was open and free, and freedom of the seas and trade was the norm. (Reid, 1980:441-444)

Throughout the 17th century the Dutch were preoccupied with establishing a monopoly over the spice trade. This included control over production; spice trees were often cut and burned in an effort to keep the European price high. The Portuguese and the Spanish introduced American crops including maize, sweet potatoes, cocoa, tobacco, and cinchona (grown for quinine). Coffee was introduced in 1707 as an export crop, and sugar and indigo were converted to export crops.

In his classic study of Indonesia, Geertz (1963:13-45) records the impact of geography on agricultural production. The island of Java (called "Inner Indonesia") was ecologically well suited for sawah cultivation (irrigated rice paddy). Volcanoes provided plant nutrients, water came regularly through run-off from the mountains, there were gentle plains and basins and a moderate, humid climate. In contrast, "Outer Indonesia" lacked these attributes, and swidden (or slash-and-burn) agriculture was the norm.

It was upon this stable agricultural system that the VOC imposed its policy of subjugation, tribute, and control of trade. Where they were able to defeat the Javanese states, tribute was imposed via forced agreements requiring deliveries of rice, timber, indigo, cotton yarn, and coffee. In west Java, for example, peasants were compelled to grow coffee and sugar and make forced deliveries to the VOC. The company tried to farm out Javanese land to the Chinese on a cash basis, primarily to grow sugar under forced labour, but this approach failed. On the outer islands, "coffee sergeants" were hired to try to police the growing and delivery of spices. However, the constant warfare and rebellion greatly disrupted agricultural production.

Dutch influence in Indonesia greatly diminished after 1780; the VOC itself became bankrupt in 1796, and its charter was not renewed in 1799. During the period of occupation (1806-1815) the British governor, Sir Thomas Stamford Raffles, tried unsuccessfully to abolish "feudalism" by introducing a land tax to raise revenues and to stimulate independent peasant agriculture. The Anglo-Dutch Treaty of 1824 partitioned the Malay world, giving the Dutch a sphere of influence south of the Sulu Sea. Between 1825 and 1830 the Dutch engaged in a long and bitter war to finally subjugate Java. It was a peasant war against foreign imperialism; when it ended, the Dutch formed their long-lasting political alliance with the Javanese aristocrats. (Ricklefs, 1981:105-113; Caldwell and Utrecht, 1979:12-17; Sievers, 1974:80-105; Furnivall, 1944:54-108)

Historians list 1830 as the beginning of direct Dutch colonial rule in Indonesia. Van den Bosch arrived as the new Governor-General, determined to make Indonesia a profitable enterprise for Holland. The key to the new colonialism was *Cultuur Stelsel,* commonly referred to as the "Culture System." Rather than pay colonial land taxes in the form of cash, the peasants were to deliver a share of their crop directly to the government. The export of the crops was monopolized by the Netherlands Trading Company (NHM) formed in 1825, backed by Dutch capital and the royal family. The village was assessed the colonial tax, calculated at 40% of the value of the main crop, usually rice. It then set aside a percentage of its land for the growing of annual export crops, mainly sugar, but also indigo and tobacco. This removed around one-third of the land from production for food consumption.

In the areas outside the sawah, plantations were created, often on "waste" land which was now owned by the Dutch government. As part payment for the colonial tax, peasant men were required to perform compulsory labour on these estates. Officially this was set at 66 days per year, but often it was longer. The key crops in this early period were the perennials: coffee, tea, spices, and cinchona.

But work on the estates was not the only compulsory labour assigned. Peasants were also assessed land taxes to be paid by forced labour and services, including work on public projects such as roads, dams, and irrigation systems. The colonial state enforced the new system by corporal punishment and significant restrictions on movement.

For the Dutch, the new system was an instant success. The value of exports rose from 11.4 million guilders in 1830 to 109.2 million in 1864. Profits escalated for NHM. The textile industry of Trente grew with exports to the islands. Between 1833 and 1878 Indonesia contributed between 800 and 900 million guilders, or roughly one-third of the national budget of The Netherlands.

On Java, the population rose from 6 million in 1830 to 12.5 million in 1860. With the withdrawal of land in food production, rice shortages appeared. The quality of the diet of the peasant declined, and in the 1840s there were famines; the widespread epidemics of the late 1840s reflected a decline in general health standards. (Ricklefs, 1981:114-119; Caldwell and Utrecht, 1979:17-22; Sievers, 1974:107-122; Geertz, 1963:65-80; Furnivall, 1944:115-147)

The sudden profitability of the East Indies brought a wave of reforms in The Netherlands, as the rising bourgeois class sought to gain the profits of mercantile colonialism. The Liberals forced through tariff reductions (1872), the Accounts Law (1864), the Agrarian Law (1870), the Sugar Law (1870), the Penal Code (1872), and finally the Capitation Tax (1882). All were designed to get the state out of colonial enterprise and to open the door to private exploitation. Revenues for colonial administration were garnered through a series of monopolies; nearly two-thirds came from the opium monopoly. Most of these sources were transferred to the private sector; the opium trade remained a state monopoly until after 1900. (Furnivall, 1944:162-172)

The question of land ownership was never finally resolved, but the colonial state now granted long-term leases to private capital, particularly on "waste" land on the Outer Islands. But the private entrepreneurs needed labour more than they needed land. First, the regulations were modified to allow private capital to contract with village headmen for "voluntary" contracts. When this proved inadequate, they turned to individual labour contracts, enforced by the Penal Code. Finally, they resorted to imported labour, at first Chinese coolies, working on the estates under the contract system. Compulsory labour on government projects was replaced by the capitation tax and the introduction of wage labour. The Liberal reforms included the special Penal Code of 1872, which applied only to Indonesian natives, formalizing the separation of the races under colonialism. (Sievers, 1974:124-125; Geertz, 1963:83-84; Furnivall, 1944:166,181-188)

The opening of the Suez Canal and the introduction of steamships stimulated the growth of exports from Indonesia to Europe. When exports of sugar and coffee declined or fluctuated, others expanded, including tobacco, tea, palm oil, agava, cassava, kapok, copra, pepper, and then rubber. But trade was not limited to agricultural products; it was not long before tin, tin ore, and petroleum became major exports. In the 19th century sugar was the dominant export, and technology and machinery for process- ing were imported. Exports boomed during the latter part of the 19th century, but the profits went to private interests, not to the government nor to the agricultural masses. (Caldwell and Utrecht, 1979:30-31)

For the peasants on the sawah system, the standard of living under liberal colonialism deteriorated. This process has been described by Geertz (1963) as a process of "involution." Village leases with private sugar companies led to the land being tied up in sugar production for one-half the time. The village tried to protect its growing population through more labour- intensive production, work sharing, and expansion of the irrigation system. Dry-land crops like cassava, maize, sweet potatoes, and peanuts were added where possible, mainly on unfertile slopes. By the 1930s only 45% of the cropped, irrigated land was in rice, a situation unique to Southeast Asia. Per capita consumption of rice declined, calorie intake declined, and so did the quality of the diet. It was a system of shared poverty; Geertz (86-97) called it "post-traditional" agriculture which produced "marginal agriculturalists, petty traders and day labourers."

The Indonesian population was increasing in the Outer Islands, and they also had less food per person. After 1873 rice rapidly became a major import. Furnivall (1944:214-216) stresses that rent declined under the Liberal system, and after 1885 there was a "strong reduction of wages" with the situation for the cultivator going from bad to worse. Indonesian unemployment rose when the handicraft industry declined because of cotton textile imports. Buchanan (1967:72,78,81) points out that the destruction of the handicraft industries led to the "agrarianization" of rural life, warping the development of villages and leading to "the gross inflation of the tertiary sector" with its chronic underemployment. The colonial system blocked industrialization.

The concept of "dualism" in economic development originates with the work of J. H. Boeke (1953), who described the relationship between The Netherlands and Indonesia. To Boeke, this was not just the clash between imported and indigenous social systems. In reality, it was a clash between European capitalism and pre-capitalist agrarian societies, usually non-Christian. Despite its advanced development, the imported capitalist system was unable to become the general system; the traditional system persisted along with the imported one. Boeke was unwilling to ascribe dualism to colonialism—only to capitalism.

Without a doubt there was a dual society in Indonesia, the racial separation of the Europeans from the Indonesians. Geertz (1963) and Buchanan (1967) also stress, in the Indonesian context, the differences between Java, with its sawah cultivation, and the Outer Islands, based first on swidden agriculture and then estate and garden cultivation (the mix of trees and food crops). There was also a form of dualism in the ecology of agriculture.

But Indonesia is probably the worst case for advancing the theory of a dual society split between a traditional subsistence sector and a modern market capitalist sector. At least from the beginning of the Culture System the peasants on Java were fully integrated into the world market for export crops. On the Outer Islands the estates were capitalist enterprises, first using forced labour, then labour contracts, and finally hired labour. But as the crops diversified, independent producers cultivated them for the export market; this form of agriculture gradually became dominant. Geertz (1963:105-115) points out that independent producers accounted for 35% of value of agricultural exports by 1930; for the Outer Islands as a whole, by 1937 they accounted for 50%.

The Indonesian case again illustrates that a substantial economic surplus can be extracted from agriculture for economic development. But the surplus was siphoned off to help develop The Netherlands; it was not available for industrial development in Indonesia. Caldwell and Utrecht (1979:30-31) point out that, in contrast to the other European colonial powers, the Dutch were at least not hypocritical; there was none of the nonsense about the "white man's burden." The Dutch openly proclaimed that colonies existed to enrich the "mother country."

Geertz (1963:124-154) and a few others note the similarity in culture, geography, agricultural ecology, and development between Japan and

Indonesia in the mid 19th century. The key difference, of course, was that Indonesia was dominated from abroad, whereas Japan was ruled by an indigenous elite. But of equal importance was the orientation of development policy: Indonesia was forced to follow a policy of exporting cash crops and minerals for the world market. In contrast, the Japanese opted for relative isolation from the world market, a balanced industrial development, and their own version of imperialism and colonialism.

The Stagnation of Agriculture and Development in China

Traditional liberal theories hold that nations develop in a progression from primitive societies to industrialization. Yet when the Europeans arrived around 1500, China was without question the most populous and most highly developed country in the world. It maintained that status for another 300 years. But by the first half of the twentieth century it was among the poorest countries in the world and famine was common. How did this happen?

In recent years mainstream social scientists have argued that the bureaucratic imperial system, with its inward orientation, produced economic stagnation. However, others have pointed out that during the Song Dynasty (960-1279) this same bureaucratic system produced an economic revolution with rising agricultural productivity, commercialization of the economy, the introduction of paper money, and the development of innovative technology. (Lippit, 1980:1-2; Elvin, 1973:159,179; Balazs, 1972:42) Reports from Marco Polo fired Europeans to seek trade with China, the most industrialized country in the world, with high-quality paper, printing, gunpowder, porcelain, silk, and cotton textiles. (Fairbank et al, 1965:10-11)

By the 13th century China also had the most highly developed and sophisticated agricultural system in the world using fertilizers, improved seed strains, steel tools including plows, irrigation and water control, and specialized production for the market. Printing enabled new techniques in agriculture to be spread rather quickly over an empire larger than Europe. (Lippitt, 1980:2)

In 1500 the population of China was over 100 million. It increased to around 275 million by 1780, 430 million by 1850, and 500 million by 1933. While China was still primarily an agricultural society, Gernet (1970:38, 84) reports that in 1270 the population of the city of Hangzhou was over one million and included a wide variety of tradesmen, artisans, merchants, and various business enterprises.

When the barbarians from Europe arrived, the Chinese imperial order had no use for them. Historians record the futile attempts of the Europeans to open China to trade; the Europeans had only inferior goods to offer in exchange. Trade was banned during the early period of the Ming Dynasty (1368-1644) and greatly restricted throughout the Qing Dynasty (1644-1912). For 200 years there was very little trade with the Europeans. In 1637 the British arrived, but the famous Canton trade did not really begin until 1699. Restricted by British protectionist legislation, the East India Company concentrated on importing silk and tea. Tea became the national drink of England, and by 1830 it provided most of the profits for the Company and one-tenth of England's revenue. (Fairbank et al, 1965:66-71; Greenberg, 1951:2-3)

At this time tea was almost exclusively grown in China. How did the British pay for it? First they used bullion, largely silver from Latin America. After the conquest of Bengal (1757), they exported opium and raw cotton. Opium was grown in Bengal under a monopoly granted to the East India Company. Its possession and trade was illegal in England and China, but that meant little when profits were involved. The export of opium to China increased rapidly; by 1828 it accounted for over one-half of the value of British goods traded. The Bengal opium monopoly provided one-seventh of the total revenue of British India. By the beginning of the first Opium War in 1839, the British controlled two-thirds of all foreign trade with China. When the Chinese began a concerted effort to stop the trade in opium, the result was war and the beginning of western imperial intrusion. (Bagchi, 1982:96-97; Greenberg, 1951:13, 105)

The class structure in China was well established by the 18th century and persisted with little change down to the successful revolution in 1949. Pre-communist China is often described as a bureaucratic state, dominated by the scholar-official class, an oligarchy that reproduced itself through the educational system. (See Balazs, 1972; Moore, 1966) However, this huge imperial state had only 20,000 senior government officials. They could rule because they relied on the power and authority of the local landed gentry. This key social class represented only 3% of the population in agriculture, but controlled around 25% of all farmland. Lippit (1980:8, 49-54) concludes that the rural landed gentry dominated both the scholar-official class and the rising merchant and industrial bourgeoisie.

There was also a class system among the peasants: the rich peasants (roughly 7%), who commonly hired agricultural labourers; the middle peasants (20-30%), who had enough land for subsistence; and the poor and landless peasants (60-70%), who were most vulnerable to crop failures and exploitation. From the Ming period on through the Qing, tenant farmers paid roughly 50% of the crop as rent to the landlords. Peasants who owned their own land paid interest on loans to the moneylenders, were subject to various taxes, were forced to perform a variety of services, and were victimized by bandits and warlords. Tax collectors extracted "presents" and numerous surcharges from the peasants. Rents from agriculture could be paid either in kind or in cash; a bushel of rice, for example, had a fixed price in silver that translated into copper currency. Famines and peasant revolts were widespread. (Lippit, 1980:8-9; 43, 62; Chesneaux et al, 1976:17-18, 23-24; Riskin, 1975:57-60)

There seems little doubt that a substantial economic surplus was extracted from the peasants, which could have been used to finance industrial development. Riskin (1975:70-75) estimates that in 1933, around 37% of net domestic product was potential economic surplus (following Baran's definition). Of this, around two-thirds was latent in the agricultural sector. Lippit (1980:42) concludes that the surplus available in 19th century China "cannot have been less than 30% of national income." What happened to it?

Much of it was used by landlords to buy large landholdings; aside from land and buildings, investment in agriculture was low. Indeed, as landlords grew rich, they regularly moved to urban areas where they purchased luxury residences. Huge expenditures were used in a wide variety of ceremonies. The gentry financed education for their sons, and, when necessary, bought titles. There were large military expenditures to put down constant peasant revolts. Gold and silver was hoarded. A considerable amount of the surplus was absorbed through bribery and corruption, widespread in the 19th century. The general conclusion, then, is that most of the surplus created from agriculture was not put to productive use. Lippit (1980:68) and Riskin (1975:81-84) argue that the exploitation of peasants and the system of corruption worsened under the rule of the new bourgeois government in the 20th century, intensifying the class conflicts that led to the revolution.

China was a highly developed country when the European imperialists arrived. At no time was China subjected to the type of colonialism that dramatically affected India or Indonesia. Why did the Chinese society, and its agricultural sector, stagnate?

Many people who have studied China stress the combination of a rise in population and the relative stagnation of agricultural technology. Without innovations in agriculture, the law of diminishing returns to labour sets in. The problem was intensified by the continued division of farmland into small parcels. Transportation was poor (mainly by river) and internal trade was limited. (e.g., see Fairbank et al, 1965:89-99) This situation conforms to the "high level equilibrium trap" theory advanced by Schultz (1964), which emphasizes technological stagnation in agriculture. (For its application to China, see Elvin, 1973.)

Nevertheless, Chinese agriculture was not stagnant in the period after western intrusion. Chesneaux (1976:26-27) argues that it was still the most advanced in the world in the 18th century, using terraced hillsides, dikes, reservoirs, canals, and farm equipment. New seed varieties were adopted that reduced the growing season and permitted multiple cropping. Land under cultivation increased with the introduction of crops from the Americas, especially sweet potatoes, groundnuts, tobacco, and maize. But the high level of exploitation left the average peasant living in wretched poverty.

Other scholars have stressed the negative impact of western imperialism. (e.g., Bagchi, 1982:94-105) As one might expect, opium had a wide-ranging negative effect on the structure of Chinese life. (Chesneaux et al, 1976:54-57; Fairbank et al, 1965:136-140; Greenberg, 1951:196-215) The first Opium War was designed to break down Chinese resistance to free trade. The Treaty of Nanking (1842) was the first of a series of "unequal treaties" that undermined Chinese sovereignty: four new ports were opened to foreign trade, Chinese duties on imports were limited to 5%, Hong Kong became a British colony, and the opium trade was to be continued. The "most favoured nation" clauses gave all the imperialist powers equal "rights" in China. Following the second Opium War in 1860, the super-vision of the Chinese customs themselves was granted to the imperialists. After first humiliating the Chinese government, the British and French then intervened militarily to help it put down the Taiping Revolution in 1864.

The total budget of the central Chinese government in the 19th century was only 40 million taels (a tael was 38 grams of silver). Foreign indemnities extracted after the Opium War (5 million taels), the Sino-Japanese War (200 million taels), and the Boxer Revolution (450 million taels), imposed an enormous hardship on the imperial government. (Chesneaux et al, 1976:18)

Japan attacked Korea in 1894, and when China tried to support her tributary state, the Imperial navy was crushed. The Treaty of Shimonoseki (1895) ceded much territory to Japan, including Taiwan and Manchuria. The Boxer Revolution of 1898, directed at imperialist intervention, was jointly suppressed by the foreign powers. Without question, at this time China was no better than a semi-colony.

The economy was adversely affected by the impact of European intrusion. After 1870 the textile industry was decimated by British imports. There was a shift to the production of commercial agricultural crops, often for export: tea, cotton, silk, opium, and even grains. After 1860 the merchant class became primarily a comprador class. Foreigners dominated the modern industrial sectors in the Treaty ports. (Chesneaux et al, 1976:214-219)

Nevertheless, many scholars feel that foreign intervention was not on a scale large enough to be the deciding factor in the stagnation of the Chinese economy. Lippit (1980:14, 28) points out that the capital drain from China was not extensive, nothing like that from India. Direct foreign investment was not a significant factor, rising to only 15% of total investment in 1933. Foreign trade was a small percentage of net domestic product.

Equal responsibility for the failure can be assigned to the Chinese class system. Lippit (1980:49-58) argues that the landed gentry were the dominant class, and they held power over both the scholar-officials and the merchant and industrial bourgeoisie. They were comfortable under the existing system and rejected the blocked outside innovations. While foreign technology was present in the Treaty ports, it did not spread to other areas under the control of the Chinese bourgeoisie.

Closely linked to this class system was the ideology of Confucianism, with its repression of women, the institutionalization of inequality, the requirement of docility and submission to authority, and the denigration of business and commerce. This ideology of the status quo received greater official sanction after the humiliations of the Opium Wars. Change towards industrialization and "modernization" was initiated by the bourgeois Kuomintang, but liberation from foreign domination and the destruction of the exploitative, old, class society required a social revolution.

Southeast Asia and Colonialism

Throughout Southeast Asia the pattern of agricultural production and development was similar to the experience of India, Indonesia, and China. Mercantile colonialism was the dominant force. The British arrived in Sri Lanka (then Ceylon) in 1796. The Dutch had introduced plantations for cinnamon, but the first major estate crop was coffee, planted for the first time in the 1830s using imported wage-labour from Tamil in south India. When coffee was destroyed by a blight in the 1870s, there was a major shift to tea production on the estates. There was some diversification into rubber in the 20th century, but the economy continued to depend heavily on tea. These export crops were primarily grown on plantations financed by foreign capital; in contrast, coconut cultivation was undertaken primarily in small holdings, although it was marketed by foreign firms. While there was a rather dramatic increase in population growth in the period after World War II, land cultivated for food crops did not increase as fast, yields from rice agriculture remained relatively low for Southeast Asia, and Sri Lanka became a major importer of rice. (Bandarage, 1983; Snodgrass, 1966)

The British drove the Dutch out of Malaysia between 1786 and 1795, and formalized complete colonial control over the area in 1909. The Chinese had planted pepper in the 18th century, but the British quickly shifted to sugar production. (After 1906 major investments were made in rubber plantations, again using Tamil labour from India.) However, in the 1850s the major export from Malaysia was tin, mined by immigrant Chinese labourers. British policy concentrated on the export of industrial raw materials to the extent that food production declined. By the 1920s Malaysia was importing over 70% of rice consumption. (Snodgrass, 1980)

The British conquered Burma through a series of wars in 1824-1826, 1852, and 1886. Lower Burma depended heavily on rice grown on rather large holdings often held by absentee landlords. Under British rule exports of rice to other Asian areas greatly increased. But after the opening of the Suez Canal in 1869, exports were re-directed to Europe; by 1870 four-fifths went to this market. Rice remained the dominant export. In Upper Burma agricultural holdings were small, with peasant producers; the main cash crop grown and exported was cotton. Under the British rule, the agricultural producer became trapped in poverty. (Christian, 1942)

While Indochina was constantly under the influence of Europeans after 1535, the process of colonialization was much more difficult. French missionary influence was the key until the first military campaign between 1858 and 1863. Tonkin and Annam were conquered in 1883, but it was not until 1893 that Laos was annexed and the French proclaimed the Indochinese Union. Full control over the region (including Cambodia) was not accomplished until 1897, when the colonial regime finally began the construction of an infrastructure. The French pursued a strict mercantilist policy: exports were mainly rice, coal, and rubber; imports were from France, and manufacturing and industrialization were greatly restricted.

Between 1880 and 1930 irrigation was expanded in the Mekong Delta, in order to produce more rice for export. The newly developed lands were sold to the landlord class, whose power greatly increased under the French. For the majority of the rural inhabitants, farmers on small holdings and landless labourers, French colonialism meant forced labour, a decline in per-capita rice consumption, heavy taxes, and usury, all of which resulted in growing poverty. (Murray, 1980)

The Spanish claimed the Philippines in 1521 and were able to gain control of much of the commercial and coastal areas by the end of the 16th century. But for 200 years little development occurred, as the Spanish were preoccupied with extracting precious metals from their American colonies. In the 18th century there were attempts to introduce cash crops: sugar, indigo, tobacco, and hemp. Rice also became an important export.

However, the Philippines were never a profitable colony and, after 1820, the Spanish adopted a policy of free trade. Quickly, the British and Americans came to dominate the economy. The Americans established large plantations for hemp. After 1859 Spanish *haciendas* began planting sugar; these evolved into plantations. Under the new policy the acreage planted to rice began to decline. The local weaving industry was destroyed by the importation of British textiles.

The seizure of the Philippines by the United States in 1898 resulted in the re-imposition of a mercantilist system of trading and production. A major emphasis was put on sugar plantation development, but copra and hemp also remained important. Tariffs tied Philippine imports to the United States. Rice production declined, food imports increased, tenant farming was expanded, and the standard of living of the majority of the people declined. (Constantino, 1943)

Thailand is an interesting case, because its rulers managed to maintain formal political independence. This was achieved via the Bowring Treaty of 1855, with the British. Thailand agreed to extraterritoriality, free trade, and the fixing of import duties at 3%. The economy was overwhelmingly based on rice production. While rice remained the main export, teak, tin, and rubber were added. However, under the free trade arrangement, the domestic textile industry was destroyed.

The example of Thailand is also of interest because of the historic terms of trade. Between 1850 and 1940 the total value of exports regularly exceeded that of imports. Furthermore, the unit price for rice rose while the price of imported textiles declined. According to orthodox economic theory, this ideal example of international comparative advantage should have led to economic development. But it didn't. In 1937 88% of the population was still in agriculture and only 1.6% in manufacturing. The rate of population growth increased. While acreage planted to rice also increased, it did not keep up with population increases; furthermore, yields declined. Between 1857 and 1941 rice exports increased more than twenty-fold, but there was very little improvement in the standard of living of the vast majority of the population. (Feeny 1982; Ingram, 1971)

Conclusion

Traditional food systems have normally produced a rational, well-balanced adaptation to the environment. Farming techniques were usually environmentally sound. They produced a varied diet that was quite balanced nutritionally. But as subsistence farmers were brought into the market system, and as they shifted to the production of cash crops for export, their nutritional status declined. The growing of export crops brought seasonal cycles of plenty and want, a decline in crop diversity, a shift to poorer quality food crops (like cassava) that required less labour time, and the cultivation of crops that could not be eaten when markets were poor. (Rider, 1983; Fleuret and Fleuret, 1980; Dewey, 1979)

The impact of colonialism on the people working in agriculture was profound. In the Americas most of the indigenous population was destroyed by war, disease, and forced labour. In Africa the capitalist quest for slaves wrought havoc on an entire continent for around four centuries. In Asia peasants were traditionally exploited by landlords and moneylenders, but this exploitation increased under the yoke of colonialism. For most people in what is now called the underdeveloped world, the effect of colonialism was impoverishment, hunger, and even famine, at least down to World War I. In all areas, colonial exploitation brought with it European racism.

Mercantile colonialism had a dramatic effect on the evolution of economic development. Budding manufacturing was characteristically destroyed and industrialization was blocked. The result was the rise of a rural semi-proletariat of poor peasants on small holdings and labourers with only scattered seasonal employment. In the urban areas the lumpenproletariat expanded as people tried to survive in the service or informal sector. A major shift of the rural population from agriculture to industry, as in Europe, was largely blocked during colonialism. The development of a national bourgeois class was hindered by the habit of the colonial powers of aligning themselves with the most reactionary pre-capitalist elements of the local ruling classes. As Banaji (1972:2502) concludes, during the colonial phase imperialism was not primarily interested in the reproduction of the capitalist mode of production within the colonies.

There were two major differences between capitalism in the metropolitan countries and in the colonies. First, capitalism introduced the generalized production of commodities. Local self-sufficiency was broken down, and production was now for the market: local, national, and international. But the specific nature of colonialism meant that the circuit of production and distribution was closely tied to the more powerful metropolitan country. Second, the economic surplus extracted from agricultural workers was not directed to local investment by local capitalists and their governments; to a large degree it was appropriated by the metropolitan country for its own development. Thus, the structure of capitalist development in the colonies was quite distinct from the development of capitalism in the metropolitan countries. (See Alavi, 1982; 1980)

World War II signalled the end for the old colonial order. With independence, could the former colonies strike out on a new path, emulating the experience of the European powers? Would they be able to fundamentally alter the structure of their economies? Would they be able to provide their people with a high quality diet and a standard of living similar to that of their former oppressors? These are some of the questions that will be addressed in the following chapters.

References

Alavi, Hamza (1982). "The Structure of Peripheral Capitalism." In Hamza Alavi and Teodor Shanin, eds. *Introduction to the Sociology of "Developing Societies."* London: Macmillan, pp. 172-192.

Alavi, Hamza (1980). "India: Transition from Feudalism to Colonial Capitalism." *Journal of Contemporary Asia*, X, No. 4, pp. 359-399.

Bagchi, Amiya Kumar (1982). *The Political Economy of Underdevelopment.* Cambridge: Cambridge University Press.

Balazs, Etienne (1972). *Chinese Civilization and Bureaucracy.* New Haven: Yale University Press.

Banaji, Jairus (1972). "For a Theory of Colonial Modes of Production." *Economic and Political Weekly*, VII, No. 52, December 23, pp. 2498-2502.

Bandarage, Asoka (1983). *Colonialism in Sri Lanka.* New York: Mouton Publishers.

Banerji, A.K. (1982). *Aspects of Indo-British Economic Relations, 1858-1898.* Delhi: Oxford University Press.

Baran, Paul A. (1957). *The Political Economy of Growth.* New York: Marzani and Munsell.

Bhatia, B.M. (1967). *Famines in India.* Bombay: Asia Publishing House.

Boeke, J. H. (1953). *Economics and Economic Policies of Dual Societies.* New York: Institute of Pacific Relations.

Buchanan, Keith (1967). *The Southeast Asian World.* New York: Taplinger Publishing Company.

Caldwell, Malcolm and Ernst Utrecht (1979). *Indonesia, An Alternative History.* Sydney: Alternative Publishing Co-operative.

Charlesworth, Neil (1982). *British Rule and the Indian Economy, 1800-1914.* London: Macmillan.

Chesneaux, Jean et al (1976). *China from the Opium Wars to the 1911 Revolution.* New York: Pantheon Books.

Christian, John L. (1942). *Modern Burma.* Berkeley: University of California Press.

Constantino, Renato (1973). *A History of the Philippines: From the Spanish Colonization to the Second World War.* New York: Monthly Review Press.

Dewey, Kathryn (1979). "Agricultural Development, Diet and Nutrition." *Ecology of Food and Nutrition*, VIII, No. 4, pp. 265-273.

Dutt, R. Palme (1949). *India Today.* Bombay: People's Publishing House.

Elvin, Mark (1973). *The Pattern of the Chinese Past.* Stanford: Stanford University Press.

Fairbank, John K. et al (1965). *East Asia; The Modern Transformation.* Volume II. Boston: Houghton Mifflin.

Feeny, David (1982). *The Political Economy of Productivity: Thai Agricultural Development, 1880-1975.* Vancouver: University of British Columbia Press, 1982.

Fleuret, Patrick and Anne Fleuret (1980). "Nutrition, Consumption, and Agricultural Change." *Human Organization*, XXXIX, No. 3, pp. 250-260.

Frank, André Gunder (1979). *Dependent Accumulation and Underdevelopment.* New York: Monthly Review Press.

Frank, André Gunder (1978). *World Accumulation.* New York: Monthly Review Press.

Freund, Bill (1984). *The Making of Contemporary Africa.* Bloomington: Indiana University Press.

Furnivall, J.S. (1944). *Netherlands India*. Cambridge: Cambridge University Press.

Geertz, Clifford (1963). *Agricultural Involution: The Processes of Ecological Change in Indonesia*. Berkeley: University of California Press.

Gernet, Jacques (1970). *Daily Life in China on the Eve of the Mongol Invasion, 1250-1276*. Stanford: Stanford University Press.

Ghosh, Suniti Kumar (1984). "Marx on India." *Monthly Review*, XXXV. No. 8, January, pp. 39-53.

Greenberg, Michael (1951). *British Trade and the Opening of China 1800-42*. Cambridge: Cambridge University Press.

Grigg, David B. (1974). *The Agricultural Systems of the World*. Cambridge: Cambridge University Press.

Ingram, James C. (1971). *Economic Change in Thailand, 1850-1970*. Palo Alto: Stanford University Press.

Lippit, Victor D. (1980). "The Development of Underdevelopment in China." In Philip C.C. Huang, ed. *The Development of Underdevelopment in China*. White Plains, New York: M. E. Sharpe.

Marx, Karl and Frederick Engels [1965]. *On Colonialism*. Moscow: Foreign Languages Publishing House.

Moore, Barrington, Jr. (1966). *Social Origins of Dictatorship and Democracy*. Boston: Beacon Press.

Murray, Martin J. (1980). *The Development of Capitalism in Colonial Indochina (1870-1940)*. Berkeley: University of California Press.

Pannikar, K.M. (1965). *Asia and Western Dominance*. London: George Allen and Unwin.

Parry, J.H. (1966). *The Establishment of the European Hegemony: 1415-1715*. New York: Harper & Row.

Reid, A.J.S. (1980). "The Origins of Poverty in Indonesia." In R. G. Garnaut and P.T. McCawley, eds. *Indonesia: Dualism, Growth and Poverty*. Canberra: Australian National University, pp. 441-454.

Ricklefs, M.C. (1981). *A History of Modern Indonesia*. Bloomington: Indiana University Press.

Rider, Leslie (1983). "Determinants of the Nutritional Impact of Cash Cropping." In Georgio R. Solimano and Sally A. Lederman, eds. *Controversial Nutrition Policy Issues*. Springfield, Ill: Charles C. Thomas, pp. 27-50.

Riskin, Carl (1975). "Surplus and Stagnation in Modern China." In Dwight H. Perkins, ed. *China's Modern Economy in Historical Perspective*. Stanford: Stanford University Press, pp. 49-84.

Schultz, Theodore (1964). *Transforming Traditional Agriculture*. New Haven: Yale University Press.

Sievers, Allen M. (1974). *The Mystical World of Indonesia*. Baltimore: The Johns Hopkins Press.

Snodgrass, Donald R. (1980). *Inequality and Economic Development in Malaysia*. New York: Oxford University Press.

Snodgrass, Donald R. (1966). *Ceylon: An Export Economy in Transition*. Homewood, Ill.: Richard D. Irwin.

Thorner, David and Alice Thorner (1962). *Land and Labour in India*. Bombay: Asia Publishing House.

Williams, Glyndwr (1966). *The Expansion of Europe in the Eighteenth Century*. London: Blendford Press.

CHAPTER SIX

The Industrial
Food System

The present system of food production and distribution is commonly referred to as "agribusiness." This reflects the reality that food is no longer primarily associated with farming or agriculture. In the developed countries, both capitalist and state socialist, the industrial system has assumed a dominant role in the production and distribution of food. The producer on the land is playing a steadily declining role in the process of providing food for the consumer.

Many who have described this situation have attributed it to capitalism's natural evolution from competition among many firms to monopoly, oligopoly, cartels, and centralization. It is certainly true that the food industry has mirrored the changes in industrial organization in the advanced market economies. But what is also significant is the development of parallel trends in the food industry in the more industrialized centrally planned (or state socialist) countries of Europe. It is for this reason that I prefer to call it "the industrial food system."

The 19th and early 20th centuries saw the rapid growth of industry and technological change in western Europe, North America, Japan, Australia, and New Zealand. This brought economies of scale, large factories, and the division of labour in the workplace.

Yet during this period of industrialization, agriculture, for the most part, remained on a cottage scale: small, family owned and operated, simple commodity production. This form of farming was based on diversity of crops, crop rotation, heavy reliance on biological energy, and farm-generated inputs. Markets were usually close and processing was minimal. Farming was more than simple commodity production — it was a "way of life" quite different from that of the urban centres. This was reflected in rural populist movements which stressed that farm life had "different values," superior to those of the urban centres.

The period after World War II saw a tremendous change with the widespread adoption of the new technologies: mechanization, irrigation, manufactured fertilizers and pesticides, and plant breeding, all involving expanded use of fossil fuel energy. Farm inputs were now supplied by large transnational enterprises; individual industries were characterized by monopoly and oligopoly, and international cartels were quite common.

Coupled with this was the shift in farming towards economies of scale, crop specialization and vertical integration with processing and distributing firms. Monoculture became the norm. Meat and egg production were transformed into a factory operation. The advanced farmers were those who separated crop production from animal production.

The fisheries industry went through similar changes. Science and technology, coupled with increased capitalization, resulted in a major redirection of the industry in the period after World War II.

Developments in food and agriculture in the United States set the pace. Food processing firms became larger, and individual industries became characterized by oligopoly. In addition, the conglomerate firm emerged, operating in a number of food and non-food areas. Wholesale and retail firms became larger, more capital-intensive, more centralized, and integrated back into food processing. In this new era, agricultural products were viewed primarily as raw materials for further processing. Profits were much higher in the "value added" area between the farmer and the consumer; where food products could be differentiated through advertising, profits were highest. (See Polopolus, 1982; Connor, 1981; Schulman, 1981; Martinson and Campbell, 1980; OECD, 1980; Parker and Connor, 1979; Perelman, 1977; U.S. NCFM, 1966)

In spite of these changes in the food system beyond the farm gate, the basic form of agricultural production remained the simple commodity producer, or, as it is popularly called, the "family farm" operation. Capitalist farming, based on wage labour, has not yet developed to any significant extent in any of the advanced capitalist states. While farms are increasing in size, in all of the industrialized capitalist countries (the Organization for Economic Co-operation and Development minus Turkey) the number of farm workers is steadily declining, replaced by capital. (Lianos, 1984:100) Meanwhile, as food production has become industrialized, farmers have become more directly integrated into a system by way of production contracts with the corporate sector.

Gonzolo Arroyo (1977:257) calls the present-day family farmer the "piece worker" for the food corporations. Ernst Feder (1982:45) likens them to the share-cropper. Michael Troughton (1982:220) describes them as a "station on the food-production assembly line." Lewontin (1982:17) likens them to the "putting out system" of the pre-factory era.

In all of the industrialized capitalist states, the simple commodity producer is caught in a squeeze between the monopoly power of the farm supply industry (including credit) and the monopoly power of the food processors, wholesalers, and retailers. Through their organizations and political efforts, farmers have fought to protect their position. But it has been a failing effort. Despite government protection, subsidies, collective marketing systems, and the exploitation of family members and hired labour, in all the advanced capitalist states the size of farms is increasing and the number of farm families is steadily declining. (Lianos, 1984:103; Goss et al, 1980:98-100)

Industrial Agriculture in Centrally Planned Economies

Similar forces tending towards large-scale food production and distribution were at work in the Soviet Union and the state socialist societies of eastern Europe. Reconstruction after World War II delayed this development. In Poland and Yugoslavia, farming remains primarily simple commodity production, but in the other centrally planned economies, the social organization of agriculture has been radically changed.

In the Soviet Union agricultural land was socialized by the government through the formation of collective and state farms between 1929 and 1934. During the 1950s and 1960s there were major horizontal consolidations of these farms, and the average size increased substantially.

Agriculture went through several general stages of development in eastern Europe following World War II. Between 1945 and 1950 emphasis was on land reform, with distribution to the peasants. But between 1950 and 1960 the governments moved to collectivize the land. In more recent years, horizontal amalgamation has occurred.

In the USSR and the other countries of eastern Europe, collectivization of land preceded the large-scale introduction of industrial agriculture. Furthermore, it was not until the 1960s that major investments were made in agriculture. In these countries, the amalgamation of farms into larger units was not the product of market forces but a conscious government policy. Communist parties hold firm to the belief that large-scale production is preferable in industry and farming; concentration is seen as an objective process, not only in agriculture, but in all areas of material production. They have introduced specialization of production, concentration of units and management, new scientific techniques, and widespread mechanization. Large fields have been created to accommodate large machinery. Specialization and concentration make it easier to use airplanes and helicopters in the application of pesticides and fertilizers.

A key development in these state socialist countries has been the introduction of the Agro-Industrial Complex (AIC), first announced by Nikita Khrushchev in 1961. This involves the formal vertical integration of agriculture and industry, deemed "a law of socialist development," an attempt to draw the labour of the farm worker closer to that of the factory worker. One of the stated aims of the AIC program is the planned decentralization of the food processing industry. It is hoped that the shift will increase the availability of year-round work for farm members and help facilitate the equalization of living standards between town and country. The progressive introduction of the AIC system in the Soviet Union and eastern Europe began around 1970.

The Agro-Industrial system consists of three separate sectors: (1) the move backwards into the farm supply sector; (2) agricultural production; and (3) downstream expansion into food processing and distribution. As the share in the second (farm) sector declines (in labour or share of total food value) compared to the first and third sectors, progress is said to be occurring.

AIC activity in the first sector has been more or less limited to Agro-Chemical Centres and Machinery Repair Stations. Horizontal joint ventures among collective and state farms have been created by contract for this kind of activity and for the creation of new enterprises for processing and distributing food products.

The AIC system is the most advanced in Bulgaria. In 1979 the government formed the National Agro-Industrial Union ministry. Now political and geographical boundaries coincide with AIC boundaries. State and collective farms have been merged with agribusiness, and a new form of national land ownership has been introduced. (Bozhinov, 1982:37-40; Jacobs, 1980:241-242; Wiedemann, 1980:109-110)

Soviet agricultural experts and party officials admire the development of large, corporate-style farms in the United States, vertically integrated into the food industry. They view this as a natural, progressive development. Thus it was not too surprising when the government of Hungary purchased a hog-corn production system from Corn Production Systems of Illinois. Under contract, the American firm actually established the Technically Operated Production System (TOPS) which operates on around 30% of all arable land. (Jacobs, 1980:247-249; Elek, 1977:175-179)

There is one major difference in food systems as between the advanced capitalist and state socialist countries. This is in the crucial area of food distribution. In advanced capitalist countries like the United States and Canada, food is available on the basis of ability to pay. The unemployed or poor have a very difficult time obtaining an adequate nutritional diet. During the great recession of the 1980s, social programs were cut back, and there was greater reliance on private charity for the poor. The number of people actually going hungry greatly increased.

In contrast, in the state socialist countries there is full employment, with personal income at an adequate level and controlled food prices. Indeed, beginning in the early 1960s, retail food prices were frozen for about fifteen years in the Soviet Union and most eastern European countries. As prices to farmers were raised steadily over this period, the result was a considerable subsidy from the central government. While consumers in these countries often complain about the lack of variety of foods, there is no shortage, and everyone has access to an adequate nutritional diet. Indeed, the major health problems in these countries have been traced to overconsumption. This has been achieved in countries whose average per capita gross national product in 1982 was less than one-half the average of the OECD countries. (World Bank, 1984:Table 1)

Industrial Agriculture and the Underdeveloped Countries

The former colonies (referred to here as the underdeveloped countries) have not escaped the expansion of the industrial food system. They have all been significantly involved in the world food market since the beginning of western colonization in the 16th century. The colonial powers established the plantation system, designed to produce special crops for export, often with slave labour. Plant material was exchanged on a world-wide basis, and new export crops were introduced throughout the colonized areas. During the mercantile period of capitalism, the emphasis was on the production of export crops for the market in the mother country.

With the expansion of free-trade capitalism in the 19th century, there was significant migration of Europeans to the colonized areas. They introduced the form and techniques of European agriculture. The white settlers acquired the best land and began production of commercial crops for both export and domestic markets. Down through the end of World War II, the colonized areas, plus Latin America, were net exporters of food and agricultural products, including cereals.

The colonial powers were interested in developing commercial agriculture in the colonies. The colonial governments characteristically used poll and hut taxes to force peasants in subsistence operations into producing for the market. While political independence was achieved in the period after World War II, most of the former colonies were left with an agricultural system heavily dependent on exporting a few luxury crops and with a neglected system of food production for local consumption. (See Dinham and Hines, 1983; Dumont and Cohen, 1980; Burbach and Flynn, 1980; George, 1979; Perelman, 1978; Beckford, 1972)

Agriculture in the underdeveloped capitalist countries is often described as a "dual system," contrasting traditional subsistence farming with modern commercial farming. The reality is much more complex. Today we find a wide variety of farming units, varying in their degree of participation in domestic and export markets. Arroyo (1976:261) identifies six basic classes in Latin America: (1) subsistence family units; (2) unintegrated market-oriented family farms; (3) family farms indirectly integrated with agribusiness; (4) the *hacienda* system; (5) plantations; and (6) modern capitalized farms.

Malassis (1975:66-76) developed a slightly different classification. First, there is the customary type of farm organization involving common ownership of land for both cultivation and grazing purposes. Second, there is the "feudal or semi-feudal" system with large estates, the *hacienda*, and the *latifundia*. Thirdly, there is "peasant agriculture" including *minifundia* (small, subsistence farms), commercial production, and share cropping. Finally, there is capitalist agriculture based on wage labour, originally plantation agriculture but, in recent years, including modern mechanized agriculture for both the export and the domestic markets.

Feder (1980) has emphasized the degree to which agriculture in the underdeveloped countries is increasingly oriented to producing luxury crops for the markets of the western industrialized states. Of particular concern to him was the American feed-poultry-meat system.

Crouch and de Janvry (1980:4-5) have classified agriculture in under-developed countries according to commodities produced: (1) wage foods, primarily cereals for the domestic market: (2) peasant foods, primarily for personal consumption; and (3) export crops, where the major market is overseas. How each sector develops is profoundly influenced by state policy and the direction of research and technology. For example, the Green Revolution involved the production of wage foods, wheat and rice, by commercial farmers. Research was directed to this end (rather than to traditional subsistence crops), and the producing farmers received a wide variety of state subsidies.

The transnational food corporations (TNCs) have played a key role in bringing the industrial food system to the underdeveloped countries. Much of the literature has emphasized the role of the TNC and foreign investment in manipulating dependent capitalist economies. In the agricultural area they have been the overseas agents for major crops exported by the capitalist underdeveloped countries, as well as the suppliers of modern farm inputs. But the main impact of the TNC has been in marketing: the creation of popular tastes through product differentiation and advertising, imposing the food habits of the industrialized countries on the underdeveloped countries. (See Arroyo, 1981; Muller, 1979)

A number of former colonies have had social revolutions and are no longer fully integrated into the world market economy. A few of these have been quite successful in increasing agricultural production and have provided a nutritional diet for everyone; most notable have been North Korea and Cuba. Enormous advances in this direction have also been made in China and Zimbabwe. But other post-revolutionary societies are having a very difficult time overcoming the legacy of their war against colonialism and imperialism and subsequent economic boycotts by the advanced capitalist states. This would include the three countries who were victims of the long U.S. war in Southeast Asia (Vietnam, Laos, and Kampuchea) as well as Angola, Mozambique, and Nicaragua.

Problems Created by the Industrial Food System

The modern industrial food system has brought with it serious problems, both ecological and social. In a natural terrestrial system there is a steady progression towards diversity of species, an increase of structural complexity, an increase in organic matter, and the development of metabolic stability. Animals, of course, are an integral part of the system.

Modern industrial agriculture runs directly contrary to the natural order. Perennials are replaced by cereals, which are weedy annuals. Cultivation, summerfallowing, and intensive grazing lead to serious erosion problems. Monoculture and uniform varieties produce pest problems and the dangers of genetic uniformity. Attempts to counter nature require the use of pesticides, manufactured fertilizers, and antibiotics, etc., which create pollution problems.

The natural biological system is self-sustaining, because the waste products of the solar energy eco-cycle are essential to its preservation. Industrial agriculture has broken this cycle; natural fertility has been reduced, natural biomass has declined, and the long-run effects of increasing consumption of fossil fuels is unknown. The costs of the industrial food system are constantly rising.

At the moment our primary attention is focused on the social effects of the system. In the advanced capitalist states the industrial system has produced an abundance of food products. But producers are caught in a perpetual cost-price squeeze that forces them deeper into debt, and each year a significant number are forced out of farming. While the exploitation of unpaid family labour has apparently declined in recent years, it appears that wives and children are seeking better-paying, off-farm employment to subsidize the farm operation. Increasingly, farmers themselves turn to off-farm employment. The reality of the industrial food system is that simple-commodity producers have little independence today. What they produce and how is determined by the corporate food sector and the lending institutions. (Lianos, 1984; Clement, 1983; Davis, 1980; Warnock, 1978)

As farms get larger and there are fewer of them, the rural areas become depopulated. Increased capitalization of farms has produced a steady decline in hired farm labour. Regional areas heavily dependent on agriculture become relatively depressed. Urban centers are forced to absorb the continuing influx of farmers and farm workers looking for alternative employment or social support. This is most evident in the United States and Canada, but it is also a reality in the western European states, where farmers receive more systematic government protection and support.

A key characteristic of the system is the steady growth and importance of a small number of large, capital-intensive farms vertically integrated into the corporate sector of food processing and distribution. Processed food is marketed on a national and international basis. Consumers complain about the decline in the quality and taste of food. The decision-making process in the industrial food system is highly centralized. At all levels of the food system under capitalism, the workplace is hierarchical, completely lacking in any sense of democracy. Producers and consumers feel powerless to deal with it.

Marxists have traditionally argued that environmental degradation is an inevitable problem under the capitalist mode of production, but that it will not exist under socialism. However, it is quite clear that the industrial food system has produced the same kind of environmental problems in the existing state socialist countries. Pollution is evident in the increasing use of pesticides and fertilizers. Large-scale animal operations have major waste problems. Crop and livestock specialization results in increased pest problems. Agricultural land is degraded by wind and water erosion, siltation, and salinization. (Komarov, 1980; Laird, 1979; Lydolph, 1977: Gustafson, 1977; Pryde, 1972; Goldman, 1972)

Economists in the Soviet Union and the eastern European states have identified problems similar to those in the advanced capitalist states. Diseconomies of scale are reported. Amalgamation has created transportation problems: long distances from markets and the source of inputs. Total factor productivity has not increased. The energy subsidy is expanding. (Dovring, 1980; Laird, 1979; Clark, 1977; Shaffer, 1977; Martynov, 1977)

The horizontal amalgamation of farms and their vertical integration into Agro-Industrial Complexes has produced social concerns in many ways similar to those found in the advanced capitalist states. State enterprises have objected to the new, government-supported farm enterprises that threaten to drive them out of business. Representatives of state and collective farms have objected to the industrial sector's domination of the farm sector through the contract system. Collective farms in particular have resented the loss of decision-making power to the state management of the AIC. Farm members feel they have lost control of joint ventures to a new level of bureaucracy. The horizontal amalgamation of farms has resulted in a loss of local democratic control; popular participation in decision-making on the level of the collective and state farms has been replaced by a system of delegate representation at a regional level. (Lazar, 1982; Wodekin, 1982; Durgin, 1980; Khan and Ghai, 1980; Wiedemann, 1980; Jacobs, 1980; Bajaja, 1980)

The Demand for Food

In the marketplace for food, two laws are in operation. It seems clear from the evidence available that they are found in both market and centrally planned economies. However, the impact of these laws on the nutritional status of a population differs greatly between existing capitalist and socialist societies.

The first law postulates that, as income rises, the amount an individual or household spends on food also rises, but not to the same degree. Thus, as real income rises, a declining percentage of total income is spent on the purchase of food items. This law is commonly identified with the German statistician, Ernst Engel, who first recorded it.

A second pattern of food consumption has been noted. It is evident in all societies, at all levels of development. As income increases there is a change in the consumption pattern. The demand for staple foods declines while the demand increases for higher quality foods, in particular meat and dairy products, eggs, fruit, and vegetables. These foods are considered higher quality not only because of taste preferences but because of more balanced protein and vitamin and mineral content.

This second law is often called Bennett's Law after the U.S. economist, Merrill K. Bennett, who pioneered in this research in the 1930s and 1940s. (Poleman, 1983:56-58) More recent research indicates that the substitution process begins among the starchy staples. Poorer peoples tend to shift first to rice and wheat and away from coarse grains and other staples like manioc and plantains. This is not only due to the impact of western culture but also because coarse grains take more time to prepare and more fuel to cook. (Delgado and Miller, 1985:57-59; Mellor, 1983:241-242; Blaylock and Smallwood, 1982:104-109)

The production of higher quality foods (particularly animals and poultry) places greater demands on land and energy. For example, in 1981, around 600 million metric tonnes of cereals were fed to animals. Grain converted to meat loses 75 to 90 percent of its calories and 65 to 90 percent of its protein. (World Bank, 1982:42)

Demand for food in societies with rising incomes can significantly exceed the annual population growth or historic average increases in the production of food. Hopper (1981:36-39) points out that, in the "rich countries," the average person consumes the equivalent of 670 kgs of grain each year, much of it indirectly in the form of meat, poultry, eggs, and dairy products. In the low-income underdeveloped countries the average annual per capita consumption is 180 kgs, most of it directly as grain. (See Table VIa) The second law of the food market is a significant factor in Hopper's estimate that global demand for food will increase at a rate of around 3% per year between 1980 and the year 2000. Mellor (1983:242-243) and the International Food Policy Research Institute make similar projections.

If food is allocated by the market system according to ability to pay, then even steady increases in per capita food production do not guarantee an improvement in the diet of families with lower incomes. Rather wide inequalities of income, wealth, and status are common characteristics of the underdeveloped capitalist countries; they are also found in several of the poorer post-revolutionary countries. Inflation rates have been much higher than in the industrialized states over the past decade, and, in many countries, the real income of the poorest 50% of the population has declined. Given such conditions, farmers will choose to produce food for those who can pay. This often means diverting grains from direct consumption to the feedgrain-livestock-poultry system preferred by higher income consumers. It can also mean shifting prime agricultural land (particularly irrigated land) to producing luxury products (even flowers) for export markets. This is most evident in the pattern of food trade on the international market. (Yotopoulos, 1984:23-25; Christensen, 1978:757-764)

The other major factor in the production and distribution of food is the role of the state. In both the industrialized capitalist and state socialist countries a high priority has been placed on maximizing food self-sufficiency. Insel (1985:909-910) stresses that food and agricultural production is a "strategic good" which, in the industrialized capitalist states, is strongly supported, primarily "to protect a major domestic economic, social and political interest"; exports are a source of foreign exchange, but this is only a secondary objective. State policies include not only direct economic subsidies to food producers but also protection in the form of tariffs and other trade barriers.

TABLE VIa   Grain Consumption Per Capita, 1982

Countries	Population Millions/1982	Consumption 1000 MT	Kilograms Per Capita
North Africa and Middle East	239.5	87,648	366
Sub-Sahara Africa	403.2	62,308	154
Central America and Caribbean	130.0	39,266	302
South America	251.7	68,686	273
Asia[1]	1,388.4	333,420	240
India	711.7	151,194	212
China	1,020.7	371,356	364
United States	231.9	190,116	819
Canada	24.5	25,505	1,034
Australia/New Zealand	17.9	11,125	618
Japan	118.4	37,944	320
Western Europe	351.8	162,471	463
USSR	270.0	206,954	776
Eastern Europe	135.9	108,875	801

[1]Excluding China and Japan.

SOURCE: Food and Agricultural Organization. *Production Yearbook*, Volume 37, 1983; *Trade Yearbook*, Volume 37, 1983.

For example, at the Tokyo Round of multilateral trade negotiations (1975-1978) the advanced capitalist states made few concessions in the area of protection of agricultural products. (World Bank, 1982:53-56; Singer and Ansari, 1982:80-81) The European centrally planned economies have always stressed national planning in food production. In recent years there has been some concession to international specialization and "comparative advantage," but emphasis is on maximizing trade within the confines of the Council of Mutual Economic Assistance (CMEA). The food deficit in trade for these countries comes from the importation of feed grains to increase beef consumption; it in no way undermines their commitment to food self-sufficiency. (Johnson, 1983b:18-20; Balaam and Carey, 1981:57-59; Clark, 1977:20-21; Shaffer, 1977:81)

The European Economic Community maintains prices that are 30 to 80 percent above world prices, and imports are strictly controlled. (Legg, 1980:215-216) In 1984 EEC subsidies totalled $16 billion, or 79% of the entire EEC budget. (Insel, 1985:900) Protection is more complex in the United States, but the World Bank (1982:54) reports that state budgetary support for agriculture amounts to 38% of agricultural value added, which is similar to that of the EEC. U.S. agricultural subsidies, which averaged $3 billion per year in the 1970s, rose to $19 billion in the early 1980s. (Insel, 1985:900) Japan has the strictest controls on food imports and a major fiscal program to support agriculture. (Donnelly, 1979:186)

In contrast, as we shall see, the governments of the advanced industrialized countries and the international lending agencies (e.g., the World Bank, the International Development Agency, and the International Monetary Fund) insist that the underdeveloped countries reject policies of self-sufficiency, promote free trade in food and agricultural products, and follow principles of "comparative advantage."

The World Food Market

The factors that affect the demand for food within the nation state also operate on the international level. The bulk of trade in agricultural products (over 70%) is by the industrialized capitalist and state socialist countries. The international trade in food serves primarily to improve the quality and diversity of food for those who are already well fed.

Trade figures for the 1979-1981 period reveal that most of the highly industrialized capitalist states were net importers of agricultural products (see Table VIb), importing around $7.7 billion more than they exported. Of the eighteen western European countries, only five (Denmark, France, Greece, Ireland, and The Netherlands) were net exporters of agricultural products. The European centrally planned economies imported around $19 billion more than they exported; only Albania and Bulgaria were net exporters.

For that same period, the underdeveloped countries with market economies exported $60.1 billion worth of agricultural products and imported $55.5 billion. Of course, the aggregate figures tend to hide even more dramatic local conditions.

Contrary to conventional opinion, many low-income underdeveloped countries are net exporters of food and agricultural products. Of the 122 underdeveloped countries covered in the 1979-81 survey of trade by the Food and Agriculture Organization (FAO), 58 were net exporters of agricultural products. (FAO, 1981)

The greatest food deficits are found among the small island states of the Caribbean and in the Middle East. With the exception of Haiti, these countries are classified as middle-income countries by the World Bank. Demand for food is greatly outstripping production.

Despite very low per capita incomes and declining agricultural output, Africa south of the Sahara is a net exporter of agricultural products. Indeed,

---

TABLE VIb   *Trade in Agricultural Products*

1979-1981 Average, US$ millions

Countries	Imports	Exports
North Africa and the Middle East	21,415	5,986
Sub-Sahara Africa	7,281	11,832
Central America and the Caribbean	6,054	11,451
South America	6,717	19,704
Asia[1]	16,699	19,282
China	7,309	3,349
All Underdeveloped	**55,552**	**60,110**
United States	18,125	41,378
Canada	4,528	6,774
Australia/New Zealand	1,225	11,759
Japan	17,643	923
Western Europe	105,986	78,972
Industrial MEs[2]	**149,127**	**142,849**
USSR	29,652	10,673
Eastern Europe	11,971	7,854
Industrial CPEs[3]	**41,623**	**18,527**

[1]Excluding China and Japan.
[2]Market Economies
[3]Centrally Planned Economies

SOURCE: Food and Agricultural Organization, *Trade Yearbook*, Volume 35, 1981.

several of the 22 countries who asked the FAO for emergency food aid in October 1983 (including Zimbabwe, Tanzania, Ethiopia, Ghana, Chad, and the Central African Republic) were major net exporters of agricultural products.

Almost all the countries of central and south America are net exporters of agricultural products, Mexico and Venezuela being the major exceptions. Most of the Asian underdeveloped countries are also net exporters. In 1979-81 even the low-income countries of India and Pakistan exported more food and agricultural products than they imported.

Egypt is one of the major food-deficit countries. In 1980 domestic cereal production accounted for only 24% of consumption. Over the 1970s, cereal production only increased, on average, 0.5% per year, well below the population growth rate. Poverty is extensive. Yet the greatest increase in plantings by farmers have been to vegetables, orchards, and clover for meat production. In 1980 vegetables were the fifth most important export. (Thomson, 1983)

India is one of the poorest countries in the world, with a per capita income around US$150 and a per capita GNP below the average for the low-income underdeveloped countries. As we have seen, the National Nutrition Monitoring Bureau has reported that close to 50% of Indians suffer from chronic undernutrition. Yet over the period 1979-81 India was a net exporter of food every year. Exports in 1981 included fruits as well as the more traditional tea, spices, sugar, and coffee. (United Nations, 1981).

There is a pattern emerging in world trade in food and agricultural products. The industrialized countries are exporting cereals to the underdeveloped countries. Even Japan, which is heavily dependent on food imports, is self-sufficient in rice and exports its surplus to Asian countries. The underdeveloped countries are continuing to export the foods and agricultural products that were introduced during the colonial period. But in recent years they have begun to increase exports of foods that are relatively high in quality in terms of vitamins, minerals, and balanced protein. This trend also parallels the shift in the international division of labour: cereals exported by the industrialized countries are capital-intensive crops, while food products being imported from the underdeveloped countries tend to be labour intensive. The availability of cheaper land is becoming a factor in shifting beef and forage production to underdeveloped countries.

The underdeveloped countries are still heavily committed to exporting the traditional plantation crops developed during the colonial period: coffee, tea, cocoa, sugar, coconuts, bananas, rubber, jute, palm oil, cotton, etc. But the terms of trade of these export crops has declined substantially over the past twenty years. A 1982 study by the FAO found that, of fifteen traditional agricultural exports, all except cocoa were trading at lower real prices than they were in 1960. (FAO, 1982) The OECD reports that the purchasing power of commodities exported by low-income countries declined substantially over the period 1972-82 in relation to the manufactured products they purchased from abroad. (OECD, 1983). Thirlwall and Bergevin (1985) conclude that, aside from petroleum and minerals, the terms of trade of primary products exported by the underdeveloped countries have deteriorated in the post-war period, "continuing the long-run historical trend."

Generally speaking, the structure of trade between the industrialized state socialist countries and the underdeveloped countries is similar. In the late 1970s, 80% of their imports from the underdeveloped countries were foodstuffs and primary materials. Almost 50% of the imports were food, beverages, and tobacco. However, the CMEA countries have not been major exporters of cereals to the underdeveloped countries; manufactured products have accounted for 65% of their exports. (Berrios, 1983:241)

Trends in protein flows are important. While fish provides only one-seventh of the animal protein in the world, it has been the only form that traditionally reached the masses. Milk products, meat, and eggs have been the protein of the higher income classes.

Most of the ocean's fish are caught by the industrialized countries, with Japan and the USSR ranking at the top. In addition, the developed countries buy much of the fish caught by the underdeveloped countries; in the early 1980s Japan, the United States, and western Europe were the major importers. (See Table VIc) Of the 36 leading exporters (over $100 million per year), half are in the underdeveloped world. One result is that the price of fish in the underdeveloped world is rising much faster than prices for other foods. The FAO projects that, for the underdeveloped countries, production will not be able to meet demand by the end of the century. (Christy, 1984:13-14)

A few examples will illustrate the pattern of the fishery trade. Fish is India's seventh largest export, most of it going to Japan. Seafood is one of the major exports of Indonesia, Thailand, the Philippines and South Korea; again, most of this goes to Japan, the remainder primarily to North America. Fish is one of Mexico's major exports, the United States being the primary market. Fish canned in Morocco and Ghana, once eaten locally, now goes to the United States for use as cat food. Increasingly, fresh fish from Africa feeds Europe. Furthermore, this pattern of trade is not limited to the capitalist world. Cuba, Vietnam, North Korea, Mozambique, and the Democratic Peoples Republic of Yemen are all major net exporters of fish that goes primarily to the advanced capitalist states. (FAO, 1982b: Table A1-6; George, 1979:47; Kent, 1982:26-28)

Production of meat, particularly beef, has been concentrated in the temperate climates, where the protein level of forage is high and surplus grain production exists. Latin America has always had extensive ranching and has exported meat, primarily to Europe. More recently, emphasis has been on the production of grass-fed beef for export to the United States for use in hamburgers and frankfurters. (Nations and Komer, 1983; Feder,

1982, 1980) Berg (1973:65-67) shows that, as the forage-beef industry expanded in Central America for export to the United States, local consumption declined. In recent years, the United States has emerged as the second largest importer of meat products in the world, slightly behind Japan.

TABLE VIc   *Fisheries Catch and Trade*

1981 Catch in Thousand Metric Tonnes

Countries	Total Catch	Imports	Exports
North Africa and Middle East	1,388.8	361.7	179.3
Sub-Sahara Africa	2,703.3	1,076.6	771.5
Central America and Caribbean	1,967.9	221.7	128.9
South America	8,549.1	209.4	1,537.1
Asia[1]	15,359.8	811.7	1,381.8
China	4,605.0	0.0	101.2
All Underdeveloped	**34,573.9**	**2,681.1**	**4,099.8**
United States	3,767.4	1,043.5	1,142.0
Canada	1,362.2	100.6	520.7
Australia/New Zealand	306.9	147.6	227.4
Japan	10,656.5	1,038.0	683.1
Western Europe	10,951.7	4,316.5	3,902.9
All Industrial/ME	**27,044.7**	**6,646.2**	**6,476.1**
USSR	9,545.9	516.2	155.0
Eastern Europe	1,296.9	57.2	418.9
All Industrial/CPE	**10,842.8**	**573.4**	**573.9**
World Totals	**72,461.4**	**9,900.7**	**11,149.8**

[1]Excluding China and Japan.

SOURCE: Food and Agriculture Organization. *Yearbook of Fishery Statistics.* Volume 55, 1982; United Nations. *Statistical Yearbook* 1982.

Japan not only depends heavily on the world's fisheries but has become the largest importer of other protein sources. Overseas joint ventures are establishing major forage, pork, and poultry operations in Thailand and Indonesia. In those countries, the staple peasant food, cassava, is being made into pellets for animal feed. (Ping, 1980:52-53)

The underdeveloped countries are also increasing their production of luxury food items for the industrialized countries. The transnational corporations play an important role here in marketing and processing. Vertical integration is common, as a standardized product is required. (Halfani and Barker, 1984:47-61; Dinham and Hines, 1983:30-35; Hawes, 1982:26-27;

Arroyo, 1977:262-265). Contract farming and joint venture investments are common. Feder has documented this in his study of the strawberry industry in Mexico. (Feder, 1978)

During the 1974 famine, ships bringing "relief" foods to Senegal departed with peanuts, cotton, vegetables and meat for Europe. Aircraft flew loads of green beans, melons, tomatoes, eggplant, and strawberries to Europe. The drought did not seem to affect export crops. (Lappé and Collins, 1977:259-261) During the 1974 and 1984 famines in Ethiopia, coffee, meat, sugar, fruits, and vegetables were exported to Europe. (Abouchar, 1985; Bondestam, 1975)

In Southeast Asia luxury crops are being promoted for export to Japan. These include poultry, pork, shellfish, pineapples, bananas, and a wide variety of fresh and processed fruits and vegetables. The *Far East Economic Review* reports that three-quarters of the food exports from Southeast Asia go to the Japanese market, with the remainder going to the United States and Europe. (Ping, 1980)

The power of market forces in international production and trade in food have been emphasized in this discussion. But most observers in this area also stress the importance of the policies of the governments of the western countries and the international lending agencies they control, and the reinforcement given these patterns by local governments in the underdeveloped countries.

Cereals and the World Food Market

For the poor of the world, a scarcity or price rise in the staple food is a crisis situation. Since the shortages of 1973-74 there has been concern that the world's producers of cereals are not keeping up with the rise in population. It is argued that world food security (measuring the reserve stocks of grain and the potential of idle cereal cropland against daily world consumption figures) has been declining. (Brown et al, 1985:36-39; Brown, 1981:92-100) In contrast, Insel (1985:892) argues that the world has entered "an era of permanent grain surpluses."

Cereals are most important to low-income people in the underdeveloped countries. Table VIa shows that the consumption of cereals in kilograms differs greatly between the industrialized countries and the underdeveloped countries. A high percentage of grain consumption in the industrialized countries is indirect, in the form of animal products. This is reflected in calorie and protein consumption figures presented in Table VId. Thus, a rise in the price of cereals has little nutritional effect for those well off. But for the poor, it can be devastating. For many of the underdeveloped countries, there is no surplus of cereal production, so a decline in supply brought about by weather or foreign exchange difficulties can mean a crisis situation, at least for those with lower incomes. In Chapter I it was pointed out that low-income people, particularly in urban areas, suffered food shortages and a decline in the quality of diet during the 1979-1984 world economic recession, even in middle income countries.

TABLE VId   *Calorie and Protein Consumption*

Per-capita, Per Day, 1978-1980

| | Calories | | Protein (Grams) | |
| | Total | Animal Products | Total | Animal Products |
Countries				
North Africa and Middle East	2852	257	75.5	25.6
Sub-Sahara Africa	2209	182	55.4	13.5
Central America and Caribbean	2690	382	66.3	22.9
South America	2601	502	67.2	30.6
Asia[1]	2115	116	46.3	7.5
India	1998	89	48.5	4.6
China	2472	254	65.4	11.9
United States	3652	1331	106.7	72.0
Canada	3358	1397	97.8	62.4
Australia/New Zealand	3256	1235	101.0	67.4
Japan	2916	622	93.4	50.1
Western Europe	3440	1152	96.7	56.3
Eastern Europe	3515	1074	100.7	49.4

[1]Excluding China and Japan.

NOTE: The FAO has no data on the USSR.

SOURCE: Food and Agricultural Organization. *Production Yearbook.*Volume 35, 1981.

During the period 1978-80 wheat production, amounting to 440 million metric tonnes (mt), was slightly higher than that of rice (384 mt) or maize (378 mt). Over the 1970s, 30% of the increase in cereal production came from expanded acreage, a condition unlikely to continue. The cultivation of marginal land areas means that cereals are "forming an increasingly susceptible production base" able to meet current effective demand in good weather but more than ever before subject to variability in climate and weather. (Barr, 1981:1089-1090) Mitchell (1985:12-14) points out that the increase in cereal production in underdeveloped countries in the 1970s was primarily due to the introduction of new, high-response varieties. This avenue of increasing production is now peaking, and future increases will have to come from additional use of fertilizers and chemicals, new technology, and genetic improvements. Historically, these largely energy-intensive inputs have not produced such dramatic improvements.

In the period from 1983 to 1985 climate and weather were relatively good, and cereal production expanded. In 1983 the world's production of coarse grains (including maize) rose to 683 mt, of which 108 mt were traded, a new record. In 1984, wheat production reached a record 519 mt, and rice rose to 470 mt. In these two years record or near-record crops were obtained in China, India, eastern Europe, Argentina, Australia, Canada, the European Common Market, and the United States. Among the major cereal producers, only the Soviet Union experienced bad weather and poor harvests. Increased production in these years came primarily from increasing production on cropped land. The shift in food consumption patterns is increasing pressure on cereal production. In the middle-income countries, and the European centrally planned countries, there is greater emphasis on meat and dairy consumption. Governments of the Soviet Union and eastern Europe have given extensive food price subsidies to encourage consumption. The middle class of the underdeveloped countries is also consuming more poultry, eggs, and pork. But greater meat, dairy, and egg consumption requires more grain production. Since the 1960s, world consumption of red meat has been growing at an annual rate of 3% and of poultry at 6%. The Worldwatch Institute points out that, on a world-wide basis, per capita production of beef has declined since 1976. (Brown et al, 1985:9; Mitchell, 1985:12-14; Johnson, 1983a:19, 28; Mellor, 1983:241-242)

The Worldwatch Institute and the *Global 2000 Report* argue that, while production increases were very good during the 1950s and 1960s, since 1970 cereal production has barely kept up with the growth in population. Brown (1981:91) presents figures showing that per capita grain production peaked in 1978 and declined in the following two years. But over the period 1979-84, total grain production increased 2% annually, while population increased at a rate of 1.7%. (Brown et al, 1985:37; Barney, 1980:Table 6-6)

There is also widespread concern over the increasing dependence of cereal importers on surplus grain from the United States, Canada, Australia, and Argentina. Before World War II, Latin America, Africa, Asia, eastern Europe, and the Soviet Union were net exporters of grain. By 1980 these areas were all major importers of cereals.

In the last few years the European Common Market has become a major net producer of grains and an exporter of wheat. There were dramatic increases in production in the United Kingdom after it came under the Common Agricultural Policy. There has also been a major increase in cereal production in France. Without question, higher prices and a wide variety of state subsidies stimulated production. To reduce coarse grain imports, the EEC raised barriers to protein feeds (soybeans etc.), feed compounds, and maize. A key factor has been the adoption of the system of "intensive farming," which has raised wheat yields from 75 bushels per acre in 1973 to 133 bushels per acre in 1983 (or from 5039 kg/ha to 8936 kg/ha). However, this approach to farming is heavily dependent on fuel, fertilizers, and pesticides, and can only be justified if the EEC maintains its artificially high prices. (*Western Producer*, March 26, 1985; Insel, 1985:894-895)

Over the 1960s and 1970s world wheat production increased, on average, 3.4% per year, well above the overall cereal increase of 2.9%. On a worldwide basis, around 18% of all wheat is fed to animals. In the underdeveloped countries, average annual consumption of wheat has increased by 4.5% per year over the past two decades against a population growth rate of 2.4%. In the developed countries, and some of the middle-income countries, per capita wheat consumption is falling as demand shifts to higher quality foods. (Byerlee and de Polanco, 1983:68-70; Ahalt, 1979:6-7)

Wheat production in sub-Sahara Africa is limited, primarily because of ecological factors. The Middle East and North Africa have little chance to increase production, primarily because of lack of water; this is a major cereal-deficit region. There is concern that China will eventually have to increase its grain imports, for lack of new arable land, declining increases in yields, and the conversion of good farmland to other uses. In South and Central America adequate cereals are produced in only a few states: since the 1970s the region has become dependent on cereal imports. While south Asia has become more self-reliant in cereal production, the newly industrialized countries, with their higher incomes, are rapidly increasing the importation of cereals. Barr (1981:1094) of the U.S. Department of Agriculture concluded in 1980 that 48% of the world's population lacked a production base adequate to maintain per capita consumption and also lacked the financial reserves to bid for grain in times of short supply or world depression.

Very little of the world's rice production is traded on the international market. Over the 1960s and 1970s rice production increased by around 2.6% per year. In the period 1978-80 less than 5% of world production was exported. Thailand has been the major exporter; the other net exporters are Pakistan, Japan, India, Burma and Australia, all exporting below one million metric tonnes. (Tetro, 1981:5-8)

Increases in maize production have been highest in the developed market economies. The rate of growth has been well above that of all cereals. Less than 25% of world production is consumed by humans. Around 9% of production is exported, and world trading patterns reflect the cereals' primary use as feed for animals and poultry. In the period 1977-1979, less than 2 mt of the 14 mt of grain exported to underdeveloped countries went for human consumption. (Byerlee and de Polanco, 1983:74)

Johnson (1983a:19-20) argues that the increased export of grain in the 1970s was largely due to the lack of virtually any increase in the consumption of feed grains in the industrialized capitalist states since the 1973/1974 period. With the drop in real prices for almost all farm commodities, and, in particular, grains, there has been increased consumption and importation by the middle-income countries.

Between 1971-1981 feed concentrate consumption rose only 2% per annum in the industrialized countries, while it rose 5% in the underdeveloped countries. However, feed production in the underdeveloped countries lagged behind demand; as a result, feed imports grew by 14.35 per annum over the ten-year period. (*Ceres*, May-June 1984:14)

Most of the cereal trade, including wheat, is between industrialized countries. But the wheat trade is changing. Over the past twenty years, the proportion of cereal calories provided by wheat in the underdeveloped countries has risen from 21% to 27%. Per capita calories supplied by wheat rose much faster than calories from rice or maize. (Delgado and Miller, 1985:55-58; Byerlee and de Polanco, 1983:73-75)

Wheat has traditionally been the major cereal in international trade. Over the past two decades the bulk of the increase in wheat imports went to the low- and middle-income countries, for human consumption. Their share of the world wheat market has risen from 49% to 59%. There are several reasons for this.

First, international prices for wheat have been cheaper than for rice or maize. Second, government policies have assisted the export of wheat through direct subsidies, manipulated exchange rates, and food assistance programs. Third, wheat and bread have become identified with the more modern lifestyle of the industrialized countries. Thus demand for wheat is increasing in countries where it has never been a part of the traditional diet. (Delgado and Miller, 1985:58-59; Byerlee and de Palanco, 1983:74-75)

Crouch and de Janvry (1980:11-13) point out the contradictions the underdeveloped countries face with the cereal trade. The need for cheap wage foods can be met either by stimulating local cereal production for the local market (as in Mexico) or by relying on imports. But food imports compete with imports of machinery and raw materials (like oil) needed for the expansion of manufacturing. For most of the low-income underdeveloped countries, the only way to increase food imports is to increase agro-industrial exports. But policies that give preference to traditional agricultural exports limit land and other resources needed for local food production.

In the 1980s a "glut" of grain appeared on the international market. Prices continued to decline in real terms, and the major exporters, particularly the European Common Market, the United States, and Argentina, resorted to a variety of state subsidies to increase exports. For those countries with the greatest need, lack of foreign exchange has been the primary problem. (Schuh, 1983:236-237; Bale and Duncan, 1983:246-247) The rise in world oil prices and the persistence of the world economic recession greatly reduced their ability to import cereals. It was estimated in 1980 that these two developments had reduced the exchange earnings of the low-income underdeveloped countries by $6 billion. (Mitchell, 1985:13; Barr, 1981:1094) The World Bank (1982:40) referred to this "paradox" of poverty in the midst of plenty. The FAO (1981:25) noted the "irony" of a world afflicted by undernutrition while the rich countries were beset with grain surpluses.

Conclusion

Today, the industrial food system exists in all states, regardless of their degree of development or political structure. It is capital- and energy-intensive. The extent of its domination is dependent on the degree of industrial development. It operates in societies based on simple commodity production or collective agriculture.

The modern industrial food system is characterized by a high degree of centralization, hierarchical structure, and the absence of democratic control. In advanced capitalist societies this appears to be normal, following the general pattern of the political culture. But these features are also found in industrialized state socialist countries. The official position in these countries is that this is part of the "law of socialist development." But it has been argued that this is a rationalization, on the grounds that advanced techniques for farming, food processing, and distribution themselves determine the system. Is the industrial food system an inevitable development determined by science and technology? Is there no other form possible in an industrialized society? This has yet to be determined.

All countries with a market economy are integrated into the world food market. The preponderate bulk of the trade is between the industrialized countries, as they seek to improve the quality and diversity of foods consumed. There is relatively little food trade among the underdeveloped countries. There *is* a net flow of food and agricultural products (in dollars) from the underdeveloped countries to the industrialized countries. For the most part the underdeveloped countries are captives of the world market. Many are dependent on selling food and agricultural products to obtain foreign exchange to buy goods they do not produce.

Several patterns of trade seem to be emerging. First, the underdeveloped countries are tied to production and export patterns that developed during the period of colonialism. Even post-revolutionary societies have difficulty in making basic policy changes. In addition, recent developments stress the export of higher quality foods (luxury crops, poultry, animal products, and fish). In contrast, the developed countries export "low quality" foods in the form of wheat and feed grains. Second, world food trade also appears to be following the pattern of the new international division of labour. The underdeveloped countries tend to export labour-intensive food products; the industrialized countries tend to export capital-intensive crops.

The degree of participation in the world food market is largely a matter of state policy. All of the industrialized capitalist countries maintain programs guaranteeing a high degree of food self-sufficiency. Their involvement in world food trade, with a few notable exceptions, is largely for luxury purposes. The USSR and the state socialist countries in eastern Europe were only marginally involved in world trade in food before they decided to embark on a policy of rapid expansion of beef consumption. This has stimulated the importation of feed grains and supplements and produced an overall deficit in their balance of food trade.

For the underdeveloped countries, the concept of food self-sufficiency can be misleading. The fact that a state has a favourable balance of trade in food, or no longer imports cereals, does not by any means suggest that it has solved its food problem. The central fact in most underdeveloped countries is the "lack of effective demand," as the orthodox economists describe it. Many countries with a high proportion of their population suffering from chronic undernutrition are nevertheless "self-sufficient" in the area of food trade, because their poor cannot compete with the buyers from the industrialized world.

Those few countries which have chosen at one time or another to opt out of the international free market in food (e.g., China, Albania, Burma, North Korea, Vietnam, Kampuchea, Angola, and Mozambique) or who have challenged outside control of their food production system (Cuba and Nicaragua) have experienced serious political, economic, and military harassment from the major capitalist countries. For a government in an underdeveloped country, adopting a policy of "food first" means an intense struggle with both internal and external opposition.

References

Abouchar, Alan (1985). "The Positive Side of the Ethiopian Situation." *The Globe and Mail* (Toronto), January 11, 1985, p. 7.

Ahalt, J. Dawson (1979). "World Food Supplies: Abundant Today, But Great Challenges Ahead." *Foreign Agriculture*, XVII, No. 1, January 29, pp. 6-7, 12.

Arroyo, Gonzalo et al (1981). "Transnational Corporations and Agriculture in Latin America." In Latin America Research Unit. *Studies*, IV, No. 21, December, pp. 23-62.

Arroyo, Gonzalo (1977). "Institutional Constraints to Policies for Achieving Increased Food Production in Selected Countries." *Proceedings of the World Food Conference of 1976*. Ames, Iowa: Iowa State University Press, pp. 255-273.

Bajaja, Vladislav (1980). "Concentration and Specialization in Czechoslovak and East German Farming." In Ronald A. Francisco et al, eds. *Agricultural Policies in the USSR and Eastern Europe*. Boulder, Col.: Westview Press, pp. 263-293.

Balaam, David N. and Michael J. Carey (1981). "Agri-Policy in the Soviet Union and Eastern Europe." In David N. Balaam and Michael J. Carey, eds. *Food Politics: The Regional Conflict*. Totowan, N.J.: Allanheld, Osmun & Co., pp. 48-80.

Bale, Malcolm D. and Ronald C. Duncan (1983). "Food Prospects in the Developing Countries: A Qualified Optimistic View." *American Economic Review*, LXXIII, No. 2, May, pp. 244-248.

Barney, G.O., ed. (1980). *The Global 2000 Report to the President*. Washington: U.S. Government Printing Office.

Barr, Terry N. (1981). "The World Food Situation and Global Grain Prospects." *Science*, CCXIV, December 4, pp. 1087-1095.

Beckford, George L. (1972). *Persistent Poverty: Underdevelopment in Plantation Economies of the Third World*. London: Oxford University Press.

Belenky, V. B. (1982). "Agro-Industrial Co-operation and the Rural Settlement: The Case of the USSR." In Gyorgy Enyedi and Ivan Volgyes, eds. *The Effect of Modern Agriculture on Rural Development*. Toronto: Pergamon Press.

Berg, Alan (1973). *The Nutrition Factor: Its Role in National Development*. Washington, D.C.: The Brookings Institution.

Berrios, Ruben (1983). "The Political Economy of East-South Relations." *Journal of Peace Research*, XX, No. 3, pp. 239-252.

Blaylock, James R. and David M. Smallwood (1980). "Analysis of Income and Food Expenditure Distributions: A Flexible Approach." *Review of Economics and Statistics*, LXIV, No. 1, February, pp. 104-109.

Bondestam, Lars (1975). "Notes on Foreign Investment in Ethiopia." In Carl Widstrand, ed. *Multinational Firms in Africa*. Uppsala: Scandinavian Institute of African Studies, pp. 125-142.

Bozhinov, Todor (1982). "The Food Problem: Search for New Solutions." *World Marxist Review*, XXV, No. 71, July, pp. 36-40.

Brown, Lester R. et al (1985). *State of the World*. New York: W. W. Norton.

Brown, Lester R. (1981). *Building a Sustainable Society*. N.Y.: W.W. Norton.

Burbach, Roger and Patricia Flynn (1980). *Agribusiness in the Americas*. N.Y.: Monthly Review Press.

Byerlee, Derek and Edith Hesse de Polanco (1983). "Wheat in the World Food Economy." *Food Policy*, VIII, No. 1, February, pp. 67-75.

Christensen, Cheryl (1978). "World Hunger: A Structural Approach." *International Organization*, XXXII, No. 3, Summer, pp. 745-774.

Christy, Francis T. (1984). "Fisheries for Food: Global Developments and Special Needs." Rome: FAO.

Clark, M. Gardner (1977). "Soviet Agricultural Policy." In Harry G. Shaffer, ed. *Soviet Agriculture: An Assessment of its Contributions to Economic Development.* N.Y.: Praeger, pp. 1-48.

Clement, Wallace (1983). *Class, Power and Property; Essays on Canadian Society.* Toronto: Methuen.

Connor, John M. (1981). "Food Product Proliferation: A Market Structure Analysis." *American Journal of Agricultural Economics*, LXIII, No. 4, November, pp. 607-617.

Crouch, Luis and Alain de Janvry (1980). "The Class Basis of Agricultural Growth." *Food Policy*, V, No. 1, February, pp. 3-13.

Davis, John Emmeus (1980). "Capitalist Agricultural Development and the Exploitation of the Propertied Laborer." In Frederick H. Buttel and Howard Newby, eds. *The Rural Sociology of the Advanced Societies.* Montclair, N.J.: Allanheld, Osmun Publishers, pp. 133-154.

Delgado, Christopher L. and Cornelia P.J. Miller (1985). "Changing Food Patterns in West Africa." *Food Policy*, X, No. 1, February, pp. 55-62.

Dinham, Barbara and Colin Hines (1983). *Agribusiness in Africa.* London: Earth Resources Research Ltd.

Donnelly, Michael W. (1979). "The Political Economy of Food in Japan." In Barbara Huddlelston and Jan McLin, eds. *Political Investments in Food Production.* Bloomington: Indiana University Press, pp. 185-201.

Dovring, Folke (1980). "Capital Intensity in Soviet Agriculture." In Ronald A. Francisco et al, eds. *Agricultural Policies in the USSR and Eastern Europe.* Boulder, Col.: Westview Press, pp. 5-26.

Dumont, René and Nicholas Cohen (1980). *The Growth of Hunger: A New Politics of Agriculture.* London: Marion Boyars Publishers.

Durgin, F. A. Jr. (1980). "The Low Productivity of Soviet Agricultural [Labour]." In Ronald A. Francisco et al, eds. *Agricultural Policies in the USSR and Eastern Europe.* Boulder, Col.: Westview Press, pp. 27-35.

Elek, Peter S. (1977). "Hungary's New Agricultural Revolution and Its Promise for the Fifth Five-Year Plan." In Roy D. Laird et al, eds. *The Future of Agriculture in the Soviet Union and Eastern Europe.* Boulder, Col.: Westview Press, pp. 171-184.

Feder, Ernest (1982). "The World Bank and the Expansion of Industrial Monopoly Capital into Under-developed Agricultures." *Journal of Contemporary Asia*, XII, No. 1, pp. 34-60.

Feder, Ernest (1980). "The Odious Competition Between Man and Animal over Agricultural Resources in the Underdeveloped Countries." *Review*, III, No. 3, Winter, pp. 463-500.

Feder, Ernest (1978). *Strawberry Imperialism.* The Hague, Netherlands: Institute for Social Studies.

Food and Agriculture Organization (1982a). "Commodity Prices Reveal Weakness over Long Term." *Ceres*, XV, No. 3, May-June, pp. 11-12.

Food and Agriculture Organization (1982b). *Yearbook of Fishery Statistics.* LV, Fishery Commodities. Rome: FAO.

Food and Agriculture Organization (1981). *Trade Yearbook.* XXXV. Rome: FAO.

George, Susan (1979). *Feeding the Few: Corporate Control of Food.* Washington, D.C.: Institute for Policy Studies.

Goldman, Marshal I. (1972). *The Spoils of Progress: Environmental Pollution in the Soviet Union.* Cambridge, Mass.: MIT Press.

Goss, Kevin F. et al (1980). "The Political Economy of Class Structure in U.S. Agriculture: A Theoretical Outline." In Frederick H. Buttel and Howard Newby, eds. *The Rural Sociology of the Advanced Societies.* Montclair, N.J.: Allanheld, Osmun, Publishers, pp. 83-132.

Gustafson, Thane (1977). "Transforming Soviet Agriculture: Brezhnev's Gamble on Land Improvement." *Public Policy,* XXV, No. 13, Summer, pp. 293-312.

Halfani, Mohamed S. and Jonathan Barker (1984). "Agribusiness and Agrarian Change." In Jonathan Barker, ed. *The Politics of Agriculture in Tropical Africa.* Beverly Hills: Sage Publications, pp. 35-63.

Hawes, Gary A. (1982). "Southeast Asian Agribusiness: The New International Division of Labour." *Bulletin of Concerned Asian Scholars,* XIV, No. 4, October-December, pp. 20-29.

Hopper, W. David. (1981). "Recent Trends in World Food and Population." In Richard G. Woods, ed. *Future Dimensions of World Food and Population.* Boulder, Col.: Westview Press, pp. 35-55.

Insel, Barbara (1985). "A World Awash in Grain." *Foreign Affairs,* LXIII, No. 4, Spring, pp. 892-911.

Jacobs, Everett M. (1980). "The Impact of Agro-Industrial Programs on East European Agriculture." In Ronald A. Francisco et al, eds. *Agricultural Policies in the USSR and Eastern Europe.* Boulder, Col.: Westview Press, pp. 237-262.

Johnson, D. Gale (1983a). "The World Food Situation: Recent and Prospective Developments." In D. Gale Johnson and G. Edward Schuh, eds. *The Role of Markets in the World Food Economy.* Boulder: Westview Press, pp. 1-33.

Johnson, D. Gale (1983b). "The Soviet Union. Agriculture—Management and Performance." *Bulletin of the Atomic Scientists,* XXXIX, No. 2, February, pp. 16-22.

Kent, George (1982). "Food Trade: The Poor Feed the Rich." *Food and Nutrition Bulletin,* IV, No. 4, October, pp. 25-33.

Khan, Azizur Rahman and Dharam Ghai (1980). *Collective Agriculture and Rural Development in Soviet Central Asia.* N.Y.: St. Martin's Press for the International Labour Organization.

Khomelyansky, B.N. (1982). "Stabilizing the USSR's Rural Population through Development of the Social Infrastructure." *International Labour Review,* CXXI, No. 1, January-February, pp. 89-100.

Komarov, Boris (1980). *The Destruction of Nature in the Soviet Union.* N.Y.: M. E. Sharpe.

Laird, Roy D. (1979). "The Plusses and Minuses of State Agriculture in the USSR." In Ronald A. Francisco et al, eds. *The Political Economy of Collectivized Agriculture.* N.Y.: Pergamon Press, pp. 3-20.

Laird, Roy D. and Betty A. Laird (1977). "The Widening Soviet Grain Gap and Prospects for 1980 and 1990." In Roy D. Laird et al, eds. *The Future of Agriculture in the Soviet Union and Eastern Europe.* Boulder, Col.: Westview Press, pp. 5-42.

Lappé, Frances Moore and Joseph Collins (1977). *Food First: Beyond the Myth of Scarcity.* Boston: Houghton Mifflin Co.

Lazar, Istvan (1982). "Hungarian Agriculture: Whither and How?" *The New*

Hungarian Quarterly, XXIII, No. 85, Spring, pp. 26-45.

Legg, Wilfrid (1980). "Agriculture in the EEC: Two Scenarios to the Year 2000." *Futures*, XII, No. 3, June, pp. 212-222.

Lewontin, Richard (1982). "Agricultural Research and the Penetration of Capital." *Science for the People*, XIV, No. 1, January/February, pp. 12-17.

Lianos, Theodore P. (1984). "Concentration and Centralization of Capital in Agriculture." *Studies in Political Economy*, No. 14, Summer, pp. 99-116.

Lydolph, Paul E. (1977). "The Agricultural Potential of the Nonchernozem Zone." In Roy A. Laird et al, eds. *The Future of Agriculture in the Soviet Union and Eastern Europe*. Boulder, Col.: Westview Press, pp. 49-77.

Malassis, Louis (1975). *Agriculture and the Development Process*. Paris: UNESCO.

Martinson, Oscar B. and Gerald R. Campbell (1980). "Betwixt and Between: Farmers and the Marketing of Agricultural Inputs and Outputs." In Frederick H. Buttel and Howard Newby, eds. *The Rural Sociology of the Advanced Societies*. Montclair, N.J.: Allanheld, Osmun, Publishers, pp. 215-254.

Martynov, Vladen A. (1977). "Production of Food and Development of Agro-Industrial Integration in the USSR." In *Proceedings of the World Food Conference of 1976*. Ames, Iowa: Iowa State University Press, pp. 233-242.

Mellor, John W. (1983). "Food Prospects for the Developing Countries." *American Economic Review*, LXXIII, No. 2, May, pp. 239-243.

Mitchell, Donald O. (1985). "Trends in Grain Consumption in the Developing World, 1960-1980." *Finance & Development*, XXII, No. 4, December, 12-14.

Muller, Ronald (1979). "The Multinational Corporation and the Underdevelopment of the Third World." In Charles K. Wilber, ed. *The Political Economy of Development and Underdevelopment*. New York: Random House, pp. 151-178.

Nations, James D. and Daniel I. Komer (1983). "Rainforests and the Hamburger Society." *Environment*, XXV, No. 3, April, pp. 12-20.

Organization of Economic Co-operation and Development (1983). "Strengthening the Export Capacity of Low-Income Countries: Commodities." *OECD Observer*, No. 122, May, pp. 13-15.

Organization of Economic Co-operation and Development (1980). "The Food Industry; Innovation and Industrial Structure." *OECD Observer*, No. 106, September, pp. 17-22.

Parker, Russell C. and John M. Connor (1979). "Estimates of Consumer Loss due to Monopoly in the U.S. Food-Manufacturing Industries." *American Journal of Agricultural Economics*, LXI, No. 4, November, pp. 626-639.

Perelman, Michael (1978). *Farming for Profit in a Hungry World*. Montclair, N.J.: Allanheld, Osmun Publishers.

Ping, Ho Kwon (1980). "Profits and Poverty in the Plantations." *Far East Economic Review*, CXVIII, July 11, pp. 52-57.

Poleman, Thomas T. (1983). "World Hunger: Extent, Causes, and Cures." In D. Gale Johnson and G. Edward Schuh, eds. *The Role of Markets in the World Food Economy*. Boulder: Westview Press, pp. 41-75.

Polopolus, Leo (1982). "Agricultural Economics Beyond the Farm Gate." *American Journal of Agricultural Economics*, LXIV, No. 5, December, pp. 803-817.

Pryde, Philip R. (1972). *Conservation in the Soviet Union*. Cambridge: Cambridge University Press.

Schuh, G. Edward (1983). "Changing Trends in World Food Production and Trade." *American Economic Review*, LXXIII, No. 2, May, pp. 235-238.

Schulman, Michael D. (1981). "Ownership and Control in Agribusiness Corporations." *Rural Sociology*, LXVI, No. 4, Winter, pp. 652-668.

Shaffer, Harry G. (1977). "Soviet Agriculture: Success or Failure?" In Harry G. Shaffer, ed. *Soviet Agriculture: an Assessment of its Contribution to Economic Development*. N.Y.: Praeger, pp. 51-99.

Singer, Hans and Javed Ansari (1982). *Rich and Poor Countries*. London: Allen and Unwin.

Stebelsky, Ihor (1978). "Soviet Agricultural Land Resource Management, Policies, and Future Food Supply." In W.A. Douglas Jackson, ed. *Soviet Resource Management and the Environment*. Columbus: American Association for the Advancement of Slavic Studies, pp. 171-186.

Tetro, Robert (1981). "World Rice Production." *Foreign Agriculture*, XIX, No. 5, May, pp. 5-8.

Thirwall, A. P. and J. Bergevin (1985). "Trends, Cycles and Asymmetries in the Terms of Trade of Primary Commodities from Developed and Less Developed Countries." *World Development*, XIII, No. 7, July, pp. 805-818.

Thomson, Anne M. (1983). "Egypt: Food Security and Food Aid." *Food Policy*, VIII, August, pp. 178-186.

Troughton, Michael (1982). "Process and Response in the Industrialization of Agriculture." In Gyorgy Enyedi and Ivan Volgyes, eds. *The Effect of Modern Agriculture on Rural Development*. Toronto: Pergamon Press.

United Nations (1981). *Statistical Yearbook*. N.Y.: United Nations.

United States. National Commission on Food Marketing (1966). *The Structure of Food Manufacturing*. Technical Study No. 8. Washington, D.C.: U.S. Government Printing Office.

Wadekin, Karl-Eugen (1982). *Agrarian Policies in Communist Europe: a Critical Introduction*. London: Allenheld, Osmun Publishers.

Warnock, John W.(1978). *Profit Hungry: The Food Industry in Canada*. Vancouver: New Star Books.

Wiedemann, Paul (1980). "The Origins and Development of Agro-Industrial Development in Bulgaria." In Ronald A. Francisco et al, eds. *Agricultural Policies in the USSR and Eastern Europe*. Boulder, Col.: Westview Press, pp. 97-135.

World Bank (1984; 1982; 1981) *World Development Report*. Washington, D.C.: World Bank.

Yotopoulos, Pan A. (1984). "Competition for Cereals: The Food-feed Connection." *Ceres*, XVII, No. 5, September-October, pp. 22-25.

CHAPTER SEVEN

The Unequal Distribution
of Population
and Foodlands

Since the publication of *The Limits to Growth* in 1972, attention has focused on the question of the world distribution of population and resources. Most of the debate has centred around whether there are adequate resources to continue the present world system of production and distribution into the near future. Much less attention has been focused on a more important question: are there enough resources available to allow the presently industrialized countries to maintain their steadily increasing high standards of living *and* at the same time allow the poor countries to close the gap and become industrialized?

The narrower perspective of this book asks a question slightly different again: Are there adequate resources available to allow *all* the population of the world to consume a diet similar to that now available to the majority in the industrialized countries? In the industrialized countries, both capitalist and state socialist, the availability of a high quality diet and a wide variety of foods is taken for granted. No one could conceive of returning to a diet of basically staple foods. In the underdeveloped world, the goals are to achieve the same food standards. Whether this is possible involves an analysis of the distribution of population, projections for population growth, land use patterns, the availability of resources needed for food production, and the patterns of end-use of these resources.

Population Distribution and Trends

At the beginning of the 18th century, Europe's population was increasing at a rate less than 0.2% per year. Over the next few decades, the population increased more rapidly: in some countries the annual rate of growth reached 1%, which results in a doubling in 70 years.

For the 10,000-year period before the 18th century, human population was controlled by famine, epidemics, and war. For example, in France between 1000 A.D. and the 19th century around 150 serious famines were recorded, about one every six years. In the early agrarian societies, before industrial development, the low rate of population growth was due to the narrow margin between a high death rate and a high birth rate. (Dumont and Rosier, 1969:27-29)

The major reason for the rapid rise in population was the discovery and use of stored fossil energy as coal, oil, and gas; this allowed the development of new machinery and technology. Population growth from this time on closely paralleled the rapid increase in the use of fossil fuel energy. Not only did the new energy source increase agricultural productivity, it fostered economic development in general, including improvements in public health.

The rate of population growth since the end of World War II has been without precedent, averaging around 2% per annum, a doubling in just 35 years. Over the 1970s the growth rate in the low-income underdeveloped countries was around 2.3%; in the middle-income underdeveloped countries it was even higher, averaging around 2.6%. Only in a few underdeveloped countries did the rate of growth drop below 2%, and in many the population was growing by more than 3% per year. In contrast, the annual growth rate in the capitalist industrialized countries was around 0.8%, and in the European state socialist countries it was even lower. (World Bank, 1984:63-65; Coale, 1983:828-832)

Table VIIa reports population trends in the world between 1965 and 1980 by geographic area and by general levels of socioeconomic development. Over this fifteen-year period the average annual population growth varied widely between areas: Sub-Sahara Africa, 3.5%; North Africa and the Middle East, 3.3%; South America, 3%; Central America and the Caribbean, 2.8%; India, 2.8%; China, 2.0%; Western Europe, 1% and Eastern Europe, 0.7%.

The primary reason for the rise in population growth in the underdeveloped countries during this period was the falling death rate achieved through improvements in sanitation, improved communications and transportation, control of epidemics, and the increased availability of antibiotics. The increase in the general availability of medical services was not large enough to have accounted for much of the change. Furthermore, given the grossly unequal distribution of food, improved nutrition could not have been a major cause in the decline. (Mauldin, 1980:148-149) For the low-income underdeveloped countries, the crude death rate per 1000 people dropped from 24 in 1960 to 11 in 1982. Over the same period the crude birth rate also declined, from an average of 44 per 1000 to 30; however, when China is excluded, the decline is much less significant. The total fertility rate is the number of children on average a woman typically would have over a lifetime. For the low-income underdeveloped countries (excluding China) in 1982, this was around 5.2. For the industrialized capitalist countries it was around 1.7, and, for the European state socialist countries, around 2.3. (World Bank, 1984:71-72, Table 20; Mauldin, 1980:148-150)

TABLE VIIa   *Population Trends*

Countries	Total Population		Agricultural Pop'n		% in Agriculture	
	1965	1980	1965	1980	1965	1980
North Africa and Middle East	149.2	222.9	84.6	103.6	56.7	46.5
Sub-Sahara Africa[1]	232.1	353.7	185.6	246.6	79.9	69.7
South Africa	18.4	29.2	5.5	8.3	29.9	28.4
Central America and Caribbean[2]	72.4	113.7	38.1	45.0	52.6	39.6
Cuba	7.6	9.7	2.7	2.2	35.5	22.7
South America	166.0	240.5	70.9	77.7	42.7	32.3
Asia[3]	944.7	1,329.6	643.9	827.1	68.2	62.2
India	483.0	684.5	338.1	432.9	70.0	63.7
China	764.0	994.9	441.0	594.7	57.7	59.8
United States	194.6	227.7	11.7	4.9	6.0	2.1
Canada	19.6	24.1	1.7	1.2	8.7	4.9
Australia/New Zealand	14.0	17.5	1.5	1.1	10.7	6.3
Japan	97.9	116.8	23.7	12.6	24.2	10.8
Western Europe	323.3	372.2	64.2	39.9	19.9	10.7
USSR	230.6	265.5	73.3	43.6	31.8	16.4
Eastern Europe	121.5	134.3	46.0	38.8	37.9	28.9

[1]Excluding South Africa.
[2]Excluding Cuba.
[3]Excluding China and Japan

SOURCE: Food and Agricultural Organization. *Production Yearbook.* Volume 20, 1966; Volume 35, 1981.

The other major factor in population growth is distribution by age. In the underdeveloped countries there is a far greater percentage of the population in the child-bearing ages than there is in the more developed countries. Around 40% of the population is under 15 years of age. Until this group passes through childbearing age, birth rates will remain high. Moreover, in the underdeveloped countries the dependency rate (the proportion of the population under fifteen and over sixty-five to those between ages fifteen and sixty-four) is on average higher than in the developed countries. (World Bank, 1984:65-66; Sai, 1984:801-802; McNicoll, 1984:183-189)

The rate of growth in population in the underdeveloped countries is no longer just the concern of population experts in the industrialized countries. The change in attitude between the 1974 International Conference on Population and the 1984 conference in Mexico City has been widely reported. At Bucharest, there was strong opposition to population control measures, even from China. Government representatives from many of the underdeveloped countries insisted that "development is the best contraceptive." However, economic development in the underdeveloped countries has been less than hoped for, and the central concern of government delegates at Mexico City, ten years later, was how to implement successful programs of control.

Much attention has been directed to the success of birth control policies in China and Cuba. This has been widely attributed to egalitarian policies, full employment, and central planning in general. But successful programs have also been introduced in Indonesia, Barbados, Hong Kong, Singapore, and Costa Rica. Crude birth rates dropped below 30 in Sri Lanka, Thailand, Jamaica, Colombia, Chile, Argentina, Malaysia, Trinidad and Tobago, Taiwan, and South Korea. This seemed to suggest that improvements could be achieved even in capitalist underdeveloped states.

Ironically, while the major voices of opposition to birth control at Bucharest were those of governments of states with centrally planned economies: at Mexico City the major dissenting voice came from the U.S. government. Its position was a reflection of the Reagan Administration's "free market" ideology. Symbolically, the head of the U.S. delegation was James L. Buckley, former Conservative Party Senator from New York state. The New Right position of the U.S. government held that, if the Third World countries wished to slow population growth, they should adopt more free-market policies. Reflecting the views of Julian Simon (1981), they argued that population growth was a positive factor in economic development. (Brown et al, 1985:200-203; Murray, 1985:9-10)

Projecting Population Trends

Planning for future food needs requires estimates of future populations. The United Nations and the World Bank, as well as other institutions, have been making projections for a number of years. The Club of Rome used a sophisticated computer model for *The Limits to Growth*; they estimated that world population would reach 6 billion people by the year 2000. (Meadows et al, 1974:34-38) The Independent Commission on International Development Issues, commonly known as the Brandt Commission, projected a population of between 6 and 6.5 billion people by the year 2000. (Brandt, 1980:105-106) The difficulty of adopting a strictly empirical approach to population projects is well known. (Coontz, 1957) For the purposes of this book, discussion will be limited to widely cited population projections.

Projecting population growth is complicated because of the many variables involved, including fertility rates, sex ratios, life expectancies, age distribution, and other demographic factors. Tribe and Belyea (1977:86) remind us that the United Nations' 1954 medium projection of the world population for 1980 was actually overtaken in 1970. Even trends are difficult to forecast. For example, after 1960 fertility rates for Costa Rica, India, South Korea, and Sri Lanka steadily declined; however, after 1975, the decline slowed and even stopped. (World Bank, 1984:71; Mauldin, 1980:154-155)

More recent projections using complex computer models have proven to be more accurate and consistent. The 1963 U.N. projection of 4.3 billion people for 1980 was only slightly under the actual total. The 1973 U.N. medium projection for total population for the year 2000 was 6.25 billion, and their 1980 projection only slightly reduced this number. (World Bank, 1984:73-74; Harrison, 1984:33; Barney, 1980:35)

One of the most sophisticated computer models is that of the U.S. Bureau of the Census. Their projections were used in the *Global 2000 Report.* (Barney, 1980, II:15) Their medium projection for the world in the year 2000 was set at 6.35 billion; this would reflect an average annual growth rate of 1.5% between 1975 and 2000.

In 1984 *World Development Report* issued by the World Bank concentrated on the population issue. Their revised projections estimate that the world's population will reach 6.08 billion people by the year 2000. These figures are reproduced here in Table VIIb. There is a widespread consensus that by the year 2000 there will be around 6 billion people on the planet.

The World Bank assumes in its projections that mortality rates will continue to decline and that fertility rates will also decline until they reach replacement levels. Given the trends, they project that the industrialized

---

TABLE VIIb *Population Distribution by Economic Category*

Millions

Economic Classification	1960	% Total	1980	% Total	2000	% Total	2050	% Total
Low Income Economics (34)	1370	46.9	2161	49.3	3097	50.9	5863	53.1
Lower Middle Income Economies (42)	397	13.6	699	16.0	1023	16.8	2391	21.7
Upper Middle Income Economies (23)	234	7.9	410	9.3	751	12.3	1434	13.0
Industrialized Market Economies (19)	594	20.3	714	16.3	780	12.8	828	7.5
Industrialized Centrally Planned Economies (8)	330	11.3	398	9.1	431	7.1	523	4.7
Total (124)	2924	—	4382	—	6082	—	11039	—

NOTE: Projections for the year 2050 are close to the estimates of the hypothetical size of stationary population.

SOURCE: Food and Agricultural Organization. *Production Yearbook*, Volume 16, 1961; World Bank, World Development Report, 1982, 1984.

capitalist countries will reach a net reproduction rate of 1 around the year 2005, with most of these countries reaching a stationary population by the year 2030. The industrialized state socialist countries are expected to reach a net reproduction rate of 1 at around the same time and to achieve a stationary population around 2070. (World Bank, 1984, Table 19:254-255)

The population projections produced by the World Bank, seen in Table VIIb, suggest that there will be little population growth in the industrialized countries by the year 2000 or even by 2050. Between 1980 and 2000, the world's population is expected to increase by 1,700 million, of which 94% would be in the underdeveloped countries. The largest increase would occur in low-income underdeveloped countries. In 1980 the World Bank estimated that the fifteen largest underdeveloped countries had a population of 2.6 billion, accounting for 78% of the total population in the underdeveloped world and 59% of the total world population. (World Bank, 1982: Table 1)

The latest U.N. medium projection estimates that the world's population will reach 7.8 billion by the year 2020. By the year 2050 world population is supposed to exceed 11 billion people. Over 96% of the increase between 1980 and 2050 is projected to occur in the underdeveloped world, with 3,702 million being added to the low-income countries. While Julian Simon insists that increases in population are a positive contribution to economic growth, the prevailing opinion is that these steady population increases are already frustrating efforts at development. (For example, see Sai, 1984; Keyfitz, 1984)

To illustrate what this means in more concrete terms, Table VIIc lists the sixteen most populous countries in 1980, reports their population growth since 1960, gives the World Bank's projections for their growth to 2000, and estimates the year when they might reach a stationary level. The large industrialized countries, with their low fertility rates, are expected to increase only marginally. But the population growths projected for the underdeveloped countries are almost beyond belief.

When Europe went through a period of rapid population growth a considerable percentage of its population permanently emigrated to the "new countries" overseas. The exodus was not insubstantial. The World Bank (1984:69) has made the following estimates: between 1851-80, 11.7 million; between 1881-1910, 19.6 million; and between 1911-40, 14.4 million. This out-migration has continued, although at a slower pace; between 1940 and 1980 another 11.9 million went overseas. Another authority (Willcox, 1985:519-520) believed that the figures for national emigration greatly underestimated the total amount of emigration. His survey of people of European origin or descent living outside Europe at the beginning of the 20th century totaled over 100 million. In contrast, between 1850 and 1980 there has been very little migration overseas from the underdeveloped countries: 8.4 million from Latin America, 1.6 million from

Asia and 0.5 million from Africa. (World Bank, 1984:69; Mauldin, 1980:149-150)

The other basic demographic feature of the underdeveloped countries is rapid urbanization, as unemployed and underemployed rural people move to the cities in the hope of finding some sort of work. In the underdeveloped countries, urban population is growing at a rate that is almost twice that of the overall population. Between 1950 and 1980 the urban population in the underdeveloped countries grew by 585 million people. In 1980 around two-thirds of the population in Latin America lived in cities; in Asia and Africa it was around one quarter. (McNicoll, 1984:185-186)

TABLE VIIc   *Most Populous Countries, 1980*

Millions

Countries	Population 1960	1980	Population Projections 2000	Stationary Level	Year, Net Reproduction 1
China	646.5	976.7	1,196	1,461	2000
India	432.6	673.2	994	1,707	2010
USSR	214.4	265.5	306	377	2000
United States	180.7	227.7	259	292	2010
Indonesia	92.6	146.6	212	370	2010
Brazil	65.7	118.7	181	304	2010
Japan	93.2	116.8	128	128	2010
Bangladesh	—	88.5	157	454	2035
Pakistan	92.7	82.2	140	377	2035
Nigeria	34.3	84.7	169	618	2035
Mexico	34.6	69.8	109	199	2010
West Germany	42.0	60.9	60	54	2010
Italy	49.4	56.9	58	57	2010
United Kingdom	52.5	55.9	57	59	2010
Vietnam	29.3	54.2	88	171	2015
France	45.5	53.5	58	62	2010
% World Total	**70.4**	**70.6**	**68**	**61**	**—**

SOURCE: Food and Agricultural Organization. *Production Yearbook*, Volume 15, 1961; World Bank, *World Development Report*, 1984.

Furthermore, the large cities of the underdeveloped countries are growing much faster than the world average. The United Nations projects that, by the year 2000, 21 of the 25 cities with populations exceeding 10 million will be found in the underdeveloped world. (World Bank, 1984:66-68) This rapid urban growth has put tremendous pressure on governments to provide sanitation, water supplies, health care, food, shelter, and employment. A growing percentage of these new urban arrivals are forced to live in "uncontrolled settlements," commonly known as shantytowns or slums, where public services are minimal at best. In 1980 the *Global 2000 Report* estimated that at least 25% of the population of Bombay, Calcutta, Mexico City, Rio de Janeiro, Seoul, and Taipei were living in such areas. (Barney et al, 1980:9)

In all the underdeveloped areas the percentage of the population living in urban centres is rising. But despite migration to urban areas, in the low-income countries of Asia and Africa the rural population continues to increase, on average, around 2% per year. (World Bank, 1984:66) Table VIIa reveals that while the *percentage* of the population in agriculture has declined between 1965 and 1980, *the absolute number* of people in agriculture has increased in all underdeveloped areas, even South America. This is in contrast to the history of development in the industrialized countries and makes the job of increasing the productivity of labour in agriculture much more difficult.

The other major characteristic of the demography of the underdeveloped countries is the rapid rise of a large service sector in the economy. When economic development advanced in the presently industrialized countries (see Chapter III), peasants moved out of agricultural areas and were absorbed in the industrial sector. Many of those who could not find work migrated overseas. It is well known that in the advanced industrialized countries, with their high level of technological development, there has been a significant rise of the service sector. Yet in 1980 the OECD countries still employed 38% of the labour force in industry. Only 6% of the labour force was in agriculture.

In the underdeveloped countries, as the percentage of the labour force in agriculture declines, there has been an increase in employment in the industrial sector. But the adoption of modern, capital-intensive technology from the industrialized countries has limited employment opportunities. For the low-income countries, the percentage of the labour force employed in industry has been roughly the same as in the service sector; in 1980 it was around 15%. But, in the lower-middle-income countries, industry accounted for only 16% of the labour force in 1980, compared to 28% in the service sector. In the upper-middle-income countries, the percentage in industry was 28%, with 42% in the service sector. (World Bank, 1984, Table 21:258-259)

Roberts (1978:127) points out that when the United States, France, and Italy each had about 50% of their population in agriculture, the service sector employed 26%, 23%, and 14% of the population respectively. In contrast, in 1960, with roughly 50% of the population in agriculture, Brazil, Mexico, and Peru had 35%, 30% and 31% respectively in the service sector.

The service sector is roughly divided into three groups: those employed by the state, those employed by commercial enterprises, and the remainder who form the "informal economy," carrying out private services. Included in the latter are small retail outlets, small-scale public transport, personal services, security services, gambling services, recycling, prostitution, begging, and theft. Bromley (1982:59-60) categorizes these as "street occupations." However, most social scientists refer to this as the "informal sector" of the economy.

The people in this sector of the economy in underdeveloped countries are commonly defined as underemployed, the subproletariat, or the marginalized. The general absence of unemployment insurance and welfare in underdeveloped countries forces people to find whatever source of income they can for mere survival. Others have noted that the informal economy is expanding in the underdeveloped world because of the capital-intensive nature of new industry, high unemployment rates in the formal sector, the small numbers of skilled workers, the lack of an urban mass market due to the high degree of inequality in income and wealth, and the concentration of people living in slum areas. (See Roberts, 1978:116-124)

The well-known British Marxist, Bill Warren, emphatically denied that these people were "marginalized" and insisted that the informal sector provided a "wide variety of essential goods and services at relatively low cost." In his view, what is taken to be underemployment "appears actually to be functional to the general growth of the urban economy." (Warren, 1980:216-217)

Other commentators are more critical. Roberts (1978:162) defines the informal sector as "marginalized people," because their activities are "risky, do not provide full-time work, and generate low incomes or very low profits." Bromley (1982:59-70) points out that workers in this area are "generally held in low esteem." His study of those in the informal sector in Cali, Colombia, found that they work relatively long hours, seven days a week, and earn around US$3 per day, which is roughly the same as for unskilled wage-workers in casual employment. He finds this one of the "worst forms of poverty and exploitation associated with work."

Petras (1984:195) concludes that in the underdeveloped countries today the informal service sector is rising faster as the industrialization process deepens. In the now-industrialized countries, as the population left the agricultural sector they entered the industrial labour force. The result was a polarization between capital and those employed on the basis of wage labour. But in the underdeveloped countries today there are three major sectors in the urban economy; capital, wage-labour, and the underemployed mass which is superior in size to the other two sectors.

Foodland Resources

It is virtual certainty that the world's population will rise to at least 6000 million by the end of the 20th century. We can also be fairly certain that around 70% of the growth in population between now and 2000 will take place in the underdeveloped countries. Obviously, these countries in particular will need to increase their food production to supply the additional people and to improve their general standard of living. The key for most of these countries will be increased production of staple foods, cereals in particular.

FIGURE VIIa *Major Limitations on Agriculture*

	Drought	Mineral stress	Shallow depth	Water excess	Permafrost	Left available
			% of total land area			
Europe	8	33	12	8	3	36
Central America	32	16	17	10		25
North America	20	22	10	10	16	22
South Asia	43	5	23	11		18
Africa	44	18	13	9		16
South America	17	47	11	10		15
Australasia	55	5	8	16		15
Southeast Asia	2	59	6	19		14
North and Central Asia	17	9	38	13	13	10
World average	28	23	22	10	5	11

SOURCE: Food and Agricultural Organization. *Ceres.* XI, No. 5, Sept - Oct , 1978, p. 5.

Historically, as world population grew the amount of land under cultivation expanded. The ability of the world to provide food was greatly increased when the "new" continents were opened to European settlement. However, today the underdeveloped countries must rely on expanding the amount of foodland within their own borders and increasing productivity on that which is presently being used.

The total land area of the world today is around 13,000 million hectares. But much of the land is clearly unsuited for agriculture. Figure VIIa, prepared by the Food and Agriculture Organization, illustrates the major limitations to agricultural use: permafrost, drought, shallow depth, water excess, and mineral stress (e.g., high aluminum content).

The United Nations Environment Programme estimates that 36.3% of the world's land is arid or semi-arid, with little chance of water for cropping or significant grazing. Another 25% of the land surface is "highlands," with an elevation over 1000 metres. Nevertheless, this land supports 10% of the world's population. (Abercrombie, 1978:18)

Table VIId provides a breakdown of world land use in 1980. Only 1,414 million hectares are presently used for some sort of cropping, representing only 10.8% of the earth's land total. Another 3,151 million hectares, or 24.1%, is used for pasture for domestic animals. Forests and woodlands amount to 4,056 million hectares, or 31% of the land total. Forest lands can often be used for grazing.

TABLE VIId   *World Land Use, 1980*

('000 hectares)

Category	Area	% Total	% Sub-total
Total Land Area	13,073,597	100.0	
Developed Market Economy	3,157,798		24.0
Developing Market Economy	6,439,705		49.3
European Centrally Planned	2,326,869		17.8
Asian Centrally Planned	1,149,225		8.8
Total Arable Land	1,414,229	10.8	
Developed Market Economy	394,860		27.9
Developing Market Economy	629,572		44.5
European Centrally Planned	277,922		17.8
Asian Centrally Planned	111,875		8.8
Permanent Pasture	3,150,862	24.1	
Developed Market Economy	880,390		27.9
Developing Market Economy	1,530,663		48.6
European Centrally Planned	389,546		12.4
Asian Centrally Planned	350,263		11.1
Forest and Woodlands	4,056,673	31.0	
Developed Market Economy	885,480		21.8
Developing Market Economy	2,057,000		50.7
European Centrally Planned	949,132		23.4
Asian Centrally Planned	165,061		4.1
Other Land	4,451,833	34.1	
Developed Market Economy	997,068		22.4
Developing Market Economy	2,222,470		49.9
European Centrally Planned	710,269		16.0
Asian Centrally Planned	522,026		11.7

SOURCE: Food and Agricultural Organization. *Production Yearbook*, Volume 33, 1980.

TABLE VIIe   *Land Use for Food Production, 1960 to 1980*

Million Hectares

Countries	Arable Land		Per Capita Ha Arable Land	
	1960	1980	1960	1980
North Africa and Middle East	82.741	87.158	0.62	0.39
Sub-Sahara Africa	213.028	156.301	1.06	0.41
Central America and Caribbean	30.460	36.394	0.46	0.29
South America	73.000	125.741	0.53	0.52
Asia[1]	266.759	288.648	0.32	0.22
India	160.738	169.130	0.37	0.25
China	109.354	99.200	0.17	0.09
All Underdeveloped	**775.342**	**793.442**	**0.39**	**0.24**
United States	184.940	190.624	1.02	0.84
Canada	40.600	44.350	2.27	1.84
Australia/New Zealand	27.521	44.853	2.17	2.56
Japan	6.072	4.881	0.07	0.04
Eastern Europe	96.216	87.200	0.31	0.23
All Industrial/ME	**355.349**	**371.908**	**0.39**	**0.24**
USSR	212.366	231.966	1.03	0.87
Western Europe	56.216	53.749	0.48	0.40
All Industrial/CPE	**277.582**	**285.715**	**0.84**	**0.71**
World Totals	**1,408.273**	**1,451.065**	**0.48**	**0.33**

[1]Excluding China and Japan.

SOURCE: Food and Agricultural Organization. *Production Yearbook*, Volume 16, 1951; Volume 33, 1980.

Tables VIIe and VIIf reveal the distribution of foodlands among geographic and economic categories and their changes between 1960 and 1980. Arable land per capita is quite high in Australia, New Zealand, Canada, the United States, and the USSR. It is noticeably low in Asia.

Between 1960 and 1980 the total amount of arable land in the world increased by 43 million hectares, for an average annual increase of only 0.15%. But over this twenty-year period, the world's population grew by 1,459 million, which reduced the world average of per capita arable land from 0.48 ha to 0.33 ha.

Table VIIf reveals that the amount of permanent pasture increased by 537 million hectares between 1960 and 1980. Nevertheless, on a per capita basis, permanent pasture declined from 0.88 ha to 0.72 ha. The amount of land classified as forest and woodlands increased slightly over the 20-year period, but on a per capita basis it also declined, from 1.38 ha to 0.93 ha.

However, the amount of arable land available on a per capita basis is not necessarily the most important factor in food production. The quality of arable land is of equal importance. For example, the generally favourable climate in the United States makes its arable land potentially more productive than land in the USSR, which has very significant problems associated with drought, acidity, and limitations on the length of the growing season. Secondly, the availability of fossil fuel imputs is a key factor. Western Europe, with a per capita arable land base 25% below the world average, is a major producer of food because of heavy capital and fossil fuel subsidies that are not available to African countries.

TABLE VIIf *Permanent Pasture, Forests, and Woodlands*

Million Hectares

Countries	Permanent Pasture 1960	Permanent Pasture 1980	Annual % Change	Forest/ Woodlands 1960	Forest/ Woodlands 1980	Annual % Change
North Africa and Middle East	197.6	233.7	0.9	44.6	58.0	1.5
Sub-Sahara Africa	541.1	719.9	1.7	766.7	685.4	(0.5)
Central America and Caribbean	87.1	90.7	0.2	123.3	72.6	(2.0)
South America	292.0	449.6	2.7	908.0	942.6	0.2
Asia[1]	102.1	213.4	3.8	377.4	356.9	(0.3)
India	13.1	12.0	(0.4)	51.8	67.5	1.5
China	177.9	220.0	1.2	76.6	116.4	2.6
All Underdeveloped	**1,397.8**	**1,927.3**	**1.9**	**2,296.6**	**2,231.9**	**(0.1)**
United States	255.0	237.5	(0.3)	258.4	284.5	0.5
Canada	21.9	23.9	0.5	442.3	326.1	(1.3)
Australia/New Zealand	455.1	466.1	0.2	49.2	114.1	6.6
Japan	0.9	0.6	(1.9)	24.9	25.0	0.0
Western Europe	56.5	64.9	0.7	101.6	116.2	0.7
All Industrial/ME	**789.4**	**793.0**	**0.2**	**876.4**	**865.9**	**0.5**
USSR	369.7	373.7	0.1	880.3	920.0	0.2
Eastern Europe	21.5	21.7	0.1	36.4	35.5	(0.1)
All Industrial/CPE	**391.2**	**395.4**	**—**	**916.7**	**955.5**	**0.2**
World Totals	**2,578.4**	**3,115.7**	**0.1**	**4,089.7**	**4,053.3**	**—**

[1]Excluding China and Japan.

SOURCE: Food and Agricultural Organization. *Production Yearbook*, Volume 15, 1961; Volume 33, 1980.

Of special importance is the amount of land planted to cereals, the basic staple food for most people. Recent figures are presented in Table VIIg. The amount of arable land in such use has increased steadily over the past two decades, but at a rate that is less than 1% per year, considerably below increases in population. Table VIIg reveals the special problem facing China, which accounts for over one-fifth of the world's population. Between 1960 and 1980 land planted to cereals in China steadily declined, at a rate of around 0.5% per year. Japan's rate of loss of arable land was higher, but, in contrast to China, it has the economic power to purchase needed food on the world market.

The productivity of land can be greatly increased through the utilization of irrigation. Changes occurring between 1960 and 1980 are found in Table VIIh. Land under irrigation increased by 73 million hectares, for an average annual increase of 2.6%, higher than the rate of population increase.

TABLE VIIg   *Land Planted to Cereals*

Countries	Million ha 1961-65	Million ha 1979-81	% Increase
North Africa and Middle East	35.523	38.025	7.2
Sub-Sahara Africa	48.244	58.712	21.7
Central America and Caribbean	11.327	12.830	13.3
South America	28.746	37.717	31.2
Asia[1]	157.565	178.599	13.3
India	93.449	103.478	10.7
China	107.016	96.073	(10.2)
All Underdeveloped	**388.421**	**421.956**	**8.6**
United States	61.812	72.621	17.5
Canada	18.234	19.430	6.6
Australia/New Zealand	9.437	16.296	72.7
Japan	4.591	2.717	(40.8)
Western Europe	41.398	41.209	(0.5)
All Industrial/ME	**135.472**	**152.273**	**12.4**
USSR	120.487	121.038	0.5
Eastern Europe	31.679	29.068	(8.2)
All Industrial/CPE	**152.166**	**150.106**	**(1.4)**
Totals	**676.059**	**724.355**	**7.1**

[1]Excluding China and Japan.

SOURCE: Food and Agricultural Organization. *Production Yearbook*, Volume 28, 1974; Volume 35, 1981

TABLE VIIh   *Irrigation of Arable Land*

Countries	1000 ha 1960	1000 ha 1980	% increase per annum
North Africa and Middle East	13,323	15,241	0.7
Sub-Sahara Africa	2,370	4,324	4.2
Central America and Caribbean	3,960	6,774	3.6
South America	3,863	7,409	4.6
Asia[1]	47,230	73,901	2.8
India	23,755	39,350	3.3
China	38,500	46,000	0.9
All Underdeveloped	**109,247**	**153,670**	**2.0**
United States	11,257	20,517	4.1
Canada	346	510	2.4
Australia / New Zealand	924	1,666	4.0
Japan	3,369	3,250	(0.1)
Western Europe	2,522	9,868	14.6
All Industrial/ME	**18,418**	**35,811**	**4.7**
USSR	9,490	17,500	4.2
Eastern Europe	1,294	4,671	13.0
All Industrial/CPE	**10,784**	**22,171**	**5.3**
Totals	**138,449**	**211,652**	**2.6**

[1]Excluding China and Japan.

SOURCE: Food and Agricultural Organization. *Production Yearbook.* Volume 19, 1965; Volume 35, 1981.

Significant increases were recorded in Asia, particularly India. However, the data reveal that the industrialized countries were much more successful in adding irrigated land over the 20-year period. For the rich countries, irrigated land was added at a rate of 4.7% per year; for the underdeveloped countries as a whole, the increase was only 2.0% per annum, below the rate of population growth.

The data on population growth and land use for food production reveals disturbing trends. Those areas with the highest rate of population growth are also the regions where the land resources are least adequate to meet present food needs. Land resources in Central America and the Caribbean were in short supply for population levels even in the mid-1970s. One quarter of the land is highlands, and many believe that it is already overpopulated for sustaining the ecology. Harrison (1984:29) argues that land shortages are crucial in 11 of the 21 countries.

Arable land is in very short supply in North Africa and the Middle East. In the mid-1970s the land could not feed the existing population, and the region is increasing its dependence on food imports. Of the sixteen countries in Southwest Asia surveyed by Harrison (1984:27-28), only Turkey could be considered as having adequate foodlands for future needs. Most of the countries in this area have paid for their food imports by selling their finite resource, petroleum, to the industrialized west.

In Africa most of the underdeveloped land resources with agricultural potential lie in the less populated areas. Food shortages have been severe in the drier and more mountainous areas. (Sai, 1984:803) The World Bank (1984:164-165) concluded that in the mid-1970s fourteen countries in sub-Sahara Africa, representing about one-half of the population, did not have enough foodlands to support the needs of their own populations.

In Asia as a whole, population growth has slowed over the past two decades. China has been more successful than the capitalist underdeveloped countries in lowering the birth rate. However, Asia already has a very high level of population in relation to its foodland resources. The amount of land remaining for possible conversion to cropping is quite limited. For the most part, raising production requires greatly increased fossil fuel subsidies and capital investment, particularly for additional irrigation. (Harrison, 1984:28-29)

Thus it is all too evident that population and foodland resources are very unevenly distributed on a world-wide basis. Projected trends for population increases and the availability of arable land suggest that it will be most difficult for the underdeveloped countries to achieve the quality and diversity of diet now enjoyed in the industrialized countries. The problems of the underdeveloped countries can be illustrated by looking at the case of China which, in 1980, contained roughly 30% of those living in the underdeveloped world.

China and the Malthusian Question

One of the major tests of Malthusian theory is China. The 1982 census found that China's population had reached 1,032 million, or roughly one quarter of the world's total. Around 22% of the world's rural population lives in China, which contains only 7% of the world's arable land. The World Bank projects that China's population will reach 1,460 million before it becomes stationary. Will it be possible to feed this many people and also provide them with a rising standard of living?

Following the success of the revolution in 1949, the new government called for the fulfilment of the basic physical needs of the society: good health, good water, and adequate food. The two major campaigns of the 1950s were (1) to improve sanitation, reduce disease, and improve health conditions; and (2) to transform nature through the containment of drought and floods in order to expand food production. (Leung, 1983:140-149)

Compared to the achievements of other underdeveloped countries, the successes of the post-revolutionary government in China were impressive. In 1929-1931, average life expectancy in China was 24 years; it rose to 40 in 1953 and 65 in 1982. Infant mortality rates are much harder to judge; the World Bank has estimated that the rate dropped from 200 per 1,000 live births in 1949 to 6.36 in 1982. But it is apparent that with increased food production and a much more egalitarian system of distribution, population has increased substantially.

The 1953 census reported 582 million people. The 1957 sample census estimated that the population had risen to 656 million, an annual increase of around 15 million. There were major disruptions during the Great Leap Forward (1958-61). The formation of the communes brought major social change; the economy was re-oriented, with an emphasis on decentralized rural industrialization. The Chinese estimate that 80% of their major irrigation and water conservation projects were started in 1958 and 1959. One result was a shortage of labour for the harvest. Unfortunately, this major step towards a more egalitarian society was accompanied by widespread natural disasters, including typhoons, floods, and droughts that destroyed crops on millions of hectares. The result was famine conditions in some areas and a temporary decline in population growth. (Ashton et al, 1984:614-620; Banister, 1984:254-255; Nolan, 1983:383, 401; Stavis, 1979:180-182)

The period after 1962 stressed modernization in agriculture, including increased production and application of fertilizers, insecticides, and herbicides, rural electrification, tubewell irrigation, and more agricultural machinery. Heavy emphasis was put on grain production. Nolan and White (1981:9) point out that this was a natural response to a number of important considerations: "the relatively rapid rate of population increase, the desire to maintain regional self-sufficiency in food-grain production (partly for security reasons), and the attempt to ensure that the basic food needs of the whole population were met."

However, tremendous pressures were put on marginal lands in order to increase land under cultivation. Deforestation became widespread. Fragile grasslands and pastures were ploughed and planted to grain. Land degradation and environmental pollution increased. Heavy reliance on China's soft coal for fuel not only polluted the urban environment, it began to produce the well-known effects of acid rain. Official concern for the state of the environment began in 1970, during the Great Proletarian Cultural Revolution. (Vermeer, 1984:7-10; Smil, 1982:18-23; Broadbent, 1976:415-421; Orleans, 1977:326)

As Seccombe (1983:22) points out, "the primary form of Marxism's traditional address to demography, dating back to Marx himself, has been through its virulent denunciation of all Malthusian versions." The leaders of the Chinese Communist Party followed in this tradition. The policy of "people are precious" and the belief that China suffered from a labour shortage remained intact down until the 1953 census. The National People's Congress in 1954 raised the issue of birth control. After the 1957 sample census a full-fledged birth control program was launched. Nevertheless, when Professor Ma Yinzhu, an economist and then president of Beijing University, published a paper in June 1957 arguing that population growth should be controlled, he was denounced in the press and in 1960 was removed from office. (Mauldin, 1980:153)

The shortage of food in 1960 and 1961 raised the issue once again. There was renewed emphasis on family planning, and in 1962 the "late marriages" campaign began. The Five Guarantees (food, clothing, shelter, medical care, and decent burial) were introduced to try to remove the ancient Chinese tradition of "many children for support in old age." (Tregear, 1980:212-214) The 1964 census revealed that China's population had risen to 696 million, but that the late marriage laws were having a significant effect. By 1971 the leadership of the Communist Party had changed its position, and birth control was made a national priority. (Banister, 1984:248-251; World Bank, 1984:178)

Officially, the Chinese leadership still opposed the Malthusian position. At the Stockholm Conference on the Environment in 1972, the Chinese delegates repeated the line that "people are precious." At the Bucharest Conference on Population in 1974, the Chinese delegation aligned themselves with the Roman Catholic Church, the Marxists, and the other left-wing elements to oppose the family planning position advanced by the U.S. government and its supporters. The Chinese delegation went so far as to demand suppression of two United Nations' reports on existing Chinese population policy. (Dyck, 1977:274; Allaby, 1977:61)

In August 1979 the new Chinese leadership launched its policy of the "one-child family" and the "multi-child tax." Bonuses were given for one-child families and late marriages. A second child resulted in a 15% loss in income; for a third child there was an additional 10% loss, and a 5% for loss each additional child. (Xinzhong, 1983:21-22)

The results of the birth control program were astounding. In 1971 the annual increase in population was estimated at 2.23%. It declined steadily to a low of 1.17% in 1979, but then rose to 1.2% in 1980 and 1.4% in 1981. (Kojima, 1982:402; *Beijing Review*, February 8, 1982:25) In 1982 the World Bank (Table 20) reported that, of all the underdeveloped countries, China had the lowest crude birth rate, the lowest crude death rate, and the lowest total fertility rate.

However, the results of the July 1982 census came as a shock to the Chinese leadership. The population had risen to 1,032 million, of which 825 million lived outside cities or towns. Over the period since the 1964 census the annual increase in population had averaged 2.1%, or close to 20 million per year. One-half of the population was under 21 years of age; 314 million were below the age of 18. The Communist Party leadership had a set a goal of only 1,200 million people by the year 2000. That meant that the annual increase had to be held to below 9.5 million per year. However, the census revealed that compared to the 1976-1980 period, the population growth rate was again increasing. (See *Beijing Review*, February 14, 1983; November 29, November 8, and February 8, 1982) Keyfitz (1984:54) concludes that given the age structure of the population, the demographic momentum will continue into the 21st century, when China's population will exceed 1,500 million.

China is a very large country, but only about 10% of the land surface is suitable for cultivation. Table VIIi shows that China's per capita arable land is now the lowest among the low-income, more populated Asian underdeveloped countries, with less than 0.10 ha per capita. In contrast, Canada has 1.85 ha per capita and the United States 0.84. While the United States has an estimated 52 million ha of land in reserve (permanent pasture or forestland which could be converted to arable land) China has exhausted its reserve of potential arable land.

China's arable land totalled 111.33 million ha in 1957, but it declined to 99.2 million ha by 1980. Furthermore, the 1980 figures included 17 million ha of arable land that had been reclaimed since the revolution. Thus Chinese officials estimate that between 1957 and 1977 they actually lost 29 million ha of arable land to other uses. As elsewhere in the world, this has

TABLE VIIi   *The Distribution of Arable Land in Asia, 1980*

Countries	Population Millions/1980	'000 ha Arable Land	Hectares Per Capita
China	994,913	99,200	0.09
India	684,460	169,130	0.25
Indonesia	148,033	19,500	0.13
Bangladesh	88,164	9,145	0.10
Pakistan	86,899	20,320	0.23
Vietnam	53,740	6,055	0.11
The Philippines	49,211	9,920	0.20
Thailand	47,063	17,970	0.38
Republic of Korea	38,455	2,196	0.06
Burma	35,289	10,023	0.28
Korean Democratic Republic	17,892	2,240	0.13
Afghanistan	15,940	8,050	0.51
Sri Lanka	14,815	2,147	0.14
Nepal	14,288	2,330	0.23
Malaysia	14,068	4,310	0.30

SOURCE: Food and Agricultural Organization. *Production Yearbook*, Volume 37, 1983; Volume 35, 1981.

generally involved the addition of marginal lands with relatively low productivity and the loss of prime farmland in the urbanized areas. (*Beijing Review*, July 19, 1982:5-6) Smil (1982:21) claims that the losses totalled 33 million ha, with 20% accounted for by conversion to other uses and 80% through environmental degradation. The overall result is that one-third of the remaining arable land is relatively marginal, with low yields.

A number of observers have pointed out that much prime farmland has been lost to capital construction projects, rural housing, new transportation systems, and the building of dams. Since 1980 there has been a boom in rural construction, both for personal housing and for new, off-farm enterprises. All of these projects have consumed large amounts of prime agricultural land. (DuRand, 1985:16; Kojima, 1982:404) In October 1985 the *China Daily* reported that in recent years urban and rural construction alone was absorbing on average 440,000 ha of arable land per year, but in 1984 this had risen to 1 million ha. (*Western Producer*, October 24, 1985)

Vermeer (1984:6) argues that Chinese figures are always suspect. The gathering of statistics in such a large and diversified underdeveloped country is most difficult. Furthermore, officials have a tendency to adjust figures to suit the policy views of those in power. He reports that local surveys show the cultivated area to actually be around 120 million hectares, but does not cite any supporting data. In contrast to Chinese figures, he notes that satellite photographs show only around one-half the forested land reported by government sources. In early 1986 the Chinese were claiming that 114 million hectares were planted to crops. (*Beijing Review*, January 20, 1986:16)

The loss of arable land has been offset by the expansion of land under irrigation. The early estimates for land under irrigation were questionable. However, in the 1960s the World Bank revised its estimates, showing an increase from 38.5 million ha in 1960 to 46 million ha by 1980. Improvements in plant breeding permitted a significant expansion of land under double and triple cropping. The other source of increased yields has come from the application of fertilizers. China is still behind Japan and North and South Korea in the application of kilograms of plant nutrients per hectare. But in 1981 they applied twice the amount of any other Asian country and five times the amount used in India. (World Bank, 1984; 1982)

The data in Table VIIj illustrate that China has already achieved a rather high level of production of cereals per hectare. For the key staple product, paddy rice, Chinese production is exceeded only by Japan and the two Koreas; these three countries are utilizing very large fossil fuel subsidies in production.

Chinese agricultural specialists have been disappointed with the results of the large-scale mechanization and chemicalization which began in the early 1960s. Between 1965 and 1977 there was an 830% increase in farm machinery available, a 260% increase in the use of manufactured fertilizers, a 130% increase in total farm input expenditure, but a total production increase of only 80%. (Nolan, 1983:399; Nolan and White, 1981:7)

Vermeer (1982:50) points out that in China there is a limitation on the farmland areas that can make use of modern technologies: "not much more than half of all farmland (but maybe three-quarters of the *sown* area) can be irrigated at reasonable cost, not much more than two-thirds of all farmland may eventually be ploughed and sown by mechanical means."

TABLE VIIj   *Asian Cereal Production*

Kilograms Per Hectare

Countries	All Cereals		Paddy Rice		Wheat	
	1969-71	1979-81	1969-71	1979-81	1969-71	1979-81
China	2379	2899	3295	4228	1168	1989
India	1108	1338	1668	1890	1231	1551
Indonesia	2005	2784	2346	3317	—	—
Bangladesh	1660	1938	1681	1976	854	1871
Pakistan	1206	1599	2246	2450	1110	1564
Vietnam	1785	1929	2018	2102	—	—
The Philippines	1295	1596	1655	2196	—	—
Thailand	2014	1933	1947	1933	—	—
Republic of Korea	3496	4918	4428	5512	2308	3119
Burma	1610	2504	1708	2538	576	770
Korean Dem PR	3119	3888	5371	6093	1948	2473
Afghanistan	1133	1273	1847	2098	978	1130
Sri Lanka	2402	2396	2402	2396	—	—
Nepal	1754	1617	1937	1828	1044	1215
Malaysia	2392	2876	2396	2833	—	—
All Asia Average	**1697**	**2019**	**2350**	**2815**	**1144**	**1682**

SOURCE: Food and Agricultural Organization. *Production Yearbook*, Volume 37, 1983; Volume 35, 1981.

The *Far East Economic Review* (October 1, 1982) reported that between 1977 and 1981 there was a 70% increase in the use of fertilizers in China, and a significant increase in the use of pesticides. They also point out that China's yields are already very high by Asian standards, and "the net cost of each successive productivity increase tends to become higher and higher."

The disasters associated with cultivating ecologically sensitive areas have been stressed by Vermeer (1984) and Smil (1984). All the problems of land and water degradation associated with industrial agriculture are found in their worst form in China. Government plans for more ecologically sensitive and diversified farming are being undermined by the widespread shortage of timber and fuel that encourages deforestation. But there is another central problem. In his widely reported critique of the shift to the social responsibility system in agriculture (the de-collectivization between 1979-83), Hinton stresses that private family farming and heavy political emphasis on maximizing individual gain has greatly increased the misuse of the basic resources, including farmland, which are still owned by the state. (Quoted in DuRand, 1984b:17)

One of the key problems for the Chinese has been the creation of employment for the steadily increasing population. During the 1950s and 1960s much of the surplus population was mobilized in the large capital construction programs: irrigation and water conservation, expansion of arable land, and road construction. In 1958 the rural population was formally tied to the commune in order to prevent the mass migration to urban areas so characteristic of the underdeveloped world. The surplus population was absorbed in agricultural labour on the communes. Employment opportunities in industry did not increase as rapidly as the population in general. Thus it is estimated that the number of actual agricultural workers rose from 190 million in 1957 to 290 million in 1977. The communes were relatively effective in providing work for everyone and a basic standard of living. (Nolan, 1983:895; Kojima, 1982:400) However, these programs disguised the extent of underemployment, and the gap in the standard of living between the rural and urban population widened. The 1982 census reported that 71% of the working population was still in the economic sector defined as "agriculture, forestry, water conservancy, and meteorology." (Banister, 1984: Table 6)

The shift in economic policy to the Four Modernizations and the Agricultural Responsibility System represents a new approach to the problem of underemployment. First, the abolition of the communes and the return to private family farming restricts the labour productivity that comes with mechanization of agriculture. Keyfitz (1984:41) points out that mechanization of agriculture is not currently being promoted. By stressing individual production on small, garden-sized plots, more labour can be absorbed during the growing season. It appears that the new Chinese leadership has opted for the Japanese model of labour-intensive agricultural development.

The abolition of the communes has also eliminated the collective support for underemployed people, and has loosened ties to the rural communities. It has permitted more people to enter into the informal economy of private services. Open unemployment is now very visible as the "floating population" drifts into the cities. Even the government estimates it at 20 million. (*The Globe and Mail*, December 21, 1982)

Cliff DuRand (1984b:11) reports that on his return visits to Dzhai, "fields that by hard work had been made large enough to farm by machine are now subdivided into strips that have to be worked by hoe." Hinton (1983:15-18) found a similar situation when he revisited the areas he knows very well. He also found that without the collective works organized by the communes, "thousands of people now idle their way through the winter months."

The new five-year plan (1986-1990) is now being formulated. It must create new jobs for 140 million people. By the year 2000 the new leadership hopes that only 30% of the total labour force will be actively engaged in crop cultivation, 20% will be working in forestry, animal husbandry, and fisheries, and another 10% will be employed in the cities. The remaining 40% are to be employed in rural areas in industry, commerce, transportation, and services. In contrast to the economic policy under the direction of Mao, the new leadership under Deng hopes these new jobs will be created by local co-operative efforts and private entrepreneurs. Private ownership of the means of production, the employment of others on a wage-labour basis, and "putting out" cottage industries are now officially encouraged. (Du-Rand, 1985:16)

There is, however, at least one major contradiction in the new approach. The Agricultural Responsibility System, emphasizing "getting rich first," makes family labour once again important. One notices in the articles in *Beijing Review* promoting the new system of individual family farming that special attention is drawn to families with incomes considerably above the local average. But invariably, in the cases cited, the family has had two to four working children! (e.g., *Beijing Review*, July 29, 1985; July 8, 1985; April 12, 1982)

Since the 1960s, the government of China has recognized that continued increases in population can pose a serious obstacle to economic development. The challenges are great because of the large population, the shortage of arable land, limited oil and natural gas resources, and the already high yields in cereal production. Roughly 80% of the population still lives in the rural areas. Few believe that it will be economically or ecologically possible for China to follow the industrialized countries and reduce this to 10%. Already the rural industrialization program of the Four Modernizations is costing the country invaluable farmland. The Japanese road to development, based on the importation of a high percentage of food requirements and most natural resources, is simply out of the question for China.

Conclusion

The present division of the world into nation states has resulted in grossly unequal political distribution of population and foodland resources. The ability of a nation state to feed its people also depends on its level of economic development. For many of the underdeveloped countries (both capitalist and post-revolutionary), the limited amount of arable land restricts the ability to be relatively self-sufficient in food production. Some countries, like Japan, have compensated for the lack of foodland resources and a large population by acquiring much of their food and fertilizer on the

References

Allaby, Michael (1977). *World Food Resources: Actual and Potential.* London: Applied Science Publishers.

Ashton, Basil et al (1984). "Famine in China, 1958-61." *Population and Development Review,* X, No. 4, December, pp. 613-645.

Banister, Judith (1984). "An Analysis of Recent Data on the Population of China." *Population and Development Review,* X, No. 2, June, pp. 241-271.

Barney, Gerald O., ed. (1980). *The Global 2000 Report to the President.* 2 volumes. New York: Pergamon Press.

Barney, Gerald O. et al (1981). *Global 2000: Implications for Canada.* Toronto: Pergamon Press.

Brandt, Willy, Chairman, 1980. *North-South: A Program for Survival.* Cambridge, Mass.: The MIT Press.

Broadbent, Kieran (1976). "Agriculture, Environment and Current Policy in China." *Asian Survey,* XVI, No. 5, May 1976, pp. 411-426.

Bromley, Ray (1982). "Working in the Streets: Survival Strategy, Necessity or Unavoidable Evil?" In A. Gilbert et al, eds. *Urbanization in Contemporary Latin America.* Toronto: John Wiley & Sons.

Brown, Lester et al (1985). *State of the World, 1985.* New York: W. W. Norton for the Worldwatch Institute.

Coale, Ansley J. (1983). "Recent Trends in Fertility in Less Developed Countries." *Science,* CCXI, No. 4613, August 26, pp. 828-832.

Coontz, Sydney H. (1957). *Population Theories and the Economic Interpretation.* London: Routledge & Kegan Paul.

Dumont, René and Bernard Rosier (1969). *The Hungry Future.* London: Methuen.

DuRand, Cliff (1985). "An Away from the Land Movement Gets Going." *Guardian,* October 23, p. 16.

DuRand, Cliff (1984a). "Hinton Unhappy with New Farm Set-up." *Guardian,* May 30, p. 17; June 6, p. 17.

DuRand, Cliff (1984b). "No Longer Learning from Dazhai." *Guardian,* October 3, pp. 10-11.

Dyck, Arthur J. (1977). "Alternative Views of Moral Priorities in Population Policy." *BioScience,* XXVII, No. 2, April, pp. 272-276.

Harrison, Paul (1984). "Achieving a Balance Constructively." *Ceres,* XVII, No. 2, March-April, pp. 33-36.

Hinton, William H. (1983). "A Trip to Fengyang County: Investigating China's New Family Contract System." *Monthly Review,* XXXV, No. 6, November, pp., 1-28.

Keyfitz, Nathan (1984). "The Population of China. *Scientific American,* CCL, No. 2, February, pp. 38-47.

Kojima, Reeitsu (1982). "China's New Agricultural Policy." *The Developing Economies,* XX, No. 4, December, pp. 390-413.

Leung, Joyce T. (1983). "China's Multiple Approach to Its Food Problem." In Georgio R. Solimano and Sally A. Lederman, eds. *Controversial Nutrition Policy Issues.* Springfield, Ill.: Charles C. Thomas, pp. 132-154.

McNicoll, Geoffrey (1984). "Consequences of Rapid Population Growth: An

Overview and Assessment." *Population and Development Review*, X, No. 2, June, pp. 177-240.

Mauldin, W. Parker (1980). "Population Trends and Prospects." *Science*, CCIX, July 4, pp. 148-159.

Meadows, Donella H. et al (1974). *Limits to Growth*; A Report of the Club of Rome on the Predicament of Mankind. New York: Universe Books.

Murray, Anne Firth (1985). "A Global Accounting." *Environment*, XXVII, No. 6, July/August, pp. 7-11, 33-34.

Nolan, Peter (1983). "De-collectivization of Agriculture in China, 1979-82: A Long-term Perspective." *Cambridge Journal of Economics*, VII, Nos. 3/4, September/December, pp. 381-403.

Nolan, Peter and Gordon White (1981). "Distribution and Development in China." *Bulletin of Concerned Asian Scholars*, XIII, No. 3, July-September, pp. 2-18.

Orleans, Leo A. (1977). "China's Environomics: Backing into Ecological Leadership." In Thomas C. Emmel, ed. *Global Perspectives on Ecology*. Palo Alto: Mayfield Publishing Co., pp. 310-333.

Petras, James (1984). "Toward a Theory of Industrial Development in the Third World." *Journal of Contemporary Asia*, XIV, No. 2, pp. 182-203.

Roberts, Bryan (1978). *Cities of Peasants*. London: Edward Arnold.

Sai, Fred T. (1984). "The Population Factor in Africa's Development Dilemma." *Science*, CCXXVI, No. 4676, November 16, pp. 801-805.

Seccombe, Wally (1983). "Marxism and Demography." *New Left Review*, No. 137, January-February, pp. 22-47.

Simon, Julian (1981). *The Ultimate Resource*. Princeton: Princeton University Press.

Smil, Vaclav (1984). *The Bad Earth; Environmental Degradation in China*. London: Zed Press.

Smil, Vaclav (1982). "Ecological Mismanagement in China." *Bulletin of the Atomic Scientists*, XXXVIII, No. 8, October, pp. 18-23.

Stavis, Benedict R. (1979). "The Impact of Agricultural Collectivization on Productivity in China." In Ronald A. Francisco et al, eds. *The Political Economy of Collectivized Agriculture*. New York: Pergamon Press, pp. 157-191.

Tregear, T. A. (1980). *China: A Geographical Survey*. London: Hodder and Stoughton.

Tribe, D.E. and J. Belyea (1977). "Energy and Agriculture: The Third World." In Ross King, ed., *Energy, Agriculture, and the Built Environment*. Melbourne: Centre for Environmental Studies, University of Melbourne.

Vermeer, E.B. (1984). "Agriculture in China — A Deteriorating Situation." *Ecologist*, XIV, No. 1, pp. 6-14.

Vermeer, E. B. (1982). "Income Differentials in Rural China." *The China Quarterly*, No. 89, March, pp. 1-33.

Warren, Bill (1980). *Imperialism: Pioneer of Capitalism*. London: Verso Editions for New Left Books.

Willcox, Walter (1985). "The Expansion of Europe and Its Influence on Population." *Population and Development Review*, XI, No. 3, September, pp. 515-527.

World Bank (1984, 1982). *World Development Report*. Washington, D.C.: World Bank.

Xinzhong, Qian (1983). "China's Population Policy," *Beijing Review*, No. 7, February 14, pp. 21-28.

CHAPTER EIGHT

The Loss of Foodland
Resources

The world's population is expected to reach 6 billion by the year 2000, a 40% increase over 1980. In order to maintain the existing pattern of food consumption and nutrition, food production will have to rise at an equivalent rate. Furthermore, a majority of the world's population are either undernourished or wish to improve the quality of their diet; to close the gap, additional food production and more equitable distribution is required.

Historically, when faced with the need for more food production, people have first looked to "wastelands" to convert to agricultural production. In the twentieth century emphasis has shifted to increasing yields on already utilized foodlands through the use of fossil-fuel-based inputs.

However, this is only one side of the food production question. While governments and international officials are pondering where they can find new arable land, the world is losing an alarming amount of existing foodlands through environmental degradation and conversion to other uses. In many cases, it is prime farmland that is being lost.

As population has risen, we have converted forests, grasslands, and rangelands to cropping. One historian (Richards, 1984:8-9) has estimated that, between 1860 and 1920, 441 million hectares of land were converted to cropping. This was mainly frontier settlement that involved putting the axe to trees. During this period fewer than 9 million hectares of land were converted from cropping to other uses. In the period from 1920 to 1978 an additional 470 million hectares was converted to cropping. However, during this second period, around 51 million hectares was converted from cropping to other uses.

Much of the reversion has been from cropland to pasture, scrubland, or second-growth forest. It has occurred primarily in North America and Europe. This has been possible because rising yields from capital-intensive farming on more productive soils have permitted the abandonment of more marginal lands. But Richards expects the rate of conversion to continue in the underdeveloped countries, due to population growth and international demand for agricultural and forest products.

Today, concern is not only for the loss of prime arable land through conversion to other uses. Of at least equal significance is the loss of foodlands through soil erosion, desertification, deforestation, the destruction of irrigation systems, the deterioration of land under irrigation, and damage from increasing pollution.

Farmland Conversion to Other Uses

As the population increases, so does the demand on land. Industry, energy projects, mining, and transportation are large users of land. Individuals also need land for living space. In one aerial survey of forty-four counties in the western United States, it was found that "built-on land" ranged from 80 to 1740 square metres per person. The authors of *The Limits to Growth* estimated that the average U.S. citizen used 800 square metres of land for housing, roads, waste disposal, power lines, industry and all the other uses that make land unusable for producing food. (Meadows et al, 1972:50-51) Brown (1978:12) estimates that between 1960 and 1970 the U.S. average of land use per capita rose from 800 to 1300 square metres.

A survey by the Organization for Economic Co-operation and Development (OECD) found that the amount of total living space needed per person in the industrialized countries varied considerably. In 1972, each new Japanese citizen required 83 square metres of living space in an urban area, whereas the figures were 800 square metres in Canada and 1500 in the United States. (*OECD Observer*, No. 83, 1976:12)

Brown (1978:12) has estimated that on a worldwide basis an individual requires 400 square metres of living space. Not as much is required in underdeveloped countries, as people are more crowded together. Given the expected population increase, this means that the world will lose another 32 million hectares of prime arable land by the year 2000, just to meet the space needs of individuals.

Differences in housing space alone are significant. For example, the average floor space of a new house built in Canada in 1975 was almost 100 square metres, twice the average size of similar units in Italy and the USSR and almost three times the size in West Germany. (Beaubien and Tabacnik, 1977:117)

In the industrialized countries, the land lost to urbanization tends to be the best farmland. Cities are placed on the most fertile soils. UNESCO estimates that in the developed countries "at least 3,000 square kilometres of prime agricultural lands are submerged every year under urban sprawl." (*UNESCO Courier*, No. 4, 1980:10) A survey by the FAO found that between 1966 and 1976 cropland in western Europe declined by 5.7 million hectares, or at a rate of 0.56% per year. (*Ceres*, No. 4, 1978:14-15)

The OECD surveyed the loss of arable land in the industrialized capitalist countries between 1960 and 1970. The annual losses ranged from a low of

0.05% in New Zealand to a high of 1.23% in Belgium. (OECD, 1977, Chapter 13) The *Global 2000 Report* extrapolated arable land loss data from 1978 to the year 2000 to project cumulative losses of arable land. The highest losses were expected to be in Belgium (24%), Japan (15%), The Netherlands (10%) and Sweden (7%). (Barney, 1980:282)

The conversion of arable land to other uses has been extensively studied (and debated) in the United States. Early studies by the U.S. Department of Agriculture estimated that 18.3 million hectares had been lost between 1945 and 1971. A 1971 survey concluded that 13 million hectares had been paved over by highways and roads. (Cook, 1980:247; Pimentel et al, 1976:149) In 1975 the Soil Conservation Service estimated that between 1967 and 1975 the U.S. had lost 9.5 million hectares of arable land to other uses: 6.75 million to urban and built-up areas and 2.7 million to the building of dams. The main loss was prime farmland. (Schmude, 1977:241-242) A subsequent survey by the U.S. Bureau of the Census reported that between 1969 and 1978 there had been a loss of 35.8 million hectares of agricultural land, calculated on reports of actual use of the land by the owners. (Cook, 1981:92)

The debate over how much land is actually being lost was not resolved by the two most recent U.S. surveys, the National Agricultural Land Survey (1981) and the National Resources Inventory (1982), as each produced different estimates. However, there is little doubt that the land that is being lost is mainly the prime agricultural land near rapidly expanding urban centres. (Lee, 1984:226-227; Lee, 1981:135-137)

The patterns seen in the United States are also reflected in Canada. Between 1951 and 1971 2.8 million hectares of farmland (nearly 25% of the total) was lost to urban conversion in the Quebec City-Windsor, Ontario population corridor. This area has a high proportion of Canada's best farmland, based on the Agroclimatic Resource Index (ACRI) established by Agriculture Canada. (Geno and Geno, 1976:15-18; Beaubien and Tabac-nik, 1977:34-35) More recent data has been provided by Environment Canada studies. Between 1966 and 1971, 54,789 hectares of prime farmland (Classes 1-3) were lost to urban conversion; between 1971 and 1976, another 38,211 hectares were lost. This seems to indicate a decline in conversion, but, on a population-change basis, "fewer people were using more prime agricultural land for urban purposes." (Warren and Rump, 1981:22-30) Over the period 1961-1976, Canada had a net loss of 1.4 million hectares of agricultural land, or 2% of the 1961 base. However, these figures present an incomplete picture of the problem. There was a loss of prime agricultural land in central Canada (with a relatively high ACRI rating), and the addition of more marginal lands in western Canada (with an ACRI rating less than half as good as that of the land lost). (McCuaig and Manning, 1982:26-35) Canada has been losing land capable of growing fruit, vegetables, and corn, and replacing it with land only suitable for growing barley or hay.

The Food and Agricultural Organization concludes that "the steady loss of good agricultural land to non-agricultural uses, almost always a permanent loss, also began to add up (between 1950 and 1980) to magnitudes constituting a significant constraint to future expansion of food production." This is most visible in the industrialized countries. They concluded that a continuation of these trends "would influence export production capacity in the long run in countries such as the United States." (FAO, 1981:7)

Land loss through urbanization is certainly not limited to the industrialized countries. The fastest growing urban centres are in the underdeveloped countries, and they are swallowing up agricultural land. However, the rate of conversion is not well documented. The expansion of villages is also a problem, particularly where locally available building materials are not strong enough to hold a second storey; as a result, more space is required per person than in urban areas. It has already been noted that the expanding population, the building of new rural housing, and the development of rural cottage industries is absorbing considerable amounts of prime agricultural land in China.

One worst-case example would be Egypt, the most populous country in North Africa and the Middle East, and one that already imports over 50% of its food supply. Between 1960 and 1980 the total amount of irrigated land remained the same, despite the building of the Aswan Dam. Old agricultural land was lost to conversion to other uses as fast as additional hectares of irrigated land were added. (Barney, 1980, II:281)

Energy products have also been major users of agricultural land. Oil refineries tend to be built on prime agricultural land, near fertile valleys, or on coastal deltas. Strip mining and coal development is now rapidly expanding, taking large amounts of water that could be used for irrigation.

A major source of farmland loss is flooding by reservoirs created by hydroelectric dams. For example, the Kariba Dam in Africa put 29,000 farmers out of business. The Volta Dam flooded some of Ghana's best farmland. The Kossou Dam flooded some of the best cropland in the Ivory Coast. (Brown, 1978:14)

The Soviet Union offers another good example of the problem of land conversion to other uses. Down to the 1960s dams were regularly being built, flooding some of the most productive agricultural land. By the 1960s around 2.3 million hectares had been lost to reservoirs; one fifth of it was the best farmland in the Soviet Union. Strong opposition from the Ministry of Agriculture actually caused the cancelling of a number of proposed dams and the relocation of others to areas where the land lost was of a lower quality for agricultural production. (Gustafson, 1979:73-77)

Losses from Soil Erosion

Loss of farmland occurs not only from conversion to other uses but through soil degradation and environmental stress. The most serious is soil erosion.

First, soil erosion leads to a decline in productivity, which, if left unchecked by conservation practices, eventually leads to deterioration to a level where abandonment takes place. Second, there are the downstream damages caused by erosion, particularly through the loss of irrigation capacity, flooding, and sedimentation.

Soil erosion is caused by the climate acting on the land. A distinction has to be made between geological erosion, caused by the natural processes of the passage of time, and human erosion, resulting from the clearing of land or poor agricultural practices. Before human cultivation, erosion was beneficial, for the most part, as it led to the formation of fertile valleys and river deltas. (Larson et al, 1983:458; Riquier, 1982:18)

The joint FAO/UNEP/UNESCO project on world soil degradation defines it as "a process which lowers the actual and/or potential capacity of soil to produce (quantitatively and/or qualitatively) goods or services." The processes are normally grouped in the following categories: (1) water erosion; (2) wind erosion; (3) excess of salts (salinization and sodication); (4) chemical degradation (e.g., acidification or rise in levels of toxic chemicals); (5) physical degradation (lowering of structural stability, etc.) and (6) biological degradation (humus mineralization).

Loss of soil through erosion has been extensively studied in the United States, following the creation of the Soil Conservation Service in the 1930's. The Universal Soil Loss Equation (USLE) was developed there in 1954; estimates are based on rainfall, soil erodibility, slope length, degree of the land slope, the type of cropping, and erosion control practices. The Wind Erosion Equation (WEQ) calculates soil erodibility, surface roughness and configuration, climate, field length, and vegetative cover. Over the years these formulas have been tested on site, to determine their accuracy.

Soil formation is a slow process. Under natural conditions, topsoil forms at a rate of one inch every 300 to 1000 years. Under well-managed agricultural conditions, topsoil is formed at a rate of one inch every 100 years, or the equivalent of about 3.5 tonnes of topsoil per hectare per year.

In measuring the effects of soil erosion, scientists have established a tolerance level or T-value. This is defined by Wischmeier and Smith of the U.S. Department of Agriculture as "the maximum level of soil erosion that will permit a high level of crop productivity to be maintained economically and indefinitely." The T-value used in the United States is 5 tons per acre per year; from this definition the international agencies have set the T-value at 11.2 metric tonnes per hectare per year. The FAO/UNEP/UNESCO project classifies degradation of less than 10 t/ha/year as "none to slight," 10-15 as "moderate", 50-200 as "high", and over 200 as "very high." (Larson et al, 1983:461; Riquier, 1982:19; Sampson, 1981:150)

In the United States extensive surveys of soil losses caused by water erosion have revealed a wide range of damage. The U.S. National Academy of Sciences concluded in 1976 that sheet and rill erosion (water moving over the land) "affects 18 million hectares in the corn belt, 15 million hectares in the Northern Plains, and 9 million hectares in the southern plains." They estimated that it would cost $4,000 million to replace the nitrogen and phosphorus lost by the eroding waters. (46) In the Palouse area in Idaho and eastern Washington, soil losses ranged from 34 to 75 tonnes per hectare. In Texas and Illinois average annual losses ranged between 17 and 25 tonnes. In Virginia and Tennessee, with their rolling topography, losses were between 30 and 75 tonnes per hectare. (Brink et al, 1977:629)

Pimentel and his associates at Cornell University College of Agriculture estimated in 1976 that 80 million hectares of U.S. cropland had been "either totally ruined for crop production or had been so seriously eroded that the land is only marginally suitable for production." (150) The 1977 survey by the Soil Conservation Service estimated that the average loss through water erosion on U.S. cropland was 22 tonnes per hectare. (Brown, 1978:24) In 1977 the U.S. General Accounting Office examined 283 farms chosen at random in the Corn Belt, the Great Plains, and the Pacific northwest; they concluded that 84% of them experienced soil losses above the T-value. (Carter, 1977:410) The 1982 National Resources Inventory (NRI) concluded that the national average for water erosion on cropland in the United States was 13 tonnes per hectare. About 44% of all cropland was experiencing losses above the T-level. (Lee, 1984:227)

The problem was set forth by Norman W. Hudson (1983:446) in an address to a convention of the Soil Conservation Society of America:

> if soil conservation cannot be made to work effectively in the United States, with all the advantages of research, extension, and conservation services, plus wealthy, educated farmers on good land with a gentle climate — if with all these benefits conservation is not successful — then what hope is there for struggling countries that have few, or none, of these advantages?

The rise in soil losses in recent decades has been attributed to the plowing of marginal lands once in pasture, rangeland, and forests, and the elimination of hay and pasture from crop rotations. In the United States erosion rates are high in areas specializing in growing corn and soybeans in rotation. (Larson et al, 1983:461; Brown, 1981:18) In the Maritime provinces of Canada continuous cropping of potatoes has led to losses exceeding 20 tonnes per hectare per year. In the Peace River area of British Columbia long slopes, summer-fallowing, high snowfall, and rapid spring runoff have led to average annual losses of 11.5 tonnes per hectare. (Agriculture Institute of Canada, 1980:27; Sparrow, 1984:42)

Serious damage can also be done by wind erosion. In the United States it is a major problem on the Great Plains, and is also significant in other areas. The introduction of tube-well centre-pivot irrigation in the High Plains areas has led to cropping on marginal lands with sandy soil and an increased wind-erosion problem. In 1968 the USDA estimated that wind erosion was the dominant problem on 22.4 million hectares of U.S. cropland. The 1976 study by the U.S. National Academy of Sciences (51) concluded that wind erosion affected 28 million hectares of land.

Pimentel and his associates at Cornell University (1976:150-151) estimate that annual U.S. losses of soil by wind erosion are close to 1 million tonnes; combined with estimates of 4 million tonnes of soil lost from water erosion, the total is a loss equal to 18 centimetres of soil from 2 million hectares.

In April, 1981, strong winds blew across the Canadian prairies, reaching 130 kilometres per hour in southern Saskatchewan. The sun was blocked out in many areas, bringing back memories of the drought of the 1930s. Ten to 15 centimetres of topsoil were blown away in many areas of southern Saskatchewan, leaving only subsoil and rocky ground exposed. (*The Globe and Mail* [Toronto], April 10, 1982; *Western Producer*, May 7, 1981)

One of the more widely publicized examples of serious wind erosion occurred in the USSR when the government decided to plow the "Virgin Lands" in northern Kazakhstan, western Siberia, and eastern Russia. Between 1954 and 1960 40 million hectares of grassland were brought under cultivation. With continuous cropping, wind erosion greatly increased. In 1963 there was a serious drought with disastrous results both in soil losses and reduced yields. (Eckholm, 1976:53-57) Even with improved conservation methods, the USSR is abandoning around 500,000 hectares of farmland every year, because they have been severely eroded by wind. (Brown, 1984:164)

Satellite photographs show large quantities of dust carried from North Africa out over the Atlantic ocean. Four studies of this phenomenon, made between 1972 and 1981, estimated the losses at between 110 and 441 million tonnes of soil annually. Similarly, soil from Asia (mainly China) is carried across the Pacific and is recorded at the Mauna Loa Observatory in Hawaii. (Brown, 1984:163)

Erosion is high on land planted to maize, because that crop is relatively poor at holding the soil. In 1980 maize was grown on 7.5% of all cultivated land and represented 20% of the world's grain. Wheat is relatively good at holding the soil, with annual soil losses in the range of 5 to 10 tonnes per hectare per year. In contrast, terraced rice production is best at controlling soil losses, where flooding can be controlled. Under such circumstances land can actually be improved, as in many areas of China, Japan, and Korea. (Barney, 1980, II:280-281)

There is very little hard data on the rate of soil erosion in underdeveloped countries. Ingraham (1975) concludes that the rate of land lost due to soil erosion is twice as high as in the United States. Hudson (1983:447-448) reports "terrifying destruction" where subsistence farmers have moved to the marginal lands on the mountain slopes in central Java, Kenya, the Himalayas of India and Nepal, and the Andes of South America. In

Venezuela erosion increases as peasants ciimb higher up the mountains; however, there are millions of hectares of unused land in the southern plains. In India and Nepal there is no opportunity to resettle on better lands.

Posner and McPherson (1982:341-345) surveyed agriculture on the steep slope areas of tropical America. In all 12 countries the mountain slopes were very important, accounting for between 15% of arable land (Dominican Republic) to 70% (Haiti). Including coffee production, the high slopes accounted for a very high proportion of agricultural production. In some areas soil losses reached 134 tonnes per hectare per year; with ditches and contour mounds, soil losses were reduced to "only" 27 tonnes. Hudson (1983:447) suggests that one approach to soil conservation would be to remove from cultivation land with a slope exceeding 15%; however, if this were done, many areas would have little arable land left. In El Salvador, for example, clean-weeded maize is produced on land with 45% slopes.

A recent article by Brown (1984:165) surveyed soil losses from erosion in the U.S., the USSR, China, and India; these four countries have 52% of the world's cropland and accounted for more than half of world food production. He estimated their total soil loss at 14.7 billion tonnes per year.

Data compiled in 1980 by Chinese scientists suggests that the Yellow River, with a drainage basin of 1.1 million square kilometres, carries 1.6 billion tonnes of soil per year out into the ocean. The Ganges, with a drainage basin of 670,000 square kilomeres, carries an annual sediment load of 1.4 million tonnes. In 1974 Indian agricultural scientists estimated that 6 billion tonnes of soil are eroded each year and that 60% of cropland is eroding above the T-level. (Brown, 1984:163-165)

A UNESCO report cites serious soil erosion from water in Pakistan, Nepal, Ethiopia, and South Africa; due to the topography of the land and the nature of the soils and rainfall the crop land is more susceptible to erosion than land in the temperate zones. (*UNESCO Courier*, No. 4, 1980:10-14) The 1977 U.N. Conference on Desertification reported that almost one-fifth of the world's arable cropland is now being steadily degraded through erosion. (Brown, 1981:21) The combined FAO/UNEP/UNESCO assessment of world land degradation (1979) concluded that, if conservation measures were not undertaken, about 20% of the land's productivity in underdeveloped countries would be lost by the end of the century. (Dudal, 1982:247)

Given the widespread loss of topsoil, how has the world managed to continually increase food production? By the steady increase in the use of fertilizers and other energy-related inputs. Pimentel and his associates (1976:152) estimate that 122 litres of fuel equivalents are used per hectare in the United States every year, solely to offset losses from soil erosion.

Desertification

Public attention was drawn to the problems of drought and desertification in the mid-1980s, when the media gave considerable coverage to crop failures, food shortages, and famine in Africa, particularly in the states bordering on the Sahara desert. Television reports of the widespread starvation in Ethiopia brought a far-reaching relief effort.

A meteorological drought occurs when rainfall is well below expectations for a long period of time. An agricultural drought occurs when rainfall and groundwater reserves combine to markedly diminish either crop or livestock yields. However, natural ecosystems usually recover from droughts. The term "desertification" implies the deterioration of arid and semi-arid lands because of human use beyond the land's carrying capacity. It is the steady impoverishment of the land by human misuse — primarily by excessive cultivation, overgrazing, and lowering of water tables, and the stripping of vegetation. (Hare, 1984:2-4; Dregne, 1978:11-13). In the Sahel area of Africa, higher than normal rains occurred during the 1950s, encouraging the expansion of human and animal population. When the more traditional patterns of low rainfall returned, this population had nowhere else to go; the land could not support them, given the available technology.

Hare (1984:4) argues that only in Africa does it seem that changes caused by human use might have permanently altered the climate. Stripping the area of vegetation created feedbacks: (1) albedo (the reflective power of the earth's surface) is increased, leading to a lower level of absorbed radiation; (2) soil temperatures are raised, and the stress on organisms increased; (3) fine materials, both mineral and organic, are lost to erosion, and organic material is oxidized; finally, (4) the water-holding capacity of the area is reduced.

The drought conditions in the Sahel-Sudan region of Africa between 1968 and 1974 brought to the attention of the world the fact that deserts are expanding. One result was the special U.N. Conference on Desertification held in Nairobi, Kenya in 1977. The Conference reported that 630 million people were living in arid and semi-arid areas. Another 78 million were living on land useless for production of food, due to erosion, dune formation, changes in vegetation, and salt buildup. (Brown, 1978:16)

In a special report to the United Nations Environment Programme (UNEP), Professor M. Kassas, an eminent Egyptian ecologist, concluded that 36.3% of the world's surface is extremely arid, arid, or semi-arid. Yet the world's soil surveys by the FAO indicate that 43% of its surface falls within these three categories. The difference, Kassas argues, is accounted for by the extent of man-made deserts. (Eckholm, 1976:60) The World Bank (1984:96) has estimated that every year an additional 200,000 square kilometres are reduced by desertification to the point of yielding nothing.

The Nairobi Conference concentrated on the area around the Sahara Desert. But almost all other desert areas are expanding. In the 1980s drought conditions were prolonged in southern and eastern areas of Africa as well. The Sahara is also pressing against the North African countries; the FAO estimates that Morocco, Algeria, Tunisia, and Lybia are losing 100,000 hectares of range and cropland each year to the expansion of the Sahara. (Brown, 1978:17)

The Middle East is experiencing desertification, particularly in Syria, Jordan, and Iraq, resulting in a reduction of cereal yields. Desert-like conditions are advancing through Iran, Afghanistan, Pakistan, and north-western India. Deserts cover over one million square kilometres of China, almost 12% of the total land area. Much of this is in sand dunes (59%) and the remainder is gravel. The expansion of cultivation for grain production in the period since 1960 has increased wind erosion and fears that the deserts may be spreading.

In Latin America the semi-arid tip of Brazil's northeast is turning into desert. Similar conditions are developing in the Argentinian states of La Rioja, San Luis, and La Pampa. The southward advance of the Atacama Desert is a major problem in Chile.

The main cause of expanding deserts is overgrazing by domestic animals. Permanent pastures (land used for five years or more for forage crops, whether cultivated or wild) are the most extensive type of land use in the world, covering 24% of the world's land surface. (see Table VIIf)

Permanent pasture lands are generally in areas of low and irregular rainfall and are generally unsuited for cropping. Their productivity is low: on fertile, well managed pastures, as in central Europe, 1 hectare can support 3 to 5 animals; at the other end of the scale, it takes 50 to 60 hectares of land to support one animal in dry areas like Saudi Arabia. (*UNESCO Courier*, No. 4, May 1980:29)

The *Global 2000 Report* (Barney II, 1980:277) noted that the population of livestock in the underdeveloped countries has been rising as fast as the human population. Between 1955 and 1976 the global cattle population rose by 38%, including 62% in the Near East and 51% in Latin America. The global sheep and goat population rose 21%, including a 53% rise in centrally planned economies in Asia and 44% in Africa. Some of this was due to the development of feedlot operations. But the report concluded that in many areas the free-ranging livestock population was pushed above the levels that could be sustained by the land, given existing pasture-management policies and the availability of technologies for protecting the range lands.

The other major cause of desertification is lack of erosion control where dryland farming is undertaken. Cropping is carried on in areas that should be left in grasses. When the permanent vegetation is removed, wind and water erosion are accelerated. Cultivation is often expanded during the years of good rainfall, particularly where there is strong population pressure on the land or when food price increases provide incentives.

Desertification is certainly not limited to underdeveloped countries. The U.S. National Academy of Sciences (1976:56) reports that overgrazing has been responsible for the deterioration of rangelands in the United States. Over 80 million hectares of once-good grassland in the southwestern United States have been replaced by brushland with much lower productivity and increased erosion. Dregne (1978:14) concludes that overgrazing on range-land in the U.S. has led to a situation where about 70% of the western grazing lands are producing less than 50% of their forage potential. He concludes that even if livestock were removed from these lands for 30 years range conditions would probably not improve.

In 1976 the U.S. Bureau of Land Management reported that of the 66.3 million hectares of rangeland under its control, 50% was in "fair condition," 28% was in "poor condition," and 5% was so poor that it could only support "low value plants." (Brown, 1981:48)

The desert area of the United States is estimated to be around 91 million hectares. An additional 80 million hectares of land are now undergoing desertification. The seriousness of this can be illustrated by the San Joaquin Basin in California. Of 1.6 million hectares of rangeland, 1.3 million are suffering from overgrazing. In 1977 a storm of very high winds stripped away as much as 58 centimetres of soil. This one storm carried away 370 tonnes of soil per hectare. (Sampson, 1981:143-145)

During the period of high prices for cereals, American farmers expanded cultivation onto marginal lands, usually converting pasture in dry areas. The result was increased wind erosion, the most serious problem on 22.5 million hectares of cropland, primarily in the Pacific northwest, the Great Plains, and the western Corn Belt. (Dregne, 1978:13)

Given present population pressures, lack of conservation measures, and the cost-price squeeze on agricultural producers, there is every reason to believe that the trend towards desertification will continue. The U.N. Conference on Desertification identified 7,992,000 square kilometres of existing land as desert. If all the land identified by the Conference as having a high or very high probability of desertification were to become desert, then the area under desert conditions would triple. (Barney, II, 1980:277)

Deforestation and Foodland Resources

The process of deforestation is also having a negative impact on the ability of people to produce food. Here our primary concern is the underdeveloped countries. In 1980 the industrialized countries, with 25.4% of the world's population, had 45.2% of the world's forests and woodlands (see Table VIId). At the current rate of conversion, by the year 2000 the underdeveloped countries will have less than half the area of forest available to industrialized countries and only about half their present forest area. (Plumwood and Routley, 1982:5) Forests in underdeveloped areas are primarily used as (1) a source of fuelwood; (2) land to be cleared for agricultural purposes; and (3) logging for use locally for paper, housing, and transportation and also for export to the industrialized countries.

The rate at which the earth has been stripped of forest is astounding. By the mid-twentieth century, around one-third of the original forested land in the world had been removed by human action. At this time one fourth of the world's land surface remained as forest. But by 1980 this area had been reduced to less than one fifth. (Baidya, 1984:258; Brown, 1981:36-37; Eckholm, 1976:37)

Forests are needed for the survival of humans and other species. They influence climates by generally making them milder. They help retain rainfall, cleanse water, and allow aquifers to be recharged. Watershed forests are most important, as they protect the soil from erosion and prevent downstream floods. Trees absorb the excessive amounts of carbon dioxide produced when fossil fuels are burned.

In 1980 tropical forests covered around 2,970 million hectares of land. Of this area 40% was closed broad-leafed forest (interlocking continuous canopy), 25% was open forest (mixed broad-leafed forests and grasslands), 21% was shrub-land, and 1% was conifer forest. In addition, 14% of the land was in fallow and 11 million hectares were in plantation production. (Hadley and Lanly, 1983:11)

Estimates of the rate of deforestation differ significantly. In 1982 the FAO estimated that 7.5 million hectares of closed forest and 3.8 million hectares of open forest were being converted each year. (Iltis, 1983:57) It is estimated that, between 1976 and 1980, 6.9 million hectares of closed broadleaf forests were being converted each year. (Hadley and Lanly, 1983:11-12) These conversion rates are about 0.6% per year. Myers, in his study for the U.S. National Academy of Sciences, put the figure at between 18 and 20 million hectares per year. Hadley and Lanly (1983:12) point out that the FAO/UNEP data is based on forestry and agricultural values; the approach used by Myers was based on the rate at which primary forests were being modified from their original state and reflects concerns over biological issues. Iltis (60) argues that it is really irrelevant whether the forests are being lost at an annual rate of 0.6% or 2.0% "because even the lower figure is an incredibly large area—1/3 as large as the state of Wisconsin." Bowonder (1983:206) points out that over the past 25 years the annual rate of population growth in the underdeveloped countries has risen at a rate of 2.3%, while the growth of wood extraction has risen at a rate of 2.76%.

On the other hand, there seems to be a consensus that fuelwood is the primary use of wood in the underdeveloped countries. In 1980 UNESCO estimated that fuelwood accounted for 80% of domestic wood use in these countries. (*UNESCO Courier*, No. 4, 1980:29) In the same year a study by the United Nations Environment Programme (UNEP) concluded that 85% of all wood is used for cooking and heating. In Africa, 90% of wood cut is burnt as fuel. (Baidya, 1984:225; 259) In a subsequent joint survey of 76 underdeveloped countries by the FAO and the UNEP, the annual production of fuelwood and charcoal was estimated at 1,100 million cubic metres, eight times the production of wood logged for industrial purposes. (Hadley and Lanly, 1983:14) Bowonder (1983:206) argues that this rate of conversion for firewood will continue, since the majority of people in underdeveloped countries have no other economic source of fuel available.

Baidya (1984:257-259) points out that, for many people in underdeveloped countries, the cost of firewood is rapidly rising and consumes a major portion of the household budget. In West Africa it takes over 25% of income. The situation is acute in most rural areas in South Asia. In Nepal between 15 and 19 work days per month are spent by a family gathering firewood. A family in rural India spends between 200 and 300 person-days per year gathering firewood. With the steady increase in population, and a continued absolute growth of rural population, it is not surprising that in Asia alone 19.5 million hectares of forest land are being cut each year.

There are major differences, however, on the question of the cause of deforestation. Hadley and Lanly (1983:13) argue that shifting cultivation accounts for 70% in Africa, 50% in Asia, and 35% in Latin America. However, they concede that this largely occurs in areas that have been previously logged. UNESCO estimated in 1980 that 200 million people in underdeveloped countries live in societies based on shifting cultivation of forest lands. (*UNESCO Courier*, No. 4, 1980:13-14) Population pressure is commonly cited as the main cause of deforestation.

However, Bowonder (1983:210) argues that one of the major causes of deforestation is the clear-cutting of productive forests, followed by the establishment of commercial plantations for coffee, cocoa, rubber, pepper, spices, and cassava. These plantations are not started on existing wasteland, but in new areas of evergreen forests.

Using Central America as their focus, Nations and Komer (1983:12-14) argue that there is a distinct pattern to deforestation. First, logging companies extract the valuable hardwoods, building roads to make the harvest. The roads open the new areas to colonization by peasants who generally plant subsistence crops. The land is cleared by the peasants, but declining fertility, invasive weeds, and noxious insects combine to force the peasants off the land. They give way to the next group of settlers who transform the land to the production of cash crops for export: sugar cane, bananas, pineapples, coffee, oil palm, or beef cattle. Often the last stage of agricultural production is beef cattle grazing; overgrazing results, and given torrential rains, the forests end up as eroded wastelands. (See also Myers, 1981:3-8)

Nations and Komer (15-16) estimate that around two-thirds of all arable land in Central America is now devoted to cattle production, most of which is exported to the United States for use in the fast-food industry. Myers (1981:5) reports that since 1960 the area of man-made pastureland in Central America has increased by two-thirds. Pastures in eastern Chiapas, Mexico, now yielding 10 kgs of beef each year, yielded 6000 kgs of shelled corn and 4500 kgs of root and vegetable crops per hectare when farmed by the Maya. Iltis (1983:57) decries the destruction of virgin tropical-dry forests in Mexico to produce a "miserable crop of sorghum for cattle feed."

While admitting that population pressure on the land base is one factor in rainforest destruction, Plumwood and Routley (1982:7-14) place much of the blame on local governments promoting colonization schemes like those in the Amazon area in Brazil, razed for American cattle ranchers. Focusing on Indonesia, they argue that the main problem there is the link between the government and large transnational corporations. Shifting cultivation affects only 200,000 hectares of forest land each year, whereas logging covers 800,000 hectares. The Indonesian government has given American and Japanese forest products corporations large concession areas for timber extraction, covering nearly all the accessible primary forests of Sumatra, West Irian, and Indonesian Borneo.

Only about 6% of the wood taken from tropical forest is exported, but its value is about $8 billion. While there are enormous unmet needs for forest products in the underdeveloped world, production goes to the highest bidder. Indeed, the United States imports 70% of all the plywood and veneer produced in tropical areas. (Hadley and Lanly, 1983:7; Plumwood and Routley, 1982:7-8)

Governments in underdeveloped countries export logs and other forest products in an attempt to acquire needed foreign exchange. (Kumar, 1982:177-192) Bowonder (1983:209-210) points out that in most underdeveloped countries the forests are owned by the government. The government in turn sells these resources to transnational forest corporations at prices considerably below world market values.

The steady decline in forest lands in the underdeveloped countries is also due to the absence of forest management programs. Hadley and Lanly (1983:16-17) report that only 4.5% of the productive closed forest in the tropics is under intensive management, and three-quarters of that is in India. While much attention has been given to reforestation efforts in China and India, Bowonder (1983:207) argues that "the area recently added has been mainly man-made forest which is qualitatively inferior." Plumwood and Routley (1982:16-17) note the scientific evidence on the extensive damage done during selective logging, the fact that the secondary forests have comparatively low value, and that their highest value is in watershed protection, and conclude that the tropical rainforest "cannot be regarded as a renewable resource."

The Siltation of Irrigation Systems

One of the results of deforestation is increased flooding, which has reached very serious proportions in the Philippines, Thailand, Indonesia, Malaysia, Nigeria, Tanzania, India, Pakistan, and Bangladesh. The extensive flooding in Bangladesh in 1974 was partly caused by the increased deforestation in Nepal and eastern India. The result was a sharply reduced rice crop and famine conditions. (Brown, 1981:38; Crosson and Frederick, 1977:103-104)

The literature is full of horror stories of deforestation, soil erosion, flooding, and siltation. Each year Argentina must spend $10 million to dredge the estuary of the Plate River to keep Buenos Aires open to shipping; the sediments originate with overgrazing along the Bermejo River. The Panama Canal is experiencing the same problem, due to the timber cut, land clearing for agriculture, and expanding forest grazing. (Brown, 1981:39; *UNESCO Courier*, No. 4, 1980:12-13)

Deforestation in the Cauca Valley of Colombia has increased the floods and the silt load of the region's rivers. Construction began on the Anchicaya Dam in 1947. Twenty-one months after it was completed, a fourth of the reservoir's capacity had already been lost to sediment, and billions of dollars are to be lost in hydroelectric benefits alone. (Crosson and Frederick, 1977:103)

El Salvador spent $100 million to build the reservoir in Cerron Grande. The hydroelectric project had a life expectancy of 100 years. But as deforestation took place, and as cultivation increased, so did sedimentation. The reservoir's life expectancy was reduced to 25 years. (Brown, 1981:38-39)

In 1969 the Kainji Reservoir was opened on the Niger River in northern Nigeria, intended to supply water and power for agricultural development. Deforestation and intensive cultivation in Mali, Niger, Upper Volta, Dahomey, and Nigeria were dumping far more sediment than expected into the river system, and the life expectancy of the reservoir has been greatly reduced. (Eckholm, 1976:130)

Some of the worst cases of sedimentation are occurring in Asia, where heavy seasonal rains make erosion a much more serious problem. In Java, as farmers move up the hillsides in search of farmland, silt runoff increases, clogging downstream irrigation canals. (Brown and Eckholm, 1974:49) The silt load of the Citarum River is rapidly filling up Indonesia's largest reservoir, at Jatiluhur. Crops are now planted in the watershed area right to the top of peaks that used to be covered with dense jungle. (Eckholm, 1976:132-133)

In the Philippines, the Ambuklao Dam was built with the expectation that it would last 62 years. But with excess logging in the upper Agno River watershed, siltation has increased to such a degree that the dam's life expectancy has been reduced to 32 years. (*UNESCO Courier*, No. 4, 1980:13)

When the Shihmen Reservoir was constructed in Taiwan, it was expected to have a life of around 70 years. Between 1963 and 1968 alone 45% of its capacity was lost due to siltation. In order to slow the process of destruction, the government halted further clearing of the forests in the watershed. (Eckholm, 1976:129-130)

The biggest dam in Pakistan, the Mangla Reservoir, was completed in 1967; it was expected to operate for 100 years. However, increased sedimentation reduced its life expectancy to 55 years. In 1975 Pakistan completed the Tarvela Dam, at the time the largest earth-rock dam in the world. By the time it was completed its life expectancy was estimated to be only 50 years, due to siltation. (Eckholm, 1976:122)

River beds in Nepal's Terai region, one of the better agricultural areas in that country, are rising between 15 and 30 centimetres per year, due to erosion, as deforestation continues. The Nepalese government estimates that the country's rivers annually carry 240 million cubic metres of soil to India. (Brown, 1978:25; Crosson and Frederick, 1977:103)

By 1980 the capacity of India's Nizamasagar Reservoir had been reduced from 900 million cubic metres to less than 340 cubic metres. There was not enough water left to irrigate the 1,100 square kilometres of sugar cane and rice that had been planted and thus not enough of a crop to supply the planned needs of the local factories. (*UNESCO Courier*, No. 4, 1980:13)

Some of the world's worst cases of siltation are occurring in India. In 1972 the Indian government surveyed 22 reservoirs and found that the annual flow of sediment was much higher than originally expected, in some cases four times as high. Thus, a reservoir site becomes a non-renewable resource: it can be replaced only at great expense, and often it is irreplaceable. (Eckholm, 1976:130) The multi-dam projects on the Damodar river were to provide hydroelectric power and water for irrigation. Sedimentation was so high that the whole system became clogged, the river flow slowed, and the river between Calcutta and the Bay of Bengal became so choked with silt that dredging is required to keep the port open. (Sundborg, 1983:16)

The Yellow River in the loess region of China carries the highest load of sediment of any major river in the world, an average of 1,640 million tonnes per year. Sundborg (1983:10; 15-16) notes that the sediment load for the Yellow River is almost one million times more than for rivers flowing out of the forested areas of Scandinavia. Sedimentation has played havoc with the dams and irrigation projects of the Yellow River system; in order to maintain them, it has become necessary to sluice sediments through the dams.

The conclusion of the *Global 2000* study team was most pessimistic. Deforestation is expected to continue in the underdeveloped world. Conservation and reforestation efforts are scattered. If trends continue as in the 1970s, these forests will be reduced by half by the year 2000 and "erosion, siltation, and erratic streamflows will seriously affect food production." (Barney, I, 1980:36)

The Degradation of Irrigated Lands

Land under irrigation is being lost and subjected to degradation. In 1980 around 212 million hectares of land were being irrigated, representing 15% of the world's arable land. Irrigated lands are the most productive and, as arable land per capita declines, it is hoped that productivity can be improved. However, the authors of the *Global 2000 Report* concluded that about half of the land presently being irrigated suffers from salinity, alkalinity, or waterlogging. (Barney, I, 1980:33)

The 1977 U.N. Conference on Desertification estimated that around 125,000 hectares of irrigated land is being lost each year from environmental degradation. At the time of the conference, the losses represented only 0.06% of the total; at this rate of decline, 2.75 million hectares, or 1.4% of the total, would be lost by the year 2000. The total amount of land under irrigation continues to rise. However, with average yields, this amount of land could feed nine million people. (Barney, II, 1980:279)

The most serious problems are alkalization and salinization, which occur when water is put on land and there is inadequate drainage. There is an increase in the underground water supply, which raises the water table. When the water table comes close to the surface, waterlogging results, and the growth of crops is usually impaired.

As the water table rises further, increased evaporation takes place through the topsoil, concentrating salts and minerals there. The salts build up and production declines. Throughout history, all civilizations that have relied on irrigation have had this problem. It is a serious problem even in the United States and the Soviet Union, where technology and capital for improvements are readily available. In the poorer underdeveloped countries, land is often abandoned.

The 1977 U.N. Conference estimated that 21 million hectares of irrigated farmland suffered from some degree of waterlogging. Where waterlogging had become a problem, yields had been reduced by about 20%. Another 20 million hectares of land was said to suffer from salinization. Drainage systems can be installed to correct this problem, but the conference estimated that this would cost, on average, US$650 per hectare. (Brown, 1978:19)

North Africa and the Middle East have had these problems from the time of the collapse of the ancient civilization of the Fertile Crescent in what is now Iraq to the newly irrigated areas in contemporary Egypt. In Latin America it is a problem in Argentina, Brazil, and Peru. Mexico has had serious salinization problems in the northwestern area, and in particular in the Yaqui Valley, where considerable land has gone out of production. Degradation is even more serious in the Colorado Delta, where four-fifths of the land is affected; by 1965, 14% had been removed from cultivation. The salinization of irrigated land in California and Mexico has made the Colorado River itself extremely salty, reducing its quality for irrigation. (Eckholm, 1976:127)

The worst case usually cited is Pakistan. By the 1960s most of the irrigated land suffered from waterlogging and salinity. Large, expensive reclamation programs were undertaken, and this has been somewhat successful in the waterlogged areas. However, reclamation of salinated areas has been slow. (Barney, II, 1980:279)

Degradation of irrigated land is certainly not limited to underdeveloped countries. Dregne (1978;14) estimates that "about 25% of the irrigated land in the U.S. suffers from some degree of salinization or waterlogging." Close to where I used to farm, the state of Washington has been planning to expand land under irrigation, drawing from the Columbia River system. But just west of Sunnyside, Washington there is a large sector of farmland that used to be beautiful orchards; it has been abandoned because of salinization.

The land under irrigation in the United States is concentrated in the 17 western states. There is a great deal of concern over the quality of the water returned from use on irrigated land. The return flow not only contains sediment and salts but fertilizers and pesticides. A 1973 study found that around one-half of all the irrigated water in these states is affected by excess salinity. (Groth, 1975:290)

Most of the irrigation in the western United States is by centre pivot sprinkler systems. Of the water used for irrigation, 17% is lost through evaporation in transport and another 59% is lost through sprinkling systems and plant transpiration. Thus, only 24% of the original water is left for return flow. However, as the irrigated water passes through irrigated lands, salts build up in the runoff. (Barney, II, 1980:143)

The most notorious example is the Colorado River. The salt builds up in it as it flows towards the Mexican border. The polluted water has seriously affected the irrigated crops in southern California, Arizona, and Mexico. Falling crop yields are reported, and new drainage systems are being installed to rehabilitate the land. Although the technology and expertise is available, the costs are quite high. (Barney, II, 1980:279-280)

Damage from Pollution

The food producing capability of the earth is also being reduced by the effects of pollution of the air, water, and soil. Much of the pollution is due to the wastes created by increased human population. But more of it is due to the use of fossil fuels in industrial society.

As petroleum production declines, it is projected that the world will increasingly shift to the use of coal for energy. The use of coal revived following the increases in oil prices in 1973. However, burning coal releases toxic pollutants into the atmosphere, raises the carbon dioxide level in the atmosphere, and is the primary source of the contaminants that cause acid rain.

Acid rain is destroying the fish populations in the fresh water lakes in North America, Scandinavia, West Germany, Eastern Europe, and the USSR. Sulfur dioxide, produced from burning either coal or oil, combines with oxygen and rain, resulting in the production of sulfuric acid. It is estimated that sulfur dioxide is responsible for two-thirds of this form of pollution, with nitric oxide accounting for the other one-third. (Postel, 1985:98-102; Barney, I, 1980:36)

Solutions with a pH level less than 7 are acidic. Normal, clean rain in eastern Canada has a pH level of 5.6; thus unpolluted rain is normally acidic. In Canada acid rain is described as rain with a pH level less than 5.6. In most of eastern Canada, rainfall has a pH level of less than 4.5, which is more than ten times as acidic as normal, clean rain. (Forster, 1984:499-500)

Acid rain from the burning of fossil fuels is now beginning to destroy forests in many areas of the industrialized countries, including eastern Canada, the Appalachian mountains in the Eastern United States, the white pine areas in Pennsylvania and Virginia, the ponderosa pine forests in California, the Black Forest in West Germany, and many forests in Switzerland, Scandinavia, and the industrial areas of the USSR. Damage appears to be even greater in eastern Europe where the sulfur dioxide emissions are much higher, due to reliance on the soft "brown" coals mined and burned in the region. Acid rain is also appearing as a serious problem in Brazil, Mexico, and Chile. (Postel, 1985:99-108; Wetstone and Foster, 1983:10-12)

Scientists are just beginning to determine the effects of acid rain on crop production. Studies in New Jersey, California, and Massachusetts have demonstrated that crop production is reduced by acid rain and other pollutants. (Brown, 1981:84-85) The first report of the joint U.S./Canada Research Consultation Group concluded that "there is every indication that acid rainfall is deleterious to crops." One study in Oregon found a 9% reduction in the yield of corn when the pH level was 4.0, similar to the rainfall in southern Ontario and parts of Quebec. Forster (1984:521) extrapolates these losses to eastern Canada and concludes that they may be costing farmers over $100 million per year. Irving (1983:442-453) found that general environmental factors interacted with acid rain to produce different effects in different areas. While most studies revealed no effect, there was reported damage to corn and soybeans, very important crops in the United States and Canada.

The most serious pollution problem to crops in eastern North America is ozone damage. Ozone is formed in the photochemical oxidation of nitrogen dioxide (released through the burning of fossil fuels) while in the presence of hydrocarbons. There is a high concentration on the north side of Lake Erie, where studies have revealed injury to Ontario crops of tobacco, beans, onions, potatoes, grapes, tomatoes, cucumbers, squash, pumpkins, endive, and peas. (Forster, 1984:507-508; Ontario, 1981:27; Beaubien and Tabacnik, 1977:46-47)

One of the effects of the introduction of high-response varieties of cereals (Green Revolution) in Asia has been the rise in water pollution from the increased use of fertilizers and pesticides. For example, production of fish in farm ponds in the Philippines, Malaysia, and Indonesia has been reduced. (Eckholm, 1976:161-162)

General pesticide use is on the increase in the underdeveloped countries, and so are the resulting pollution and health problems. In the tropical areas there are more numerous pests, no freezing temperatures to offer some control, and the insects' natural development of resistance to pesticides is accelerated. This encourages heavier use than in the temperate zones. Furthermore, many pesticides banned in the advanced industrialized countries for their adverse health or environment effects are nevertheless manufactured in industrialized countries and sold to underdeveloped countries. The widespread use of organochlorines (the DDT family), banned in almost all of the western industrialized countries, has resulted in the building up of residues in the food system. (Weir and Schapiro, 1981)

The World Health Organization reports that pesticide poisonings are on the increase. The newer organophosphate pesticides may be less persistent in the environment, but they are more acutely toxic than the organochlorines. (Pimentel and Edwards, 1982:595-600; Barney, I, 1980:35; Barney, II, 1980: 286; Pimentel and Pimentel, 1979:142; Crosson and Frederick, 1977:81-82)

Much of the world depends on ocean fisheries as a source of protein. But the ocean fish and shellfish resource is being depleted. This is not only due to overharvesting; the fisheries industry is also being destroyed by pollution. Between 60% and 80% of the food resources of the oceans use the estuaries, salt marshes, and mangrove swamps as habitat in their life cycles, and these are rapidly being polluted. (*UNESCO Courier*, No. 4, May 1980:28; Eckholm, 1976:160-162) While this is most noticeable in the United States and Japan, the disaster is being repeated in the underdeveloped countries. (Brown, 1984:81-83; Barney, I, 1980:35)

Conclusion

It is difficult to quantify the loss of foodlands on a global scale. Even in the industrialized countries good data is limited. The FAO and UNEP estimated in 1978 that losses from environmental deterioration alone were in the range of six to twelve million hectares per year. This was more than was being added to the existing cropland base. (*Ceres*, No. 4, 1978:16) In 1980 UNESCO estimated that, if current trends of land losses due to conversion and degradation continued, close to one-third of the world's arable land would be lost over the next twenty years. (*UNESCO Courier*, No. 4, 1980:10)

This concern was reiterated in the FAO's report, *Agriculture: Toward 2000* (1981:28; 129-130). They concluded that productivity would be permanently reduced, if the degradation of natural resources used for food production was not reversed. The FAO called for the investment of $25 billion between 1980 and 2000 to reclaim deteriorated agricultural lands.

Why is this degradation continuing when it is so widely recognized? There are several explanations generally advanced. The one most commonly cited is the steady rise in the world's population. For example, this has been the central focus of the Worldwatch Institute: in many areas of the world, the level of population is exceeding the carrying capacity of the ecosystem. In *Building a Sustainable Society* (1981:51-54) Lester Brown argues that the strain on the world's biological resources is caused by population increases. He cites figures indicating that per-capita production from the forests, fisheries, and the grasslands (beef, mutton, and wool production) peaked during the 1960s and is now in decline. High fertility rates have often been cited by the Worldwatch Institute as the primary cause of desertification, decline in food production, and famine in Africa.

In Chapter VII I argued that the classic overpopulation thesis is being put to the test in contemporary China. Widespread deterioration of foodlands and water resources have been reported in recent years. This has been attributed primarily to the cultivation of very marginal lands in an effort to maintain per-capita food consumption levels. The post-Mao leadership has also decided to place first priority on augmenting the forces of production, the "Four Modernizations" campaign. But China's capital is limited, and likewise its advanced technology, and the result has been a dramatic increase in all levels of industrial and urban pollution.

A second explanation for loss of foodland resources stresses the social organization of a particular country. One example would be Brazil. The colonization of the Amazon and the destruction of huge areas of tropical forest to expand cattle production for export is not necessary: Brazil has one of the highest ratios of arable land per capita in the world. But the colonization program helps divert attention from political demands for restructuring the existing system of agricultural production, with its grossly unequal distribution and misuse of arable land.

Another example would be Central America. Environmental destruction is directly linked to ownership and control of most of the prime arable land by a tiny minority of the rich who have strong ties to repressive, dictatorial governments. Much of this land is underused. A more equitable distribution of land resources and better management would permit more sustainable use of fragile areas where poor peasants are now forced to live.

A third explanation places the blame on the forces of the market economy itself. In a market economy foodlands are just another commodity to be bought and sold to the highest bidder. Under this system the responsibility for soil conservation has been left to the individual farmer. Long-term crop rotations including the use of legumes, pasture, and animals usually improve the quality of the soil. However, the cost-price squeeze of the market economy puts enormous pressure on farmers to increase production to try to stay in the business of farming. As a number of studies in the United States and Canada have shown, individual farmers cannot afford to operate their enterprises on a sustainable or ecological basis; market pressures demand that foodlands be intensively used. The inevitable result is the deterioration of foodlands through overintensive use.

Finally, there are those who place the primary blame on government policy. In the industrialized countries there are adequate capital sources available and the advanced technology that would permit sustainable agriculture. In the capitalist countries, where the means of production (including foodlands) are privately owned, governments are reluctant to pass legislation requiring ecological use of natural resources. There is a fundamental contradiction between the concept of private ownership of natural resources and government management for the benefit of the society as a whole.

But what about existing state socialist or centrally planned economies? Private ownership of natural resources does not exist. Furthermore, these countries are no longer poor; they are investing heavily in agriculture and have all the advanced technologies. Yet the evidence indicates that environmental degradation in agricultural production is widespread. Why is this the case? In Chapter VI I argued that it was largely due to the acceptance of the system of industrial agriculture, modelled after corporate agriculture in the United States. But there is another factor. Government economic plans place tremendous pressure on individual collective or state farms to continually increase production through intensive use of the land. These pressures are not unlike those found in the market in capitalist societies. Furthermore, the incentives offered for increasing production are much more significant than the incentives and penalties designed to encourage sustainable practices.

It seems evident that all four of the explanations are tenable. It is possible to cite particular cases where each appears to be the dominant cause.

References

Agriculture Institute of Canada (1980). "Soil Erosion on Agricultural Land in Canada; The Task Force Report." *Agrologist*, IX, No. 4, Fall, pp. 23-28.

Baidya, Kedar N. (1984). "Firewood Shortage: Ecoclimate Disasters in the Third World." *International Journal of Environmental Studies*, XXII, pp. 255-272.

Barney, Gerald O., ed. (1980 *The Global 2000 Report to the President* Volume I; The Summary Report. New York: Pergamon Press.

Barney, Gerald O., ed. (1980). *The Global 2000 Report to the President*. Volume II; The Technical Report. Washington, D.C.: U.S. Government Printing Office.

Beaubien, Charles and Ruth Tabacnik (1977). *People and Agricultural Land*. Ottawa: Science Council of Canada.

Biswas, Margaret R. and Asit K. Biswas (1980). *"Desertification": Environmental Sciences and Applications*. New York: Pergamon Press.

Bowonder, B. (1983). "Forest Depletion: Some Policy Options." *Resources Policy*, IX, No. 3, September, pp. 206-224.

Brink, R. A. et al (1977). "Soil Deterioration and the Growing World Demand for Food." *Science*, CXCVII, No. 4304, August 12, pp. 625-630.

Brown, Lester R. (1985). "Maintaining World Fisheries." In Lester R. Brown et al. *The State of the World, 1985*. New York: W. W. Norton for the Worldwatch Institute, pp. 73-96.

Brown, Lester R. (1984). "The Global Loss of Topsoil." *Journal of Soil and Water Conservation*, XXXIX, No. 3, May-June, pp. 162-165.

Brown, Lester R. (1981). *Building a Sustainable Society*. New York: W. W. Norton for the Worldwatch Institute.

Brown, Lester R. (1978). *The Worldwide Loss of Cropland*. Washington, D.C.: Worldwatch Paper 24.

Brown, Lester R. and Eric P. Eckholm (1974). *By Bread Alone*. New York: Praeger, Publishers for the Overseas Development Council.

Carter, Luther (1977). "Soil Erosion: The Problem Persists Despite the Billions Spent on It." *Science*, CXCVI, April 22, pp. 409-411.

Cook, Kenneth A. (1981). "The National Agricultural Land Study Goes Out with a Bang." *Journal of Soil and Water Conservation*, XXXVI, No. 2, March-April, pp. 91-93.

Cook, Kenneth A. (1980). "The National Agricultural Lands Study." *Journal of Soil and Water Conservation*, XXXV, No. 5, pp. 247-249.

Crosson, Pierre R. and Kenneth D. Frederick (1977). *The World Food Situation*. Washington, D.C.: Resources for the Future.

Dregne, Harold E. (1978). "Desertification: Man's Abuse of the Land." *Journal of Soil and Water Conservation*, XXXIII, No. 1, January-February, pp. 11-14.

Dudal, R. (1982). "Land Degradation in a World Perspective." *Journal of Soil and Water Conservation*, XXXVII, No. 5, September-October, pp. 245-249.

Eckholm, Erik P. (1976). *Losing Ground; Environmental Stress and World Food Prospects*. New York: W. W. Norton for the Worldwatch Institute.

Food and Agriculture Organization (1981). *Agriculture: Toward 2000*. Rome: FAO.

Forster, Bruce A. (1984). "An Economic Assessment of the Significance of Long-Range Transported Air Pollutants for Agriculture in Eastern Canada." *Canadian Journal of Agricultural Economics*, XXXII, November, pp. 498-525.

Geno, Barbara J. and Larry M. Geno (1976). *Food Production in the Canadian Environment.* Ottawa: Science Council of Canada.

Groth, Edward (1975). "Increasing the Harvest." *Environment*, XVII, No. 1, January-February, pp. 28-39.

Gustafson, Thane (1979). "Environmental Conflict in the USSR." In Dorothy Nelkin, ed. *Controversy: Politics of Technical Decisions.* Beverly Hills, California: Sape Press, pp. 69-83.

Hadley, Malcolm and Jean-Paul Lanly (1983). "Tropical Forest Ecosystems." *Nature and Resources*, XIX, No. 1, January-March, pp. 2-19.

Hare, F. Kenneth (1984). "Climate, Drought and Desertification." *Nature and Resources*, XX, No. 1, January-March, pp. 2-8.

Hudson, Norman W. (1983). "Soil Conservation Strategies in the Third World." *Journal of Soil and Water Conservation*, XXXVIII, No. 6, November-December, pp. 446-450.

Iltis, Hugh H. (1983). "Tropical Forests; What Will Be Their Fate?" *Environment*, XXV, No. 10, December, pp. 55-60.

Ingraham, E. W. (1975). *A Query into the Quarter Century.* Colorado Springs: Wright Ingraham Institute.

Irving, Patricia M. (1983). "Acidic Precipitation Effects on Crops: A Review and Analysis of Research." *Journal of Environmental Quality*, XII, No. 4, pp. 442-453.

Kumar, R. (1982). "World Tropical Wood Trade: Economic Overview." *Resources Policy*, VIII, No. 3, September, pp. 177-192.

Larson, W. E. et al (1983). "The Threat of Soil Erosion to Long-Term Crop Production." *Science*, CCXIX, No. 4585, February 4, pp. 458-465.

Lee, Linda K. (1984). "Land Use and Soil Loss: A 1982 Update." *Journal of Soil and Water Conservation*, XXXIX, No. 4, July-August, pp. 226-228.

Lee, Linda K. (1981). "Cropland Availability: The Landowner Factor." *Journal of Soil and Water Conservation*, XXXVI, No. 3, May-June, pp. 135-137.

McQuaig, J. D. and E. W. Manning (1982). *Agricultural Land-Use Change in Canada: Process and Consequences.* Ottawa: Environment Canada.

Meadows, Donella H. et al (1972). *The Limits to Growth.* New York: Universe Books.

Myers, Norman (1981). "The Hamburger Connection: How Central America's Forests Become North America's Hamburgers." *Ambio*, X, No. 1, pp. 3-8.

Nations, James D. and Daniel I. Komer (1983). "Rainforests and the Hamburger Society." *Environment*, XXV, No. 3, April, pp. 12-20.

Ontario (1981). *Energy and Agriculture.* Toronto: Queen's Park.

Organization of Economic Co-operation and Development (1977). *Interfutures.* Paris: OECD.

Pimentel, David et al (1976). "Land Degradation: Effects on Food and Energy Resources." *Science*, XCCIV, No. 4261, October 6, pp. 149-155.

Pimentel, David and Clive A. Edwards (1982). "Pesticides and Ecosystems." *BioScience*, XXXII, No. 7, July-August, pp. 595-600.

Pimentel, David and Marcia Pimentel (1979). *Food, Energy and Society.* London: Edward Arnold.

Plumwood, Val and Richard Routley (1982). "World Rainforest Destruction—The Social Factors." *Ecologist*, XII, No. 1, pp. 4-22.

Posner, Joshua L. and Malcolm F. McPherson (1982). "Agriculture on the Steep Slopes of Tropical America." *World Development*, X, No. 5, pp. 341-353.

Postel, Sandra (1985). "Protecting Forests from Air Pollution and Acid Rain." In Lester R. Brown et al. *State of the World, 1985*. New York: W. W. Norton for the Worldwatch Institute, pp. 97-123.

Richards, John F. (1984). "Global Patterns of Land Conversion." *Environment*, XXVI, No. 9, November, pp. 7-13, 34-38.

Riquier, J. (1982) "A World Assessment of Soil Degradation." *Nature and Resources*, XVIII, No. 2, April-June, pp. 18-21.

Sampson, R. Neil (1981). *Farmland or Wasteland: A Time to Choose*. Emmaus, Pennsylvania: Rodale Press.

Schmude, Keith O. (1977). "Perspective on Prime Farmland." *Journal of Soil and Water Conservation*, XXXII, No. 5, September-October, pp. 240-242.

Sparrow, Herbert O., Chairman (1984). *Soil At Risk: Canada's Eroding Future*. Ottawa: Senate Committee on Agriculture, Fisheries and Forestry.

Sundborg, Ake (1983). "Sedimentation Problems in River Basins." *Nature and Resources*, XIX, No. 2, April-June, pp. 10-21.

U.S. National Academy of Sciences. *Climate and Food*. Washington, D.C.: USNAS.

Warren, C. Leigh and Paul C. Rump (1981). *The Urbanization of Rural Land in Canada: 1966-1971 and 1971-1976*. Ottawa: Environment Canada.

Weir, David and Mark Schapiro (1981). *Circle of Poison: Pesticides and People in a Hungry World*. San Francisco: Institute for Food and Development Policy.

Wetstone, Gregory S. and Sarah A. Foster (1983). "Acid Precipitation: What is it Doing to our Forests?" *Environment*, XXV, No. 4, May, pp. 10-12; 38-40.

CHAPTER NINE

How Much Food
Can the World Produce?

There are several basic approaches to dealing with the reality of the persistence of hunger in a world of plenty. The most common solution advanced is to increase the amount of food produced. In theory, this will reduce food prices and permit a greater percentage of the population to acquire an adequate diet. If there is a bigger overall pie, then the total amount going to the poor will also be bigger, and absolute poverty will be reduced. This solution, often referred to as the "supply side" approach, is most commonly advanced by orthodox economists, development experts in the west, and international organizations associated with the United Nations. It is a convenient approach, because it avoids the most difficult issue, distribution.

This chapter will look at the supply-side factors in modern food production and distribution. Is there additional land that can be added to the amount now being farmed? Are there adequate energy resources available? Are there adequate mineral resources to provide the essential support? And finally, will adequate capital resources be made available to the presently underdeveloped countries? A political economy approach must also deal with the question of distribution and access to these resources. At the same time, it is necessary to seriously consider the ecological consequences of reproducing the industrial food system on a world-wide basis.

Adding Arable Land

Food production can be increased by bringing under cultivation land that is not being used for that purpose. For quite some time, numerous experts have been speculating on how much land there is in the presently underdeveloped world that could be converted to cropping. Estimates vary considerably.

In 1967 the U.S. President's Scientific Advisory Committee on the World Food Problem estimated the world's potential arable land at 3,190 million hectares. (U.S., 1967:434) The authors of *The Limits to Growth* cited these figures in their own projections. (Meadows et al, 1972:50) Using the 1974

FAO/UNESCO soil maps of the world as a starting point, Buringh and Norse also placed estimates in the same range as the President's report. (Norse, 1979:19-21) An estimate made by Mesarovic and Pestel (1975:168-169) for the Club of Rome put the figure at a somewhat lower level, 2,425 million hectares. In 1977 the U.S. Department of Agriculture estimated that there were 1,648 million hectares of potential arable land in the underdeveloped market economies. (Crosson and Frederick, 1977:36)

More recent projections were done for the *Global 2000 Report* (Barney, I, 1980:16). Under Alternative I, the medium series projection, arable land is expected to rise from 1,477 million hectares in 1975 to 1,539 million by the year 2000. This would be a total increase of only 4%. They note that "in the early 1970s one hectare of arable land supported an average of 2.6 persons; by 2000 one hectare will have to support 4 persons."

Table IXa reports actual changes in arable land between 1960 and 1980. In the underdeveloped world (including China) arable land increased from 775.3 million hectares to 793.4 million hectares. This was a total increase of only 2.3%, or an annual increase of a mere 0.1%. There were substantial net losses of arable land in Africa south of the Sahara and in China. Only in Latin America was there any substantial increase in arable land. Very little arable land was added in the industrialized countries either, with the only substantial increases coming in Australia, the only continent with an actual per capita increase.

Thus it is not surprising that the major report by the FAO, *Agriculture: Toward 2000* (1981:19, 28), concludes that the achievements of the last twenty years have been "fundamentally unsatisfactory" and that the current trends "must be changed." Their hope for "sustainable growth in production" calls for the addition of up to 150 million hectares of land for cultivation by the year 2000. Without a doubt, a 20% increase in arable land would require a dramatic change in current trends.

The most thorough analysis of potential cropland has been Land Resources for Future Populations, begun in 1978 by the FAO and the U.N. Fund for Population Activities. The key to this was the completion of the new FAO/UNESCO Soil Map of the World, a 17-year project. While the maps are not very detailed, there is a series of ten volumes providing detailed backup information. The main achievement of the exercise was the standardization of world soil classifications. (Dudal and Batisse, 1978:2-6)

The second component of the survey was the FAO's Agro-ecological Zones Project, completed between 1978-1981. The climate inventory was superimposed on the soil maps, and from this inventory specialists selected crops that matched soil, temperature, and moisture conditions. Using a computer, they estimated the rain-fed potential of presently uncultivated lands and the number of people that an area could possibly support, according to three levels of production inputs under three different scenarios for trade and self-sufficiency. The team was assisted by the Holcomb

TABLE IXa   *Additions of Arable Land, 1960-1980*

Millions Hectares

Countries	Arable Land 1960	1980	Land Added 1960-1980	% Annual Change 1960-1980
North Africa and Middle East	82.7	87.2	4.4	0.27
Sub-Sahara Africa	213.0	156.3	(56.7)	(1.33)
Central America and Caribbean	30.5	36.4	5.9	0.97
South America	73.0	125.7	52.7	3.61
Asia[1]	266.8	288.6	21.9	0.41
China	109.4	99.2	(10.2)	(0.46)
All Underdeveloped	**775.3**	**793.4**	**18.1**	**0.12**
United States	184.9	190.6	5.7	0.15
Canada	40.6	44.4	3.8	0.46
Australia/New Zealand	27.5	44.8	17.3	3.15
Japan	6.1	4.9	(1.2)	(0.98)
Western Europe	96.2	87.2	(9.0)	(0.47)
All Industrial/ME	**355.3**	**371.9**	**16.6**	**0.23**
USSR	221.4	231.9	10.6	0.24
Eastern Europe	56.2	53.7	(2.5)	(0.22)
All Industrial/CPE	**277.6**	**285.7**	**8.1**	**0.15**
World Totals	**1,408.3**	**1,451.2**	**42.8**	**0.15**

[1]Excluding China and Japan. Some FAO data for 1960 are estimated.

SOURCE: Food and Agricultural Organization. *Production Yearbook*, Volume 35, 1981; Volume 16, 1961.

Research Institute of Indianapolis and Professor Roger Revelle. (Higgins et al, 1984, 1982, 1981; Higgins and Kassam, 1981)

From this exercise the project directors concluded that the underdeveloped world in 1975 contained 2,028 million hectares of land that could support rain-fed agriculture; at the time, the cultivated area was 670 million hectares. Even under their category of "low levels of inputs" (only hand labour, no fertilizers or pesticides) they concluded that the underdeveloped world could support twice the population of 1975 and 1.6 times the projected population for the year 2000. Africa could feed nearly three times its present population. However, this scenario presumes the use of all potential farmland in staple food production for local consumption (no agricultural exports); it also assumes massive and unlimited movement of food surpluses between and within countries. The total population of the 117 underdeveloped countries covered in the study (which excludes China) is projected to increase from 1,956 million in 1975 to 3,598 million by the year 2000. If "high levels of inputs" are achieved (as in the industrialized states), only 96.6 million people (or less than 3% of those living in the underdeveloped world) would be living in "critical areas." (Higgins et al, 1984:6-8; 1981:19) These optimistic conclusions were similar to those advanced by Revelle in his widely cited article in *Scientific American* in 1974.

A second, less extreme, scenario assumes the movement of surplus food production within individual countries but not between countries. This approach found that in 1975 of the 117 countries studied 55 had insufficient land resources to feed their own populations at the level of low-input production. With no increase in farm inputs, this number would rise to 65 by the year 2000, representing a population of over 2 billion. (Higgins et al, 1984:7-8; 1982:vii-x)

There are some obvious technical shortcomings with the exercise, if it is to be perceived as a planning document; the scale and the categories are too broad. For example, there are only three texture classes for soils (coarse, medium, and fine) and there are only three slope categories. The second slope category, "rolling to hilly," covers land ranging between 8% and 30%, slope levels prone to serious erosion.

The scenarios do not include the necessity of growing crops like fruits and vegetables needed for vitamins and minerals. There is no provision for growing fibre, fodder for animals, or forestry. On the other hand, the potential for irrigation is not included. (See Harrison, 1984:25-36) The exercise does not try to deal with the problem of food distribution within countries, nor does it calculate the cost of making these lands available for cropping.

Nevertheless, the results of the project underline the concerns that have been raised in similar exercises. First, in the underdeveloped world around 80% of the soils have some form of constraint to rain-fed crop production. Second, foodland resources are immobile and unevenly distributed; food trade between underdeveloped countries is desirable. Third, most of the land with cropping potential is in the humid tropical forests of Africa and South America. Fourth, without introducing conservation measures, the potential cropland in the underdeveloped countries shrinks by 17.7% by the year 2000. (Higgins et al, 1984:3-9)

While the report concludes that there are great reserves of land in Africa, most of the potential lies in the less populated central and southern areas of the continent. Around half of the existing population lives in the drier and mountainous areas where population density already exceeds the carrying capacity of the land. Furthermore, there is the fact that over the 1970s yields for the four major crops grown in Africa (maize, millet, sorghum, and cassava) have been poor. (Harrison, 1984:26-27; Higgins et al, 1981:19-21)

The problem of resources for food production is even more evident for the region of Southwest Asia. Of the sixteen countries covered, only one, Turkey, has adequate foodland resources. Even using intermediate technology (improved cultivars, some fertilizers and pesticides, some fallow and conservation measures, and some animal traction) it was concluded that 12 of the 16 countries would remain critical as far as food production was concerned. (Harrison, 1984:27-28; Higgins et al, 1982:vii)

The region defined as Southeast Asia (from Pakistan to the Philippines) has limited additional potential. For 1975 the report concludes that 6 of the 16 countries had insufficient land resources to feed their people at low levels of inputs; the population of the six totalled 770 million, or 69% of the regional total. Of the 898 million hectares of land in this region, 262.5 million were being cropped in 1975. The report concludes that only 31.5 million hectares of reserve land has cropping potential. (Higgins and Kassam, 1981:16-23)

In Central America only one-quarter of the land is suitable for cultivation, but in 1975 only one half of that was actually being cropped. South America has an abundance of land available for agricultural purposes. As Harrison (1984:29) points out, the primary problem in this area is the full utilization of existing cropland resources. Large estates, which cover 80% of the arable land, leave a great deal of land uncultivated. But if any significant conversion to cropping occurs in South America, it will involve the clearing of substantial amounts of the 943 million hectares of tropical rainforest.

The conclusion of the study emphasizes the uneven distribution of foodland resources between and within countries. Reflecting the ideological approach of the FAO, the authors say that the first priority is to "raise input levels." These include not only the use of fertilizers but the introduction of conservation measures. The second task is the "implementation of major land improvements to enhance the land resource base." These include irrigation development and land reclamation. They note that a great deal of the potential arable land is in the humid tropics "with special clearing, fertility and conservation requirements." This necessitates "sound land-use planning." (Higgins et al, 1984:9-10)

It is generally recognized that the best farmland in the world is presently being cultivated and grazed. The remaining potential lands are marginal with serious constraints. Drought is a major problem for much of the potential arable land. In South America, this includes the west coast, the pampas, and northern Argentina. Southern Brazil has adequate rain and a good growing season, but the soils are infertile without extensive treatment. (Shrader, 1977:128-130) Cropping is difficult in the savanna zones in Africa, because of poor soils commonly lacking nitrogen, sulfur, and phosphates, and because of unreliable rainfall and poor water supplies. (Anthony et al, 1979:123-126)

A great deal of controversy surrounds the practice of clearing forests in the humid tropics. Myers (1981:8-9) insists that development means "wise use"; in this case, the forests would be of greater utility when left virtually intact. Jordan and Herrera (1981:7-13) point out that forest ecosystems in the tropics are mostly oligotrophic, characterized by soils with low fertility. As long as the thin layer of humus and tree root layer is maintained, tree growth can continue. But when the trees are cleared for agricultural use, "nutrients are quickly lost because the humus is destroyed, and the mineral soil does not have the capacity to retain the leached nutrients or to supply new nutrients." In the Amazon region, soils are much lower in nutrients than in the temperate zones and cannot support agriculture without extensive fertilization and efforts at conservation. Jordan (1982:395-399) argues that cultivation in the Amazon Basin should be limited to clearing on a small scale, on the patches of better soils.

Around 75% of the soils in the Amazon Basin are acidic and infertile oxisols and ultisols. Only around 6% of them have no major limitations to agriculture; yet this amounts to 32 million hectares. On the better soils, continuous cultivation has proven feasible where there is good crop rotation, conservation efforts, the use of agro-forestry on slopes and hills, and modern weed-control methods. In certain test areas the soil improved where there were regular applications of lime, fertilizers, and trace minerals. (Nicholaides et al, 1985; Sanchez et al, 1982)

Nevertheless, the actual experience of colonization in the Amazon Basin has been discouraging. Heavy rains leached the cleared lands quickly and created serious erosion problems. Poor soils have produced poor agricultural yields. Farmers have suffered from the buildup of pests and plant diseases that quickly develop resistance to pesticides. Furthermore, a very high proportion of the settler population annually experiences malaria. The number of farmers who have continued to farm in the settlement areas has been far below the government's expectations. (Smith:1981:757-759)

Experiments at the International Institute of Tropical Agriculture at Ibadan, Nigeria reveal that sustainable agricultural production can be achieved in the humid tropics of Africa under certain conditions:

> [if] chemical nutrients lost during cultivation are continually replenished; physical conditions of soil are maintained at a favourable level with adequate levels of soil organic matter; soil is kept constantly covered and erosion controlled; increase in soil acidity and presence of nutrient deficiencies and toxic constituents are continually corrected; and buildups of pests, weeds and diseases are prevented. (Okigbo, 1981:41)

Not surprisingly, the problems in humid Africa are similar to those in the Amazon. The most fertile soils in Africa are in the savannah and the alluvial valley bottoms and make up only 6% of the arable soils. Most soils are weathered, with low fertility. In the humid areas the most successful methods are those involving minimum soil disturbance. Pest problems are serious constraints. Mulching is considered necessary because of torrential rains; maize farmed as in the temperate zones produces significantly lower yields. Between 40% and 70% of labour time is spent controlling weeds, thus the use of herbicides is recommended. (Okigbo, 1981:42-44; Anthony et al, 1979:119-121)

Ruthenberg (1976:118-120) argues that there are few examples of economically viable systems of permanent cultivation in the humid tropics. Commercial cropping depends on tractors and fertilizers, and economic returns have been low. More successful have been gardens: small plots close to home, with dense plantings, intensive use of land, using hand implements. However, to be successful there has to be cheap labour, fairly reliable markets, and infrequent changes in crops.

The United Nations World Food Conference in 1974 set goals for adding around 200 million ha of new arable land over a ten-year period. The costs of the program were also estimated by region. It was hoped that 34 million hectares could be added in Africa, 85 million in Latin America, 10 million in the Near East, and 24 million in the Far East. The cost for bringing this land under cultivation was estimated at between $44 per hectare for Africa and $396 for the Far East. (Norse, 1979:41; Crosson and Frederick, 1977:51) Earlier, the U.S. President's Science Advisory Panel on the World Food Crisis concluded that the cost of developing new land for farming ranged from $215 to $5,275 per hectare. (Meadows et al, 1972:48)

Norse (1979:23, 41) reports that in 1971 the cost just for land clearance was more than $200 per hectare. The cost of preparation for irrigation was set by the UN Conference at $1,467 per hectare for the Far East. Yet Norse points out that in 1971 levelling costs alone were between $200 and $500 per hectare. He concludes that the development cost estimates used by the United Nations were too low.

The FAO's major study, *Agriculture: Toward 2000* (1981:63-65), presented new estimates on the cost of conversion to arable land. The average was set at $424 per hectare, ranging from $50 for the conversion of savannah pasture to $1,000 for clearing rainforest land. The cost of preparing land for irrigation ranged from $300 per hectare for controlled flooding to $7,000 for a full sprinkler system. The average cost was set at $2,380 per hectare.

The latest expert surveys of potential new foodlands conclude that there is considerable land that could be brought into cultivation in the underdeveloped world. However, land reserves are concentrated in the humid tropics, particularly in Africa and South America, and not where populations are pushing on the resource base. Furthermore, the financial costs of conversion are high for underdeveloped countries with shortages of capital and foreign exchange. Finally, there is widespread recognition that these lands are marginal for cropping. Many believe that they cannot be cleared and cultivated without causing serious environmental problems. The FAO/

UNFPA team stresses that well-planned conservation techniques are required, or the land will suffer serious degradation. The alternative is to place a higher priority on increasing food production on lands already being cultivated. Both approaches depend on the existence of capital for investment as well as on the availability of energy and material inputs.

Energy and Agriculture

The modern industrial approach to farming has always seemed efficient. How often we hear it repeated that the individual farmer in Canada or the United States now feeds fifty or more people! However, since the first round of price increases for oil in 1973, we have become much more aware of the role of non-renewable fossil fuel energy in making this productivity possible.

Traditionally, the very term "efficiency" has been linked to the effective use of energy. It is a comparison of production in relation to the cost of energy — the ratio of energy produced by a system compared to the amount of energy required to make it run. In judging food production it is necessary to measure the amount of kilocalories (kcal) used in the food system against the amount of energy consumed as food; the result is the energy-out energy-in ratio.

A few examples will illustrate the point. Primitive tribes, producing food by hand from gardens, yielded an average of 20 kcal of food energy for every kcal of energy used. The sun's energy was captured in an efficient manner. Primitive slash-and-burn agriculture in tropical areas has provided a return in the range of 16 kcal for every one expended. In the past Chinese wet-rice farmers were considered among the most efficient of all; they produced an average of 50 kcal of energy for every one used in production. (Rappaport, 1971:116-132)

Maize production by traditional farmers in the Yucatan area of Mexico produced between 13 and 29 kcal for every one used. The taro-yam gardens among primitive peoples in New Guinea produced 20 kcal for every one used in production. (Leach, 1975:152) While these were societies of very efficient farmers in the basic sense of capturing energy from the sun, their labour-intensive systems produced only a relatively low level of civilization.

The modern system of industrial agriculture depends heavily on the use of fossil fuels. Following the first "energy crisis" in 1973, studies of energy efficiency in the food system blossomed. In the face of considerable criticism, agricultural economists tried to demonstrate that the system was still energy efficient, at least on the farm. (For example, see Paarlberg, 1980:175-183) In a widely cited study, Gerald Leach (1975:150-153) concluded that in the United Kingdom wheat, oats, and barley produced a net of around 2.0 in the energy-out/energy-in ratio. But all meat products fared poorly, using between two and three times as much energy as they produced. The worst case commonly cited is the production of frozen fish from trawlers, which has an energy ratio of around 0.05.

Many modern farming systems are net energy consumers. The factory production of eggs, poultry, hogs, milk, and cattle requires extensive feeding of grain. Vegetables and fruits are also very energy-intensive food products — particularly where they are grown under irrigation. (Belyea and Tribe, 1977:106-107; Heichel, 1976:65-66; Slessor, 1974:65-66)

Between 1952 and 1972 the total energy inputs into agriculture in the industrialized capitalist states increased by around 70%, but food production increased only 30%. The new technology brought higher yields but "a marked decline in energetic efficiency." (Belyea and Tribe, 1977:103) Researchers at Cornell University found that between 1945 and 1970 corn yields in the United States had risen by 138%; but energy inputs had increased three-fold. (Pimentel et al, 1973:443-449) When beef production was transformed from rangeland grazing to feedlot operations, energy efficiency ratios declined to between 0.2 and 0.4. (Belyea and Tribe, 197:106)

Gifford (1978:93-98) reports that when Hong Kong shifted from the traditional Chinese method of vegetable production to western high-energy technology, yields increased by 8% but energy costs rose by 500%, and the net energy ratio dropped to 0.3. Gifford also estimates that the amount of food lost in the modern industrial food system ranges between 30% and 50% of what is produced on the farm.

However, farming is only one aspect of food production in industrialized societies. In a widely cited article, the Steinharts (1974:307-316) estimated in 1970 that the on-farm use of energy was only around 25% of the total energy used in the American food system. The other 75% of the energy consumed went into processing, storage, distribution, and home preparation. A survey of the industrialized capitalist countries undertaken by the Organization of Economic Co-operation and Development (OECD) found that on average the food system used 20% of all energy, and that within the food system, 75% of the energy was utilized beyond the farm gate. (Simantov, 1980:339-340) On average, the Steinharts and Gifford argue that, in the industrialized capitalist countries, it takes 10 kcal of energy to put 1 kcal of food energy on the table. Norman Borlaug, often referred to as the "father of the Green Revolution," described the American food system as an "energy sink." (Perelman, 1977:12)

One of the basic differences between living standards in the industrialized and the underdeveloped states is the energy used in the food system. The Pimentels (1979:137) made some rough calculations on this for 1975. In that year the United States used around 4.25 litres of oil per capita per day for the food system alone. That was about twice the total daily per capita fossil fuel consumed in all underdeveloped countries. To feed a world of 4,000 million in 1975 on the U.S. diet would have taken 5,760 billion litres of fuel annually; using the world's oil for the food alone would have consumed all of the proved oil reserves in just eleven years.

Leach made a similar calculation at around the same time. (1975:161) To provide the underdeveloped world with a European-level diet, based on the fossil fuel energy subsidies used in the British system of food production, would have required a *doubling* of the *total* energy consumption in these countries just for food production and consumption. Feeding a world of 8 billion people at this level would have required 70% of the world's 1972 consumption of energy for all purposes.

Controlling Fuel Resources

Energy resources will be needed in increasing amounts if agricultural production is to be increased in the underdeveloped countries. The goal set by the FAO in *Agriculture: Toward 2000* (1981:73) calls for "a steep increase in the use of commercial energy." The scenario for an improved standard of living calls for a growth in energy consumption of 2.4% per year, in order to yield a 1% increase in agricultural production.

However, these figures may be too optimistic. Bhatia (1985:331-334) reports that between 1972 and 1980 commercial energy consumption in agriculture in the major South Asian countries and China rose 117%, while agricultural output increased by only 28%. This suggests that a 1% increase in agricultural output requires a 4.2% increase in energy use. Bhatia argues that this pattern is true for all the developing regions, although the energy requirement drops to 1.8% for Latin America. Increased energy use comes with high-response seed varieties, irrigation, and then mechanization.

The fundamental characteristic of the world's energy resources is the unequal distribution in consumption, production, proved reserves, and ultimate resources. Furthermore, over the past twenty-five years there has not been any change in the general pattern of consumption; there has been no significant shift in distribution to aid the underdeveloped countries.

Pearce (1981:343) shows that between 1960 and 1979 the share of total world energy consumption controlled by the industrialized capitalist and state socialist countries fell only slightly, from 87% to 79%. This was in spite of increased consumption in the oil-rich countries (OEPC states) and the upper middle-income underdeveloped countries. His breakdown also reveals that oil and coal remain the most commonly used sources of energy. Over the 20-year period the share of total energy provided by natural gas rose from 14.6% to 18.6%; that provided by electricity rose from 2.1% to 8.1%.

Nevertheless, in spite of oil price increases, energy consumption has steadily increased, even in the oil-importing, underdeveloped countries. Choe (1985:304) reports that between 1973 and 1982 the average annual increase in energy consumption in the oil-importing underdeveloped countries was 5.2%. O'Keefe and Kristoferson (1984:168) report that commercial energy consumption in Africa rose between 1972 and 1982 at an annual rate of 6.6%. But the gap remained enormous: the average North American consumed 336 gigajoules while the average African consumed only 14 gigajoules of commercial energy.

Petroleum fuels are the normal fuel used in agriculture, everywhere. Oil is the preferred fuel because of its adaptability, regular quality, easy transportability and storage, and a well-organized world market. It is also widely recognized that the underdeveloped countries have a very limited capacity to shift from conventional oil to other forms of energy. Coal has been competitive in terms of price, if not utility. Natural gas, while an important source of energy in the industrialized countries, is not expected to be a major factor in energy use in underdeveloped countries; two-thirds of the world's reserves are in the USSR and Iran. Synthetic oil, lignite gasification, shale oil, liquids from coal, and biomass energy from crops are all more expensive than conventional oil or coal. Electricity from hydroelectric or nuclear generators has been more expensive because of the capital costs involved in the construction phase. (Dafter, 1982:12; Pearce, 1981:341; Caldwell, 1977:17-22)

Table IXb shows trends in the per capita distribution of commercial energy between 1960 and 1980. Over that twenty-year period energy consumption almost doubled in industrialized capitalist countries. Per capita consumption in industrialized state socialist countries increased even more rapidly. Though per capita energy consumption increased in low-

TABLE IXb *Per Capita Commercial Energy Consumption, 1960-1980*

Countries	Kg Coal Equivalent		% Ind/ME Average	
	1960	1980	1960	1980
China	683	736	15.0	9.8
India	142	197	3.1	2.6
Other Low Income States (34)	58	107	1.3	1.4
Lower Middle Income States (39)	218	504	4.8	6.7
Upper Middle Income States (21)	798	1677	17.6	22.4
Industrial Market Economy States (19)	4540	7495	—	—
USSR	2896	6422	63.8	85.7
Eastern European States (7)	2858	5733	62.9	76.5

NOTE: 1980 figures for China and India are estimates from World Bank data.

SOURCE: World Bank, *World Development Report, 1983, 1982*, Table 8; Food and Agricultural Organization, *Production Yearbook*, 1961, 1981, Table 3.

TABLE IXc   Oil Extraction, Reserves and Trade, 1978-1982

Million Metric Tonnes

Countries	Extraction		Crude Exports		Crude Imports		Reserves, 1985	
	Tonnes	% Total	Tonnes	% Total	Tonnes	% Total	Tonnes	% Total
North Africa and Middle East	1,049.9	35.4	944.9	64.4	42.8	2.9	59,341.8	62.0
Sub-Sahara Africa	110.7	3.7	104.5	7.1	19.1	1.3	2,839.3	2.9
Central America and Caribbean	110.8	3.7	53.3	3.6	55.8	3.8	6,800.1	7.1
South America	176.8	6.0	73.6	5.0	52.9	3.6	4,613.0	4.8
Asia[1]	134.7	4.5	79.2	5.4	123.0	8.3	2,213.4	2.4
China	103.7	3.5	11.6	0.8	—	—	2,616.4	2.7
All Underdeveloped [2]	**1,686.6**	**56.8**	**1,267.1**	**86.3**	**293.6**	**19.9**	**78,424.0**	**81.9**
United States	436.1	14.7	3.4	0.2	290.8	19.7	3,739.7	3.9
Canada	71.4	2.4	12.1	0.8	28.2	1.9	969.2	1.0
Australia/New Zealand	21.8	0.7	0.2	—	12.3	0.8	217.3	0.2
Japan	0.5	—	—	—	220.9	15.0	7.7	—
Western Europe	134.5	4.5	63.5	4.3	522.5	35.4	3,345.9	3.5
Industrial MEs	**664.3**	**22.3**	**79.2**	**5.3**	**1,074.7**	**72.8**	**8,279.8**	**8.6**
USSR	596.4	20.1	122.0	8.3	4.9	0.3	8,630.1	9.0
Eastern Europe	21.2	0.7	—	—	100.9	6.8	273.9	0.3
Industrial CPEs	**617.6**	**20.8**	**122.0**	**8.3**	**105.8**	**7.1**	**8,904.0**	**9.3**
World Totals	**2,963.5**	**100.0**	**1,468.3**	**100.0**	**1,474.1**	**100.0**	**95,607.8**	**100.0**

[1] Excluding China and Japan.
[2] Underdeveloped Countries.

SOURCE: *International Petroleum Encyclopedia, 1985; British Geological Survey, World Mineral Statistics, 1978-1982.*

income underdeveloped countries, the gap between them and the already-industrialized countries remains. The upper-middle income countries, including the oil-rich countries of North Africa and the Middle East, have closed the gap slightly and now consume around one-quarter of the energy of the industrialized west.

The basic data on oil extraction, trade, and proved reserves are presented in Table IXc. The main area of extraction and proved reserves is in North Africa and the Middle East. In sub-Sahara Africa the only major known reserves are in Nigeria. In Latin America the only major known reserves are in Mexico and Venezuela. The largest Asian reserves are in Indonesia, where they are limited and declining, and in China, where they are small on a per capita basis.

The only major European source of oil already discovered is in the North Sea and controlled by Norway and the United Kingdom. Canada's reserves are limited and declining. The United States has substantial reserves, but, in terms of consumption patterns, they are limited. The USSR has extensive reserves, but even here extraction is peaking and the discovery of new reserves is slowing. (*International Petroleum Encyclopedia*, 1985:258-259, 316-320; *World Oil*, February 15, 1985:167-170; *Oil & Gas Journal*, September 9, 1985:59-62)

Oil has been the key to industrialization, a higher standard of living, and the advanced technology of the modern military machine. The most striking figure revealed in Table IXc is the extent to which the industrialized capitalist countries rely on petroleum imports from the underdeveloped countries. Over the 1978-1982 period they were annual net importers of almost 1,000 million tonnes of oil. The eastern Europe countries, very short of oil, obtain their supply primarily from the Soviet Union.

The regions of sub-Sahara Africa, Central America, and Latin America are net exporters of oil. Only Asia shows a deficit. But these data mask the fact that most of the countries in the underdeveloped world are net importers of petroleum products.

The key question is whether the underdeveloped countries will be able to obtain the fossil fuels they need to increase food production, to industrialize, and to provide a general improvement in the standard of living, given that the industrialized states control the energy markets. One approach to the question of resource scarcity has been that of the orthodox economists (see Chapter II): all that is needed to expand mineral reserves is additional exploration and better technology. Is this true in the case of petroleum resources?

Since the first discovery of oil, more than 30,000 gas and oil fields have been found. However, the rate of discovery of new reserves is slowing while the amount of exploration and drilling is increasing. Most of the world's sedimentary basins have been explored. The number of large fields discovered peaked in the 1950s and has declined drastically in the 1970s. The main remaining sources of potential new oil fields are the deep offshore areas or polar regions. (Schumacher, 1983:50-51) The 1985 report of the U.S. Geological Survey on world petroleum resources concludes that discoveries of oil appear to be on a permanent decline, and extraction and consumption are outpacing new discoveries by almost two to one. (*The Globe and Mail*, September 26, 1985) Erickson (1985:3-4) points out that, over the last decade, additions to proved world reserves have run at about 50% of world extraction. The new discoveries tend to be in "hostile and/or remote environs."

There is a significant gap between the actual oil in the ground and what is commonly referred to as "ultimately recoverable oil." Success in extraction depends on science, technology, economics, and energetic constraints. Since the 1970s there has been a convergence of opinion on what is actually ultimately recoverable. The 1980 World Energy Conference set the figure at around 2,000 billion barrels or 275 billion tonnes. (Schumacher, 1983:51; Brown, 1981:69-70; Barney, I, 1980:27)

The reserves cited in Table IXc are "proved reserves," defined as "known deposits which can be extracted, given existing technical and economic capabilities." Since the rise in oil prices in 1973 and 1979 there has been a shift to the development of other energy resources, particularly in the industrialized countries. Nevertheless, at 1984 levels of extraction and consumption (2,698 million tonnes) the world's proved reserves of conventional oil would last only 33 years. (*International Petroleum Encyclopedia*, 1985:259, 320)

The other major source of energy is coal, and figures on extraction and recoverable reserves are cited in Table IXd. At the present time, world trade in coal is marginal, accounting for only 6.5% of the total extracted over the 1978-1982 period. The major exporters are the United States, Australia, South Africa, Poland, and the USSR. Japan, western Europe, and eastern Europe are the major importers. World extraction and recoverable reserves are concentrated in the Northern hemisphere; from a geological perspective, the southern hemisphere has significantly fewer large sedimentary basins. While it is more economical to mine coal through open pit or strip mining methods, most of the world's deposits can only be mined through underground operations.

The World Energy Conference classifies coal deposits into two main categories based on energy content: (1) hard coal, including bituminous coal and anthracite and (2) brown coal, including sub-bituminous coal and lignite. However, individual countries have their own classifications.

As with petroleum resources, world extraction of coal is highly concentrated: 10 countries account for 98% of the world's extraction and 90% of the world's reserves. Of these ten, only China, India, and South Africa are in the underdeveloped category. The *World Coal Study* listed the top four countries in terms of percentage of world reserves as the United States

TABLE IXd   *Coal Extraction and Reserves, 1978-1982*

Million Metric Tonnes

Countries	Extraction Tonnes	Extraction % Total	Reserves 1980	% Total
North Africa and Middle East	25.9	0.2	1,182	0.1
Sub-Sahara Africa	121.5	3.2	34,904	2.5
Central America and Caribbean	7.2	0.2	882	0.1
South America	11.8	0.3	10,098	1.0
Asia[1]	198.5	5.3	41,696	4.2
China	627.4	16.6	109,130	10.9
All Underdeveloped	992.3	26.3	197,892	19.8
United States	714.5	18.9	246,100	24.6
Canada	36.5	0.9	6,510	0.6
Australia/New Zealand	125.8	3.3	65,410	6.5
Japan	17.9	0.5	—	—
Western Europe	424.5	11.2	118,940	11.9
Industrial MEs	1,319.2	35.0	426,960	43.7
USSR	711.9	18.9	256,840	25.7
Eastern Europe	747.4	19.8	108,090	10.8
Industrial CPEs	1,459.3	38.7	364,930	36.5
World Totals	3,770.8	100.0	999,782	100.0

[1]Excluding China and Japan

SOURCE: *International Petroleum Encyclopedia, 1985;* British Geological Survey, *World Mineral Statistics, 1978-1982;* Loftness, *Energy Handbook,* 1984.

(25.2%), the USSR (16.4%), China (14.9%) and Poland (9%). (Wilson, 1980:161) However, in 1982 the U.S. Department of Energy listed the USSR as having the largest reserves, 26.3% of the total. (Loftness, 1984:35-36)

In contrast to petroleum, all regions in the underdeveloped world are net importers of coal. The *World Coal Study* estimated that the underdeveloped countries had only 25.6% of recoverable reserves; the U.S. Energy Department puts the total even lower, at 18%. The number with significant known reserves is very limited: China, India, Brazil, Botswana, and Vietnam. (Greene and Gallagher, 1980:523-525; Loftness, 1984:36)

There are, of course, other potential sources of energy. The World Energy Conference in 1980 estimated total resources of oil shale at 330,000 million tonnes, of which 46.3 million tonnes were deemed to be recoverable. These are concentrated in the United States, the USSR, Morocco, and Thailand. The main constraints are the environmental costs of the extraction process and the fact that more energy might be required in extraction than would be recovered by it. (Schumacher, 1983:54-55; Loftness, 1984:47)

The world's resources of petroleum from tar sands are estimated at around 116,000 million tonnes, of which 40,000 million tonnes are considered proved recoverable resources. These are almost all in the Athabasca deposit in Canada and the Orinoco belt in Venezuela. At the Alberta Syncrude operation it is necessary to mine and heat two tonnes of tar sand just to produce one barrel of oil. Because of the high capital costs involved, the energy needed for the extraction process, and the enormous environmental problems associated with it, it is doubtful if the tar sands will make any significant contribution to world energy resources. (Schumacher, 1983:54-55; Loftness, 1984:44)

Because of the extensive amount of coal available, coal liquification has been promoted as an alternative source of oil. But this process is also capital- and energy-intensive and requires an enormous amount of water. The synfuel plant at Cattlesburg, Kentucky requires 250 short tons of coal to produce 625 barrels of oil.

Projections for energy use in the underdeveloped countries were made at the 1983 World Energy Conference. Two scenarios were proposed. The first assumed that the world economy would revive following the 1981-83 recession and "business as usual" would return. The second scenario assumed increasing international tensions, especially between the industrialized world and the Third World.

The Conference assumed that the demand for energy would continue to increase in the underdeveloped world, if only because of expected population growth. Under the first (or favourable) scenario, they projected an increase in demand for commercial energy of around 2.4% per annum. But even here the Conference concluded that energy use would continue to grow in the industrialized world and that there would not be any "catching up."

In sub-Sahara Africa it was noted that in 1978 around 80% of all energy sources used were non-commercial (mainly firewood and dung); the total commercial energy consumed by the entire region was about equal to that of Norway. While there is hydroelectric potential, even under the best scenario the region's share of world energy production was expected to remain low, around 3%.

Per capita consumption of energy in South Asia is very low. Their primary source of commercial energy is low grade lignite coal, which is highly polluting. The Conference projected that Southeast Asia would increasingly depend on energy imports, both oil and coal. Latin America was the only region with adequate energy sources, mainly oil. But even these would be decreasing by the year 2020. (Frisch, 1983:xxix-xlx)

The overall long-term picture is not very encouraging. Recoverable reserves of oil are limited. In the underdeveloped world, 75% of the proved petroleum reserves are in one area, North Africa and the Middle East. The already industrialized countries have close to 80% of the recoverable coal reserves. But, in addition, the industrialized capitalist countries are rapidly consuming the Third World's energy resources.

The Key Role of Mineral Resources

It can be misleading to concentrate on the role of energy in agriculture and economic development. As Skinner (1980:160) points out, energy and mineral extraction and use are closely intertwined. Modern industrial agriculture depends on the use of farm machinery and the key fertilizers: phosphorus, nitrogen, and potassium. "A failure in the supply of one resource will inevitably influence the use of others." Without the metals we derive from minerals, we would not be able to build the machines that replace human and animal muscle.

The question raised here is whether there are enough energy and mineral resources to sustain the ever-growing demand for consumer goods in the industrialized countries and at the same time allow the majority of people in the underdeveloped countries to close the gap in the standard of living. A brief survey of extraction and consumption patterns reveals that the already industrialized countries not only are quickly exhausting their own reserves of key minerals, they are becoming more and more dependent on imports from the underdeveloped world. In the past, imperialism and colonialism allowed the western countries to acquire the raw materials necessary for their development. Today, the resources of the underdeveloped countries are sold on the world market where the industrialized countries can outbid the poor countries. Under either system, the end result is not very different; the resources of the underdeveloped world feed the industrial system of the rich countries.

This brings us back to the ideological debate on the cause of world hunger, as introduced in Chapter II. The publication of *The Limits to Growth* (1972) centred public attention on the question of non-renewable resources, including minerals. The Club of Rome's general position was that which Malthus had applied to agricultural land: there is a fixed amount of mineral resources, and as it is used up it becomes more costly to obtain the next unit of extraction. Eventually, the world would run out of key minerals.

The most widely cited alternative view was that expressed earlier by Barnett and Morse (1963), reflecting the optimistic view of orthodox economists. The optimists argue that (1) science and technology will continually improve, reducing the cost of mineral extraction; (2) minerals are widely dispersed in the earth's crust, and the true extent of resources is unknown because much of the world remains unexplored; (3) the market-place will solve the problem by making possible the extraction of lower grade ores as prices rise; (4) as the prices of metals rise because of scarcities, the market guarantees a shift to recycling and the development of substitutes; and (5) as higher grade ores are exhausted, lower grade ores are made available in greater abundance.

There are some obvious problems with the orthodox resource model advanced by Barnett and Morse. First, the data base for the study was limited to the experience of one country, the United States, from 1870 to 1957. This was a unique period in a resource- and capital-rich country, and it is obviously quite different from a world model. Second, there is inadequate attention given to the fact that, as the United States began to deplete its own reserves of high grade ores, it shifted to importing them from other countries. Third, in a world model the substitution of scarce minerals by other mineral resources can only be a short-term solution. Furthermore, it can also result in decreased quality of performance, as in the use of aluminum for copper in wiring and plastic for copper in plumbing. Fourth, they failed to recognize the central role of energy in mineral extraction. Finally, the free-market approach to resource allocation does not take into account existing inequalities of income, wealth, and power, nor the needs of future generations.

In Chapter II it was pointed out that many scientists, and, in particular, geologists, are very skeptical of what they often call the naive optimism of economists who are generally ignorant of geology and the mining process. For example, Chapman and Roberts (1983:24-26) recount the experience of a conference of scientists and economists meeting in Sweden in 1976 to discuss the resource issue. The economists were puzzled by the insistence of the scientists and engineers that energy was not just one factor of production in mineral extraction but a special one for which there was no substitute and for which there were minimum requirements. The scientists were surprised to find that the economists knew relatively little about the laws of thermodynamics.

There are 88 natural elements widely dispersed in the earth's crust. However, only 12 of them are present in amounts equal to or greater than 0.1% of the whole; these 12 elements account for 99.23% of the total. Of the 12, only aluminum, iron, magnesium, titanium, and manganese are widely used in industrial production. The other 76 elements, many of which are key ingredients to modern industrial production, are geochemically scarce.

Furthermore, when prospectors and miners seek mineral sources for metals they do not go to the average crustal rock but seek concentrations formed by some special natural process. The desired mineral is often in a concentration normally less than 0.5%; the point at which the element becomes a mineral in an economic sense is usually at a concentration of 0.01 to 0.1 percent. For example, in 1977 the minimum concentrations of ore actually being mined were many times higher than the average concentrations found in common crustal rock. The following are a few examples: tin, 62; copper, 100; nickel, 160; manganese, 200; cobalt, 275; zinc, 300; chromium, 928; molybdenum, 2275; and tungsten, 4150.

After the ore is mined, the concentration process removes the unwanted minerals. The high-grade ore is smelted and refined and the desired metal is recovered. This is a very energy-intensive part of metal production. Again, to keep energy requirements as low as possible, mining companies do not seek minerals from the common silicate sources that are the bulk of the earth's crust; they seek minerals concentrated in the form of sulfides, oxides, hydroxides, and carbonates. The extraction of minerals from silicates increases the energy requirement by a factor of 100 to 1,000. For geochemically scarce minerals, rich concentrates are even more important. As geologists point out, what makes an ore body worth mining is its very *uncommon* characteristics. (Brobst, 1979:119-123; Cloud, 1977:277-279; Skinner, 1976:160-162)

The key factor in the extraction of mineral ores (including energy minerals) is the energy required. Cloud (1977:277-278) uses the cases of aluminum, iron, copper, and titanium to demonstrate that as the grade of the ore declines the energy cost of metal production rises dramatically, creating "cutoff grades — concentrations below which ores of a given type will not yield metals at tolerable prices and existing technologies." Recent studies show that fuel use in mining in the United States has increased per unit of output over the period 1954-1972. (Chapman and Roberts, 1983:21) In 1975 16% of all energy use in the United States took place in mineral extraction and refinement. (Cloud, 1977:277)

Chapman and Roberts (1983:192-196) conclude their study of metal resources and energy by arguing that the Malthusian model is inappropriate for the question of metal availability. It is impossible to determine the ultimate stock of mineral resources, the size of future populations, the demand for metals, and the development of technology. The earth's crust and water contain enormous quantities of low-grade minerals. Chapman and Roberts argue that the model advanced by Ricardo is much more appropriate. Ricardo was not concerned about the ultimate limit of a resource. Instead, he observed that there was a wide range in the *quality* of the resources available. As the higher quality resources are utilized, the quality of the remaining resources declines, necessitating a greater use of inputs to extract the next equivalent unit. In mineral extraction or land use for agriculture, this is reflected in "diminishing returns" or higher costs. Chapman and Roberts and many others note that the key factors in mineral extraction are the grade of the ore, its accessibility, and the energy costs required to convert it to metal.

The only factor that could possibly offset lower grades and increasing costs would be an exponential increase in technology and efficiency of extraction. This is a key assumption in the resource model set forth by Barnett and Morse (1963:197-201), and is usually found in the more recent studies by their ideological disciples. For example, Goeller and Zucker (1984) of the U.S. Oak Ridge National Laboratory conclude that there are adequate reserves of non-renewable resources to last until at least 2050, which provides adequate time to develop substitutes and new methods of extraction of low-grade resources. Surprisingly, the energy factor is left out of their analysis. A key assumption in their model is that "science and technology are capable of altering the human condition in unforeseeable ways and that many of the technical solutions which are now but dimly perceived will prove to be realistic." (456)

In contrast, Chapman and Roberts (1983:78-95) note that technologists are "strongly aware" of the limits to engineering efficiency and the difficulty of continually achieving improvements. They conclude that, whether one uses the ultimate thermodynamic limits to energy use or the more practical limit of capital-to-fuel-cost ratio, most of the improvements in technical efficiency have already been made. Thus, *the law of diminishing returns also applies to technology*, and exponential improvements simply cannot occur.

Any analysis of the world's mineral resources begins with a definition of reserves and resources. What is defined as a reserve is that quantity of the total stock of a mineral proven to exist and commercially exploitable, given existing technologies. Of course, reserves can change with the introduction of new technologies. (Ray, 1984:76; Chapman and Roberts, 1983:44-45) A resource (or potential resource) is merely an estimate of what proportion of the total stock of the mineral may possibly be extracted in the future under different technologies and at higher capital and energy costs. Cloud (1977:279) concludes that we can estimate with some confidence the resources of some minerals whose geological occurrence is well understood, such as coal, oil, natural gas, iron, aluminum, magnesium, and the silicates. For the other minerals, the potential is much more uncertain and much less ample.

Nevertheless, Skinner (1980:165-167) argues that our experience in mining ores provides us with enough evidence to argue that the available resource is directly proportional to the geochemical abundance of the element. The evidence indicating that discovered reserves of scarce metals are proportional to crustal abundance was first pointed out by McKelvey (1960). In addition, Skinner has found that the size of the largest known deposit of each scarce metal and the number of deposits that contain a million or more tonnes of a given metal are also proportional to the average content of the continental crustal abundance of the element.

The geochemically scarce minerals, including mercury, gold, silver, copper, and lead, are being used at a much faster rate than the abundant minerals. Skinner (1976:167-169) argues that this "unbalanced situation" cannot long continue the calls for a "second iron age" where technology is concentrated on making use of the more abundant minerals.

Chapman and Roberts (1983:169-172) point out that industrialization depends on a continuous supply of ferrous and non-ferrous metals. The commonly used metals like iron and aluminum depend on a variety of alloys, the "vitamin elements," which greatly improve their properties; without these additives, modern metal industries could not meet the specifications required for most end products. Thus the successful utilization of the common metals depends on the availability of the scarce minerals.

Of concern to economists and geopoliticians is the relative insecurity of supply of certain key or critical metals. Of the 36 key minerals surveyed by Ray (1984:79-80), fourteen are highly concentrated in a small number of countries. South Africa leads the list with five: the platinum group, 80%; chromium, 70%; and gold, manganese, and vanadium, 50%. Zaire is the next most important state with 50% of the world's tantalum and 40% of the world's diamonds and cobalt. Chile has 50% of the lithium and 40% of the rhenium, and Brazil has 70% of the world's niobium. For many of the other key mineral resources, the largest reserves are in the Soviet Union. (Chapman and Roberts, 1983:170-173)

All of these factors are important in assessing whether or not the presently underdeveloped countries will be able to close the gap with the industrialized countries in food production and standard of living. Skinner (1980:169) notes that 150 years ago England was a major exporter of copper, lead, tin, and other scarce metals, but is now a major importer of minerals. The same trend is evident for the United States. Cloud (1977:278) lists the key minerals in U.S. industrial production in 1975 and reports that for twenty-one of them over 50% of consumption is imported. The major sources of its mineral imports are U.S. client states in the underdeveloped world, plus Canada and Australia.

Ray (1984:80) points out that of the 36 minerals covered in his survey, the European Economic Community is totally dependent on imports for 13 and, for another 8, imports account for only slightly less than 100% of consumption. Chapman and Roberts (1983:183) list import dependence for eight commonly used industrial minerals. With three exceptions (U.S. imports of lead, 13%; copper, 15%; iron ore, 36%), the United Kingdom, the European Economic Community, Japan, and the United States are all heavily dependent on imports, ranging between 60% and 100% of total consumption.

The Brandt Report (1980:154) pointed out that about 70% of the world's imports of fuel and non-fuel minerals comes from the underdeveloped world. The consumers are the already industrialized countries. For six of the most important minerals used in industrialization, Goeller and Zucker (1984:457) calculate that in 1980 consumption by the underdeveloped countries was only 15% of total world demand. On a per capita basis, demand in the underdeveloped countries was only 6% of the demand in the industrialized countries.

My own survey (Table IXe) covers seven key minerals for industrial development plus phosphate rock, the most essential element in modern industrial agriculture and the one input for which there are limited reserves and no substitute. The data in this table are confined to ores and concentrates, excluding the refining process. Nevertheless, the data reveal that the underdeveloped countries are major extractors of key minerals and that a large percentage of the raw material is exported. If one expands the table to include refinement of the ore to an unwrought state, the percentage of the mineral that is exported rises dramatically: copper, almost 100%; zinc, 82%; tin, 76% and lead, 57%. For all eight of the minerals, the industrialized capitalist states are heavily dependent on imports from the underdeveloped countries. Despite the vast resources in the Soviet Union, the industrialized state socialist countries are now also beginning to import significant amounts of key minerals from underdeveloped countries.

TABLE IXe   *Mineral Extraction and Trade, 1978-1982*

Thousand Metric Tonnes

Minerals	Under-Developed Countries	Industrialized Market Economies	Industrialized Centrally Planned
(1) Bauxite Ore	40,774	32,303	11,436
Exports (Imports)	23,565	(22,631)	(4,195)
(2) Copper Ore	3,986	2,451	1,550
Exports (Imports)	1,541	(3,843)	(119)
(3) Iron Ore	332,693	280,638	259,209
Exports (Imports)	149,783	(135,400)	(5,267)
(4) Lead Ore and Concentrates	1,053	1,630	745
Exports (Imports)	351	(650)	(35)
(5) Nickel Ore	318	270	186
Exports (Imports)	3,342	(3,729)	—
(6) Tin Ore and Concentrates	193	16	38
Exports (Imports)	(10)	(36)	(2)
(7) Zinc Ore	1,654	3,185	1,181
Exports (Imports)	719	(1,808)	(165)
(8) Phosphate Rock	63,012	51,831	25,500
Exports (Imports)	22,799	(17,227)	(1,890)

NOTE: "Underdeveloped countries" include all Asian centrally planned economies. "Industrialized market economies" are the members of the OECD except Turkey. "Industrialized centrally planned" economies include the USSR and eastern Europe (including Yugoslavia).

SOURCE: U.S. Department of the Interior, Bureau of Mines. *Minerals Yearbook, 1983.* British Geological Survey. *World Mineral Statistics, 1978-1982.*

Given these patterns of extraction and consumption, Trainer (1983) attempts to determine whether there are enough mineral resources available to allow the underdeveloped world to move towards an American standard of living. Using a scenario based on a world population of 11 billion by the mid-21st century (the World Bank projection), and U.S. consumption rates for minerals at a mid-1970s level, he concludes that for the 27 most commonly used minerals the rate of discovery would have to average 9.4 times what it was during the period 1950-1974. (45-46) Water consumption would be 12.5 times that of 1975. Wood consumption would be seven times 1977 production. Fertilizer extraction and production would have to increase 13 times. (47) Energy production would have to rise to nine times what it was in 1979, and all mineral reserves would be consumed in around 18 years. (48-49) The overall picture presented is that the underdeveloped world is poor and is likely to remain so, if "business as usual" continues, because at current rates of extraction and consumption "the West will soon have used up most of what is left to use." (51)

Financing Agricultural Development

The third key factor in increasing food production is the availability of capital. In the major study, *Agriculture: Toward 2000* (1981:58-60), the FAO hoped that agricultural production would increase at an annual rate of 3.7% between 1980 and 2000. To reach this target, it estimated that a capital investment of $1,690 billion would be required. Most of this would come from domestic sources. Yet it concluded that the average annual external assistance to the underdeveloped countries would have to rise to $12.5 billion by 1990 and $18 billion by the year 2000. If the underdeveloped countries continue to have serious foreign exchange problems, then this assistance would have to rise by an additional $5 billion per year.

However, the FAO noted (117) that in the mid-1970s average annual capital and technical assistance to the underdeveloped countries for agriculture was running less than $5 billion. While there are some differences in defining assistance to agriculture, the World Bank (1982:51) reports that official assistance to agriculture peaked in 1978. The percentage of gross national product devoted to foreign assistance in general by the OECD countries peaked in 1960 at 0.51%; by the early 1980s it had levelled off at around 0.38%. Total assistance from OPEC countries peaked at 2.92% of GNP in 1975 and declined to 1.65% in 1982. (World Bank, 1984: Table 18, 252)

More recent reports indicate that assistance to agriculture is falling behind stated goals. In 1983 the FAO reported that direct assistance to agriculture (land and water development, crop production and livestock) was still 40% below the target set by the member countries, $8.3 billion at 1975 prices. The level of actual assistance ($5.1 billion) was only 40% of the goal of $12.5 billion set for 1990. The world-wide recession led to an actual decline in total assistance in 1981 and 1982. (FAO, 1983:34-36)

The increase in the general rate of inflation began around 1965, largely as a result of the U.S. government's massive spending on the Vietnam war. Inflation received an additional push with cereal shortages in 1972-3 and the rise in oil prices in 1973-4. In the mid-1970s the central bankers of the industrialized capitalist countries concluded that inflation was the most serious economic problem facing the world. They, and the newly elected conservative governments, began introducing tight money policies and cutting back spending on social programs. The result was the great recession of 1981-1983, the worst the capitalist world had seen since the 1930s. The economies in the more industrialized middle-income countries in Asia continued to grow at acceptable levels. Economic performance was better in those underdeveloped countries which rejected monetarist policies, were less dependent on exporting raw materials, and had a tradition of strong state intervention in the economy. Most notable in this category were India and China. In contrast, most of the countries of Latin America and Africa had declining rates of growth and a drop in per capita income. (World Bank, 1983a:1-9)

Throughout the 1970s economic growth rates were relatively high in the underdeveloped countries. Much of this was due to a large inflow of capital in the form of loans from western banks, recycling royalties paid to the oil-exporting states. Prices for primary products rose until late 1975, because real interest rates were low. However, by the time the second round of oil price increases came, in 1979, the central banks of the industrialized capitalist countries had already introduced monetarist policies. This year was a watershed for borrowers in the underdeveloped countries: real interest rates rose sharply, prices for primary commodities began to fall, and trade deficits rose significantly. Governments continued to borrow in order to pay for imports. The prolonged recession in the industrialized capitalist countries and their protectionist measures against imports reduced overseas markets for the underdeveloped countries. (Goldsbrough, 1985:31-32; Naylor, 1983:95-99) Beginning in the third quarter of 1980, the terms of trade for most agricultural products experienced a steep decline in comparison to other major commodities and, in "income terms of trade," the relationship between prices for agricultural export commodities and the manufactured goods and crude petroleum they had to import. (FAO, 1982:20-22; 1983:31-33)

The external debt of all the underdeveloped countries rose from $332 billion to $865 billion between 1977 and 1985. Annual debt service payments rose from $39 billion to $139 billion. The total external debt in 1985 was the equivalent of 148% of all exports of goods and services; debt service payments had risen to 23% of all exports. For the indebted underdeveloped countries, the external debt had risen from 24.9% of gross domestic product in 1977 to 36.7% in 1985; for Africa south of the Sahara, it had risen to 68.9%. (IMF, 1985: Tables 44, 48)

Western banks reaped high returns on their investments in the 1970s. Interest rates were high. For example, in the early 1980s, Brazil, with the

largest external debt in the underdeveloped world, was paying 2.25% above
the world inter-bank rate. Many loans had floating interest rates. (Pratt,
1983:18) Between 1970 and 1982 the average rate of interest on loans to
the low-income underdeveloped countries rose from 2.8% to 4.9%. But
these loans were primarily from international institutions at concessional
rates. For the lower middle-income countries the average rate rose from
4.5% to 9.8% and, for the upper middle-income, from 6.9% to 13.2%. The
latter included the enormous loans made to Brazil, Mexico, Argentina, and
South Korea. During the same period of time the average length of maturity
of loans dropped significantly. (World Bank, 1984: Table 17)

Thus the 1970s produced some significant changes in foreign investment
in underdeveloped countries. First, there was a significant shift from direct
foreign investment in the form of equity to lending on the financial markets.
Second, there was a relative decline in official (government) lending and an
increase in private lending through the large western banks. Third, most of
the new lending by the financial institutions was directed to the middle-
income underdeveloped countries, particularly those that had shown high
growth rates in the 1960s and 1970s, were now diversifying into industrial
manufacturing, or were expanding exports of oil and other mineral resources. But for the borrowing countries, their debt position worsened
during the world recession of the early 1980s. In poor economic times,
returns on direct equity investments are also low because profits are low.
But bank loans have fixed payments that borrowers are obliged to pay
regardless of the world economic situation.

What we have seen in the late 1970s and early 1980s is something of a
return to the lending practices of the old colonial period, where portfolio
investments were the norm, and collection of interest was guaranteed by the
colonial power and its local agents. Now the international banks rely for this
on their governments, the official international lending institutions, the
international consortium of private financial lenders, and the local authori-
tarian governments. As Hoogvelt (1981:3-4) notes, the "degree of exploitation of labour and resources" is reminiscent of the old colonial days when
the imperial state directly intervened on behalf of capital to suppress wages,
make land grants to foreign enterprises, and control trading rights so as to
be sure of making profits outside the more competitive world market.

Several radical economists have pointed out that the process is leading to
debt peonage or enslavement, because most of the countries were borrowing to balance their current account trading deficits and/or to pay off
existing debt service commitments. Citing World Bank statistics, Sweezy
and Magdoff (1984:3-5) showed that debt service consumed 56.3% of all
new borrowing in 1972; by 1981 this percentage had risen to 75.3%. For
Latin America as a whole, it had risen to 85% of all new loans by the end of
1981. (World Bank, 1983b: Table 6)

Unless the underdeveloped countries were to start to obtain foreign
exchange through an expanded excess of exports over imports, borrowing
would have to increase. Pool and Stamos (1985:10, 14) have noted that the

underdeveloped countries are almost totally dependent on the importation of capital goods and technology in order to maintain their capacity to increase exports. Using Mexico as an example, they show that in 1982 interest and amortization on the external debt finally reached and exceeded the amount of new public loans. Chinweizu (1985:33) argues that of the $16 billion that Nigeria borrowed between 1978 and 1984, only around $4 billion was invested in productive enterprise; most of it was "squandered," primarily to finance the military and the luxury goods imported for the elite classes in the urban centres.

TABLE IXf   *Major Debtor Countries, 1982*

Country	Population Millions 1980	External Debt US$ Billions		Debt Service as a Percentage			
				GNP		Exports	
		1970	1982	1970	1982	1970	1982
Mexico	73	3.2	50.4	2.0	5.5	23.6	29.5
Brazil	127	3.2	47.6	0.9	3.5	12.5	42.1
South Korea	39	1.8	20.1	3.0	5.2	19.4	13.1
India	717	7.9	19.5	0.9	0.7	20.9	7.1
Indonesia	153	2.4	18.4	0.9	2.6	6.9	8.3
Turkey	47	1.8	15.9	1.3	3.4	16.3	19.6
Argentina	28	1.9	15.8	2.0	4.4	21.5	24.5
Egypt	44	1.6	15.5	4.1	6.4	28.7	20.2
Israel	4	2.3	14.9	0.7	9.2	2.7	20.8
Algeria	20	0.9	13.9	0.9	9.8	3.2	24.6
Venezuela	17	0.7	12.1	0.7	4.6	2.9	15.6
Philippines	51	0.6	8.8	1.4	2.6	7.2	12.8
Peru	19	0.9	6.9	2.1	7.4	11.6	36.7
Nigeria	91	0.5	6.1	0.6	1.9	4.2	9.5
Colombia	27	1.3	6.0	1.8	2.2	11.9	17.5
Zaire	31	0.3	4.1	2.1	2.6	4.4	n.a.
Low Income Underdeveloped				1.5	1.6	5.7	9.9
Lower Middle Income Underdeveloped				1.6	3.7	9.2	16.8
Upper Middle Income Underdeveloped				1.5	4.4	10.7	16.9

SOURCE: World Bank. *World Development Report, 1984:* World Bank, *Annual Report,* 1984.

With the world-wide recession, the international bankers cut back loans to the underdeveloped countries, particularly to those with serious debt problems. A critical point was reached for the world financial system, when in stepped the U.S. government, the Bank for International Settlements, the International Monetary Fund, the World Bank and the mysterious Club of Paris. The result has been the rescheduling of loans, rolling over the debt. As

Sweezy and Magdoff stress (1984:2, 8), the "rescue operation" was designed to save the overextended western banks and the international financial system and not the underdeveloped countries. For example, by 1982 the nine largest American banks had loaned $78 billion to the debtor countries; these loans amounting to 341% of their total equity capital.

The result of the intervention was to shift part of the risk from the banks to the general public. The banks collected fees for rescheduling the loans. The settlements followed the practice of the notorious Household Finance Corporation: loans were consolidated and spread over a longer period of time (usually eight to 10 years), and a higher interest rate was charged. An example would be the landmark settlement with Mexico; it stretched $48 billion of their total external debt over 14 years at an interest rate 1.12% above the interbank rate. Twenty-five countries rescheduled part of their debt in 1982; the amount totalled around $20 billion. (*The Globe and Mail* [Toronto], December 19, 1984; September 26, 1985)

In return for the restructuring of debt, the debtor country surrendered considerable sovereignty over internal economic decision-making. While the major debts of the underdeveloped countries are now held by the private banks, the IMF is given the responsibility of overseeing the settlement. Recounting Nigeria's experience in trying to negotiate a rescheduling agreement, Chinweizu (1985:23-24) reports that the IMF team arrives to inspect the books, approve the budget, and decide which social and economic programs are acceptable — just like the Colonial Office in the old days. The standard package of rescheduling includes (1) devaluation of the local currency; (2) elimination of exchange controls, import restrictions, and controls on foreign investment; (3) reduction of government spending on social programs but not on the military or the police; (4) wage restraints and the removal of price controls; (5) the elimination of central government budget deficits; (6) limitations on government borrowing and credit creation; and (7) a move to a "free market" economy. (Bernal, 1983:237-139; Perpinan, 1983:170-175; Loxley, 1983:204-207; Phillips, 1983:69-75) The result has been a serious deterioration in the standard of living of the ordinary people in the countries affected. As noted above, this often led to "IMF riots," particularly when food subsidies were reduced.

By 1985 even the conservative governments in office in the major capitalist countries began to admit that things were not going all that well. As a response to rather weak recovery from the long recession and continued high unemployment, they abandoned the policy of tight money. By the first quarter of 1985 the narrow money supply (or M1) was rising at an annual rate of 14% in the OECD countries. (*Times-Colonist* [Victoria], October 10, 1985) In September 1985 the Group of Five representatives (the United States, Japan, West Germany, France, and the United Kingdom) met to plan new ways to improve exchange rates, block rising protectionist pressures, and reduce the strength of the American dollar. (*The Globe and Mail* [Toronto], September, 23, 1985)

In the underdeveloped countries, the tough policies of the international bankers had prolonged the recession, reduced demand, and caused civil unrest. Real interest rates remained high; the average inflation rate rose from 25% in 1977 to 38% in 1984. Economic growth was non-existent in Latin America and declined for the fourth consecutive year in sub-Sahara Africa. To try to balance current account deficits, purchases of goods from the industrialized countries had been reduced. Furthermore, exports were expected to grow at only 0.25% in 1985. As a result, the debtor countries were still having a difficult time paying their interest charges on their external debt. (Applegate and Fennell, 1985:50) In September the Inter-American Development Bank released a detailed report by professor Albert Fishlow, highly critical of the tough line on debtors pursued by the international bankers, the U.S. government, and the IMF. (*The Globe and Mail* [Toronto], September 17 and 20, 1985)

At the October 1985 meeting of the Boards of the IMF and the World Bank at Seoul, Korea the U.S. government put forth a three-point program (known as the Baker Plan after the U.S. Secretary of the Treasury) to support "sustained growth." First, over the next three years the international banks were to extend an additional $40 billion in loans to the 15 most indebted countries; half would come from the private banks and half from the international institutions and government lending. Second, the debtor countries would continue to follow "comprehensive macroeconomic and structural policies" as specified in the terms of the conditional agreements. Third, the IMF would continue to police the accords with increased support from the World Bank. The proposal, which represented a major change of policy by the Reagan Administration, was accepted by the Boards. (Applegate and Fennell, 1985:50-51; *The Globe and Mail* [Toronto], December 13, 1985) However, the private banks have been unwilling to extend additional new credit; in the spring of 1986 they were limiting additional loans to the servicing of existing debts. Lending to the major debtor countries fell from $40 billion in 1984 to around $30 billion in 1985; at the same time, interest payments rose to $50 billion, resulting in a net outflow of around $22 billion. (*The Globe and Mail* [Toronto], April 8, 1986)

Thus the ability of the underdeveloped countries to reach the goals outlined by the FAO in *Agriculture: Toward 2000* has been seriously undermined by the economic and financial crisis of the first half of the 1980s. Debt payments have drained the underdeveloped world of foreign exchange and capital and reduced investment in agriculture. For a great many people in the underdeveloped world, the crisis has brought a reduced standard of living and a poorer diet. As Professor Fishlow pointed out in his report to the Inter-American Development Bank, the payment of interest and amortization on external debts worsened inflationary pressures and undermined long-term growth prospects in these countries.

Natural Limitations to Increasing Food Production

The need to increase agricultural production in the world is also constrained by some natural forces. One of the major limitations is the availability of water, both for rainfed agriculture and for irrigation. The FAO (1981:64-65) concludes that water resources will be in increasingly tight supply toward the end of the twentieth century. Water management in general has been a limiting factor in agricultural production in the past in the underdeveloped countries. The *Globe 2000 Report* estimated that over 50% of all investment in land development in the 1960s and 1970s went for irrigation, flood control, drainage, and soil-erosion control. The major problem with future water use is the increasing demand made on the already limited supply by other population and energy needs. (Barney, II, 1980:100-101)

As with other natural resources, the distribution of water is very uneven. Postel (1985:44-45) reports that Asia, with 58% of the world's population, receives only 26% of the world's average annual runoff of rainfall. In contrast, South America, with only 6% of the world's population, receives 27% of the runoff. But these regional figures are also misleading. For example, in South America 60% of the runoff flows through the Amazon river system, remote from most people and difficult to use. The Soviet Union and Canada are both blessed with a large share of the world's total runoff, but the major river systems flow north, far from centres of population and agricultural need.

In most areas of the world, agriculture is still the primary user of freshwater supplies. On a worldwide basis, the average is 70%. Irrigated land produces much higher yields, and increasing the amount of land under irrigation has been a primary goal of agricultural policy. However, the rate at which irrigated land has been added has been steadily declining over the period from 1950 to 1980. Much of the new irrigation has come from the use of tubewells, drawing on underground aquifers. In southern India, northern China, and many other areas of the world, water tables are falling, due to the mining of the resource, extracting more water than can be naturally replenished. (Postel, 1985:43, 47, 54)

Concerns about water quality are even greater in the underdeveloped countries than in the advanced industrialized countries. Water pollution is increasing rapidly, because of the lack of capital for water treatment systems. For example, in China only about 2% of the wastewater discharged per year is treated. In Latin America virtually all municipal and industrial effluents are discharged into local rivers without treatment. (Postel, 1985:50-51)

Finally, there is the question of competing use for already scarce water resources. The World Health Organization estimated in 1980 that 75% of rural households and 29% of urban households in the underdeveloped world were not served with drinking water. In most of the advanced industrialized countries, industry consumes between 60% and 80% of water withdrawals; in the underdeveloped countries, industrial use usually accounts for less than 10%. The largest consumers are power plants; two thirds of the remaining industrial use is accounted for by five industries: primary metals, chemical products, petroleum refining, pulp and paper manufacturing, and food processing. (Postel, 1985:48-51)

Agricultural production in underdeveloped countries is also constrained by biological limits on plant yields. Pimentel and Pimentel (1978:7), Crosson and Frederick (1977:62-63) and Brown (1981:100) have all noted that the average rate of increase in yields in cereals in the United States and Europe began to decline in the 1970s, despite a rapid increase in high-energy inputs. But the decline in the rate of increase of yields is not limited to the industrialized countries. For example, Egypt and China also reported declines in the 1970s. (Brown, 1981:27-28)

Jensen (1978:317-320), a plant breeder at Cornell University, points out that there are biological ceilings to yields that can be obtained from any land, and that there are limits to increases that can be obtained by additional farm inputs and research. Brown (1981:121) has argued that the major breakthroughs in agricultural technology have already been made: mechanization, hybrid cereals, fertilizers, and irrigation. Comparable advances in the future will be much harder to realize.

Other factors commonly cited for the decline in the rate of increase of yields are the expansion of cropping on marginal lands, the shortening of rotation cycles, cutting back on fallow periods, reduced fertility of the soil due to erosion, and the development of a less stable climate.

If the standard of living of peoples in the underdeveloped countries is to rise, then agricultural production and productivity must rise. When the output per hectare rises, there is an increase in agricultural production. But total factor productivity increases only if the output per hectare increases at a greater rate than all the inputs. Sampson (1981:177) points out that today's American farm family produces more food than their parents, but this is no proof that they work any harder or any more efficiently. The sole reason for increased production is the use of many more manufactured inputs.

It is widely recognized that the significant increase in agricultural production in the industrialized countries in the 1950s and 1960s was largely due to increased use of fertilizers. It now takes much more fertilizer to produce the same increase in crop yield. (Barney, II, 1980:99-100) Brown (1981:119) argues that on a world-wide basis the grain/fertilizer response has been steadily declining from 14.8 in the 1934-38 period to 6.8 in the 1978-80 period.

This evidence of diminishing returns is also widely reported in studies of fossil fuel energy substitutes in agricultural production. For example, Belyea and Tribe (1977:103) point out that fossil fuel subsidies in the form of agricultural inputs increased by 70% between 1952 and 1972, but the production of energy in food for human consumption rose by only 30%.

Climate is a factor in agricultural production, even though it is unfashionable to raise the point these days. The variation of precipitation is greater in the tropical areas than in the temperate zones. Rainfall is often too much or too little for crop production. In countries depending on the annual monsoon, its time of arrival can mean the difference between a good crop and a poor one. The long dry seasons increase wind erosion. When the heavy seasonal rains come, they result in much greater water erosion than is found in the temperate zones. Where tropical forests are cleared, flooding and erosion are even greater.

It has already been noted that pest problems are much greater in the tropical and semi-tropical areas than they are in the temperate zones. The diversity of species is much greater, and there are many more pests, including weeds. Monoculture, identified with modern agriculture, is more susceptible to attack from pests. The grasses used for grazing are often inferior to those in the temperate zone, due to low nitrogen levels, and domestic animals are more susceptible to intestinal parasites. Irrigation also tends to spread water-borne diseases. (Biswas, 1979:188-195; Pimentel and Pimentel, 1979)

Crop yields are also affected by the general variation in weather. For example, there has been a cooling trend in the northern hemisphere since around 1938. If this continues, it could reduce the growing season and production in the more northerly areas of Canada, China, and the USSR and perhaps re-establish the climatic patterns found in the early 19th century. Many have attributed this to the buildup of particles in the atmosphere during the period of industrialization and land clearing. (Idso, 1983:160-162; Boville and Doos, 1981:3-5; Moran et al, 1977:80-81; U.S. NAS, 1976:26-27)

However, the primary concern in recent years has been the buildup of carbon dioxide in the atmosphere as a result of burning fossil fuels. The general view of the scientific establishment is that continued burning of fuels, and continued deforestation, will double the carbon dioxide concentration in the atmosphere by the year 2065, and a "greenhouse effect" may result, producing a general rise in the earth's surface temperature of two to three degrees centigrade. A second result would be a wider variation in temperature increases and greater climatological uncertainty. This could produce a "climatic revolution" in the next century. A warming of the planet could render many agricultural areas too dry for cultivation; one area commonly cited is the great plains that stretch from the United States through the Canadian prairies. (U.S. NRC, 1983; Seidel and Keyes, 1983; Schware and Kellogg, 1982:40-42; Hare, 1980:113-115; Kellogg, 1978:14-17) However, a dissenting minority believe that the "greenhouse effect," if it happens, will be beneficial to agriculture through increased photosynthesis and more efficient use of existing water resources (although more nitrogen would be needed). (Idso, 1983:160-162; Wittwer, 1980:116-120)

While the scientists have not reached a consensus on the issue of carbon dioxide buildup in the atmosphere, the controversy emphasizes the fact that humans are already heavily dependent on producing food from marginal farming areas. As Hare (1980:113-114) stresses, climate has always varied; what has changed is the increased vulnerability of the human economy.

Conclusion

There is no reason to believe that food production will not continue to increase in the underdeveloped world. However, there is a tremendous task at hand if production is to expand to meet the needs of the expected increase in population *and* to improve the general quality of diet. These are commonly cited goals. Over the long run it is clear that there are considerable constraints.

The academic experts can produce maps and figures to indicate that we can double or triple the amount of land under cultivation. But anyone with any experience in farming can understand why this land is not presently being farmed. Aside from the important economic questions, most of the potential new farmland lies in the hostile humid tropics or semi-tropical areas where water shortages are well known. There are good reasons why these areas are scantily populated. The reality is that the best farmland in the world is already being farmed.

The best hope for improving food production in the underdeveloped world is to increase yields on land already under cultivation. This will require heavy fossil fuel subsidies as more fertilizers and pesticides are applied, more land is brought under irrigation, and mechanization is expanded. As this chapter has stressed, there are indications that the necessary energy and mineral resources may not be available. At present, the central problem is that these key resources are consumed by the already industrialized countries who are able to control world markets through their superior purchasing power.

The ability of the underdeveloped countries to finance their own agricultural expansion has been limited by their mounting external debt, debt service requirements, and lack of foreign exchange. The huge outflow of capital in the 1980s has seriously limited domestic investment. Unless this debt burden is removed, agricultural and other necessary development will be significantly restricted.

Finally, the long-term constraints have been noted. In many areas where there is good soil, the key problem is lack of water. There are also biological limits to yields on any farmland. In most underdeveloped countries there is the reality of a climate both hostile and variable. We don't know how much pollution the world can absorb. All of these constraints point to the need to put a high priority on the sustainable use of existing foodland resources and the conservation of key non-renewable resources. The most difficult problem remains: how do we abolish poverty and hunger in a world where governments are hostile to the ethical ideal of egalitarianism?

References

Anthony, Kenneth R.M. et al (1979). *Agricultural Change in Tropical Africa*. Ithaca: Cornell University Press.

Applegate, Charles and Susan Fennell (1985). "Cooperating for Growth and Adjustment." *Finance & Development*, XXII, No. 4, December, pp. 50-53.

Barnett, H.J. and C. Morse (1963). *Scarcity and Growth*. Baltimore: Johns Hopkins Press for Resources for the Future.

Barney, Gerald O., ed. (1980). *The Global 2000 Report to the President*. Volume I: The Summary Report. New York: Pergamon Press.

Barney, Gerald O., ed. (1980). *The Global 2000 Report to the President*. Volume II: The Technical Report. Washington, D.C.: U.S. Government Printing Office.

Belyea, J. and D.E. Tribe (1977). "Energy Use in Agricultural Systems." In Ross King, ed. *Energy, Agriculture and the Built Environment*. Melbourne: Centre for Environmental Studies, pp. 103-108.

Bernal, Richard L. (1983). "Jamaica: Democratic Socialism Meets the IMF." In Jill Torrie, ed. *Banking on Poverty; The Global Impact of the IMF and World Bank*. Toronto: Between the Lines, pp. 217-240.

Bhatia, Ramesh (1985). "Energy and Agriculture in Developing Countries." *Energy Policy*, XIII, No. 4, August, pp. 330-334.

Biswas, Asit K. (1979). "Climate and Economic Development." *Ecologist*, IX, No. 6, September-October, pp. 188-195.

Boville, B.W. and B.R. Doos (1981). "Why a World Climate Programme?" *Nature and Resources*, XVII, No. 1, January-March, pp. 2-7.

Brandt, Willy (1980). *North-South; A Program for Survival*. Cambridge, Mass.: The MIT Press.

Brobst, Donald A. (1979). "Fundamental Concepts for the Analysis of Resource Availability." In V. Kerry Smith, ed. *Scarcity and Growth Reconsidered*. Baltimore: Johns Hopkins Press for Resources for the Future, pp. 106-142.

Brown, Lester (1981). *Building a Sustainable Society*. New York: W.W. Norton.

Caldwell, Malcolm (1977). *The Wealth of Some Nations*. London: Zed Press.

Chapman, P.F. and F. Roberts (1983). *Metal Resources and Energy*. London: Butterworths.

Chinweizu (1985). "Debt Trap Peonage." *Monthly Review*, XXXVII, No. 6, November, pp. 21-35.

Choe, Boum-Jong (1985). "World Energy Markets and the Developing Countries." *Energy Policy*, XIII, No. 4, August, pp. 304-309.

Cloud, Preston (1977). "Mineral Resources and National Destiny." *Ecologist*, VII, No. 7, August/September, pp. 273-282.

Crosson, Pierre R. and Kenneth D. Frederick (1977). *The World Food Situation*. Washington, D.C.: Resources for the Future.

Dafter, Ray (1982). "Energy Projects in Peril World-Wide." *The Globe and Mail* (Toronto), April 26, B-12.

Dudal, Rudy and Michel Batisse (1978). "The Soil Map of the World." *Nature and Resources*, XIV, No. 1, January-March, pp. 2-6.

Erickson, Edward W. (1985). "Prospects for a Tighter World Oil Market." *The Energy Journal*, VI, No. 1, January, pp.3-7.

Food and Agricultural Organization (1983, 1982). *State of Food and Agriculture.* Rome: FAO.

Food and Agricultural Organization (1981). *Agriculture: Toward 2000.* Rome: FAO, 1982.

Frisch, J.R., ed. (1983). *Energy 2000-2020: World Prospects and Regional Stresses.* Report of the World Energy Conference. London: Graham & Trotman.

Gifford, R.M. (1977). "Energy in Modern Agriculture and the Rural-urban Relationship: a One-way Cul-de-sac?" in Ross King, ed. *Energy, Agriculture and the Built Environment.* Melbourne: Centre for Environmental Studies, pp. 91-102.

Goeller, H.E. and A. Zucker (1984). "Infinite Resources: The Ultimate Strategy." *Science,* CCXXIII, February 3, pp. 456-462.

Goldsbrough, David (1985). "Foreign Direct Investment in Developing Countries." *Finance & Development,* XXII, No. 1, March, pp. 31-34.

Greene, Robert P. and J. Michael Gallagher, eds. (1980). *Future Coal Prospects: World Coal Study.* Cambridge, Mass.: Ballinger Publishing Co.

Hare, F. Kenneth (1980). "Climate and Agriculture: The Uncertain Future." *Journal of Soil and Water Conservation,* XXXV, No. 3, May-June, pp. 112-115.

Harrison, Paul (1984). "A New Framework for the Food Security Equation." *Ceres,* XVII, No. 2, March-April, pp. 25-36.

Heichel, G.H. (1976). "Agricultural Production and Energy Resources." *American Scientist,* LXIV, No. 1, January-February, pp. 64-72.

Higgins, G.M. et al (1984). "Land, Food and Population in the Developing World." *Nature and Resources,* XX, No. 3, July-September, pp. 2-10.

Higgins, G.M. et al (1982). *Potential Population Supporting Capacities of Lands in the Developing World.* Rome: FAO/UNFPA.

Higgins, G.M. et al (1981). "Africa's Agricultural Potential." *Ceres,* XIV, No. 5, September-October, pp. 13-21.

Higgins, G.M. and A.H. Kassam (1981). "Regional Assessments of Land Potential: A Follow-up to the FAO/UNESCO Soil Map of the World." *Nature and Resources,* XVII, No. 4, October-December, pp. 11-23.

Hoogvelt, Ankie M.M. (1982). *The Third World in Global Development.* London: Macmillan.

Idso, Sherwood B. (1983). "Carbon Dioxide and Global Temperature: What the Data Show." *Journal of Environmental Quality,* XII, No. 2, April-June, pp. 159-163.

International Monetary Fund (1985). *World Economic Outlook.* Washington, D.C.: IMF.

Jensen, Neal F. (1978). "Limits to Growth in World Food Production." *Science,* CCI, July 28, pp. 317-320.

Jordan, Carl F. (1982). "Amazon Rain Forests." *American Scientist,* LXX, No. 4, pp. 394-401.

Jordan, Carl F. and Rafael Herrera (1981). "Tropical Rain Forests: Are Nutrients Really Critical?" *Nature and Resources,* XVII, No. 2, April-June, pp. 7-13.

Kellogg, William A. (1978). "Facing Up to Climatic Change." *Ceres,* XI, No. 6, November-December, pp. 13-17.

Leach, Gerald (1975). "The Energy Costs of Food Production." In Forrest Steele and Arthur Bourne, eds. *The Man/Food Equation.* London: Academic Press, pp. 139-163.

Loftness, Robert L. (1984). *Energy Handbook.* New York: Van Nostrand Reinhold Co.

Loxley, John (1983). "Tanzania: Origins of a Fiscal Crisis." In Jill Torrie, ed. *Banking on Poverty: The Global Impact of the IMF and World Bank.* Toronto: Between The Lines, pp. 203-216.

McKelvey, V.E. (1960). "Relation of Reserves of the Elements to their Crustal Abundance." *American Journal of Science,* CCLVIII, pp. 234-241.

Meadows, Donella H. et al (1972). *The Limits to Growth.* New York: Universe Books.

Mesarovic, Mihajlo and Eduard Pestel (1975). *Mankind at the Turning Point.* London: Hutchinson and Company.

Moran, Joseph M. et al (1977). "Agricultural Implications of Climatic Change." *Journal of Soil and Water Conservation,* XXXII, No. 2, March-April, pp. 80-83.

Myers, Norman (1981). "Stand and Deliver; Tropical Moist Forests." *IDRC Reports,* X, No. 1, April, pp. 8-9.

Naylor, R.T. (1983). "The World Debt Crisis: A Scenario." In Jill Torrie, ed. *Banking on Poverty: The Global Impact of the IMF and World Bank.* Toronto: Between The Lines, pp. 93-113.

Nicholaides, J.J. et al (1985). "Agricultural Alternatives for the Amazon Basin." *BioScience,* XXXV, No. 5, May, pp. 279-285.

Norse, David (1979). "Natural Resources, Development Strategies, and the World Food Problem." In Margaret R. Biswas and Asit K. Biswas, eds. *Food, Climate and Man.* Toronto: John Wiley & Sons, pp. 12-51.

O'Keefe, Phil and Lars Kristoferson (1984). "The Uncertain Energy Path — Energy and Third World Development." *Ambio,* XIII, No. 3, pp. 168-170.

Okigbo, Bede N. (1981). "Alternatives to Shifting Cultivation." *Ceres,* XIV, No. 6, November-December, pp. 41-45.

Paarlberg, Don (1980). *Farm and Food Policy.* Lincoln: University of Nebraska Press.

Pearce, David (1981). "World Energy Demand and Crude Oil Prices to the Year 2000." *Journal of Agricultural Economics,* XXXII, No. 3, September, pp. 341-354.

Perelman, Michael (1977). *Farming for Profit in a Hungry World.* New York: Universe Books.

Perpinan, Mary Soledad (1983). "The Philippines: Collision Course." In Jill Torrie, ed. *Banking on Poverty: The Global Impact of the IMF and World Bank.* Toronto: Between The Lines, pp. 169-188.

Phillips, Ron (1983). "The Role of the International Monetary Fund in the Post-Bretton Woods Era." *Review of Radical Political Economics,* XV, No. 2, Summer, pp. 59-81.

Pimentel, David et al (1973). "Food Production and the Energy Crisis." *Science,* CLXXXII, November 2, pp. 443-449.

Pimentel, David and Marcia Pimentel (1979). *Food, Energy and Society.* London: Edward Arnold.

Pool, John C. and Stephen C. Stamos (1985). "The Uneasy Calm: Third World Debt — the Case of Mexico." *Monthly Review,* XXXVI, No. 10, March, pp. 7-19.

Postel, Sandra (1985). "Managing Freshwater Supplies." In Lester R. Brown, ed. *State of the World 1985.* New York: W.W. Norton & Co., pp. 42-72.

Pratt, R. Cranford (1983). "The Global Impact of the World Bank." In Jill Torrie, ed. *Banking on Poverty: The Global Impact of the IMF and World Bank.* Toronto: Between The Lines, pp. 55-66.

Rappaport, Roy A. (1971). "The Flow of Energy in an Agricultural Society." *Scientific American,* CCXXV, September, pp. 116-132.

Ray, George F. (1984). "Mineral Reserves: Projected Lifetimes and Security of Supply." *Resources Policy,* X, No. 2, June, pp. 75-80.

Revelle, Roger (1974). "Food and Population." *Scientific American,* CCXXXI, No. 3, September, pp. 160-171.

Rifkin, Jeremy (1980). *Entropy,* New York: Viking Press.

Ruthenberg, Hans (1976). *Farming Systems in the Tropics.* Oxford: Clarendon Press, 2nd edition.

Sampson, R. Neil (1981). *Farmland or Wasteland: A Time to Choose.* Emmaus, Pennsylvania: Rodale Press.

Sanchez, Pedro A. et al (1982). "Amazon Basin Soils: Management for Continuous Crop Production." *Science,* CCXVI, May 21, pp. 821-827.

Schumacher, Diana (1983). *Energy: Crisis or Opportunity?* London: Macmillan.

Schware, Robert and William W. Kellogg (1982). "How Climatic Change Could Affect Food Production Patterns." *Ceres,* XV, No. 2, March-April, pp. 40-42.

Seidel, S. and D. Keyes (1983). *Can We Delay a Greenhouse Warming?* Washington, D.C.: U.S. Environmental Protection Agency, U.S. Government Printing Office.

Shrader, William D. (1977). "Soil Resources — Characteristics, Potentials, and Limitations." In E.R. Duncan, ed. *Dimensions of World Food Problems.* Ames: Iowa State University Press, pp. 118-135.

Simantov, A. (1980). "Agriculture and the Energy Challenge." *Journal of Agricultural Economics,* XXXI, No. 3, September, pp. 339-350.

Skinner, Brian J., ed. (1980). *Earth's Energy and Mineral Resources.* Los Altos, California: William Kaufmann.

Slessor, Malcolm (1974). "How Many Can We Feed?" *Agriculture and the Energy Question.* Ottawa: Agricultural Economics Research Council of Canada, pp. 65-69.

Smith, Nigel J.H. (1981). "Colonization Lessons from a Tropical Forest." *Science,* CCXIV, November 13, pp. 755-761.

Steinhart, J.S. and C.E. Steinhart (1974) "Energy Use in the U.S. Food System." *Science,* CLXXXIV, April 19, pp. 307-316.

Sweezy, Paul M. and Harry Magdoff (1984). "The Two Faces of Third World Debt: A Fragile Financial Environment and Debt Enslavement." *Monthly Review,* XXXV, No. 8, January, pp. 1-10.

Trainer, F.E. (1983). "The Relationship between Resources and Living Standards." *Resources Policy,* IX, No. 1, March, pp. 43-53.

United States (1967). *The World Food Problem: A Report of the President's Science Advisory Committee.* Washington, D.C.: U.S. Government Printing Office.

United States National Academy of Sciences (1976). *Climate and Food.* Washington, D.C.: U.S. NAS.

United States National Research Council (1983). *Changing Climate.* Report of the Carbon Dioxide Assessment Committee. Washington, D.C.: National Academy Press.

Wilson, Carroll L., Director (1980). *Coal — Bridge to the Future. Report of the World Coal Study.* Cambridge, Mass.: Ballinger Publishing Co.

Wittwer, Sylvan H. (1980). "Carbon Dioxide and Climatic Change: An Agricultural Perspective." *Journal of Soil and Water Conservation*, XXXV, No. 3, May-June, pp. 116-120.

World Bank (1984, 1983a, 1982). *World Development Report*. Washington, D.C.: IBRD.

World Bank (1983b). *Annual Report*. Washington, D.C.: IBRD.

CHAPTER TEN

Developing Food
and Agriculture
under Capitalism

World War II was the beginning of the end of colonialism. In much of Asia the old European powers had been displaced by the Japanese invaders, and nationalist forces grew, demanding independence. In August of 1945 the people of Indonesia declared an independent republic, but it took three more years of conflict to drive the Dutch out. In 1946 the United States granted conditional independence to the Philippines. The Vietminh forces declared Indochina to be a free republic in March 1946, but the French returned, and a major anti-colonial war ensued. The nationalist forces in the Indian subcontinent escalated their demands, and the British granted independence to the jewel of the Empire, divided, mainly along religious lines, into Pakistan and India. Ceylon was granted independence in 1947; a major general strike led to Burmese independence in 1948. Racial and political conflicts between Malays and the Chinese minority delayed independence for Singapore, Malaysia, and Borneo, but this was resolved, and full independence came in 1957-8. In North Africa Lebanon and Syria obtained independence during World War II and Jordan in 1946. Strong national forces and a weakened French government permitted Morocco and Tunisia to gain independence in 1956. But for the rest of Africa, the end of colonialism came in the later 1950s and 1960s.

The Cold War between international capitalism and the Soviet Union had been interrupted by the war against fascism, but by 1946 it was once again well under way. The most serious setbacks for world capitalism (and colonialism) came in the underdeveloped world: the victory of the Communist forces in the Chinese civil war in 1949, the stalemate in the Korean civil war of 1950-54, the victory of the Vietminh forces over the French in 1954, and the Algerian war for independence, which lasted from 1954 to 1962. In all these cases the forces for liberation were led by agrarian political movements strongly influenced by Marxism and Leninism. This had a profound effect on orthodox liberal theory on development.

Despite relatively high rates of economic growth in the period since World War II, the problem of poverty, deprivation, and hunger persists. The 1975 World Conference on Employment, Income Distribution and Social Progress, sponsored by the International Labour Office, concluded that 67% of the population in the underdeveloped world was "seriously poor" and 39% "destitute." The absolute number of poor people was increasing. Open unemployment was estimated at 8% of the labour force, and an additional 36% were classified as underemployed, people working less than regularly or in a job yielding inadequate income. The ILO concluded that in order to achieve a basic level of human needs within the time-frame of one generation, the underdeveloped countries would have to grow at a rate double that of the 1960s and early 1970s. (ILO, 1976:18-23, 40-41)

In the 1970s international agencies and most western governments concluded that development assistance should be directed towards meeting the basic needs of the poorest people in the underdeveloped world. However, the "basic human needs" approach was largely abandoned after the onset of the world economic crisis in the late 1970s. Ruttan (1984:399) argues that the programs were not solving one of the most fundamental rural problems, "achieving a reliable food supply." In the 1980s there was a shift to emphasizing rapid growth, to be achieved by private investment in a free-market atmosphere.

Growing Concern about Food Distribution

In 1967 the World Bank created the Commission on International Development, headed by Lester B. Pearson, former Prime Minister of Canada. Its job was to undertake a "grande assize" of two decades of effort by international agencies and lending countries. Its report, issued in 1969, noted the mixed record, but concluded that in the 1960s the overall rate of economic growth in the underdeveloped countries had been around 5%; on a per capita basis, it had been around 2.5%, which represented "by any historical standard of comparison, a remarkable acceleration." (12) They advocated a continuation of existing policies: the promotion of free trade (14), reliance on private foreign investment (16), external aid, particularly for infrastructure (16), the maintenance of low wages in the industrial sector (59), and the promotion of exports where comparative advantage existed (17).

Despite the glowing tone of the report, a few problems were noted. There was the "widening gap" between the developed and the underdeveloped countries. (3) The debt problem was increasing. (72-76) Between 1953 and 1968 the net barter terms of trade had turned against primary exports from the underdeveloped world. (45) The share of world exports had declined, particularly for agricultural products. (46-47) Manufacturing was not absorbing new workers entering the labour force. (243) Finally, there was the problem of prolonged malnutrition, pervasive poverty, and low "effective demand" for food. (62-63) The Commission concluded that the "unemployment problem" might lead to social and political turmoil that could "arrest the development process." (60)

Despite impressive economic growth rates, there was a proliferation of empirical studies revealing that a very large percentage of the population was not sharing in the results. (Some of these are cited in Chapter I.) The result was a shift in emphasis to policies that would increase the standard of living of the poor in the underdeveloped countries through government-sponsored welfare programs. Hoogvelt (1981:96) has described this as the rise of "global social democracy," an alliance between progressive elements within the underdeveloped countries and certain enlightened "internationalist" political opinion-makers in the industrialized west:

> Neither of these groups as a rule wields direct political power inside its own national community. Rather, they converge in the secretariats, commissions, and *ad hoc* groups of experts and "eminent persons" of the international organizations. In these organizations they themselves do not even have voting power. Yet they establish the parameters of the discourse, because it is they who prepare the documents and the background papers that ultimately inform the various "resolutions."

The key alternate approach to the problem of poverty and undernutrition is "basic human needs." It was adopted as a declaration of principles and a program of action by the 1975 World Conference on Employment organized by the International Labour Organization. The ILO estimated that 40% of the labour force in the underdeveloped countries was either unemployed ("open unemployment") or underemployed. Using a model of "purchasing power parity," they argued that in 1972 around 67% of the population of the underdeveloped countries was "seriously poor" and that 39% of these were "destitute." (ILO, 1976:16-20) The ILO conference calculated that achieving the goals of basic human needs in one generation under the present strategy of "trickle down" welfare within the market economy would require doubling the rates of economic growth in the underdeveloped countries; it would require annual growth rates of around 11% in Africa. (40-41)

The basic human needs strategy was to provide minimum subsistence in two general areas. First, there is personal consumption, including food, shelter, and clothing. Secondly, there are the essential services of water, sanitation, transport, health, and education. In the area of agricultural production, emphasis was to be shifted to improving the status of small farms and the income of the rural poor, as opposed to the larger and more commercial farms, ranches, and plantations. Landlessness and peasant farmers' low productivity were to be corrected by creating new rural employment. The goal was to eliminate "absolute poverty"; the new crusade was launched by Robert McNamara, President of the World Bank, in 1973. (Srinivasan, 1977:11-28)

Paul Streeton, one of the main advocates of the basic needs approach, argues that its advantage is that the poor are targeted and the projects are specific. Unemployment, he adds, is not the main problem in underdeveloped countries; the full employment option is "an example of the transfer of an inappropriate intellectual technology from modern societies to developing countries." The results in Sri Lanka demonstrate that a basic human needs strategy is appropriate to poor countries and that "gradual reform *is* possible." (Streeton, 1982:33, 46) Marcelo Selowsky (1981:73-92) of the World Bank argues that for south Asia the unmet needs of the majority are so great that progress towards basic needs will be slow, whereas in Latin America, with its already significant level of economic development and adequate resources, poverty is purely a distributive problem, as there is no lack of resources. Thus, in this view, the welfare approach is appropriate, and there is really no need for structural change.

As a result of this new direction, many of the underdeveloped countries introduced a wide variety of welfare programs designed to deal with the problem of hunger among the poor. These included direct subsidies for staple foods, supplementary feeding programs for children and pregnant mothers, rationing, and the establishment of government food outlets where the poor could obtain certain staple foods at low cost. In some cases the subsidies were available to everyone; in other cases there were attempts to target special groups. (See McNaughton, 1983; Reutlinger, 1982; Harvard, 1981)

Sri Lanka: Social Democracy in a Poor, Underdeveloped Country

Sri Lanka is a relatively small island state off the southeastern tip of India. In many ways it is more similar to the Indian subcontinent than to Southeast Asia. For example, in 1980 the estimated per capita income and per capita gross national product were similar to that of India, Bangladesh, and Pakistan; all four countries were among the poorest 30 in the world, well below Indonesia and the Philippines. Energy consumption is very low, only one-half that of the average of the low-income countries. In 1982 the FAO estimated that the average per capita daily consumption of calories was 2249, above that of Bangladesh and India but behind that of Pakistan. Protein consumption was similar to that of India, 44 grams per day, and animal products supplied only 15% of the total. In 1982 agriculture still accounted for well over 40% of gross domestic product; 57% of exports by value were agricultural products; and 53% of the population was classified as agricultural. (FAO, 1983: Annex Tables 11, 13) Around 33% of all land is cultivated or in permanent crops. Following the pattern of plantation agriculture as established under British rule, more than half of all arable land is still planted to permanent crops for export: tea, rubber, and coconuts. Irrigated paddy rice remains the dominant food crop, occupying 80% of all arable foodland. (FAO, 1981)

Sri Lanka is regularly cited as the best example of the success of the basic human needs strategy. It has ranked very high on the Physical Quality of Life Index (PQLI), which measures the rate of literacy, the infant mortality rate, and average life expectancy at one year of age. However, as is often the case in the history of development, the key example appears to be more of a special than a general case.

First of all, Sri Lanka has had relatively favourable ecological conditions, compared to most underdeveloped areas. Until recently there was adequate land to support the level of population. In the wetter, southwest part of the island, paddy rice cultivation is well developed, including multiple cropping. The construction of dams on the many rivers flowing out of the mountains has permitted the expansion of irrigated farming, particularly in the drier northern areas. With colonialization, a large plantation system was introduced; when the indigenous peoples refused to leave their paddy fields to work on the plantations, the British imported indentured Tamil labourers from adjacent India. For a long period of time, export earnings and taxes from the three major cash crops were adequate to expand local services. (Isenman, 1980:237-238)

In the 19th century the British began to introduce a broad-based primary health system. Life expectancy rose from 30 in 1900 to 45 by World War II. In 1945 there was a concerted campaign to wipe out malaria; infant mortality rates dropped dramatically, and morbidity declined. The British introduced universal adult suffrage in 1931. Public education was introduced for women as well as men. Secondary schools were opened throughout the colony in the 1940s, and education became a free public service. By 1946 70% of males and 44% of females were literate. As the school curriculum included instruction in nutrition and hygiene, infant mortality continued to decline, and life expectancy increased. Finally, a system of food rationing and price subsidization was introduced during World War II and continued thereafter. Sri Lanka has been described as "the model colony." (Bjorkman, 1985:542-546)

Sri Lanka was given independence "from above" in 1948; there was no strong grass-roots nationalist movement as existed in India. Following independence, the United National Party (UNP), which represented the westernized upper classes, was elected and formed the government. In 1956, the 2500th anniversary of the death of Bhudda, a Sinhalese coalition of rural-based landlords, rich peasants, and others formed the Sri Lanka Freedom Party (SLFP), headed by S.W.R.D. Bandaranaike. In a United Front Coalition with the pro-Moscow Communist Party and the Trotskyites (LSSP), they won the 1956 election and governed the country until 1977. (Omvedt, 1984:24-25; Samaraweera, 1981:154-159)

Under the United Front government the welfare state system was expanded. While some have described Sri Lanka as a "small socialist developing country" (Morawetz, 1980), the economy has always been capitalist. It was, however, the first attempt to apply the principles of social democracy, including western liberal democratic institutions, to an underdeveloped country. Expenditures on health and education continued to rise. A universal rice ration was introduced, and prices for wheat and sugar were subsidized. Food subsidies alone accounted for 20% of government expenditures. In contrast, military expenditures were very low, around 0.5% of GNP. Government expenditures on social welfare programs rose to around 50% of the total national budget. (Bjorkman, 1985:547; Jayawardena, 276-279)

The UF government was also active in the agricultural area. The large foreign-owned plantations were nationalized, and most of them were kept as state institutions. The government guaranteed a floor price for paddy rice, but it was low; the UF chose instead to subsidize farm inputs. (Moore, 1984b:116) The World Bank emphasizes the agricultural reforms brought in by the UF government: legislation protected the rights of tenant farmers, limited rents to 30% of the crop, placed ceilings on landholding at 10 hectares, set an income "ceiling" of 2000 rupees per month, instituted taxes on income and wealth and expanded irrigation and land reclamation projects. (Jayawardena, 1974:275-276) In contrast, studies by the International Labour Office conclude that the reform legislation was not enforced and was ineffective. (Richards, 1981:215-216; Lee, 1977:169-173)

The UF government undertook an import substitution policy. Domestic industries would be assisted through policies which protected them against foreign competition. Merchandise imports were covered by licenses and quotas. Foreign exchange controls were introduced. During the 1960s the growth rate for domestic industry was 8% per annum. Despite the drop in price for the key primary exports, the rise in the price of imported cereals, and the 1973 oil price increases (all petroleum products were imported), the economy performed adequately during the 1970s, growing at an annual rate between 1% and 4%. Nevertheless, open unemployment grew to 20% of the labour force. Dissatisfaction with the parties of the left and with unemployment led to the formation of the National Liberation Front (JVP); in 1971 they revolted and were brutally suppressed by the UF government. The UNP won a sweeping victory in the 1977 election. (Moore, 1984a:1088; Omvedt, 1984:25-26; Isenman, 1980:245; Lee, 1977:164)

Both the UF and the UNP government have placed considerable emphasis on increasing food production through land reclamation, the extension and improvement of irrigation, and the introduction of new cereal varieties which not only increased yields but permitted double cropping. Irrigated land increased by 42% between 1962 and 1980. Cereal production doubled between 1961 and 1981. But population rose from 9.8 million in 1960 to 15 million in 1982. The World Bank (1984:Table 1) projects that Sri Lanka's population will rise to 21 million by the year 2000 and stabilize at 32 million in the next century. However, by 1981 Sri Lanka was already importing 30% of domestic consumption of cereals. Furthermore, the FAO reports that the average per capita consumption of calories in the 1978-80 period was lower than that in both the base periods of 1966-68 and 1968-71. (FAO, 1983:Table 97)

Much of the debate over Sri Lanka has centred on the question of whether the policies of pre-1977 governments actually resulted in a more egalitarian distribution of income and wealth and whether the PQL Index is an appropriate guide for judging the existence of malnutrition. In the World Bank's widely cited study of "redistribution with growth" (Chenery et al, 1974:279), it is argued that between 1963 and 1973 the per capita real income of the poorest decile of the population more than doubled, and that of the richest quintile fell by 17%. In his study for the ILO, Lee (1977:161-184) presents a devastating critique of these figures, which are based solely on income data produced by the Central Bank of Ceylon. Using other data and consumption surveys, Lee concludes that the World Bank underestimated the real inflation rate, that the consumption levels of the poor declined and the rich increased over the period, that the decline in per capita consumption of rice was concentrated in the lowest income classes, that real wages fell in all employee categories, that the rich consistently understated their income, and that paddy rice land units declined in average size through fragmentation. Agricultural terms of trade after 1970 favoured rice producers against export crops, lowering the standard of living of plantation workers. Lee argues that the reported decline in income of the upper quintile most likely was due to the fall in prices for export crops and a resulting decline in rent and investment income. The standard of living of Tamils working as wage labourers in the estate (plantation) sector fell steadily over the period.

The second major question concerns the relationship between the widely used "physical quality of life" index and the level of malnutrition. Between October 1975 and March 1976 the Center for Disease Control of Atlanta, Georgia carried out a very extensive nutritional survey of Sri Lankan children 6 months to 72 months of age, using three anthropometric indices. (Brink et al, 1978:41-47) The survey covered all 15 health districts on the island. Between 3.7% and 8.8% of rural children were found to be suffering from acute undernutrition; between 20.7% and 49.6% were experiencing chronic undernutrition. Among the children of families working on the estates, 62.4% were found to be suffering from chronic undernutrition. The medical team concluded that "a problem of undernutrition of an impressive magnitude exists in the rural Sri Lankan population."

More recent evidence is presented in two conflicting studies. Gunatilleke and Kurukalasuria (1984:313) of the Marga Institute in Colombo report that an ad hoc survey of pre-school children conducted by the Medical Research Institute from 1979 to 1982 found that acute undernutrition was around 5% and that chronic undernutrition ranged between 13% and 34%. Jayawardena (1984:317-319; 327), an employee of UNICEF based in Colombo, concludes that policy changes instituted by the UNP government after 1977 have increased poverty and have led to a decline in nutrition, particularly among women and children who work and live on the estates. The UNICEF survey of 1980-82 revealed an increase in undernutrition among infants and young children in the estate sector, attributed to diet deficiencies caused by the inflation of food prices. In 1974 infant mortality rates among estate families rose dramatically by over 40%, from famine conditions caused by the sudden rise in prices of rice and wheat flour; rural workers in the rice-producing areas were not as badly affected.

This finding is not that surprising. The Indian state of Kerala is also commonly cited as having a good PQL Index, thanks to the progressive social policies introduced by several Marxist state governments. Gopolan (1983:2165-2168) argues that there is a major difference between "social development" and "economic development." Despite having the highest PQL ratings in India, Kerala is one of the poorest of the states, the average dietary intake in terms of both calories and protein is very low even by Indian standards, and poverty is widespread. He stresses that literacy, family planning, and health facilities are no substitute for food nor an antidote to poverty; mere "child survival" is not the same as the eradication of undernutrition.

The election of the UNP under the leadership of J.R. Jayewardene in 1977 brought a major change in Sri Lanka. The new government was committed to a radical change in economic policy, following the economic model of export-orientated industrialization. The policies associated with East Asian newly industrializing countries were adopted: encouragement of foreign investment, subsidies for private investors, free trade zones, the abolition of exchange controls, tax and other credits for investors, and legislation tough on trade unions and the right to strike. As labour, political, and ethnic strife escalated, martial law was imposed. The Public Security Act and the Essential Services Act were used to repress the opposition parties and movements on the left. The new policy direction did attract private foreign investment, plus American and international aid denied the UF government.

To shift policy towards economic growth, basic social services in Sri Lanka were cut to 15.9% of the budget by 1982. The food ration and subsidies were replaced by a food stamp program with a means test. Spending on housing rose, but the budgets for health and education were progressively cut. Inequalities of income and wealth increased. With large government subsidies offered to private investors, the budget deficit rose significantly. By the mid-1980s the escalating conflict between the UNP and the Tamil minority brought the country close to chaos: Tamil demands for political autonomy were supported by guerrilla forces, and the UNP government responded with military repression, even including aerial attacks on Tamil villages and towns. The basic human needs experiment appeared to be over. (Gunatilleke and Kurukulasuria, 1984:310-313; Pfaffenberger, 1984:15-22; Omvedt, 1984:23-26; Martin, 1983:19-21; Moore, 1984a:1087-1092; Ponnambalam, 1980:127-167)

In a general sense, there is a fundamental contradiction in the social democratic approach of basic human needs. First, it has been determined by empirical studies that in the underdeveloped capitalist countries the existing economic and political system is preventing the poor from sharing in economic development. But what is the solution? Somehow, the governments and ruling classes of these countries are to be convinced that they are guilty of a moral error, that they should change their ways, and that they should adopt new policies requiring increasing taxes on themselves. This does not mean that we should dismiss the *goals* of supplying basic human needs for everyone. These are certainly legitimate. The question is how to achieve them.

This theme has been explored by Makhoul (1983) of the Faculty of Medicine of The Hebrew University in her comparative study of human nutrition in Brazil, Cuba, Israel, and the United States. She concludes that there are fundamentally different approaches to a basic human needs strategy. The approach advocated by the World Bank and other supporters of the "trickle down" approach to economic development, she says, "represented a reorientation in nutrition policy — from one of eradicating malnutrition as an aim in and of itself, derived from the concept of basic human rights and prioritizing the nutritionally most vulnerable, to one of eradicating malnutrition when and where such intervention promises the highest rate of return." Thus, under the values of the capitalist system, a basic human needs policy is a form of *crisis management*; it is approached from the position of what is best for the preservation of the capitalist system and not what is in the best interests of all human beings. Therefore, it is a form of "triage." As such, "it eliminates from nutritional programmes (in the name of optimal use of scarce resources) those who are unlikely to become directly integrated into the process of capital accumulation and whose nutritional-status improvement is thus likely to result in no productivity changes." (Makhoul, 1983:15-31)

Growth with Equity under Capitalism

Orthodox economists regularly cite the newly industrializing Asian countries (mainly Hong Kong, Singapore, South Korea, and Taiwan) as the prime examples of how underdeveloped countries, maintaining a capitalist economy, can overcome their relative poverty and move on to a modern society. But in addition there is a group of development experts who also argue that these countries demonstrate that it is possible to have rapid economic growth *and* equity at the same time.

The capitalist "growth with equity" position is most commonly associated with Irma Adelman. In 1973 Adelman and Morris published a very influential study, *Economic Growth and Social Equity in Developing Countries*, which examined data from 43 underdeveloped capitalist countries over the period from 1957 to 1968. They concluded that even with high levels of economic growth, increasing inequality was typically the case. Furthermore, their survey indicated that the income share of the lower 60% of the population not only declined in a relative sense but very often absolutely.

Adelman argues that the goals of development are central; from a moral perspective they must include a move towards the full realization of the human potential of all members of a society. Not only is it necessary to provide the material base, but the barriers to self-realization must be removed. She calls this "depauperization": a weighted combination of equity and growth, most successfully achieved in the non-Communist countries of Japan, Israel, Singapore, South Korea, and Taiwan. According to Adelman, these countries have all gone through three stages of development: (1) a radical redistribution of productive assets; (2) a major investment in human capital; and (3) stress on rapid labour-intensive growth. (Adelman 1975a, 1975b, 1973)

Ten years later, after the onset of the world economic crisis, Adelman (1984) revised her development theory. As a result of the economic crisis and high unemployment rates, the industrialized countries were raising barriers to manufactured export from underdeveloped countries. The economic strategy of export-led industrialization, identified with the Asian NICs (Newly Industrializing Countries), appeared to be faltering. While continuing to oppose import-substitution as a development strategy, Adelman now supports a program led by agriculture, with its links to the local market. She calls this an "agricultural-demand-led-industrialization" program. While this has similarities to the strategies advanced by Beckford (1972) and Thomas (1974), and the general linkages theory advanced by Hirshman (1958), Adelman holds firm to her position that development must be within the framework of capitalism. The ideal model advanced by Adelman is South Korea in 1963, described by her as "typical of a large class of low-income less developed countries." (Adelman, 1984:940)

It is therefore imperative to look at the experience of "growth with equity" in South Korea and Taiwan. How successful has the strategy been? Just how typical are South Korea and Taiwan of underdeveloped countries? Can the experience be replicated in other countries?

South Korea and the State Capitalist Model

In the latter part of the 19th century Korea was forced to sign commercial treaties with the major imperial powers and open its markets to trade and foreign investment. When the farmers rebelled in 1894, Japan intervened via a war against China and established its hegemony. In 1905 Japan intervened militarily, and by 1910 Korea was absorbed as a colony. Japanese colonial rule was very repressive. The government and the economy were directly run by the Japanese. Japanese citizens even replaced local landlords; between 30% and 50% of the rice crop was siphoned off to Japan, and Korean farmers experienced extreme deprivation and starvation. During World War II there was compulsory delivery of grain. Public lands were sold to Japanese immigrants, who reached one million by 1945. Koreans were banned from influential positions. The mining industry was greatly expanded, serving Japan's needs. In the period just before World War II, a heavy industrial sector was begun, to serve Japanese military interests. Japanese cultural imperialism was brutal, with the Korean language and writing banned in schools and Korean newspapers closed. Koreans were even forced to change their family names to conform to the Japanese style. (Barone, 1983:54-56; Kihl and Bark, 1981:48; Brun and Hersch, 1976:39-63)

Korean resistance to Japanese colonialism emerged early in the regime. The spontaneous demonstrations of March 1, 1919 were brutally repressed by the Japanese military. In the 1920s and 1930s the independence movement came under the leadership of socialist and communist political elements. Demonstrations and strikes were common. The most important development was the formation of the Anti-Japanese Guerilla Army in 1931, led by Kim Il Sung and the Korean Communist Party. Operating out of the mountains on the Manchurian border, they launched successful attacks on the Japanese army. When the Japanese surrendered, People's Committees sprang up everywhere, and by the time the U.S. Army arrived, they had disarmed the Japanese and organized local provisional governments. (Brun and Hersch, 1976:67-73; Burchett, 1968: 94-101, 107-110)

Soviet troops and the Korean Anti-Japanese Army marched into Korea in 1945. As there was no American presence in Korea, the U.S. government asked Stalin to stop its advance at the 38th parallel and wait for the arrival of American troops to take control of the rest of Korea. Stalin agreed. Between 1945 and 1948 Korea was occupied by American and Soviet armies. The Japanese were expelled in 1946, and the productive assets they controlled were seized by the state. In the north, the left-wing opposition to Japanese rule formed a provisional government, began restructuring the area along socialist lines and awaited unification of the country. In the south the Americans were determined to establish a capitalist economy with a supporting government. Japanese business and farm assets were distributed to Koreans on a relatively equitable basis. Farm tenancy was reduced from 70% to 33%. In 1948 Korea was formally divided by a U.S.-supported resolution pushed through the United Nations. In a phony election in 1948 (the major parties refused to participate), Syngman Rhee, brought to Korea by the U.S. government, was "elected." The Land Reform Act of 1949 gave ownership of land to those who were tilling it and limited individual ownership to 3 hectares. In 1950 the Grain Management Law was enacted, which provided for government purchase of rice at set prices. Lacking a Korean capitalist class, the government assumed the major role in developing production. (Barone, 1983:56-59; Kihl and Bark, 1981:49; Lee, 1979:493-495; Chen, 1979:166; Brun and Hersch, 1976:73-93)

It is important to understand the special relation of South Korea, Taiwan, and even Thailand to the overall strategic policy of the U.S. government after the success of the revolution in China. The central focus of U.S. policy was the containment of the Chinese revolution. These countries are "front line" states, and they have received major economic and military assistance from the U.S. government. For example, between 1953 and 1974 South Korea received $4 billion in economic *grant* aid from the United States; over this period it was the equivalent of 7% of GNP and accounted for 60% of all investment. Between 1963 and 1974 the government received concessionary loans from the U.S. government and international institutions. Military assistance was even greater: between 1946 and 1975 South Korea received $8.9 billion from the U.S. government. (Bunge, 1982:149-150; Halliday, 1980:6-8; Lee, 1979:513-514) U.S. government interest in these key states is primarily political, not economic. They have been quite willing to support the development of strong state capitalist governments that reject basic "free market" principles. They are not at all worried about the very repressive policies of these governments towards internal political opposition; they have never insisted that they be democracies.

From the beginning, the Rhee government set the pattern of state direction of the South Korean economy. An import substitution policy was initiated. Not only did the government directly establish key industries, it provided numerous subsidies to private entrepreneurs. The government still controls finance through state banking, control over interest rates, extension of credit, foreign exchange controls, and the allocation of capital for investment. Beginning in 1962, regular five-year plans were instituted, implemented by the Economic Planning Board. The result has been relatively integrated economic growth, the creation of a strong national bourgeois class linked to the state, and quite significant controls on foreign-owned transnational corporations. This does not mean that South Korea has developed along lines similar to Japan. There has been very extensive dependence on foreign capital, technology, and trade with the industrialized capitalist countries. However, the state-capitalist governments in South Korea have been much more successful than most governments in underdeveloped countries in directing and controlling economic growth. (Koo, 1984:1035-1036; Landsberg, 1984:181-193; Barone, 1983:47-61)

Following the military coup of 1961, the new government under Park Chung Hee shifted to a policy of "unbalanced growth" based on the export of labour-intensive manufactured goods. This coincided with a period of rapid economic growth throughout the world, stimulated by massive U.S. government spending on the war in Indochina. All of the Asian capitalist states greatly benefitted from the U.S. war effort. Between 1965 and 1975 exports of manufactured products rapidly expanded; around 60% went to the United States and Japan, who also accounted for around 65% of all imports. (Long, 1977:31) The economy grew very rapidly. When the economic crisis of 1979 caused a slowdown in exports, the government responded by a shift to a more open market system with greater reliance on the large internal market. (Suh, 1984:330-331, 337)

The state also has a preponderant role in the agricultural area. Compulsory deliveries of rice and barley were begun in 1948, and the government still purchases most cereals at a fixed price. The supply and price of fertilizers and pesticides is controlled by the state through the National Agricultural Co-operatives Federation. All farm credit is through the Agricultural Bank, a state institution. With limitations on the extent of ownership and a prohibition on tenancy, a free market in land has been greatly limited.

Under the first three five-year plans (1962-1976), investment in agriculture lagged well behind industry. Because of international price differences, rice was exported and wheat imported. A survey in 1976 found that the rate of return on investment in farming was 4.4%, well below the bank interest rate of 16.2%. Lee (1979:312-315) notes that between 1959 and 1975 the government procurement price for grain was below the free market price; up to 1961 it was below the cost of production. Even after a significant increase in procurement prices in 1971, the internal terms of trade for agricultural produce improved only moderately. Kihl and Bark (1981:51-53) argue that the relative neglect of the agricultural sector led to (1) a widening food gap as the overall per capita consumption of grain declined; (2) increasing reliance on imported food, particularly wheat from the United States; and (3) increasing urban-rural disparity in household income. Between 1974 and 1982 cereal imports rose from 2.7 to 5.5 million metric tonnes; by 1982, South Korea was the third largest importer of cereals in the underdeveloped world, behind only China (20.3 mmt) and Egypt (6.7 mmt).

The structure of Korean agriculture has hardly changed since the end of World War II. At the time of the expulsion of the Japanese landlords, over 93% of the farms were less than 2 hectares, and 41% were less than 0.5 hectares. (Lee, 1979:494) Since then there has been no significant change in the distribution of farms by size. Rao (1978:384) reports that in 1974 67% of the farms were under one hectare. This is certainly dwarf agriculture, not much different from gardening. Between 1970 and 1983, the percentage of the total population in agriculture dropped from 51% to 35%. Furthermore, South Korea is one of the very few underdeveloped countries (the only one in Asia) where the absolute number of people in agriculture is also dropping. Nevertheless, with the use of new varieties, multiple cropping, and a high input of fertilizers, cereal yields are among the highest in the world; rice yields are exceeded only by Japan and North Korea. (FAO, 1983: Tables 3, 11, 15)

Without a doubt, there is relative equity in rural assets in South Korea, even today. However, all the current available evidence indicates that there is a wide gap in the distribution of wealth in the urban areas. Koo (1984:1032-1035) notes that inequalities of wealth and income have been fostered by government policies that have consistently repressed the income and working conditions of wage labourers, provided enormous public subsidies to a small class of capitalists, followed monetary policies encouraging inflation that has hurt people living on wages and salaries, and emphasized regressive, indirect taxes falling hardest on the poor.

Figures supplied by the government-financed Korean Development Institute indicate that absolute poverty is on the decline but persists among the inhabitants of the urban squatter areas and the rural population that is either landless or exists on very small parcels of land. The considerable underemployment in the rural area leads to migration to the rapidly expanding urban centres. Furthermore, the proportion of government expenditures for social welfare is "well below the level for other countries with similar per capita incomes." (Suh, 1984:332-335) A 1976 study cited by the World Bank found the bottom quintile of the population with only 5.7% of national income and the highest quintile with 45%. (World Bank, 1982:Table 25) For most capitalist countries, this would appear to be a rather egalitarian distribution. However, it should be remembered that these figures include the egalitarian agricultural sector, representing around 35% of the population.

The variety of conclusions reached by other surveys reflects the weakness of the data. Chen (1979:167) points to the increasing inequality of business income and the growing importance of large capitalist enterprises. Rao (1978:385-386) of the World Bank stresses the high levels of growth of employment and low levels of open unemployment. The study by Lee (1979:505) for the ILO concludes that over the period from 1963 to 1975 real incomes have increased significantly for all income groups in the rural area. On the other hand, Koo (1984:1029-1031) argues that newer data suggest that income inequality is increasing and so is relative poverty. The distribution of the labour force in 1982 indicates rather significant under-employment: primary sector, 32%; industrial sector, 24%; service sector, 40%, with the remaining 4% open unemployment.

But there are factors other than income distribution that must be included in any discussion of equity. As Barone (1983:43) notes, it is difficult to cast South Korea as "capitalism with a human face." The string of right-wing dictators have been flagrant violators of human rights. For workers, the conditions of employment are "among the worst in the world." The repression of political opposition and labour organizations is widely known.

Only company-controlled unions are allowed. Dissident workers can be sent to "re-education" camps. Citizens face jail terms for holding unauthorized meetings, even in private homes. No unions are permitted in government-run enterprises. Strikes are widely prohibited. (Shorrock, 1981:9) Women in the labour force are grossly exploited, primarily through long hours of work at piece rates. (Rosenberg, 1980:304-305; Long, 1977:37-38) As I write this, South Korean government prosecutors have demanded jail terms of between three and five years for seven leaders of an illegal but peaceful strike at the textile giant, Daewoo Corporation. (*The Globe and Mail* [Toronto], October 28, 1985).

State Capitalism in Taiwan

The development of Taiwan closely parallels that of South Korea. Historically, the island of Fòrmosa (Taiwan) was a province of China, but it was ceded to Japan after the war of 1895. As in South Korea, the colonial masters invested in infrastructure, education, and agriculture in order to expand rice and other food exports. Manufactured goods were imported from Japan, and local industrialization was retarded until the approach of World War II. In addition, around 300,000 Japanese migrated to Taiwan where they assumed a dominant role in the government and the economy. At the end of World War II, the Japanese were expelled and their assets seized by the Chinese Nationalist government.

There was, however, one major difference between South Korea and Taiwan. Following their defeat by the Communist forces in the civil war, Chiang Kai-shek, the leaders of the Kuomintang, and their army moved to the island. Taiwan had always been relatively free from control by the Chinese governments. The newcomers (currently around 15% of the island's population) spoke Mandarin, whereas the Taiwanese mainly spoke Fukien and Hakka. Beginning in 1945 the Kuomintang not only replaced the Japanese but also drove locals from important positions in business. In 1947 the Taiwanese rebelled against their new masters, and they were brutally crushed.

Hoping to consolidate their position of power on Taiwan, between 1949 and 1953 the Kuomintang government initiated a land reform virtually identical to that of South Korea: tenancy was eliminated, and a class of small independent farmers was created. As in South Korea, the Kuomintang initiated an import substitution policy which lasted until 1961. The state assumed a major role in the economy, first building an infrastructure and then establishing government corporations in capital-intensive areas including electricity, petroleum and natural gas, fertilizer, aluminum, shipbuilding, sugar processing, and some areas of mining. The more labour-intensive areas of the economy were left to private capital, supported by various government subsidies. Government development plans were implemented, giving emphasis to decentralized and labour-intensive industrialization. The Taiwanese, blocked from any role in the government or the military, expanded their domination of the business class. After a relatively strong national bourgeois class was created, in 1965 the government launched a policy of encouraging foreign investment, including export processing zones. By 1973 manufactured goods accounted for 85% of exports.

Developments in Taiwan cannot be understood except in the context of U.S. foreign policy. Taiwan is a front-line state in the battle against the spread of communism. Between 1953 and 1968 Taiwan received $1.7 billion in economic aid from the U.S. government — all in the form of grants. In addition, the U.S. provided $2.3 billion in military grants. (Barrett and Whyte, 1982:1068) Despite the protection provided by the U.S. Seventh Fleet, and the military commitment by the U.S. government, Taiwan was considered to be a risky place for investment until after the Korean War was settled. Foreign investment expanded in the 1960s, but by that time the national bourgeoisie, supported by the state, was the dominant force in the economy.

The Kuomintang government was also deeply involved in the agricultural sector. The government controlled the price of rice. Rice was exchanged for fertilizer, controlled by a government monopoly. As in South Korea, the government's purchase price was below the market price. Nevertheless, because of the relative equality of productive assets, the income of the average rural family in the period down to the mid-1970s was only around 15% below that of the average urban family. Income from private property in other sectors was relatively limited. Indeed, between 1953 and 1972, the distribution of income appears to have become more egalitarian, according to government figures. (Galenson, 1979;126-129; Chen, 1979:172-173; Thorbecke, 1979:184-190)

However, by the 1980s this had changed significantly. There was a rising gap in income between the rural and urban sectors. The farm population continued to rise until around 1969; then it stabilized at around 1.65 million. The average size of a farm declined to 1.04 hectares by 1980. In that year farm families obtained around 75% of their income from off-farm employment, and more than 90% of all farmers farmed only part-time. Whereas in 1970 Taiwan was a net exporter of agricultural products, by 1980 it was only 60% self-sufficient in calories and 45% in protein. There has been a steadily increasing deficit in agricultural trade, which reached $1.5 billion in 1980. While government price supports have led to a surplus of rice, Taiwan is importing increasing amounts of feed grains to support the rising demand for meat. The demand for fruits and vegetables is also rising. The government is now faced with dwarf agriculture, producing mainly rice, while increasing real incomes have led the population to seek a more diversified western diet.

Galenson (1979:386-425) reports that between 1953 and 1975 labour force participation rates slightly declined from 57.8% to 55.8%; however, female participation rates rose from 29% to 40%. Relative to other Asian underdeveloped countries, unemployment and underemployment are low. Food is abundant and relatively cheap. However, the wage differential between skilled and unskilled workers is widening, and the differential between male and female workers is widening even faster.

Again, equity is not determined solely by distribution of income. Government welfare and social services are rudimentary for an upper middle-income country. Strikes and other labour disputes are strictly illegal. The Kuomintang political system is a form of corporate state, similar to the fascism that persisted for so long in Spain and Portugal. There are individual company "unions" controlled by the Kuomintang Party; by the constitution, they are required to "co-operate" with their employers. In reality, they have no say in the setting of wages. Working conditions are very poor, and women are grossly exploited in the new labour-intensive export industries. In any case, the Kuomintang denies that there is any conflict of interest between the owners of capital and those who work for a wage or a salary.

There is only one political party permitted, the Kuomintang. Some elections have been permitted since 1977, but those outside the party must run as individuals. The "Opposition" is divided into two factions, the "moderates" (those who have not yet been arrested) and the "radicals" (the wives and lawyers of those who have been arrested). One of the historic key demands of the Opposition is the removal of rule by martial law. Following the 1978 "elections," many of the Opposition leaders were arrested or forced into exile. (Winckler, 1984:493-496; Barrett and Whyte, 1982:1081-1083; Shapiro, 1981:11-13; Galenson, 1979:387-388; Thorbecke, 1979:192-197)

The success of export-led industrialization is based on cheap labour and the absence of regulations protecting workers and the environment. In the East Asian experience, this is achieved by repressive dictatorial governments. While this may appear to be "growth with equity" in the eyes of economists at Berkeley, Yale, and Harvard, it is doubtful if it is seen that way by ordinary farmers and workers.

Export-Oriented Industrialization and the Philippines

In the late 1960s and early 1970s, a group of economists identified with Yale University's Economic Growth Center advanced a theory of development based primarily on the relative success of Taiwan and South Korea. (Paauw and Fei, 1973; Fei and Ranis, 1964) The countries of Southeast Asia are described as having "open dualistic economies." They are "open" because trade plays a large role in gross domestic product and "dual" because of the difference between their agricultural and industrial sectors. When colonialism ended, they were all heavily dependent on exporting primary products to the metropolitan countries.

The first stage in the change in development policy for the newly independent countries comes with a shift to import-substitution industrialization. This experiment creates a group of local capitalists and a sector of the labour force with training and experience. However, productivity remains low in the largest sector of the economy, agriculture. This depresses further development, because the underdeveloped countries lack a growing domestic market. To break out of the "stagnation trap," it is necessary to find new markets for manufactured products; these are abroad, primarily in the industrialized countries. The first stage of the new, export-oriented industrial policy is the introduction of labour-intensive production; the "international comparative advantage" is provided by the large low-paid labour force. These new industries would absorb the excess rural population and allow the introduction of techniques to improve agricultural productivity. Following the Japanese experience, the model assumes that as labour becomes scarcer, the general standard of living will rise.

The key question, of course, is whether the success stories of East Asia can be extended to the underdeveloped countries as a whole. It would require a willingness by the already industrialized countries to accept a new international division of labour, with manufacturing shifting to the underdeveloped world. In general, this strategy has been supported by the United Nations Conference on Trade and Development (UNCTAD), which is dominated by the governments of the underdeveloped world. (Hoogvelt, 1981:73-83; Sampson, 1980)

The Yale model has raised some serious questions. Sampson (1980:113) notes that between 1970 and 1978 eight underdeveloped countries accounted for 77% of the increase in manufactured exports from the underdeveloped world. The major successes were the East Asian newly industrialized countries: South Korea, Taiwan, Hong Kong, and Singapore. Tyler (1976:369), noting that unemployment and underemployment are very high (close to 30%) in many of the underdeveloped countries, concludes that this strategy is really limited to "relatively small economies." Exports would have to be increased by close to 100% in order to reduce the unemployment level to 10%. Cline (1982:88-89) argues that there is a real limit to the amount of imports that developed capitalist countries can absorb before labour and other interests begin to demand protectionist measures; in 1976, manufactured exports from the underdeveloped world accounted for around 17% of their total of manufactured imports. Following the strategy of the East Asian NICs would require exports from all underdeveloped capitalist countries to rise seven-fold; this would increase their share of manufactured imports into the developed countries to 60%. An additional problem is the narrow composition of the imports, particularly high in processed foods, textiles, clothing, footwear, and electronics. Cline concludes that it is "seriously misleading" to hold up the East Asian NICs as a model for development, because it would surely provoke a protectionist response.

A similar position is taken by Landsberg. (1979:52-58) He notes that eight countries account for around 75% of the total manufactured exports of the underdeveloped world. The fifth largest exporter is India, whose population in 1980 was 30% greater than that of western and eastern Europe combined. Yet India's value added to manufacturing in that year was $16 billion, about the same as that of Sweden or Belgium. Landsberg argues that export-led industrialization policy blocks the development of an internal, self-expanding economy. Nayyar (1983:1821) points out that in 1980 the top ten underdeveloped countries accounted for 63% of all value added in manufacturing, 63% of all manufactured exports, and that this has hardly changed since 1965. On a per capita basis, even the top ten are far behind the industrialized countries in value added in manufacturing.

In the early 1970s the Philippines were chosen by the World Bank as a major test case for the new policy of export-oriented industrialization. (Elinson, 1983:156-157) Import-substitution industrialization increased production from 1945 to the early 1960s. However, growth began to stagnate because of the lure of highly-advertised U.S. brands, dependence on imported technology, the capital-intensive character of much of the manufacturing, the failure to develop "backward linkages" in the economy, and the grossly unequal distribution of income that limited the market. The U.S. government forced their client state to abolish import and exchange controls, and the International Monetary Fund forced a 100% devaluation of the peso. (Perpinan, 1983:170-172; Bello et al, 1982:127-132)

Academic endorsement for the new export-oriented industrialization policy for the Philippines came from the Yale group (Ranis, 1974; Ranis et al, 1974) in studies done for the International Labour Organization. The strategy was supported by the World Bank, the Asian Development Bank, the International Monetary Fund, and the U.S. government. (Bello et al, 1982:131) Full implementation of the development package was made easier after 1972, when President Ferdinand Marcos assumed dictatorial powers and declared Martial Law. Incentives for foreign investment were increased. Exporting manufacturers were given special tax exemptions and subsidized loans. Export Processing Zones were developed, providing an even greater range of subsidies to capital. Strikes were banned in "vital industries." Following the Singapore example, most trade unions were dissolved and the militant leaders purged or killed. The Labour Code was made more acceptable to business interests. Left-wing political opponents were jailed, killed, or "disappeared." Given this favourable investment climate, between 1973 and 1981 the World Bank lent the Philippines $2.6 billion for 61 special projects. (Elison, 1983:159, 164-165: Bello et al, 1982:140-146)

The overall growth record of the Philippines between 1946 and 1979 was good, with gross domestic product increasing in real terms by 5.7% per annum and per capita income rising at a rate of 2.4%. Trade was diversified after independence; dependence on the U.S. market for imports and exports declined from over 80% in 1946 to around 25% in 1980. But the food and agricultural sector has some serious problems. The land frontier suitable for crop production has been exhausted; there has been widespread degradation of the resource base, particularly in forestry; there has been over-exploitation of the inshore fisheries; and there has been a rapid increase in the population and the labour force. (Golay, 1983:254-255)

In the agricultural sector of the economy, emphasis was placed on increasing exports of sugar, coconuts, bananas, and pineapples. (Perpinan, 1983:174-175) However, as there was very little new land for cultivation, this meant diversion from food crops; by 1979, 30% of the country's 10 million hectares of arable land was planted to export crops. Following Martial Law, President Marcos announced that a land reform policy would be implemented, based on the World Bank's new policy of aiding small commercial producers. Aid was given to "efficient" producers; little land was given to the major sector, tenant farmers. The larger farmers were given access to credit and were able to buy fertilizers and pesticides to enhance the production of the high-yielding rice varieties. New irrigation projects displaced additional tenant farmers. The new policies tended to increase the unequal distribution of agricultural land.

Unemployment grew in both the rural and urban areas. Khan's study for the International Labour Office (1977:242-247) found an absolute decline in the income of the poorest 20% of the rural population between 1957 and 1974; only the top 20% increased their share of total income. There was also a decline in the real wages of all rural workers. This was also true in the urban areas, as the economy could not create an adequate number of jobs for the people entering the labour force. More recent data demonstrates that real wages increased slightly between 1950 and 1970, but declined by about 40% between 1970 and 1979. However, retail prices increased at an average annual rate of 12.2% in this latter period; food prices rose at a rate of 14.6%. (Golay, 1983:259)

The World Bank's own *Poverty Report* concluded that the rural development program, with its emphasis on increasing production of cash crops for export, was contributing to greater inequality. By the end of the 1970s the Philippines were exporting rice, yet the majority of Filipinos were eating less than they had been ten years earlier. While agricultural growth rates were very good, the number of families living below the poverty line increased by 23% between 1965 and 1975. Between 1971 and 1980 the real income of the bottom 30% of the population declined to US$.25 per day. (Elinson, 1983:160-161, 179, 185; Bello et al, 1982:678-99)

Overall, the World Bank's strategy of export-orientated industrialization was not very successful in the Philippines. Between 1950 and 1979 the net barter terms of trade continued to decline. The deficit in the trade balance grew until it totalled 35% of export earnings by 1980. Furthermore, the current account deficit rapidly increased to a level of 45% of total export earnings by 1980. The net outflow of investment income steadily increased between 1960 and 1978. In order to balance the deficit, the Philippines acquired a very large foreign debt; by the end of 1980 the annual debt service reached the level of 20% of foreign exchange earnings. Furthermore, fearing additional devaluation of the Philippine peso, there was a major flight of capital to safer havens abroad. (Golay, 1983:256-259)

Under mounting pressure to end his dictatorial rule, Marcos called a presidential election in early 1986. When the results appeared to be blatantly rigged in favour of Marcos, a broad-based popular movement forced him out of office and into exile. Mrs. Corazon Aquino, backed by the U.S. government, assumed the Presidency. She appointed a blue ribbon commission, dominated by academics, to draft an alternative economic plan. The preliminary report, released in May 1986, recommended the introduction of some fiscal policies to stimulate the depressed economy. However, its broad orientation was not significantly different from that of the Marcos regime. It called for less protection for domestic industry, less private support for business and large commercial agriculture, more support for free enterprise, the removal of import controls, and continued emphasis on manufacturing for export. The report was welcomed by the U.S. government, which had expanded aid to the new Philippine government.

The example of the Philippines certainly raises doubts about the potential for extending the export-orientated industrialization policy to additional underdeveloped countries. The social impact has been quite different in the Philippines than in South Korea or Taiwan. When imposed on a society already characterized by high underemployment and a high degree of inequality of income and wealth, it could only lead to even greater disparities.

Conclusion

The experience of Sri Lanka illustrates the limitations of social democracy in low-income underdeveloped countries. The UNP government elected in 1977 has chosen to follow the free-market, Southeast Asian model of development. In the competition for private foreign investment, it advertises its low wages, lack of environmental controls, and minimal regulations to protect workers. The disciplined work force is guaranteed by the one-party state and the use of "emergency powers." The persistent inequalities between the Tamil minority and the Sinhalese majority have obviously contributed to the dramatic increase in ethnic violence.

Both South Korea and Taiwan demonstrate that a relatively equitable distribution of income can result from a redistribution of productive assets. However, if capitalism and the market economy remain central to the system, it is inevitable that inequalities of income, wealth, status, and power will re-emerge. Adelman (1975b:70) notes that when Yugoslavia introduced a more liberal and decentralized economy, inequalities in the distribution of income started reasserting themselves rather quickly. She attributes this to "human nature." Leaving aside the question of original sin, recent evidence indicates that the gap in income between rural and urban workers, between skilled and unskilled workers, and between men and women is increasing in both South Korea and Taiwan. In Japan there was a redistribution of assets after the end of World War II, but it did not take long before the trend to income inequality reappeared. Chen (1979:161) reports that the share of income going to the bottom 20% of the Japanese population steadily dropped between 1956 and 1971 from 7.2% to 3.8%.

Among the members of the Association of Southeast Asian Nations (ASEAN), which includes the Philippines, the real incomes of workers in agriculture and manufacturing declined between 1966 and 1977. Indonesia had the best record of these states, yet the bottom 20% of the population received only 6.6% of the national income. (Limqueco, 1983:300) In all of these countries, the Gini coefficient of inequality has been rising over the 1960s and 1970s. (See *The Developing Economies*, XXIII, December 1985)

The dramatic changes in the world economy in the 1970s and 1980s resulted in a re-assessment of development strategies and theories. The period between 1974 and 1979 was characterized by high inflation rates yet also by rising unemployment and declining real wages. During this period the central bankers of the major industrialized capitalist states concluded that inflation was a greater threat than unemployment, and began to implement tight money policies through higher interest rates. At the September 1979 meeting of the International Monetary Fund at Belgrade, Yugoslavia, the governments of the major capitalist countries agreed to adopt conservative monetary and fiscal policies.

The response of the international agencies and banks to the debt crisis of the early 1980s was outlined in Chapter IX. The primary thrust of the International Monetary Fund has been to insist that the debt-ridden governments in the underdeveloped world reduce their spending on social programs, those which have been central to the basic human needs and "growth with equity" policies. The World Bank's commitment to basic human needs and the abolition of absolute poverty has been replaced by the ideology of monetarism, the central theme of their major report on development policies for sub-Saharan Africa (IMF, 1981). Emphasis is now on economic growth, best achieved by relying on the forces of the free market. The underdeveloped countries are advised to take advantage of the "international comparative advantage" of their resources and cheap labour, to cut restrictions on foreign private investment and imports and to reduce other government regulations. These policies will do little to help solve the problems of persistent poverty and undernutrition.

References

Adelman, Irma (1984). "Beyond Export-Led Growth." *World Development*, XII, No. 9, September, pp. 937-949.

Adelman, Irma (1975a). "Development Economics — A Reassessment of Goals." *American Economic Review*, LXV, No. 2, pp. 302-309.

Adelman, Irma (1975b). "Growth, Income Distribution and Equity-oriented Development Strategies." *World Development*, III, Nos. 2 & 3, February-March, pp. 67-76.

Adelman, Irma and Cynthia T. Morris (1973). *Economic Growth and Social Equity in Developing Countries*. Palo Alto: Stanford University Press.

Barone, Charles A. (1983). "Dependency, Marxist Theory, and Salvaging the Idea of Capitalism in South Korea." *Review of Radical Political Economics*, XV, No. 1, Spring, pp. 41-70.

Barrett, Richard E. and Martin K. Whyte (1982). "Dependency Theory and Taiwan: Analysis of a Deviant Case." *American Journal of Sociology*, LXXXVII, March, pp. 1064-1089.

Beckford, George L. (1972). *Persistent Poverty*. New York: Oxford University Press.

Bello, Walden et al (1982). *Development Debacle: The World Bank in the Philippines*. San Francisco: Institute for Food and Development Policy.

Bjorkman, James W. (1985). "Health Policy and Politics in Sri Lanka." *Asian Survey*, XXV, No. 5, May, pp. 537-552.

Brink, E.W. et al (1978). "Sri Lanka Nutrition Status Survey, 1975." *International Journal of Epidemiology*, VII, No. 1, March, pp. 41-47.

Brun, Ellen and Jacques Hersh (1976). *Socialist Korea: A Case Study in the Strategy of Economic Development*. New York: Monthly Review Press.

Bunge, Frederica M. (1982). *South Korea: A Country Study*. Washington, D.C.: The American University for the U.S. Department of the Army.

Burchett, Wilfred G. (1968). *Again Korea*. New York: International Publishers.

Chen, Edward K.Y. (1979). *Hyper-growth in Asian Economies*. London: Macmillan.

Chenery, Hollis et al (1974). *Redistribution with Growth*. Oxford: Oxford University Press for the World Bank and the Institute of Development Studies.

Cline, William R. (1982). "Can the East Model of Development be Generalized?" *World Development*, X, No. 2, February, pp. 81-90.

Elinson, Elaine (1983). "The Philippines: The Failure of Bank Strategy." In Jill Torre, ed. *Banking on Poverty*. Toronto: Between the Lines, pp. 154-168.

Fei, John C.H. and Gustav Ranis (1964). *Development of the Labor Surplus Economy*. Homewood, Ill.: Richard D. Irwin.

Food and Agriculture Organization (1983). *The State of Food and Agriculture*. Rome: FAO.

Food and Agriculture Organization (1982; 1981). *Production Yearbook*. Vol. 35. Rome: FAO.

Galenson, Walter (1979). "The Labour Force, Wages and Living Standards." In Walter Galenson, ed. *Economic Growth and Structural Change in Taiwan*. Ithaca: Cornell University Press, pp. 384-497.

Golay, Frank H. (1983). "Economic Challenges Facing the Philippines." *Journal of Southeast Asian Studies*, XIV, No. 2, September, pp. 254-261.

Gopolan, Coluther (1983). "Development and Deprivation: the Indian Experience." *Economic and Political Weekly*, XVIII, No. 51, December 17, pp. 2163-2168.

Gunatilleke, Godfrey and G.I.O.M. Kurukulasuria (1984). "The Global Economic Crisis and the Impact on Children in Sri Lanka." *World Development*, XII, No. 3, pp. 309-316.

Halliday, Jon (1980). "Capitalism and Socialism in East Asia." *New Left Review*, No. 124, November-December, pp. 3-25.

Harvard Institute for International Development (1981). *Nutrition Intervention in Developing Countries: An Overview*. Cambridge, Mass.: Hain Publishers.

Hirshman, Albert O. (1958). *The Strategy of Economic Development*. New Haven: Yale University Press.

Hoogvelt, Ankie M.M. (1982). *The Third World in Global Development*. London: Macmillan.

International Labour Office (1976). *Employment, Growth and Basic Needs: A One-world Problem*. Geneva: ILO.

Isenman, Paul (1980). "Basic Needs: The Case of Sri Lanka." *World Development*, VIII, No. 3, pp. 237-258.

Jayawardena, Kumari (1984). "The Plantation Sector in Sri Lanka: Recent Changes in the Welfare of Children and Women." *World Development*, XII, No. 3, pp. 17-328.

Jayawardena, Lal (1974). "Sri Lanka." In Hollis Chenery et al. *Redistribution with Growth*. Oxford: Oxford University Press for the World Bank and the Institute of Development Studies, pp. 273-279.

Khan, Azizur Rahman (1977). "Growth and Inequality in the Rural Philippines." In *Poverty and Landlessness in Rural Asia*. Geneva: International Labour Office, pp. 233-249.

Kihl, Young Whan and Dong Suh Bark (1981). "Food Policies in a Rapidly Developing Country: The Case of South Korea, 1960-1978." *The Journal of Developing Areas*, XVI, No. 1, October, pp. 47-70.

Koo, Hagen (1984). "The Political Economy of Income Distribution in South Korea: The Impact of the State's Industrialization Policies." *World Development*, XII, No. 10, pp. 1029-1037.

Landsberg, Martin (1984). "Capitalism and Third World Economic Development: A Critical Look at the South Korean 'Miracle'." *Review of Radical Political Economics*. XVI, Nos. 2/3, Summer-Fall, pp. 181-193.

Landsberg, Martin (1979). "Export-Led Industrialization in the Third World: Manufacturing Imperialism." *The Review of Radical Political Economics*, XI, No. 4, Winter, pp. 50-63.

Lee, E.L.H. (1979). "Egalitarian Peasant Farming and Rural Development: The Case of South Korea." *World Development*, VII, Nos. 4 & 5, April/May, pp. 493-517.

Lee, E.L.H. (1977). "Rural Poverty in Sri Lanka, 1963-73." In International Labour Office, *Poverty and Landlessness in Rural Asia*. Geneva: ILO, pp. 161-184.

Limqueco, Peter (1983). "Contradictions of Development in ASEAN." *Journal of Contemporary Asia*, XIII, No. 3, pp. 283-302.

Long, Don (1977). "Repression and Development in the Periphery: South Korea." *Bulletin of Concerned Asian Scholars*, IX, No. 2, April-June, pp. 26-41.

McNaughton, Jean (1983). "Nutrition Intervention Programmes: Pitfalls and Potential." *Ceres*, XVI, No. 2, March-April, pp. 28-33.

Makhoul, Najwa (1983). "Agricultural Research and Human Nutrition: A Comparative Analysis of Brazil, Cuba, Israel and the United States." *International Journal of Health Services*, XIII, No. 1, pp. 15-31.

Martin, Josh (1983). "Sri Lanka." *Multinational Monitor* IV, No. 5, May, pp. 19-21.

Moore, Mick (1984a). "On 'The Political Economy of Stabilization'." *World Development*, XIII, No. 9, September, pp. 1087-1092.

Moore, Mick (1984a). "Categorizing Space: Urban-Rural or Core-Periphery in Sri Lanka." *Journal of Development Studies*, XX, No. 3, April, pp. 102-122.

Morawetz, David (1980). "Economic Lessons from Some Small Socialist Developing Countries." *World Development*, VIII, August, pp. 337-369.

Nayyar, Deepak (1983). "International Relocation of Production and Industrialization in LDCs." *Economic and Political Weekly*, XVIII, No. 31, July 30, pp. PE13-PE26.

Omvedt, Gail (1984). "The Tamil National Question." *Bulletin of Concerned Asian Scholars*, SVI, No. 1, January-March, pp. 23-26.

Paauw, Douglas S. and John C.H. Fei (1973). *The Transition in Open Dualistic Economies: Theory and Southeast Asian Experience.* New Haven: Yale University Press.

Perpinan, Mary Soledad (1983). "The Philippines: Collision Course." In Jill Torrie, ed. *Banking on Poverty.* Toronto: Between the Lines, pp. 169-187.

Pfaffenberger, Bryan (1984). "Fourth World Colonialism, Indigenous Minorities and Tamil Separatism in Sri Lanka." *Bulletin of Concerned Asian Scholars*, XVI, No. 1, January-March, pp. 15-22.

Ponnambalam, Satchi (1980). *Dependent Capitalism in Crisis: The Sri Lankan Economy, 1948-1980.* London: Zed Press.

Ranis, Gustav (1974). "Employment, Equity and Growth: Lessons from the Philippines Employment Mission." *International Labour Review*, CX, No. 1, pp. 1-17.

Ranis, Gustav et al (1974). *Sharing in Development: A Programme of Employment, Equity and Growth for the Philippines.* Geneva: International Labour Office.

Reutlinger, Shlomo (1982). "World Bank Research on the Hunger Dimension of the Food Problem." *World Bank Research News*, III, No. 1, Winter, pp. 3-9.

Richards, P.J. (1981). "Comment on Isenman, 'Basic Needs: The Case of Sri Lanka'." *World Development*, IX, No. 2, February, pp. 215-218.

Rao, D.C. (1978). "Economic Growth and Equity in The Republic of Korea." *World Development*, VI, No. 6, June, pp. 383-396.

Rosenberg, W. (1980)."South Korea: Export-led Development — Sewered and Unsewered." *Journal of Contemporary Asia*, X, No. 3, pp. 300-308.

Samaraweera, Vijaya (1981). "Land, Labour, Capital and Sectional Interests in the National Politics of Sri Lanka." *Modern Asian Studies*, XV, No. 1, pp. 127-162.

Sampson, Gary P. (1980). "Contemporary Protectionism and Exports of Developing Countries." *World Development*, VIII, pp. 113-127.

Scott, Maurice (1979). "Foreign Trade." In Walter Galenson, ed. *Economic Growth and Structural Change in Taiwan.* Ithaca: Cornell University Press, pp. 308-383.

Selowsky, Marcelo (1981). "Income Distribution, Basic Needs and Trade-offs with Growth: The Case of Semi-Industrialized Latin American Countries." *World Development*, IX, pp. 73-92.

Shapiro, James E. (1981). "Taiwan: Young Women Risk Health." *Multinational Monitor*, II, No. 6, June, pp. 11-13.

Shorrock, Tim (1981). "South Korea." *Multinational Monitor* II. No. 6, June, pp. 8-10 et seq.

Smirnov, V. (1984). "Development of Foreign Economic Ties of the Democratic People's Republic of Korea." *Far Eastern Affairs*, No. 4, pp. 37-45.

Srinivasan, T.N. (1977). "Development, Poverty and Basic Human Needs: Some Issues." *Food Research Institute Studies*, XVI, No. 2, pp. 11-28.

Streeton, Paul (1982). "Growth, Redistribution and Basic Human Needs." In Claes Brundenius and Mats Lundahl, eds. *Development Strategies and Basic Needs in Latin America*. Boulder, Col.: Westview Press, pp. 31-54.

Suh, Sang Mok (1984). "Effects of the Current World Recession on the Welfare of Children: The Case of Korea." *World Development*, XII, No. 3, March, pp. 329-338.

Thomas, Clive Y. (1974). *Dependence and Transformation*. New York: Monthly Review Press.

Thorbecke, Erik (1979). "Agricultural Development." In Walter Galenson, ed. *Economic Growth and Structural Change in Taiwan*. Ithaca: Cornell University Press, pp. 132-205.

Tyler, William G. (1976). "Manufactured Exports and Employment Creation in Developing Countries: Some Empirical Evidence." *Economic Development and Cultural Change*, XXIV, No. 2, pp. 355-373.

Winkler, Edwin A. (1984). "Taiwan: From Hard to Soft Authoritarianism?" *China Quarterly*, No. 99, September, pp. 481-499.

World Bank (1984, 1982). *World Development Report*. Washington, D.C.: World Bank.

World Bank (1981). *Accelerated Development in sub-Saharan Africa: An Agenda For Action*. Washington, D.C.: IBRD.

CHAPTER ELEVEN

Alternatives for
Underdeveloped Countries

The persistence of inequality, poverty, unemployment, and undernutrition in both developed and underdeveloped capitalist states has convinced many to seek an alternative form of development. The vast majority of the underdeveloped capitalist states face many obstacles to development with equity, including extensive foreign ownership and control of the economy, reliance on the technology of the large capitalist corporations, the net outflow of capital due to external debt commitments, the historic dependence on the export of a few primary commodities, declining terms of trade for exports, unstable foreign markets, and the general ideological, social, and cultural impact of the world of advanced capitalism. Furthermore, almost all of the underdeveloped capitalist countries have dictatorial governments that regularly use repressive measures against working people and the political opposition. These governments, closely tied to the local and international business classes, maintain their control through military support from the formal colonial powers, and in particular, the U.S. government. Throughout the underdeveloped capitalist world there is a growing movement for an alternative, socialist road to development.

This chapter will look at the most prominent examples of the alternate road to development: China, North Korea, Cuba, and Nicaragua. Much of the theory and strategy for social change has emerged from the experience of these revolutionary governments. Special emphasis will be laid on how these governments have dealt with the issues of food, agriculture, and hunger.

The revolutionary movements in the underdeveloped countries have been greatly influenced by the writings of Marx, Engels, Lenin, and Mao. In addition, one of the main contributions to the theory of transition to socialism is Clive Y. Thomas's book, *Dependence and Transformation* (1974). For Thomas, only a planned socialist approach can lift the dependent former colonies up to the level of the industrialized countries while introducing democracy and equality.

The key to transformation is the creation of a worker-peasant alliance. While most underdeveloped countries are primarily agricultural, the struggle of organized labour is part of a *national* struggle to retain domestic income for local investment. In the drive to disengage from international capitalism, the underdeveloped states now have several options including "a drive to dynamic self-sufficiency, economic integration with the socialist group of countries, integration with other Third World countries, or some planned combination of these alternatives." (69) Trade can be maintained, as there is a widening area of available options.

For countries in the transition stage, it is necessary to have comprehensive planning, state ownership of the dominant means of production, and the state playing the key role in foreign trade. The first priority should be to serve local needs, which requires balancing output and demand. Import substitution should begin with the consumer goods needed by the local population. In contrast to many economists, Thomas insists that first priority should be placed on industrialization, particularly in agricultural industries and textiles. Emphasis should be on social and collective consumption combined with active support for the development of democracy and popular participation in the economy and the society.

In the area of agriculture, Thomas is strongly opposed to depending on the export of cash crops; it is a trap for underdeveloped countries, as the Tanzanian experience demonstrated to him. Emphasis should be on modernizing agriculture and moving into the production of higher quality food commodities. Basic self-sufficiency in food production is essential to break dependence on international capitalism.

As a general guide to planning, Thomas believes that the index of prices for food should not rise faster than the index for industrial goods. The barter terms of trade must remain in favour of industrial goods and against agriculture; this is an "inescapable condition" for financing industry. Yet Thomas insists that disparity in terms of trade should not be anywhere near as great as it was in the Soviet Union, or there will be a negative impact on production. Food production should increase "at a comfortable margin above consumption requirements." The move towards socialist organization of agriculture should be voluntary, to ensure maximum democratic participation in agricultural planning. In the long run, agricultural production must be rationalized and mechanized, and follow the path of capital and skill-intensive production and distribution. However, Thomas is convinced that the success of socialism in the transition phase rests on (1) avoiding hostile capitalist and imperialist intervention and the fall of marketable agricultural surpluses and (2) the success of the new state in systematically applying innovations in co-operation with a highly motivated peasantry. These are very difficult tasks, given the hostility of the capitalist countries. (Thomas, 1974:143-164)

China: Socialism in an Agrarian Underdeveloped Country

The triumph of the Communist Party in the civil war in China was a political event of enormous significance. China is a huge country, equivalent in size to Europe from Iceland to the Ural mountains. In population, it is twice that of western and eastern Europe combined and greater than that of all the capitalist states that now make up the Organization of Economic Co-operation and Development. The provinces of China are larger in size and population than many European states; Szechwan province has a greater population than any country in Europe. Thus, the revolution was a major defeat for world capitalism. The U.S. government, which had granted massive economic and military support to the Nationalists, went through a traumatic internal crisis trying to find someone to blame. Not only had one-quarter of the world's population been removed from the world capitalist market, there was the distinct possibility that China would serve as a model for other underdeveloped peasant countries. U.S. government policy, stressing the "containment" of communism in the Soviet Union and eastern Europe, now had to cope with the Asian giant. What follows here is a description of Chinese development strategy between 1949 and 1978, often called the Maoist theory of development. In Chapter VII reference was made to the changes made after 1978; they have been quite fundamental and clearly represent a reversal of the Maoist strategy of building socialism.

Rural mainland China was significantly different from Korea and the island province of Taiwan; there was a much greater polarization of wealth and income. In 1934 landlords (3% of the population) controlled around 26% of all land, and their average size of holding was around 11.5 hectares. They did not work the land but leased it to tenants. In contrast, the poor peasants and farm workers (68% of the population) controlled only 22% of the land, and their average size of holding was 0.5 hectares. The middle range of peasants, who hired labour and also worked the land, controlled the remainder. (Khan, 1977:254-258; Bergmann, 1975:185-187)

While Mao Tse-tung was a Marxist-Leninist, the political movement he led was greatly influenced by the Chinese revolutionary tradition, the philosophy of the People's Livelihood of Sun Yat-sen, and the realities of a society where a large majority of the population were agricultural workers and semi-proletarianized poor farmers. With the ideological split in the Kuomintang in 1927, the Nationalists under General Chiang Kai-shek became even more closely tied to the landlords, businessmen, and financiers; they could not carry out a program of land reform because of their class base. Rents collected by landlords remained between 50% and 70% of the total crop. On the other hand, where the revolutionary forces were in control, land reform and other popular changes were instituted. The turning point in the revolution probably came in the 1930s, when the Nationalists drove the Communists out of Kiangsi province; the land reforms and other changes introduced by the revolutionary forces were repudiated, and the property of the landlords was returned. This action stimulated the revolt against the landlords and the Kuomintang. Furthermore, the failure of Chiang and his forces to direct their military effort against the Japanese also assisted the Communist movement. Lacking support from the peasant masses, all the military help from the U.S. government could not save the old regime.

Recalling the experience of the Soviet Union, the Chinese Communists were cautious in the area of land reform. Before 1949, in the areas they controlled, this was limited to reduction of rents, limitations on the size of landholdings, expropriation of pro-Japanese landlords, and partial redistribution. In the first official reform (1949-1952) only around 50% of the land was redistributed. The landlords as a class were removed and their land was redistributed to the landless, the poor, and the middle peasants. By 1955, the average size of peasant holdings was between 2 and 4.35 hectares, and income was very egalitarian.

However, the leadership of the Communist Party did not believe that dwarf agriculture based on the family farm was the answer. Beginning in 1952 they expanded participation in producer or "elementary" co-operatives based on pooling; by 1956 close to 90% of all households belonged to "advanced co-operatives," where land and other major means of production were owned in common, and distribution was on the basis of work performed. Within seven years of the success of the revolution, a major social change had been achieved in the rural areas with very little opposition. Furthermore, during the period of socialization of agriculture, production steadily increased. This was a remarkable achievement, very different from the experience of the Soviet Union.

The Chinese leaders largely came from an agricultural background. Their long struggle against the Nationalist government had been as an agrarian revolutionary movement, working with the peasants on a daily basis. In addition, the Communist Party had twenty years of experience in land reform and government in the liberated areas. But Mao, like the Communists in the Soviet Union, believed that large units of production would provide more efficient use of land and other farm inputs, result in better organization of labour, and make the task of collecting agricultural taxes and food for the urban areas easier. However, equally important was the commitment of the Communist Party to equity: if private ownership of the means of agricultural production were continued, with renting and selling, this would simply re-create the inequalities of the past. This was already beginning to happen in the 1950s. To continue to support private household agriculture would be to follow the capitalist road. (Stavis, 1979:169-173; Kahn, 1977:258-264; Wong, 1976:486-488; Bergmann, 1975:187-190)

Between 1958 and 1960 the co-operatives were abolished and the People's Communes were introduced. The commune system was a structure for rural development encompassing three levels of ownership. For the great majority of the communes, the ownership of land, farming implements, and animals was at the lowest level, the team, which in 1959 averaged around 42 households. The team organized farming tasks and calculated and divided farm income. The second level was the production brigade, in 1959 averaging around 264 households; at the highest level were the communes, averaging around 6,000 households. By 1963 the number of communes had been increased to 76,000 each with a population of around 7,000. These two higher units provided general management and planning, were responsible for investment, owned large inputs and water resources, and mobilized labour for construction and large rural-development projects.

At the time of the revolution, the average farmer in China worked only 110 to 120 days a year. The task of the commune was to make better use of labour in the off season. Communes were responsible for the construction and maintenance of large water storage and flood control systems, land reclamation and reforestation, as well as the development of rural industries. They also provided local community services such as education, nurseries, health centres, and public security, as well as most of the functions of the old township. But equally important to Mao was the role of the commune as the central institution in a policy of increased local self-reliance, decentralization of power and decision-making, and participatory democracy. (O'Leary and Watson, 1983:593-596; Kojima, 1982:400-401; Stavis, 1979:177-180; Bergmann, 1975:189-194; Wong, 492-493)

In 1974 a team of agricultural scientists from the U.S. National Academy of Sciences toured China and were impressed by the brigade system, mainly organized on an ecological basis, supported by scientists and technicians working at the local level integrating applied research and demonstration work. They concluded that this decentralized approach had "obviously been effective in raising crop yields in all the areas we visited." (Wortman, 1975:20)

Aside from the creation of the communes, the Great Leap Forward (1958-1960) brought other major changes. First, there was the experiment with allocating personal income more on a basis of need than work contribution. It is widely agreed that this was a major failure; it was too great a change in too short a period of time. (Nolan, 1983:383; Khan, 1977:265-266) The problems caused by such major policy changes were made more difficult by the very adverse climatic factors of 1960-1962. (See Chapter VII) But of much greater significance was the decision taken on industrialization. While there was a split in the Communist Party at this time, the faction led by Mao wanted to distribute industry more equitably throughout the country rather than to continue the pattern of development concentrated on the coast. First, policies were adopted that limited the migration of people from rural to urban centres. Secondly, there was encouragement to develop industries at the commune level. The Maoist faction felt that labour-intensive local industries would more effectively use local resources and help provide off-season work for underemployed peasants. These fell into three broad categories: (1) the "five small industries": iron and steel, cement, fertilizers, energy, and machinery; (2) repair and manufacture of agricultural machinery and tools; and (3) plants for processing agriculture and sideline products. By 1973 63% of fertilizers and 50% of cement came from the rural industries. Nevertheless, the relatively unplanned transfer of labour to non-agricultural employment disrupted the harvest. (Gek-boo, 1979:57; Wong, 1976:493; Paine, 1976:280-282)

One major difference between the experience of the USSR and China has been in the pricing system for agricultural products and the internal terms of trade. Since the 1950s, agricultural products have been placed in three categories: (1) major crops essential to the livelihood of the population (grains, cotton, soybeans, rapeseed, and peanuts); (2) industrial products (hemp, sugar cane, tea, wool, etc); and (3) local and sideline products that can be sold on the free market or through barter exchange. Only the first two categories have been covered by quotas or agricultural taxes. During the 1960s and 1970s, around 25% of peasant income came from the third category. (Nolan, 1983:386; Hsu, 1982:639-640)

As in Japan, the compulsory quota (or agricultural tax) remained fixed in physical terms. It was established from average yields, taking into account ecological conditions. In the early 1950s, the tax was around 13% of agricultural income; by the mid-1970s, it had declined to only 4-5%. In the case of crop failure, the tax was remitted. For communes in poor ecological areas, the quotas were minimal; when production fell below this level, the tax was exempted. Nevertheless, the delivery prices for the basic quota were estimated to be 25-50% below free market prices. However, from the early 1950s until 1979, the state paid a bonus of 30% for deliveries of foodgrains and major cash crops over the basic quota.

The other major factor in rural development was the barter terms of trade with industrial goods, particularly farm inputs. Prices charged for agricultural production goods have steadily declined from the outset. The fixing of basic prices by the state also has the effect of virtually eliminating inflation. The result was a steady increase in the use of modern agricultural inputs and production, in direct contrast to the "scissors effect" so characteristic of the USSR. In revolutionary China, the agricultural terms of trade were set to favour the agricultural sector. (Nolan, 1983:386-389; Hsu, 1982:639-643; Kojima, 1982:395-403; Gek-boo, 1979:53; Wong, 1976:490; Paine, 1976:285-287)

Stavis (1979:175; 188) concludes that the collective approach to agriculture in China produced both steady growth and improving equity. Household consumption data for the 1960s and 1970s indicate that the ratio of the top 20% of income earners and the bottom 20% was the lowest in Asia, including Japan, South Korea, and Taiwan. Paine (1976:291) concludes that per capita consumption down to 1975 increased at a rate of around 2.4% per annum. Furthermore, this was on top of a *consumption floor* that included universal health and education, a guaranteed level of consumption of food, cheap housing, rationing of scarce goods when necessary, and a system of relative prices that discriminated against luxury goods. Full employment was a key to Chinese success.

From the beginning, there was rationing of cereals, cooking oil, and cotton cloth. Coupons were attached to residence cards, and the ration was available at the individual's consumer unit. In determining rationing requirements, the Team used the standards set in 1973 by the Food and Agriculture Organization and the World Health Organization. (See Chapter I) The basic ration provided the average working adult with about 1500 kcal of grain per day. (Rada, 1983:522-524; Klatt, 1983:18-19)

Nevertheless, disparities in personal income persisted. In his study for the International Labour Office, Khan (1977:167-276) noted the difference in incomes at the team level between men and women and between households. Given the workpoint system (remuneration according to either piece work or labour time), household income differed because of demographic factors (the number of male workers, children, and the elderly, and the presence of illness in the family). The skills of workers also differ, and this was reflected in the workpoint system of remuneration. The other major factor was the difference in resources available to the team in terms of quality of land and crops suitable to location. Differences in household income ranged as high as 2 to 1. Secondly, there was inter-commune inequality of income, most of which was due to resource differences. Again, inequalities were significant.

Ironically, the principles of decentralization contributed to these inequalities. First, the central government encouraged communes to save and invest; the rich communes grew much faster than the poorer ones, had higher labour productivity rates, and were able to diversify into sideline industries. Second, the agricultural tax was fixed, not progressive. Thus the richer communes paid a lower percentage of total income in taxes and had more to distribute as income or to invest. Third, the state paid a premium of 30% for deliveries over the basic quota; the communes with the richer resources were again able to take better advantage of the pricing system. (Gek-boo, 1979:52-55; Khan, 1977:267-271)

The leadership of the Communist Party was very aware of this situation. During the latter period of the Cultural Revolution, experiments were made to try to equalize income within the borders of the commune. On several experimental communes, food was distributed according to actual need rather than simply by work points. There were attempts to aid the poorer communes by allocating them more farm machinery, giving them extra help in infrastructure programs, instituting joint state-commune enterprises, and state aid to develop local industries.

The Maoist leadership recognized that these inequalities would persist as long as Chinese society accepted the "two bourgeois rights" as described by Marx. First, there was inequality of rental income from the use of the basic resources of land and water. Second, there was the right of individual remuneration according to work, regardless of the social situation. However, the lesson from the Great Leap Forward was that the peasants were not ready for a major change.

In Chapter VII it was noted that beginning in 1978 there was a major change in policy direction. Approximately one year after Mao's death, Deng Xiaoping was restored to high office. During the Great Proletarian Cultural Revolution he and Liu Shaoqi had been the leaders of the right-wing or "capitalist road" faction of the Communist Party; originally expelled for this open opposition, he was restored to his party positions in 1973, only to be expelled again in 1976. In contrast to most of the leaders of the Party, Deng came from a rich family and had been isolated from workers and peasants. When Hua Guofeng stepped down from leader of the Party in December 1980, it signalled the consolidation of Deng's power. The significant re-direction of policy after 1978 towards the free market strongly supports Mao's position that agricultural and food policy is not just a question of "modernization" or what is the best technology; it is an ideological and political question, a "two-line struggle" between left and right. (Nolan and White, 1981:4-6; Gek-boo, 1979:58-61; Khan, 1977:286-280)

Nevertheless, the quality of life had greatly improved under the revolutionary government. A key factor in the success prior to 1979 was guaranteed full employment. This helped to "take care of calories first." All benefitted from improvements in sanitation and hygiene, education, better nutrition, and the egalitarian rationing of basic needs in times of crisis. An adequate, nutritional diet was considered a basic human right — not a welfare program. Leung (1983:140-150) cites the emphasis on preventative medicine, and points to the longer average life span (now up to 70), and lower infant mortality rates. Hospital statistics from 1972 reveal that the infant death rate in Shanghai was considerably below that of New York City. Furthermore, figures on the cause of death for Shanghai are very similar to those in the United States, with cancer and cardiovascular disease heading the list. She notes that one of the health advantages that China has had over capitalist underdeveloped countries was the absence of advertising of "junk" foods by multinational corporations.

In revolutionary China there was no isolated food or nutrition policy. There was an overall development policy with emphasis on "agriculture as the base," linking traditional methods with new technology. It was an integrated policy with expansion of the industrial sector closely linked to agriculture and providing first the basic needs of the population. Growth with equity was possible because of the social ownership of the means of production and a policy of full employment.

The new policy of Deng Xiaoping stresses "the full scope of the market's regulatory role," individual family farming, private ownership of the means of agricultural production other than land, and the development of small-scale rural industries by private entrepreneurs using hired labour. Agricultural land is now leased by the townships to individual families. The lease is for five years and is automatically renewed; furthermore, family members now have hereditary tenure rights to this piece of public property. If a family chooses not to farm their land, they can rent it to other families. Critics see this as a major step back to the situation that existed before the collectivization of the early 1950s. Under the leadership of Deng, the Communist Party has apparently opted for the Japanese/South Korea/Taiwan model of labour-intensive family farming on small plots of land. This is one way of utilizing underemployed labour. It is tacit recognition that mechanization of agriculture has largely been abandoned.

The consensus of outside observers seems to be that the new policy of "getting rich first" is beginning to produce very visible inequalities between a few favoured individuals and families and the majority of the people. In contrast, official government figures claim that the gap in the standard of living between rural and urban families is narrowing. (*Beijing Review*, March 10, 1986; July 22, 1985)

North Korea: Socialism and Self-reliance

The northern part of divided Korea is slightly larger than the south in total area, but the population is only half that of the south. The Korean peninsula is quite mountainous, and arable land is limited. While both areas have about the same amount of arable land, the warmer southern zone permits double cropping of rice in many areas, while this is practically unknown in the north. There, almost 98% of arable land is planted to cereals; 36% is planted to rice, with the remainder in hardier grains. Under Japanese colonial rule, most of the mining and industrial development took place in the northern zone, which has a relative abundance of natural resources.

In 1946, the North Korean Interim People's Committee adopted the first Land Reform Act, which abolished tenancy, confiscated land held by the Japanese and Korean landlords, prohibited mortgages and the buying and selling of land, and put an upper limit of 5 hectares on the amount of land any farm family could own. The reforms took only three weeks to implement, and there was no resistance; Korean landlords were moved to other areas and permitted to farm. The recipients of the free land were poor peasants and landless farmworkers. A Farmer's Bank was established, which granted credit at low interest rates. Mutual aid teams were formed to share some work and draft-animals, and service co-operatives were established. Rural production teams were organized to undertake irrigation and reclamation projects, and a program of rural housing and education. From the beginning, the North Korean provisional government, led by Kim Il Sung, was committed to a policy that would change the economy from exporting food and raw materials to self-reliant industrialization. These goals were interrupted by the civil war of 1950-1953. (Halliday, 1981:890-893; Foster-Carter, 1977:45-46; Brun and Hersch, 1976:126-140)

The civil war was devastating to North Korea. The U.S. airforce destroyed almost everything that was standing north of the 38th parallel. In the city of Pyongyang, only two buildings were left standing; its population was reduced from 400,000 to 80,000. Between 12% and 15% of the population was killed, a higher percentage than the USSR lost in World War II. Industry was destroyed. Hydroelectric and irrigation dams were bombed, as were North Korea's elaborate system of dikes, flooding huge areas of farmland. Around 90% of North Korea was ravaged by the South Korean and American armies before they were pushed back by the intervention of the Chinese People's Army. In many areas, the demarcation lines between farms were completely destroyed. (Halliday, 1981:893; Gittings, 1977:32-35; Foster-Carter, 1977:47; Brun and Hersch, 1976:163-167)

Over the period from 1954 to 1958, agriculture in North Korea was completely re-organized, with the formation of co-operative farms based on collective ownership. The size of the co-operative farms increased; by 1980 they averaged 1,000 ha with between 400 and 500 households. The basic unit of production is still the work team and the even smaller sub-team. These are usually organized according to crop specialization; in addition, work groups are organized for certain seasonal tasks. In contrast to the experience in China, the co-operatives have allocated work to the teams and subteams on the basis of individual physical ability in an effort to try to equalize income. Teams working on easier tasks are composed mainly of women and the elderly. Income payments are made according to a work point system, and both prestige and material incentives are widely used. Private family plots and local peasant markets have been maintained. (Hendry, 1983:33-34; Bunge, 1981:140-146; Brun and Hersch, 1976:194-206)

Agricultural production and yields rose steadily through the period of collectivization. The agricultural tax was set at 25%, but it was completely abolished in 1966. Despite its limited area of arable land and a relatively short growing season, North Korea has basically maintained food self-sufficiency, a major policy goal. The FAO estimates that in 1980 North Korea was a net importer of agricultural products, mainly wheat, worth $82 million. In contrast, South Korea's deficit in agricultural trade in that year was $2.7 billion. North Korea's success in agriculture is the result of significant investment in the form of irrigation, land reclamation, complete rural electrification, large-scale use of fertilizers and pesticides, and mechanization. In 1983 the FAO reported that North Korea had 14 tractors per 1,000 hectares of arable land, compared to 2 in South Korea. However, by the time of their 1980 mission to North Korea, it was well above that figure. Farm tractors in North Korea are sit-down models, not just the walk-behind variety commonly found in dwarf agriculture in Asia. There is a high level of technical expertise, supported by an extensive system of post-secondary education and on-farm educational programs. The FAO mission reported that each co-operative farm had between 55 and 60 trained people on staff. By 1980 rice yields were reported to have reached 6,000 kg/ha, equivalent to those of Japan. Wheat yields had reached 2500 kg/ha, 33% higher than yields in China and 75% higher than in India; in fact, average yields were higher than those in the U.S.A. or Canada. Meat production concentrates on poultry and pigs, with cattle, sheep, and goats being raised in the more mountainous pasture areas. (Hendry, 1983:34; Bunge, 1981:137-139; Halliday, 1981:893-894; McCormack, 1981:52; Foster-Carter, 1977:48-50; Brun and Hersch, 1976:217-227)

North Korea's development strategy placed top priority on the development of heavy industry; between 1954 and 1970, this sector grew by an average of 23.5% per annum. Defying orthodox economic theory, the emphasis was put on capital goods and infrastructure. North Korea now produces all its own locomotives and rolling stock, tractors, trucks, buses, bulldozers, ships, manufacturing machinery and engines, and is now rapidly expanding in the consumer goods areas of television sets, radios, appliances, watches, etc. By the mid-1960s farm implement factories existed in all provinces; there has been considerable decentralization of light industry to try to achieve a level of provincial self-reliance.

North Korea's major raw material shortage has been the lack of oil. It has compensated for this by developing its coal reserves and building an extensive system of hydroelectric power. North Korea depended on the USSR for its imported oil (5-10% of energy use) so, when the USSR raised the price of oil by 130% in 1975, they responded by building an oil pipeline to China. Public transportation in urban areas stresses underground electric trains, and heating in urban centres is by the extremely efficient central hot water system. (White, 1982:337-339; McCormack, 1981:53-54; Halliday, 1984:894-895; Foster-Carter, 1977:49-50; Brun and Hersch, 1976:256-272)

The ideological basis for this development strategy is *juche*, which is commonly thought to mean self-reliance. However, it means much more than that. Close observers of North Korea explain that it is a form of psychological decolonization, which includes the need to transform nature and society by being independent and creative. The national strategy calls for 60-70% self-sufficiency in all sectors of the economy, wherever possible. Substitution has played a key role in this policy. The most widely known example has to do with energy, but equally significant is the use of coal for fertilizers and limestone for textiles. *Juche* is not a call for autarchy. North Korean policy emphasizes proletarian internationalism, but without becoming integrated into the Soviet-dominated COMECON system. North Korean development policy takes the position that national specialization can only work when trading nations have achieved relatively equal levels of development under socialism. (McCormack, 1981:54; Halliday, 1981:892-893; Brun and Hersch, 1978:19-23; Foster-Carter, 1977:48-49)

There are three basic principles to North Korean self-sufficiency. (1) Sources of accumulation should be generated internally; foreign assistance should clearly be in an auxiliary role. (2) The economy should be comprehensive, diversified, and organically linked. (3) Emphasis should be placed on achieving as much self-reliance in raw materials and fuels as possible. In practice, the government's policies have stressed import-substitution industrialization, diversification of external economic ties, and self-sufficiency in food production through heavy investment. (White, 1982:335, 343-345)

Nevertheless, it is known that during and after the civil war North Korea received considerable economic and military assistance from the USSR, China, and the eastern European states. One U.S. source, which relies heavily on data from the U.S. Central Intelligence Agency, estimates this at $2.8 billion between 1945 and 1978, about one-half of which came from the USSR. (Bunge, 1981:p. 255) Recently the Soviet Union has published figures on the extent and nature of this assistance in *Far Eastern Affairs*. (Smirnov, 1984:37-45) They claim that between the years 1954 and 1960 "free assistance" from the socialist countries accounted for 77% of North Korea's total imports and about 75% of its total capital investment. After 1960 the USSR granted credits at 2% interest rates. Furthermore, the USSR accepted repayment in barter goods produced by the enterprises that had been built. The USSR argues that enterprises it helped to build "are responsible for 63 per cent of the DPRK's electric energy, 50 per cent of its coal, 33 per cent of its steel, 42 per cent of its iron ore, 44 per cent of its organic fertilizers, 50 percent of its petroleum products, and 20 per cent of its fabrics." Nevertheless, North Korea successfully refused to have its economy integrated with COMECON. (White, 1982:332-336)

After 1971 North Korea adopted a policy of trading more with the capitalist countries. Many observers believe that by this time North Korea was at least equal to the USSR in industrialization and technology, was facing a labour shortage, and needed to look elsewhere for highly developed technology. Imports from Japan and other Asian countries expanded; exports also increased, particularly to Japan and Saudi Arabia. However, the price for certain key North Korean exports (particularly tungsten, tin, and zinc) fell, while the price for imported oil increased. By 1975 total foreign debt rose to around $1.8 billion, of which $700 million was to the USSR;

South Korea's debt, by comparison, rose to around $8 billion in that year. In spite of pressures from the international financial community, the North Koreans refused to open their books to the International Monetary Fund to meet their usual demands, refused to cut social spending, and simply announced that they would have to defer some of their payments, made in goods rather than currency. High growth rates were maintained during this period of financial adjustment, and the debts proved not to be a major problem. However, the problems associated with the rescheduling of debt payments has hindered the expansion of trade with the west. (White, 1982:347-349; Halliday, 1981:896-897; McCormack, 1981:53; Brun and Hersch, 1978:22-27)

North Korea is perhaps the least known of the underdeveloped countries, and the government has been quite secretive. Thus, independent data on the standard of living, per capita income, and income differentials is simply lacking. The only sources are the official figures produced by the government and outside observation. McCormack reports that in 1980 a delegation of Japanese scholars concluded that the per capita claim of $1920 was probably accurate. Others have concluded that this understates the level of standard of living. The 1980 FAO mission estimated that the average income of co-operative members was between $1200 and $1500 per annum, *over and above the social wage.* It is difficult to put a figure on the value of the very extensive social wage available to all citizens: free education through a widespread system of post-secondary education, a highly developed free health service, heavily subsidized housing and public utilities, a well developed system of modern public transportation, food price controls and heavy government subsidies for rice, a social security system as good as that in the industrialized countries, the absence of any taxes on the individual, and extended government investment in culture, sport, and entertainment. Workplaces, co-operatives, and schools have extensive cafeterias, nurseries, health services, libraries, and recreation centres. With extensive investment, subsidies, and high prices for crops, the standard of living of those on co-operative farms is considered to be as high as, if not higher than, in the urban areas. The high "physical quality of life" data, accepted by international institutions, are consistent with a very egalitarian, developed economy. (Hendry, 1983:35; McCormack, 1981:50-51; Halliday, 1981:898-901; Foster-Carter, 1977:51-52; Brun and Hersch, 1976:289-292)

In 1946 the provisional government passed a Law on the Equality of the Sexes, granting equal rights in all areas and banning prostitution. Women now make up 50% of the workforce and receive generous maternity and other child benefits. However, since the civil war, the political leadership has been very concerned about South Korea, with a population twice as large as North Korea's and a very large standing army. As a result, women are encouraged to work until they are 30 and then have children. This policy of encouraging an increasing population includes the absence of birth control and abortion services. The large standing army in North Korea is part of a militarization of the society which is not unlike that of South Korea, with the resulting emphasis on male qualities. Furthermore, as is common in the states with Marxist-Leninist parties in control, women are not found in leadership positions in either the government or the Korean Workers Party. (Halliday, 1985:46-56; Halliday, 1981:898)

North Korea does provide an experience which must be of considerable interest to other underdeveloped countries. But it is not likely to be a model that can be widely duplicated. It has achieved a high degree of self-reliance, but this has been greatly aided by extensive economic support from other socialist countries and the availability of adequate energy and other raw materials needed for industrialization. Gross exploitation by the Japanese, the Cold War, and the Korean civil war have produced a society not only dominated by the military but run by a political system that does not appear to permit real open discussion of important political questions. Furthermore, the glorification of political leaders seems to be more characteristic of a traditional kingdom than a socialist society.

Cuba: The Plantation Economy and Socialism

Cuba, the largest island in the Caribbean, was integrated into the world mercantile colonial system at an early period. The indigenous peoples were almost completely eliminated, and the island was transformed by the Spanish into *latifundia* cattle estates. The plantation system, based on sugar and slave labour from Africa, was later in coming, expanding rapidly after the revolt of the slaves in Haiti in 1791. The other major crop at this time was coffee. Cuba has a tropical climate, and a fairly high percentage of the land is suitable for agriculture: in 1980, 28% of it was under cultivation and 22% was in permanent pasture. While free from frost, Cuban agriculture has the problems characteristic of tropical agriculture: the persistence of pests and diseases. In addition, the island regularly experiences very damaging hurricanes. Furthermore, Cuba has no fossil fuel energy resources.

Cuban planters and merchants did not join the Latin American revolt against Spain between 1810 and 1820, because they were afraid of a slave revolt. In 1868 a war for independence erupted, lasted ten years, and was disastrous for the economy. The second war for independence (1894-1902) brought military intervention by the U.S. government. The result was quasi-independence. The U.S. military occupied Cuba for three years. When an agreement was reached on the removal of U.S. troops, under the provisions of the peace treaty, the U.S. government retained the major naval base at Guantanamo Bay and the right to intervene directly, at will. The U.S. government and military regularly intervened in the internal affairs of Cuba until the military coup of 1934, headed by General Fulgencio Batista.

In the period after 1902 Cuba had been transformed into a classic example of underdevelopment as described by André Gunder Frank and the world-system theorists. U.S. capital took control of the cash crop plantation economy, the financial system, and other major sectors of the economy. Cuba received a sugar quota from the United States that provided a guaranteed market at prices higher than the world price; in return, American imports entered Cuba without tariffs or quotas. Sugar accounted for around 85% of all exports, and 60% of all trade was with the United States. Around one-third of all food and almost all manufactured goods were imported from the United States. Havana was a playground for rich Americans, with organized crime dominating one of the worst examples of the tourist industry in any underdeveloped capitalist country. A large middle class developed, mainly in Havana, dependent on the close relationship with the United States.

Poverty was widespread. In 1953 70% of the economically active people in rural areas were labourers. They worked between 135 and 180 days a year and were unemployed for the rest of the time. Farm labourers were generally denied land to grow their own food, and many gravitated to the urban slums in the off season. Large areas of land suitable for cultivation were held in pasture by the cattle ranches; in the fall Cubans were hired to cut the brush. A study by the World Bank in 1950 concluded that 30% to 40% of the urban population and 60% of the rural population were undernourished. (Benjamin, 1984:2-14; Pollitt, 1982:12-13; Eckstein, 1981:179-180; Beckford, 1972:84-113; O'Connor, 1972:52-73; Dumont, 1970:1-23)

In 1953 Fidel Castro and his small band of middle-class reformers began their armed rebellion against the brutal dictatorship headed by Batista. They were soon joined by the peasants and farm workers. The rebellion was opposed by the U.S.-controlled trade unions and the Communist Party. On January 1, 1959 the revolutionary army entered Havana and took control of the government.

The first major act of the new government was the Agrarian Reform Law of May 1959. It abolished all rents in lands and gave tenant farmers, sharecroppers, and squatters (around 100,000) title to the land they farmed. The government guaranteed prices for their crops and granted low-interest credit. No individual farm could exceed 400 hectares. Twelve thousand large plantations and ranches were nationalized and transformed into state farms; the owners were compensated by 20-year government bonds at a 4.5% interest rate. The large sugar estates were deemed best suited for cash crop production and mechanization; they were not divided into small individual holdings but retained as state farms. There was no pressure to do so from farm labourers. However, wage-earners on the new state farms could now grow their own food on the land where they lived. Individual small farmers were granted additional land to bring their minimum holdings up to 27 hectares and given the option to buy an additional 40 hectares. By

1961 one-half of the farmland had been adjusted by the new law, and the state now controlled 44% of the land.

In March 1960 Cuba signed a barter deal with the USSR, trading sugar for needed oil. When the foreign-owned oil companies in Cuba refused to refine Soviet oil, they were nationalized. In response to this, the Eisenhower Administration cancelled Cuba's sugar quota. Facing a potential economic disaster, the revolutionary government responded by nationalizing all American-owned businesses and land holdings. The U.S. government retaliated with an embargo on trade with Cuba. In April 1961 a group of U.S.-trained Cuban exiles landed at the Bay of Pigs in an effort to overthrow the Castro government; they were easily defeated by the Cuban militia. As many commentators have noted, the U.S. government succeeded in trans- forming a populist reform movement into a socialist regime closely tied to the USSR. (Alroy, 1972:3-17; Blasier, 1972:18-49; O'Connor, 1972:73-81; Dumont, 1970:23-26)

In 1961 the National Association of Small Farmers was formed, limited to farmers with less than 67 hectares. They received special treatment from the Cuban government, including interest-free loans. This set the stage for the Second Agrarian Land Reform of 1963. All land holdings over 67 hectares were nationalized and transformed into state farms; this comprised around 10,000 farms and 20% of the agricultural land. The private farming sector consisted of around 170,000 farms covering roughly 30% of the arable land.

As a result of the cancellation of the sugar quota in the U.S. market, a boycott that cut off the traditional source of imported food, and the American military intervention, the new Cuban government decided to diversify agriculture and emphasize self-reliance in food production. This was reflected in the first Five Year Plan, often called the "early Cuban model." By 1962 well over 175,000 hectares of land had been reclaimed and planted to new food crops. The redistribution of farmland led to significant increases in on-farm consumption; when combined with the effects of the U.S. blockade, there was not enough food to meet the demand in the urban areas. Ironically, one of the major new problems in the rural areas was a shortage of labour, particularly at harvest time. (Benjamin, 1984:150-164; Pollitt, 1982:13-17; Eckstein, 1981:190-193; Dumont, 1970:27-58)

Cuba's highly dependent economy could not change overnight. By 1962 there was a serious balance of payments problem. Sugar exports were dropping, and there was no other available export to earn needed foreign exchange. Beginning in 1961, the USSR and the eastern European countries bought sugar on a barter basis at prices fixed above the world level. Between 1963 and 1972 the price paid by the USSR was slightly above 6 cents a pound; over that ten-year period the world price fluctuated between 1.8 and 8.3 cents a pound, averaging out at just above 4 cents a pound. After 1973 the price of Cuban sugar exported to the USSR was tied to an index of imported commodities, including oil. This form of "socialist trade" resulted in sugar export prices well above the world market price. As a result of this trading arrangement, the Cuban government shifted back to heavy emphasis on sugar as a cash crop export. In 1982 it was estimated that the Soviet Union was subsidizing the Cuban economy by about $3 billion annually, through the guaranteed sugar price. To see this in proportion, Puerto Rico receives around $4 billion in aid from the U.S. government each year, four times more, per capita, than Cuba receives from the USSR. The U.S. government still allocates sugar quotas to politically friendly states and sets the price several times above that of the free market. (Benjamin, 1984:128-129, 143, 180-182; Radell, 1983:365-382; Pollitt, 1982:17-19; Eckstein, 1981:187-188)

In order to combat the problem of the labour shortage, and to reduce the drudgery of hand-cutting sugar cane, Cuba put a high priority on mechanization of this key industry. Massey-Ferguson combines had been imported from Canada, but the trade embargo and foreign exchange problems threatened this source. At one point, combines were imported from the Soviet Union. Then Soviet and Cuban technicians developed the KTP-1 combine, which is now manufactured in Cuba and exported. Between 1970 and 1979 the percentage of the harvest cut by hand was reduced from 99% to 58%. (Pollitt, 1982:19-20)

The new revolutionary government also undertook a broad range of reforms outside of agriculture. In 1960 urban rents were reduced by up to 50%; in 1962 rents were limited to 10% of the income of the head of the household. A massive program of expanding education, daycare and nurseries, health and medicine was undertaken. The minimum wage was raised. Gambling and prostitution were outlawed. Retirement ages were lowered to 60 for men and 55 for women. Water, power, and public transportation rates were lowered. First priority was placed on expanding the social wage. (Benjamin, 1984:18, 87; Valdes-Brito and Henriquez, 1983:479; Brundenius, 1982:148-153)

But some of the more imaginative programs were in the area of distribution of food. These are detailed in the study by the Institute for Food and Development Policy, *No Free Lunch: Food and Revolution in Cuba Today*. A program of price controls on food was instituted just three months after the revolutionaries took office. The wholesale food industry was nationalized, as were many retail stores. The government established a string of people's stores in the rural areas to supply food and other basic consumer goods at official prices. By 1982 around 20% of the population received at least one hot meal a day in cafeterias at schools, workplaces, and hospitals. Children at daycare centres receive two hot meals a day plus two snacks. In rural areas, students at boarding schools get all their meals free.

One of the most important socialist policies of the Cuban government has been the food rationing system. Many underdeveloped capitalist countries have had some form of food rationing or subsidy program, usually limited to certain staples and certain target groups. This is the social welfare approach favoured by the international institutions. In contrast, the Cuban rationing system is based on the socialist principle of food as a human right; it includes all the basic foods considered necessary for an adequate diet. The ration is available at government-owned neighbourhood stores. Prices for these basic foods were frozen between 1962 and 1981. The basic ration is the equivalent of around 1900 kilocalories per day. Over and above the daily ration, food is available from the state-run parallel market outlets, at restaurants (which are also government owned and operated), directly from farmers, or from independent sellers on the black market. Farmers' markets were approved in 1980, but when the prices charged by the small farmers for preferred goods went high, urban workers openly expressed considerable resentment. Nevertheless, the markets have been continued. (Benjamin, 1984:26-57)

There are still shortages of certain foods highly prized by Cubans; the system of food production and distribution is still evolving on a path to greater self-reliance. Nevertheless, everyone is guaranteed an adequate diet. This is reflected in health statistics. Life expectancy has risen from 58 in 1958 to 73 in 1981. Over the same period, infant mortality rates per 1000 live births declined from 70 to 18.5. By 1982 the crude death rate had fallen to 6, the lowest of any underdeveloped country. The average height of the population at different ages is also increasing. The cause of death has changed from infectious and acute diarrheal diseases to heart disease and cancer, as in industrial societies. The average adult daily intake of calories has risen to around 2800, and obesity is becoming a problem. (Benjamin, 1984:96-97; Valdes-Brito and Henriquez, 1983:480-484)

Rapid improvement in the standards of basic needs supplied the whole population has not been made at the expense of economic growth. Despite the difficulties of economic transformation, the economy has been growing at an acceptable rate; between 1972 and 1977 it grew at an average annual rate of 8.3%. Open unemployment dropped from 11.8% in 1958 to 1.3% in 1978. (Brundenius, 1982:147, 158) By 1980 the agricultural labour force had declined to 23% of the total, and the rural population was diminishing in absolute numbers. In contrast to the rest of Latin America, displaced agricultural workers are not found in huge urban slums but in productive employment in industry and a service sector that pays regular wages. The revolutionary government in Cuba has demonstrated that hunger can be completely eliminated and that economic growth can occur with an equitable system of distribution. But the key difference between Cuba and other Latin American states is the existence of a planned, socialist society, where most of the productive assets are owned by the people as a whole or by co-operatives.

Nicaragua: Christian Socialism v. American Imperialism

In 1821 Central America declared its independence from Spain and formed a federation of provinces. The Central American Union was disbanded in 1838, and Nicaragua emerged as an independent state. Nicaragua's sad history can only be understood within the context of rising American imperialism, nationalism, and commercial interests in the Caribbean. In 1823 U.S. President James Monroe issued his famous "Monroe Doctrine," declaring that the European states were to keep out of the American continents. While it was quite some time before the U.S. government was strong enough to enforce the doctrine, Van Alstyne and others have noted that this was "the birthday announcement on behalf of the American Leviathan State," unilaterally declaring that the entire western hemisphere was a U.S. sphere of influence. (See Nearing and Freeman, 1966; Dulles, 1963; Van Alstyne, 1960)

The special U.S. interest in the Caribbean and central America came as a result of the policy of "Manifest Destiny": the United States was chosen by God to rule over all of North America. As U.S. military forces pushed west to California, it was only too evident that it would be necessary to build a canal across central America to facilitate movement of the U.S. navy and commerce. Unfortunately for Nicaragua, the U.S. government concluded that it was one of the prime areas for a proposed canal. Imperial interventions followed, beginning with the U.S.-British conflict of 1850 and then an effort made in 1855 by William Walker and a group of Americans to establish an American slave state. Direct intervention by the U.S. government, in league with business and commercial interests, began after the building of the canal through Panama.

Between 1909 and 1933, U.S. marines occupied Nicaragua on and off, protecting American interests and putting down rebellions. Between 1927 and 1934 Nicaraguans under the leadership of Augusto Cesar Sandino fought a guerrilla war against U.S. occupation. U.S. troops left in 1933, replaced by the puppet dictatorship of Anastasia Somoza Garcia and the National Guard. Sandino was assassinated, and the Nicaraguan people suffered forty-five years of brutal rule by the Somoza family and their American supporters. In 1961 the Sandinista Liberation Front (FSLN) was founded, and armed resistance to Somoza began. In July 1979 Somoza and his closest supporters fled to the United States, and the FSLN became the government.

The economy under the Somoza dictatorship had followed the pattern of the central American "banana republic." The ruling military class was closely tied to large commercial landowners and financial interests. It was an export economy, in which coffee, cotton, sugar, tobacco, rice, and livestock provided over 70% of all foreign exchange earnings. Peasants existed largely at a subsistence level, and when new land was needed by the planters, the National Guard drove them from their land to the more marginal growing areas in the mountains. While Somoza and his close political allies were engaged in large-scale agricultural production, Nicaragua was not a simple case of *latifundia-minifundia*. A significant portion of the agricultural product was supplied by poorer peasants involved in commercial agriculture (grossly exploited by rents and Somoza's control over finance and credit) and a significant number of medium-sized farmers. (Austin et al, 1985:16-17; Fitzgerald, 1985:209-213; Collins, 1982:15-19; Deere, 1981:195-196)

The civil war took a heavy toll on the Nicaraguan people. Out of a population of only 2.5 million, 50,000 were killed and another 100,000 were wounded. Somoza and the National Guard destroyed much of the productive base of the economy near the end. There was an enormous flight of capital from Nicaragua in all forms (including the removal of cattle) just before the victory of the FSLN; around $500 million was taken directly from the banking system. In addition, the Sandinistas inherited a foreign debt of $1.6 billion, which they chose to honour; in 1977, this was the equivalent of 40% of gross national product. While additional, badly-needed loans were initially obtained from the Inter-American Development Bank, the World Bank, West Germany, the Netherlands, Sweden, Mexico, Venezuela and even the United States, they increased the debt problem and the country's dependence on the capitalist countries. The Sandinistas soon found that debt servicing was absorbing an increasing amount of foreign exchange, while external terms of trade were steadily deteriorating. (Fitzgerald, 1985:220; Irvin, 1983:130-133; Collins, 1982:10, 46-47; Petras, 1980:103-105)

With the election of the Reagan Administration in the United States, an economic and military war was launched against the Sandinista government. The food system was almost completely dependent on the import of technology, capital goods, machinery and farm inputs; as with Cuba, the boycott by the U.S. government was devastating. The U.S. government cancelled Nicaragua's wheat credits in March 1981. Standard Fruit Corporation ended its marketing contract for bananas in 1982. In May 1983 the U.S. government reduced the Nicaraguan sugar quota by 90%. By 1983 the U.S. was openly backing a right-wing counter-revolutionary force (the "Contras") based in Honduras. They even mined Nicaraguan harbours. By 1986 one-half of the national budget was being diverted to resisting the murderous attacks of the Contras. (*Envio*, 1983:42; Ambrose, 1983:31; Collins, 1982:83)

When the Sandinistas took power, they nationalized what was left of the banking system as well as the abandoned property owned by Somoza and his key circle of supporters. This included large mechanized farms and much of the food processing sector. This sector now comprises the Areas of People's Property (APP). Most of the farmland was retained as state farms run by landless farm workers; by 1984, this sector controlled 19% of the farmland. All idle land and land rented within the previous two years was given to tenants and landless farmworkers. The Association of Rural Workers (ATC) was formed in 1978, and the minimum wage for farm work was raised and enforced. In 1980 the smallholders formed the National Union of Farmers and Ranchers (UNAG), which excluded the large producers; by 1984 they owned around 38% of the farmland. The Sandinista government encouraged the formation of credit-service and production co-operatives; by 1984, the co-operative sector owned 17% of the farmland. Between 1978 and 1984 the share of farmland owned by large individual farmers (holding over 140 hectares) fell from 52% to 26%. (Fitzgerald, 1985:212-219; Austin et al, 1985:18-20)

There was no mass nationalization of land by the Sandinistas. There was no ideological opposition to rights of private property in the means of production. Instead, they stressed the obligations of ownership. The first agrarian reforms included extension of credit at interest rates below inflation, guaranteed prices for export crops, rent decreases, and low taxes. However, during the first years of the new government, the large private farmers decapitalized their assets. They cut back on land under cultivation, sold off machinery and livestock, manipulated prices on invoices used to import farm machinery, paid themselves and their families excessive salaries, borrowed extensively from the government, and sent cash abroad to foreign bank accounts. In March 1980 a law was adopted prohibiting decapitalization; but despite the reports and warnings from the ATC, the government was ineffective in curbing the abuse. Furthermore, the agrarian law forbade land seizures by peasants and workers; where land was legally seized for neglect, the owners were still granted compensation. (Collins, 1982:39-50, 90-91) The Sandinistas chose to support the small farmers, who produce most of the country's corn and beans, by granting extensive credit and a guaranteed purchase price; in 1980, the farmers received seven times the credit they had received in 1978. However, the "spilling of credit" to the small farmers did not lead to an increase in production. (Collins, 1982:51-54)

In spite of all the difficulties, by 1983-84 production of export crops exceeded that of 1977-78 except for cotton, for which the falling world market price had discouraged planting. Production of the four main food crops (maize, rice, sorghum, and beans) had increased by 57%. Beef and milk production was down, reflecting the loss of herds during the war and decapitalization. But the production of pork, poultry, and eggs had more than doubled. (Austin et al, 1985:24-26)

The main objective of the Sandinista government has been the implementation of a socialist basic needs program. Heavy emphasis has been put on abolishing illiteracy and extending the educational system; by 1981 school enrollment at all levels was above the average for underdeveloped countries. Government expenditures on health increased significantly, and the number of physicians and nurses per capita was high by the standards of other lower middle-income underdeveloped countries. The infant mortality rate fell, as did the child death rate. Life expectancy rose. Spending on housing and infrastructure increased. By 1985 the rural basic wage had been brought up to the urban equivalent. (World Bank, 1984: Tables 23-25; Collins, 1982:153)

The National Food Program (PAN) stresses self-sufficiency in food production and more equitable distribution. Central to this policy is the National Foodstuffs Enterprise (ENEBAS) which controls imports and exports of food products and has established a variety of food distribution outlets. These include (1) People's Stores, in low-income areas with no supermarkets; (2) People's Outlets: private outlets, chosen by the local community, where basic commodities are made available at guaranteed prices; (3) Mobile Stores: trucks serving neighbourhoods without stores; (4) Workplace Commissaries, organized by the trade unions; (5) the seven Managua supermarkets, now state owned; and (6) the Rural Outlets and Rural Supply Centres, operated with the support of the UNAG and the ATC. The Ministry of Health and Education also carries out nutritional intervention programs for children of low-income families and pregnant and nursing mothers. In 1982 ENABAS introduced "Guarantee Cards," a system for rationing sugar, cooking oil, and soap, which had been in short supply. (Austin et al, 1985:29-31; Collins, 1982:121-130)

When the Sandinistas achieved power, Nicaragua was a very poor country, but one with a very large agricultural potential. A study by the U.S. Economic Commission for Latin America for 1978 reported that the top 20% of income earners in Nicaragua received 60% of all income and the bottom 50% only 15%. (Irwin, 1983:129-130) In 1977 Nicaragua reported an average per capita income of $966, but the average for the bottom 50% of the population was only $286. (Deere, 1981:196) The FAO estimates that in 1978 the average per capita consumption of calories was only 2284, low by the averages for Central America and the Caribbean. (FAO, 1981: Table 97) But per capita figures distort the reality. A special outside survey reported in 1971 that the poorest 50% of the population were consuming on average only 1767 kcal per day; in contrast, the top 5% consumed on average 3931 kcal per day and the next richest 15% consumed 3255 kcal. (Collins, 1982:157) A 1975 survey by the U.S. Agency for International Development reported that 42% of the children under four were malnourished. (Austin et al, 1985:32) The average annual rate of population growth between 1970 and 1982 was 3.9%, the fourth highest rate among the 125 largest underdeveloped countries. (World Bank, 1984: Table 19)

Has this improved? Fitzgerald (1985:219) concludes that since the revolution there has been a levelling out of consumption between social classes. Import restrictions have drastically cut the non-basic consumption goods favoured by the more well-to-do urban population. Off the farm, there is a shortage of beef, milk, maize, and beans. Austin and his associates from Harvard agree. But they believe that the one-third of the population with some access to land is now better fed. (Austin et al, 1985:32-33) Collins (1982:136) found no evidence that the urban poor in Managua had improved their diet; they had been hard hit by inflation and were eating more of the less expensive foods. There are other reports that the diet of the majority of the population is characterized by nutritional imbalances, heavy on carbohydrates and sugar, and short on protein and vitamins. (*Envio*, 1984:49) Petras (1980:99) reports that in spite of the rapid expansion of trade unions after the revolution, real wages for the industrial urban workers have been declining.

It is easy to cite the problems that remain for the Sandinista government. The Reagan Administration is escalating the conflict at a tremendous cost to the Nicaraguan people. The debt and foreign exchange problems are most serious. Outside economic help has dropped off in the face of U.S. government pressure. The bulk of the export crops in 1985 were produced by the middle-sized private farmers, whose commitment to the Sandinista cause is tenuous. If the revolution is to succeed, the urban majority of the population, including unionized workers, must benefit from the changes. In all socialist countries, there has been a problem with labour discipline and efficiency in the state farm sector, and Nicaragua is certainly no exception.

The roots of the Sandinista revolution are in the Christian base communities developed in the 1970s by the priests and nuns of the Roman Catholic Church. In contrast to the Leninist example, the new government is trying to rely on decentralized popular movements. The guiding principles in the rural area are co-operation and volunteerism. Pragmatism, flexibility, and the mixed economy remain the central characteristics of government policy. Over 80% of the farmland is still privately owned; 60% of the non-farm economy is outside the sphere of the state. While a high priority is being placed on food self-sufficiency, the agricultural export sector is recognized as essential.

The Sandinista government has resources that it can draw upon. It has considerable legitimacy in the minds of the Nicaraguan people as the force that overthrew the brutal Somoza regime. This was reflected in the 1984 election, where the Sandinistas won over 60% of the popular vote. The Communist left received less than 2% of the vote, and the traditional parties, the Conservatives and the Liberals, took the rest. Independent observers concluded that this was the most democratic election ever held in Central America. (The right-wing opposition, including the hierarchy of the Catholic Church, is inevitably forced to take the side of the U.S. government.) The army and the militia are well organized, and the local business class is relatively weak. Barring an invasion by the U.S. military, there is a chance that Nicaragua will show that there is a third approach to development, Christian socialism.

Conclusion

The experience of the post-revolutionary societies illustrates how wrong it is to judge the equity of a society on one single indicator, income distribution. A much more important question is: Who owns the productive assets? Furthermore, per-capita income or gross national product figures cannot accurately portray the status of people living in a society where a very large part of the standard of living is provided via the social wage. For example, in 1969 it was reported that the average monthly income of a worker in North Korea was 150 won, at that time roughly the equivalent of $60. On first glance, this seems rather low. But the cost of housing, power, heat, and public transport totalled only 3 won per month. Beyond that, the state provided all the basic social services free of charge to the individual. Furthermore, the prices of consumer goods were fixed, and food prices were substantially subsidized. (Brun and Hersch, 1976:289-292)

There are also very significant differences between agricultural systems based on collective work and individual family work. For example, in Vietnam the women were the main supporters of the move from family farming to production co-operatives. When farm work is collective, all participants receive work points and individual remuneration. That is not the case when agriculture is on a family unit basis. (White, 1982:44-51) This is one of the problems emerging with the Agricultural Responsibility System introduced in China after 1978. Furthermore, collective agriculture provides women with a much better support system through free nursery and day care services; these are not available in individual family farming, as in South Korea and Taiwan.

Growth with equity must also include a policy of full employment. In contrast to newly industrializing countries of Asia (NICs), the post-revolutionary societies have adopted policies leading to full employment. The result is quite visible to even the casual observer: the urban centres do not have shanty towns, or people sleeping in the streets, or a myriad of peddlers and street hawkers working long hours for very little pay. With the major redirection of Chinese policy since 1978, toward the free market, there has been a revival of unemployment (20 million people are "waiting for work") and the re-emergence of the informal economy in urban centres. Equity must include the right to employment for all who wish to work, and remuneration must be at a level that can provide a decent standard of living.

Finally, the examples of post-revolutionary governments used in this chapter reveal the great difficulties that any people face when choosing to opt out of the world capitalist system. The inevitable result is a wide range of imperialist pressures, including military intervention, which make reconstruction of the economy extremely difficult. For the smaller underdeveloped countries, the most difficult problem has been their historic dependence on exporting primary products and importing capital and consumer goods. Acquiring foreign exchange in the face of an imperialist boycott has proven to be a most difficult problem. (Fitzgerald, 1985:5-14) North Korea and Cuba have relied on support from the Soviet Union and the eastern European governments. But Nicaragua has not had the same degree of support and is facing enormous problems. The Indochinese countries experienced thirty years of military conflict. Angola and Mozambique have not only faced an international boycott, they have had to contend with a prolonged period of drought as well as military destruction by right-wing forces backed by the white regime in South Africa and the United States. The elimination of poverty and hunger comes at a high price.

References

Alroy, Gil Carl (1972). "The Peasantry in the Cuban Revolution." In Rolando E. Bonachea and Nelson P. Valdes, eds. *Cuba in Revolution.* Garden City, N.Y.: Anchor Books, pp. 3-17.

Ambrose, Robert (1983). "Agricultural Research and Breaking the Cycle of Dependency." *Science for the People*, XV, No. 6, November/December, pp. 6-7 et seq.

Austin, James et al (1985). "The Role of the Revolutionary State in the Nicaraguan Food System." *World Development*, XIII, No. 1, January, pp. 15-40.

Beckford, George L. (1972). *Persistent Poverty.* New York: Oxford University Press.

Benjamin, Medea et al (1984). *No Free Lunch: Food & Revolution in Cuba Today.* San Francisco: Institute for Food and Development Policy.

Bergmann, Theodor (1975). *Farm Policies in Socialist Countries.* Lexington, Mass.: D.D. Heath & Co.

Blasier, Cole (1972). "Social Revolution: Origins in Mexico, Bolivia and Cuba." In Rolando E. Bonachea and Nelson P. Valdes, eds. *Cuba in Revolution.* Garden City, N.Y.: Anchor Books, pp. 18-51.

Brun, Ellen and Jacques Hersh (1978). "North Korea: Default of a Model or a Model in Default?" *Monthly Review*, XXIX, No. 9, February, pp. 19-28.

Brun, Ellen and Jacques Hersh (1976). *Socialist Korea: A Case Study in the Strategy of Economic Development.* New York: Monthly Review Press.

Brundenius, Claes (1982). "Development Strategies and Basic Needs in Revolutionary Cuba." In Claes Brundenius and Mats Lundahl, eds. *Development Strategies and Basic Needs in Latin America.* Boulder, Col.: Westview Press, pp. 143-164.

Bunge, Frederica M. (1981). *North Korea: A Country Study.* Washington, D.C.: The American University for the U.S. Department of the Army.

Burchett, Wilfred G. (1968). *Again Korea.* New York: International Publishers.

Collins, Joseph (1982). *What Difference Could a Revolution Make?* San Francisco: Institute for Food and Development Policy.

Deere, Carmen D. (1981). "Nicaraguan Agricultural Policy: 1979-81." *Cambridge Journal of Economics*, V, No. 2, June, pp. 195-200.

Dulles, Foster Rhea (1963). *America's Rise to World Power, 1989-1954.* New York: Harper & Row.

Dumont, René (1970). *Cuba: Socialism and Development.* New York: Grove Press.

Eckstein, Susan (1981). "The Socialist Transformation of Cuban Agriculture: Domestic and International Constraints." *Social Problems*, XXIX, No. 2, December, pp. 178-196.

Edelstein, Joel C. (1981). "The Evolution of Cuban Development Strategy." In Heraldo Munoz, ed. *From Dependency to Development.* Boulder, Col.: Westview Press, pp. 225-266.

Fitzgerald, E.V.K. (1985a). "Agrarian Reform as a Model of Accumulation: The Case of Nicaragua since 1979." *Journal of Development Studies*, XXII, No. 1, October, pp. 208-226.

Fitzgerald, E.V.K. (1985b). "The Problem of Balance in the Peripheral Socialist Economy: A Conceptual Note." *World Development*, XIII, No. 1, January, pp. 5-14.

Food and Agriculture Organization (1983). *The State of Food and Agriculture.* Rome: FAO.

Food and Agriculture Organization (1982; 1981). *Production Yearbook.* Vol. 35. Rome: FAO.

Foster-Carter, Aidan (1977). "North Korea: Development and Self-Reliance, A Critical Appraisal." *Bulletin of Concerned Asian Scholars,* IX, No. 1, January/ March, pp. 45-56.

Gek-boo, Ng (1979). "The Commune System and Income Inequality in Rural China." *Bulletin of Concerned Asian Scholars,* XI, No. 3, July/September, pp. 51-63.

Gimenez, Martha E. et al (1977). "Income Inequality and Capitalist Development: A Marxist Perspective." In William Loehr and John P. Pawelson, eds. *Economic Development, Poverty and Income Distribution.* Boulder, Col.: Westview Press, pp. 231-265.

Gittings, John (1977). "The War before Vietnam." In Gavan McCormack and John Gittings, eds. *Crisis in Korea.* London: Spokesman Books, pp. 26-40.

Halliday, Jon (1985). "Women of North Korea: An Interview with the Korean Democratic Women's Union." *Bulletin of Concerned Asian Scholars,* XVII, No. 3, July/September, pp. 46-56.

Halliday, Jon (1981). "The North Korean Model: Gaps and Questions." *World Development,* IX, Nos. 9/10, September/October, pp. 889-905.

Hendry, Peter (1983). "Waiting and Changing: the Democratic People's Republic of Korea and the People's Republic of China." *Ceres,* XVI, No. 4, July-August, pp. 33-38.

Hsu, Robert C. (1982). "Agricultural Financial Policies in China, 1949-1980." *Asian Survey,* XXII, No. 7, July 1982, pp. 638-658.

Irvin, George (1983). "Nicaragua: Establishing the State as the Centre of Accumulation." *Cambridge Journal of Economics,* VII, No. 2, June, pp. 125-139.

Khan, Azizur Rahman (1977). "The Distribution of Income in Rural China." In International Labour Office, *Poverty and Landlessness in Rural Asia.* Geneva: ILO, pp. 253-280.

Klatt, W. (1983). "The Staff of Life: Living Standards in China, 1977-81." *China Quarterly,* No. 93, March, pp. 17-50.

Kojima, Reeitsu (1982). "China's New Agricultural Policy." *The Developing Economies,* XX, No. 4, December, pp. 390-413.

Leung, Joyce T. (1983). "China's Multiple Approach to Its Food Problem." In Georgio R. Salimano and Sally A. Lederman, eds. *Controversial Nutrition Policy Issues.* Springfield, Ill.: Charles C. Thomas, pp. 132-154.

McCormack, Gavan (1981). "North Korea: Kimilsungism — Path to Socialism?" *Bulletin of Concerned Asian Scholars,* XIII, No. 4, October-December, pp. 50-61.

Nearing, Scott and Joseph Freeman (1966). *Dollar Diplomacy.* New York: Monthly Review Press.

Nolan, Peter (1983). "De-collectivisation of Agriculture in China, 1979-82: A Long Term Perspective." *Cambridge Journal of Economics,* VII, Nos. 3/4, September/December, pp. 381-403.

Nolan, Peter and Gordon White (1981). "Distribution and Development in China." *Bulletin of Concerned Asian Scholars,* XIII, No. 3, July-September, pp. 2-18.

O'Connor, James (1972). "Cuba: Its Political Economy." In Rolando E. Bonachea and Nelson P. Valdes, eds. *Cuba in Revolution.* Garden City, N.Y.: Anchor Books, pp. 52-81.

O'Leary, Greg and Andrew Watson (1983). "The Role of the People's Commune in Rural Development in China." *Pacific Affairs,* LV, No. 4, Winter, pp. 593-612.

Paine, Suzanne (1976). "Balanced Development: Maoist Conception and Chinese Practice." *World Development,* IV, No. 4, April, pp. 277-304.

Petras, James (1980). "Nicaragua: The Transition to a New Society." *Contemporary Marxism,* No. 2, Winter, pp. 92-106.

Pollitt, Brian H. (1982). "The Transition to Socialist Agriculture in Cuba: Some Salient Features." *IDS Bulletin,* XIII, No. 4, September, pp. 12-22.

Rada, Edward L. (1983). "Food Policy in China." *Asian Survey,* XXIII, No. 4, April, pp. 518-535.

Radell, Willard W. Jr. (1983). "Cuban-Soviet Sugar Trade, 1960-1976: How Great Was the Subsidy?" *Journal of Developing Areas,* XVII, No. 3, April, pp. 365-382.

Smirnov, V. (1984). "Development of Foreign Economic Ties of the Democratic People's Republic of Korea." *Far Eastern Affairs,* No. 4, pp. 37-45.

Stavis, Benedict R. (1979). "The Impact of Agricultural Collectivization on Productivity in China." In Ronald A. Francisco et al, eds. *The Political Economy of Collectivized Agriculture.* New York: Pergamon Press, pp. 157-191.

Thomas, Clive Y. (1974). *Dependence and Transformation.* New York: Monthly Review Press.

Valdes-Brito, Jorge and Jorge Aldereguia Henriquez (1983). "Health Status of the Cuban Population." *International Journal of Health Services,* XIII, No. 3, pp. 479-485.

Van Alstyne, Richard W. (1960). *The Rising American Empire.* Oxford: Basil Blackwell.

White, Christine P. (1982). "Socialist Transformation of Agriculture and Gender Relations: The Vietnamese Case." *IDS Bulletin,* XIII, No. 4, September, pp. 44-51.

White, Gordon (1982). "North Korean Juche: The Political Economy of Self-Reliance." In M. Blienefeld and M. Godfrey. eds. *The Struggle for Development: National Strategies in an International Context.* N.Y.: John Wiley, pp. 323-354.

Wong, John (1976). "Some Aspects of China's Agricultural Development Experience: Implications for Developing Countries in Asia." *World Development,* IV, No. 6, June, pp. 485-497.

World Bank (1984, 1982). *World Development Report.* Washington, D.C.: World Bank.

Wortman, Sterling (1975). "Agriculture in China." *Scientific American,* CCXXXII, No. 6, June, pp. 13-21.

CHAPTER TWELVE

Summary and Conclusion

Hunger and undernutrition are found throughout the world where poverty and inequality persist. While most evident in countries with a relatively low level of economic development, hunger is also found among the poor in the most highly industrialized capitalist societies. On a world-wide basis, there is certainly no shortage of food. We know that there is enough food presently being produced to provide everyone in the world with a fully adequate diet. But while millions of people suffer from chronic undernutrition, many of the industrialized capitalist countries are producing more food than they can consume or sell on the world market. Thus, the key bottleneck appears to be the system of food distribution within countries and between countries. In the short run at least, the persistence of hunger is clearly a political problem.

The drought in Africa in the 1980s centred public attention on that continent. By 1986 the rains had begun to return, many of the countries hardest-hit were once again producing regular harvests, and the western media shifted public attention to other headline stories. The media's concentration on Africa, and in particular Ethiopia, allowed the industrialized west to ignore the increasing problem of hunger in other underdeveloped countries hard hit by the economic crisis of the early 1980s. Hidden in the back pages of the financial reports one could find the occasional reference to the decline in real income of the poor in the rest of the underdeveloped world, particularly in the debt-ridden middle-income states of Latin America. Occasionally, the "IMF riots" made the front pages. But the dramatic increase in urban hunger in the 1980s was largely ignored in the west.

On the other hand, more public attention was directed in those years to the problem of increasing poverty and hunger in the industrialized capitalist countries. The economic crisis resulted in a massive increase in unemployment in the most highly developed capitalist states. By 1982 official levels of unemployment in the majority of the industrialized OECD countries had risen to over 10%. (U.N., 1982: Table 22) In Great Britain, the official unemployment rate stood at 5.1% when the Conservative government headed by Margaret Thatcher took office in 1979; by early 1986 it was over

13%. In Canada official unemployment rose to 12% and then began to slowly decline, dropping to 10% by 1986. In the industrial west economic growth began to revive near the end of 1982, but unemployment remained at unusually high levels. In typically free-market countries like the United States, Great Britain, and Canada, the polarization of income and wealth increased. Bread lines did not diminish with "economic recovery"; they actually intensified as unemployment insurance benefits expired and greater numbers of people were forced to exist on social welfare.

The Malthusian Questions

In this political and economic climate the concerns of the neo-Malthusians were lost. Governments emphasized the expansion of production to end the crisis; even the existing weak efforts at environmental protection were slackened in order to free the entrepreneurs to do their job. The World Bank, the Worldwatch Institute, and other groups publicized the decline in the average annual growth of population in most of the underdeveloped countries. How could there be a hunger problem when there was a "glut" of grain on the world market and prices were dropping? During the economic crisis of the 1980s, the price of almost all natural resources declined. The crucial ingredient for production, energy, was in abundant supply; in late 1985 the price of oil began a precipitous drop as the leaders of OPEC changed policy and expanded production in an effort to maintain their share of the world market. Who could be concerned about the loss of agricultural land to other development, soil erosion and siltation, the degradation of irrigated land, desertification, deforestation, and even acid rain?

Nevertheless, the issues raised by the neo-Malthusians remain. The World Bank and other institutions project that despite expanded government family planning programs the world's population will exceed 6,000 million by the year 2000 and will stabilize some time in the 21st century at around 11,000 million. By the year 2000 80% of the world's population will be living in the underdeveloped world. Between 1960 and 1980 the amount of arable land only increased by an average of 0.15% per annum; the amount of land under cultivation per capita dropped from 0.48 ha to 0.33 ha. In the underdeveloped world where population growth is highest, additional land being cultivated increased at a slightly lower rate, 0.12% per annum.

In their major report, *Agriculture: Toward 2000*, the FAO called for the addition of 150 million hectares of new arable land in the underdeveloped world by the end of the century. This goal would require an average annual increase of 7.5 million hectares, almost 1% per annum; there would have to be a dramatic change. In Chapter IX it was noted that the UN/FAO project, Land Resources for Future Populations, estimated that the potential arable land in the underdeveloped countries was 2,028 million hectares; at the time, only 670 million was under cultivation. If we assume that all the potential arable land can be brought into production by the 21st century, and that the world's population will stabilize at the lower projected level, 9,688 million, we would still have only 0.21 hectares of arable land per capita in the underdeveloped countries. Furthermore, this land is very unequally distributed, and the areas with the highest population have the least amount of land in reserve. Given the quite marginal nature of the potential new arable land, the high capital costs involved in bringing it into production, the higher costs of production, and the lower and more unstable returns, it is only too obvious that greater emphasis must be placed on increasing food production on the higher quality existing land.

Raising agricultural production requires increased use of labour, fertilizers, chemicals, irrigation, and mechanization. All modern farm inputs are heavily dependent on fossil fuels, particularly petroleum. The data on per capita consumption of commercial energy reveals that between 1960 and 1980 the low-income countries, with two-thirds of the population of the underdeveloped world and the most serious food and hunger problem, increased their commercial energy consumption by only 1.3% per year, well below that of the industrialized capitalist and state socialist countries. The middle-income countries had an annual per capita increase of 6.5%. The distribution of commercial energy consumption did not change significantly between 1960 and 1980. (World Bank, 1983: Table 7)

Furthermore, fossil fuel reserves are very unevenly distributed throughout the world. In 1985 62% of proved petroleum reserves were in North Africa and the Middle East; oil reserves are limited in the rest of the underdeveloped world. Coal reserves are concentrated in the northern hemisphere, and only around 20% are found in the underdeveloped countries. In addition, it is clear that the industrialized capitalist countries have been able to maintain control over the consumption of energy and key minerals through their superior economic and political power. Thus, the poorer underdeveloped countries, both capitalist and post-revolutionary, desperate for foreign exchange to import capital goods, remain heavily dependent on a neo-colonial pattern of economic development, exporting their non-renewable resources to the already highly industrialized capitalist and state socialist countries. As the price of most of the primary commodities declined over the 1970s and 1980s, the underdeveloped countries borrowed extensively (mainly from the private banks in the industrialized capitalist countries); much of this new capital was used for servicing outstanding debt and to finance additional imports rather than to invest in productive ventures. Thus, in the first half of the 1980s, many of the underdeveloped countries faced balance of payments problems that left them short of capital for investment in development projects, including agriculture.

Agriculture and Economic Development

Agriculture has always played a central role in economic development. Production of food was the first social economic activity. The development of a nation has always been the process of moving from an agricultural society to a more complex and advanced society where there is a steadily increasing percentage of the population employed in other economic, service, and cultural areas.

The European experience has served as the model for both capitalist and socialist theories of economic development. The agricultural sector contributes to the process by increasing the level of food production; improvements in agricultural productivity lower food costs for the non-rural sector of the economy; labour is released for employment in the urban centres; food producers provide a ready market for manufactured goods; and the farming sector also provides needed capital in the early period of industrialization. While the industrial revolution was unfolding in Europe there was a relative abundance of arable land. The temperate climate was ideal for mixed farming. As industrial development progressed, the agricultural population declined both as a percentage of the labour force and absolutely, permitting the shift to larger, more capital-intensive farms. To a significant degree, western Europe was characterized by balanced development between agriculture and industry. New technology was introduced into both sectors simultaneously. In manufacturing, the production of consumer goods rose along with capital goods.

There were other general characteristics of the western European experience. First, it was capitalist development, led by an indigenous capitalist class that relied heavily on the state for support in the accumulation process. Infrastructure was oriented to integrated national development. Capital markets were created, and there was a relatively stable monetary system. Production was primarily oriented to the domestic market. Although external trade was not a major component of gross national product, it made a critical contribution to the early accumulation of capital for investment. Additional capital was obtained by the exploitation of overseas colonies. For a number of the European states, a considerable portion of the original capital for investment came from what can only be described as tribute, theft, and piracy. There was no shortage of natural resources in the European countries; what was lacking could be obtained from overseas sources. Energy was cheap. Population growth rates were below 1% per annum throughout the 18th and 19th centuries. The new technologies introduced into industry were relatively labour-intensive. A large percentage of the population that left the rural areas, and that could not find employment in industry, emigrated to overseas lands.

This is not to suggest that economic development in Europe was a homogeneous process of modernization. The nation-states had historically different development experiences. The social impact of early industrialization was devastating. The factory system destroyed traditional ways of life and made workers appendages of the machines. In the 19th century, men, women, and children worked 14- to 18-hour days in the factories and the mines. The labouring class was confined to slums without services, where life was short, due to hunger, epidemics, and persistent diseases. The living standards of the poor fell dramatically in the 19th century, compared to the rich and the middle class. No one would wish this experience on any people today. But within these countries the working class was able to organize into trade unions and political movements and to force concessions from the capitalists and the state to greatly improve their standard of living.

The Impact of Colonialism and Mercantilism

In contrast, almost all the countries generally classified today as underdeveloped went through a long period as colonies; a few were semi-autonomous countries dominated by mercantile imperialism. While industry and technology were advancing in Europe, the mercantile colonial system was maintained in these areas through state policy and coercion. The population remained overwhelmingly agrarian. Production often declined as the handicrafts and other budding industries were destroyed by direct colonial policies and/or more technically advanced European commodities. The best agricultural land was often taken for developing plantations or was granted to white settlers. As much as possible, trade was directed to the mother country; natural trading patterns were disrupted. The role of the colony was to export raw materials and import manufactured goods from the mother country. Capital was extracted through a system of taxation, finance, and the monopoly system of trade.

Political development was arrested in these areas. Indeed, the colonial powers often arbitrarily set political boundaries dividing national communities. The colonial powers formed alliances with the most reactionary social classes. While representative government, political democracy, and trade union rights were expanding in Europe, they were blocked in the colonies. The local educational system was undermined; illiteracy actually increased in many colonized areas. Slavery and bondage were introduced on a large scale. Missionaries brought the new European religions. Racialism became a central aspect of colonial domination. Infrastructure such as transportation and communications was re-orientated to serving the interests of the mercantile colonial system. Taxation was used to finance colonialism and further colonial wars. The imperial powers even recruited locals for the police and the military for use in their own repressive rule.

Both Marx and orthodox economists concluded that the intrusion of the capitalist system would destroy the existing pre-capitalist forms of production. This is certainly what has happened. But capitalist development in the colonies was significantly different from capitalist development in Europe. The basic structural characteristic of colonial capitalist development was internal disarticulation and external integration. Local industry gave way to imported manufactured goods. There was an absence of local industrial capitalist expansion during the period of rapid expansion in Europe. The area of merchant capital remained dominant; moneylending and trade were highly profitable because of monopoly power, supported by state coercion. The colonies were captive markets for European manufactured goods. Local accumulation of capital took place, but it was blocked in many areas, and a considerable amount was siphoned off to the metropolitan countries. The European powers were not at all interested in reproducing the industrial revolution in the colonies.

Commercial agriculture was fully integrated into the mercantile colonial system. Production shifted to cash crops for export to the metropolitan country. The development of a "middle peasantry" was stifled; the vast majority of the peasants were in the lower strata, living at a subsistence level. Landlordism and sharecropping were not destroyed; they were re-inforced. The surplus extracted from peasant labour was most often invested in non-productive ventures like luxurious personal properties. The overall result of colonialism was a distorted and retarded economic and social development. A number of theorists have argued that this form of capitalism was so specifically different from the European experience that it could be described as a "colonial mode of production" or "colonial capitalism." (See Shanin, 1984; Ghosh, 1984; Bagchi, 1982; Alavi, 1982, 1980; Banaji, 1972)

It was widely believed in the colonies that political independence was a necessary precondition to constructing a modern society and narrowing the gap in the standard of living with the western industrialized states. But was political independence sufficient? The first real test came in Latin America. After some 300 years of colonial rule, the Napoleonic wars in Europe offered the opportunity for breaking with the French, Portuguese, and Spanish colonial masters. By 1824 almost all of Latin America had achieved independence. Natural resources, including land suitable for cultivation, were abundant. Surely, there was every opportunity to follow the path of development set by the United States and Canada.

However, this did not happen. The local ruling classes were agricultural and livestock exporters, mining entrepreneurs, and merchant capitalists; they were primarily interested in expanding trade with other European countries, particularly Great Britain. They adopted the liberal ideology of the time, and, in particular, free trade. In this they were strongly supported by British interests who quickly came to dominate trade with Latin America. By the latter part of the 19th century, British capital began to invest in infrastructure, mining, and related manufacturing. In agriculture, the newly independent states continued to stress the production of "colonial staples" for the European market. Where local political and capitalist elements tried to shift to an import-substitution policy, the British and the French resorted to military intervention to preserve free trade. After 150 years of independence, most of Latin America was hardly more advanced than many Asian countries that were still colonies.

As many have noted, the major export of Britain at this time was the policy of free trade. (e.g., Semmel, 1970) In his study of Ricardo's theory of international comparative advantage and the relationship between Britain and Portugal, Sideri (1970:6-7) concludes that there is not much difference between mercantilism and free trade. Free trade becomes the mercantilism of the strongest power, and it leads to imperialism, which is not very different from a state-oriented commercial policy. Robinson (1979:104) argues that the free trade doctrine "suits the interests of whichever nation is in the strongest competitive position in world markets." At the time it was Great Britain. Bagchi (1982:53) refers to this period of Latin American history as the era of "voluntary colonialism." As the United States grew in political and economic power, it exerted greater influence over Latin America. It is not surprising that the theory of dependency or dependent development first arose among Latin American scholars.

The World Food System

The modern system of food production and distribution is commonly called "agribusiness" in the western industrialized countries. This is a reflection of the fact that it is energy- and capital-intensive, and organized on a hierarchical corporate basis. At the farm level, there is a high degree of mechanization, irrigation, dependence on manufactured fertilizers, the use of chemical pesticides, and advanced plant breeding and genetic engineering. The trend is clearly towards specialization of production and monoculture, with a separation of the production of crops and animals. Animals and poultry are raised in a factory system. At the farm level, the same methods are used in both the advanced capitalist and state socialist countries.

In capitalist societies farms continue to increase in size and decline in number, but they still remain primarily family-run enterprises, referred to by social scientists as "simple commodity production." The capital-intensive nature of modern farming has allowed most farmers and their families to increase the size of the operation and at the same time reduce their dependence on hired labour. In all of the OECD countries, the number of farmers and farm workers is steadily declining. With the exception of Poland and Yugoslavia, farming in the industrialized state socialist countries has been collectivized. In the 1960s, horizontal amalgamation of farms began, resulting in large co-operative and state farms. Management is increasingly based on professionals, and local direct democratic decision-making has been largely replaced by a representative system. Nevertheless, the collective farm system provides full employment for farm workers on a year-round basis, and gives them relatively high standards of living and extensive services normally unavailable to individual farmers and hired workers in the west.

In the advanced capitalist countries food processing and distribution sectors are characterized by monopoly, oligopoly, and vertical integration with individual farmers. The result has been the loss of any real independence for producers and a declining ability to influence decisions within the system. The structure of food production in the industrialized state socialist countries is not really that different. With the steady expansion of the Agro-Industrial Complex after 1961, state and collective farms are increasingly tied to manufacturing and distribution enterprises through horizontal and vertical contracts. The organization of the food processing and distribution enterprises is on a hierarchical basis, with management taking the primary role in meeting quotas and organizing the production system. The major difference between the AIC system and private corporate agribusiness in the west is in the area of economic development. In the state socialist countries, the AIC system is being developed as part of a national plan; one of the key goals is to decentralize production and to provide off-farm employment for people in rural areas. In advanced capitalist societies, the forces of the market lead to the centralization of production.

Both political systems consider the trends toward specialization, centralization, hierarchy, and decision-making by a professional management to be logical developments brought about by science and technology. However, there are significant differences between farming, which is a biological process, and the operation of a manufacturing industry. The ecological problems caused by industrial agriculture are similar in both systems. The modern, technological food system requires heavy fossil fuel subsidies. Under the pressure to increase production, the resource base is being depleted and pollution is increasing. Many, including the author, believe this system to be unsustainable in the long run.

Finally, there is the most important issue of food distribution. In most of the advanced capitalist states a significant percentage of the population remains unemployed; in many of these states, the level of social support for the unemployed does not provide for an adequate nutritional diet. While in the USSR and some of the eastern European state socialist societies complaints are made about the variety of food and the system of distribution, there is full employment at adequate wages, food prices are controlled and subsidized, and no one fails to receive an adequate nutritional diet.

The underdeveloped countries are integrated into the world food market. The pattern of production of cash crops for export to the metropolitan centres, initiated during the long period of mercantile colonialism, persists. The advanced technologies of the industrial food system have been exported to all of the underdeveloped countries. The introduction of advanced transportation systems and the transnational agribusiness corporation has further integrated the underdeveloped countries into the world market. Food tastes in these countries have been significantly influenced by advertising and promotion by the transnational corporations.

The bulk of international trade in food and agricultural products (over 70%) is carried out by the industrialized capitalist and state socialist countries. Trade between the state socialist and the underdeveloped capitalist states is not that significant. The primary trade is between the industrialized and underdeveloped capitalist countries; the main purpose is to enhance the quality and diversity of food for those who are already very well fed. The data presented in Chapter VI reveal that most of the underdeveloped capitalist countries with large numbers of people living in poverty and hunger are nevertheless major exporters of food and agricultural products. It was also noted that the industrialized western countries are the key exporters of cereals, produced under capital-intensive agriculture, and are importers of plantation and luxury crops that are relatively labour intensive. In the underdeveloped countries, despite the existence of substantial numbers of people lacking adequate protein, the export of meat and fish is steadily increasing. This is the logic of the capitalist market.

The uneven distribution of foodlands, other natural resources, and population makes trade in food products practical and often necessary. In Africa around one-half of the present population lives in the drier or mountainous areas, with limited prospects for increasing local food production. Of North Africa and the Middle East combined, only one country, Turkey, has adequate foodland resources for its own population; the other fifteen countries in the area are steadily increasing their dependence on imported food. The central, limiting, factor in food production in North Africa and the Middle East is the lack of water. In Asia, the ratio of humans to arable land is already quite high, population is steadily increasing, and potential new arable land is limited. Japan is heavily dependent on the importation of agricultural products and fish, and South Korea and Taiwan are following in the same pattern. China has run out of land to convert to food production, has already achieved relatively high yields, and will need to increase imports to feed the expected addition of 400 million people. The only area of the underdeveloped world with a relatively large amount of potential arable land is South America. It is obvious that international trade in food and agricultural products will continue. The major question is whether it will always be dominated by the laws of the capitalist market, where access to food is based on the ability to pay.

The Search for Alternatives

The orthodox model of development holds that capitalism evolves in a linear manner, and that underdeveloped countries are simply going through a phase experienced by the now-industrialized countries. It is assumed that eventually all of the underdeveloped countries will become modern industrial societies with a high standard of living. The diffusion of capital and technology to these countries is considered to accelerate the process. This general theory of development is not limited to orthodox economists, but is also supported by many Marxists.

However, the linear/diffusionist model underestimates the adverse impact of colonialism and the difficulties of late development. The data presented in Chapter IX demonstrate that the gap in the standard of living between the rich and poor capitalist countries is not narrowing. In 1982 the 34 low-income countries, which account for 50% of the world's population, had an average, per capita gross national product of only $280, one-fortieth that of the industrialized capitalist countries. In the 28 upper middle-income countries, the per-capita GNP was about one-fourth that of the average of the industrialized capitalist countries. (World Bank, 1984: Table 1) But even here, the gap is not closing. Furthermore, income inequality is greatest in these countries. Over the past two decades the average rate of growth of GNP in most of the underdeveloped countries has been relatively high by historic standards. Why have the overall results been so disappointing? While the differences among countries in the underdeveloped world are often emphasized, some generalization is necessary in order to comprehend the persistence of extensive poverty, unemployment, and hunger. These countries face problems significantly different from those the advanced capitalist countries faced during their period of industrialization.

Primarily because of success in controlling disease, the rate of population growth has been much higher than it ever was in the industrialized countries. While the percentage of the labour force in the agricultural sector is declining, in the vast majority of the underdeveloped countries the rural population is still increasing absolutely. This has resulted in considerable underemployment in agriculture and has made it much more difficult to increase labour productivity. The urban areas are characterized by high levels of open unemployment and a very large service sector, most of it in the informal economy, where labour productivity and income are low.

Both the production and marketing sectors of the economy are integrated into the world capitalist system. The capitalist class in most underdeveloped countries is relatively weak; the leading sectors are often linked to the export economy. The commercial sector in agriculture tends to be oriented to the export market, with food production for general consumption receiving a lower priority. Natural resources, including foodlands and energy, are limited, and prices are relatively high. Technology is largely imported; furthermore, it comes as a complete package, supplied by the transnational corporation, which limits links to the local economy. Being a product of research and development in the advanced countries, technology is oriented to economies of scale and the emphasis on capital over labour. Capital goods for production are largely imported. In many of the low-income underdeveloped countries there is virtually no internal capital market; they are heavily dependent on private foreign capital and the lending of the international agencies. For most of them, a relatively large sector of the economy is dependent on external trade, the bulk of which is in primary products having a low elasticity of demand. Trade is still mainly with the former colonial powers.

In the underdeveloped countries the state plays a central role in the economy. This is not surprising. Gerschenkron (1962) has argued that the classic western European model of development, which relied on private entrepreneurs, is inappropriate to "late development." There are two general approaches to state activity in "backward" economies. First, the state can create a suitable climate for private investment. Frank (1972:120-122) calls this "the Canadian model of development," where tariffs are established and private foreign investment is encouraged. The other model conforms to Gerschenkron's argument: in most backward economies, the state must play a dominant role in capital formation and investment. This is the model identified with Japan, South Korea, and Taiwan. Under either model, the state must control the peasants and the labour movement through a combination of ideology and repression.

In Chapter X it was shown that the industrialization occurring in the underdeveloped world is highly concentrated. In the World Bank's survey of value added to manufacturing for seventy-five underdeveloped capitalist countries in 1980, five countries (Brazil, Mexico, Argentina, India, and South Korea) accounted for 55% of the total. *The total value added to manufacturing for all seventy-five was less than that of Japan.* (World Bank, 1983: Table 7) Petras (1984:188-194) demonstrates that the aggregate growth of manufacturing output and trade in the capitalist underdeveloped world is still quite small and "growing at a snail's pace." Those few countries which have been most successful are those where the state is playing a major role in the development of basic industry and resources. Of the seven with a significant capital goods industry (the above five, plus Kenya and Singapore), all but one have a large internal market. Petras points out that in the underdeveloped capitalist countries the marginalized informal sector of the labour force is growing faster than the industrial sector. Thus, in contrast to the experience of the now-industrialized capitalist states, there is no primary polarization between labour and capital but a division of classes between capital, labour, and the larger underemployed sector. In the underdeveloped capitalist countries, industrialization has not been able to absorb the displaced peasantry.

Can the underdeveloped countries break out of this structure and move toward equitable development? Over the years critics of orthodox development theory have put together an alternative package of policies. First, it is important to get away from traditional economic dependence on the former colonial powers. The competition among the advanced industrialized countries that accelerated during the economic crisis of the 1970s has made it possible to expand trade and financial links with underdeveloped capitalist, post-revolutionary socialist, and industrialized state socialist countries. For small countries, regional alliances have been advocated, a policy of "collective self-reliance." Second, the state must play a central role in finance and trade. This requires controls on foreign exchange and imports. Economic planning and state enterprises are needed to direct investment to the most productive areas of the economy. Emphasis should be on backward and forward links to existing industries, particularly agriculture and food. Third, countries with a large enough internal market must stress import substitution. Import substitution can work when it is combined with a more egalitarian distribution of income and wealth. The more successful capitalist underdeveloped countries achieved rather high rates of economic and employment growth behind protective barriers. Emphasis must be placed on raising income on a broad basis, increasing domestic demand for locally produced goods. Technology should be "appropriate," geared to putting the underemployed labour force to work. The process of capital accumulation should stress local sources, minimizing foreign aid and investment, because these perpetuate dependent relationships and outside control.

In the agricultural area, the alternative advanced is self-reliance in food production. The current trend toward increased imports of grain from the United States and the European Common Market undermines local production and can only limit freedom of action. In addition, it is widely agreed that emphasis should be placed on diversification of agricultural production and trade, using long-term barter agreements wherever possible. Thus it is appropriate for governments to manage this trade through marketing boards. (See Jones, 1984; Chakravarty, 1983; Cardosa, 1981; Galtung, 1981; Oteiza, 1979; and Parmar, 1975)

However, there are *no examples* of underdeveloped capitalist countries that have successfully pursued this alternative strategy. The nearest example would be the Popular Unity government in Chile under Salvador Allende. It lasted three years (1970-73) before there was a U.S.-backed military coup. The implementation of a fundamentally new policy cannot come without radical social transformation. The major obstacle has proven to be the local government and the classes it represents. Thus, mass mobilization is required if new social forces are to control the government and the economy. Class alliances must be formed among the peasantry, the urban working class, and the marginalized peoples in the informal economy. But such changes are certainly not easy. Local governments in the underdeveloped world, backed by the advanced capitalist states, have acquired rather sophisticated and brutal systems of state repression. Chile is just one notable example.

Nevertheless, the existence of a number of post-revolutionary countries in the underdeveloped world does give hope for real change. China, North

Korea, and Cuba have clearly demonstrated that it is possible to have equitable development, including full employment and the elimination of poverty and hunger for everyone. Furthermore, as Petras (1984:195-196) has pointed out, the post-revolutionary governments have been more successful than the capitalist underdeveloped countries in shifting the population from agriculture to the industrial sector. Historically, the tremendous advances made in science and technology, the abundance of capital available, and the development of democracy mean that it is not necessary to repeat the horrors of early nineteenth century industrialization.

However, imperialism did not end with formal colonialism. The major capitalist countries, led by the United States, have used their extensive economic and military power to try to overthrow the revolutionary governments of China, North Korea, Cuba, and Nicaragua. The low-income post-revolutionary governments in Southeast Asia have been badly hurt by the economic boycott led by the U.S. government. In Africa, the people of Angola and Mozambique have suffered from the economic boycott and the disruption caused by the counter-revolutionary forces backed by the racist regime in South Africa and the U.S. government. After the revolution in Iran, the U.S. government led the capitalist countries in seizing all of Iran's overseas assets to pay off their international debts; again, the boycott led to serious economic difficulties. Eradicating poverty and hunger not only requires revolutionary social change in the underdeveloped countries, it also requires change in the advanced capitalist countries.

The Limits of Technology

How are we going to provide enough food and a high standard of living for an additional 5 billion people? How are we going to deal with the deterioration of the earth's resource base? The standard response is to look for a new technological solution. But the scientific solution proposed is invariably a new supply-side innovation. The most recent example would be the development of the high-response varieties of cereals widely introduced into the underdeveloped world in the 1960s and 1970s. Without question, increased cereal production helped to keep down the international price of grain and thus tended to benefit low-income peoples.

However, in capitalist underdeveloped countries food is still distributed according to the ability to pay, and the poor have not significantly improved their diet. Furthermore, there have been drawbacks. The new varieties have primarily benefitted the larger, more prosperous farmers; the small farmers did not normally have access to the necessary inputs and credit sources. (Pearce, 1979; Yapa, 1979; Griffin, 1974; Frankel, 1971) Furthermore, the new varieties have required increased dependence on the import of energy-intensive farm inputs, largely controlled by transnational corporations. (Dahlberg, 1979:110-112) South Asia was widely cited as the best example of the success of the new cereals, but as the pace of mechanization was accelerated, more tenant farmers were evicted from their land, and the number of landless hired labourers, employed on a casual basis, increased. The underdeveloped capitalist countries were not able to absorb the displaced farmers and farm workers in alternative employment. (Jose, 1984:A97-A103; Mundle, 1983:767-778)

There were also ecological problems associated with the new cereal varieties. The higher yields resulted in a lower protein content in the grain; higher cash returns to farmers encouraged them to cut back the planting of pulses. The new varieties were less resistant to drought and floods, and the native strains were more resistant to insects and diseases. As more fertilizers and pesticides were required, the result was increased water pollution. Finally, the widespread planting of the new varieties reduced the diversity of the cereals planted, making the crops more vulnerable to disaster. Plant breeders began to express concern over the loss of genetic resources. (Swaminathan, 1984:92; Reichert, 1982:11, 39; Prescott-Allen, 1982:15-20; Mooney, 1979; Yapa, 1979:374-375)

The new cure-all for the world's food problem is biotechnology, the "biorevolution" in plants and animals to be accomplished by the manipulation of genes. According to reports in the popular media, the possibilities of gene-manipulation are endless. Current research includes the development of hormones, growth regulation and hybridization; cereals that can fix nitrogen; plants that are more tolerant to drought, cold weather, and hostile soils; plants with enhanced photosynthesis; and plants more tolerant of herbicides. As researchers emphasize, biotechnology is only a natural extension of plant and animal breeding.

However, we have already gone a long way down the road toward crop and animal specialization. For example, in Canada only Holsteins are used in the commercial production of fluid milk. With embryo transplants, the genetic base is being narrowed further by selective breeding. Canada has only one primary turkey breeding operation; using genetic technology, artificial fertilization uses only the top-grade males. One poultry operation in Ontario accounts for one-third of all chicks produced in Canada, exports its breeding stock to 90 countries, and is now moving into biotechnology. In British Columbia, orchardists used to grow fifty varieties of apples; commercial growers are now down to five, all that the retail food chains want to handle. Furthermore, the trees themselves are now even more genetically uniform as nurseries clone them from the tissue culture of a single tree. The concern of ecologists over these developments is fully justified.

In addition, there are two major differences between the Green Revolution and the new biotechnology. First, the research for the Green Revolution was done in public institutions, and the results were made available to all countries. Biotechnology, while dependent on large financial subsidies from governments, is overwhelmingly concentrated in the private corporate sector. It will be available according to the ability to pay. Second, almost all the genetic material for plant breeding comes from countries in the underdeveloped world. The industrialized countries have taken the genetic material from these countries, are using it to create new life forms, and are granting patent rights to corporations who then sell the product back to the farmers in the underdeveloped countries. It is no wonder that the governments of the underdeveloped world are demanding the removal of patent rights on food products. Significantly, the governments of the United States and the USSR stand together supporting the patenting of food resources. (Wilson, 1985:30; Buttel, 1984:15-16; McGrath, 1984:10)

The alternative to corporate agriculture is a shift to sustainable agriculture. But what is sustainable agriculture in the era of huge fossil-fuel subsidies to the food system? As a minimum, sustainable agriculture is the ability to provide enough food for future populations. The solution is usually seen to be more efficient use of land and other factors of production. The problem of the degradation of foodland resources is inevitable as long as there is monoculture, crop specialization, and the separation of animals from crop production. The alternative requires a new scientific approach to food production, working with nature rather than trying to completely transform it. The key to this change of direction is the re-introduction of polyculture and a mix of crops and animals. Organic farming is often advocated, because it largely excludes the use of manufactured fertilizers, pesticides, growth regulators, and feed additives. It relies on crop rotation, crop residues, animal manures, the use of legumes and green manures, and stresses the enhancement of the tilth and biological activity of the soil. It is more labour- and less capital-intensive.

Modern organic or ecological farming is anything but a return to primitive farming. It is more difficult than monoculture specialization, because farmers have to be much more knowledgeable about the biological processes of different plants and animals. A similar high level of scientific research is required, but it has to be shifted from its commodity orientation to an ecological, site-specific, interdisciplinary orientation. (Hill, 1985; Horwith, 1985; Cacek, 1984; Altieri et al, 1984; Lowrance et al, 1984; Kiley-Worthington, 1980)

What are the social requirements for sustainable agriculture? American advocates generally support a return to the small family farm under a decentralized system of production. But few suggest that a fundamental change in the present system of monopoly capitalism is necessary. Many of the supporters exhibit a nostalgic return to a past era when things were supposedly better. Unfortunately, there is no analysis or understanding of why there is a corporate food system. Because of this, there are no strategies advanced on how to change to a sustainable agriculture. (See Jackson et al, 1983; Rodale Press, 1981; Jackson, 1980; Berry, 1977; Merrill, 1976)

What is the alternative to individual family farming? Most often the answer is seen to be the large co-operative and state farms in the Soviet Union and eastern Europe. But it is known that they are as energy- and capital-intensive as farms under monopoly capitalism. Furthermore, there is no evidence that there is any trend in these countries towards ecological or sustainable agriculture. The evidence cited in Chapter VI indicates that problems of erosion and pollution are as great in these countries as in the advanced capitalist countries.

However, there have been some very positive developments in the experience of collective farming. There has been greater decentralization of food-related manufacturing. The rural communities are being re-organized, modernized, and provided with facilities and services that have been lacking to individual family farms under capitalism. In the west, young people are deterred from farming because of the lack of the modern amenities of life found in large urban centres. Collective and state farms generally provide modern recreational and cultural facilities, libraries, schools, and technical institutes, and free day care and nursery services. Farm workers are well paid, work regular hours, have paid vacations, and have year-round employment. Farm women actually are paid for the work they do. Housing is virtually free. This is made possible by co-operation. None of this can be found in farming under capitalism.

On the ecological level, farming under state socialism leaves much to be desired. Over the long run, it may change. But this is not the only alternative to corporate agribusiness. There is the possibility that farming and food production in other countries can be re-directed under a system of socialism and direct democracy. For example, in the new Nicaragua, considerable emphasis is being placed on ecological farming and voluntary co-operatives. Capitalism is characterized by the concentration of ownership and power, centralization of production, and the hierarchy of command. Given this system of production, it cannot solve the long-run problems of population growth, inequality and exploitation, resource distribution, and environmental degradation.

References

Alavi, Hamza (1982). "The Structure of Peripheral Capitalism." In Hamza Alavi and Theodor Shanin, eds. *Introduction to the Sociology of "Developing Societies."* London: Macmillan, pp. 172-192.

Alavi, Hamza (1980). "India: Transition from Feudalism to Colonial Capitalism." *Journal of Contemporary Asia*, X, No. 4, pp. 359-399.

Altieri, Miguel A. et al (1984). "The Requirements of Sustainable Agro-ecosystems." In Gordon K. Douglas, ed. *Agricultural Sustainability in a Changing World Order*. Boulder, Col.: Westview Press, pp. 175-189.

Bagchi, Amiya Kumar (1982). *The Political Economy of Underdevelopment*. Cambridge: Cambridge University Press.

Banaji, Jairus (1972). "For a Theory of Colonial Modes of Production." *Economic and Political Weekly*, VII, No. 52, December 23, pp. 2498-2502.

Berry, Wendell (1977). *The Unsettling of America: Culture & Agriculture*. New York: Avon Books.

Buttel, Frederick H. et al (1984). "Biotechnology in the World Agricultural System." Paper presented to the American Association for the Advancement of Science, New York, May 27.

Cacek, Terry (1984). "Organic Farming: The Other Conservation Farming System." *Journal of Soil and Water Conservation*, XXXIX, No. 6, November-December, pp. 357-360.

Cardosa, Fernando H. (1981). "Towards Another Development." In Heraldo Munoz, ed. *From Dependency to Development: Strategies to Overcome Underdevelopment and Inequality*. Boulder, Col.: Westview Press, pp. 295-313.

Chakravarty, Sukhamoy (1983). "Trade and Development: Some Basic Issues." *International Social Science Journal*, XXXV, No. 3, pp. 425-440.

Dahlberg, Kenneth A. (1979). *Beyond the Green Revolution*. New York: Plenum Press.

Food and Agriculture Organization (1981). *Agriculture: Toward 2000*. Rome: FAO.

Frank, André G. (1972). *Lumpenbourgeoisie and Lumpendevelopment*. New York: Monthly Review Press.

Frankel, Francine (1971). *India's Green Revolution: Economic Gains and Political Costs*. Princeton: Princeton University Press.

Galtung, Johan (1981). "The Politics of Self-Reliance." In Heraldo Munoz, ed. *From Dependency to Development: Strategies to Overcome Underdevelopment and Inequality*. Boulder, Col.: Westview Press, pp. 173-196.

Gerschenkron, Alexander (1962). *Economic Backwardness in Historical Perspective*. Cambridge, Mass.: MIT Press.

Ghosh, Suniti Kumar (1984). "Marx on India." *Monthly Review*, XXXV. No. 8, January, pp. 39-53.

Griffin, Keith (1974). *The Political Economy of Agrarian Change*. Cambridge, Mass.: Harvard University Press.

Hill, Stuart B. (1985). "Redesigning the Food System for Sustainability." *Alternatives*, XII, Nos. 3/4, Spring/Summer, pp. 32-36.

Horwith, Bruce (1985). "A Role for Intercropping in Modern Agriculture." *BioScience*, XXXV, No. 5, May, pp. 286-291.

Jackson, Wes et al, eds. (1984). *Meeting the Expectations of the Land.* San Francisco: North Point Press.

Jackson, Wes (1980). *New Roots for Agriculture.* San Francisco: Friends of the Earth.

Jones, J.V.S. (1984). "Food, Agricultural and Trade Policy to the Year 2000." *Food Policy,* IX, No. 4, November, pp. 374-384.

Jose, A.V. (1984). "Farm Mechanization in Asian Countries." *Economic and Political Weekly,* XIX, No. 26, June 30, pp. A97-A-103.

Kiley-Worthington, M. (1980). "Problems of Modern Agriculture." *Food Policy,* V, No. 3, August, pp. 208-215.

Lowrance, Richard et al, eds. (1984). *Agricultural Ecosystems: Unifying Concepts.* New York: John Wiley.

McGrath, Paul (1984). "The Seeds of Disaster?" *The Globe and Mail* [Toronto], December 1, p. 10.

Merrill, Richard, ed. (1976). *Radical Agriculture.* New York: Harper & Row.

Mooney, Patrick R. (1979). *Seeds of the Earth.* Ottawa: Canadian Council for International Co-operation.

Mundle, Sudipto (1983). "Labour Absorption in Agriculture and Restricted Market for Manufacturing Industry." *Economic and Political Weekly,* XVII, Nos. 19-21, May, pp. 767-778.

Oteiza, Enrique (1979). "Collective Self-Reliance: Some Old and New Issues." In Jose J. Villamil, ed. *Transnational Capitalism and National Development.* Sussex: Harvester Press, pp. 289-305.

Parmar, Samuel L. (1975). "Self-Reliant Development in an 'Interdependent' World." in Guy F. Erb and Valeriana Kallab, eds. *Beyond Dependency.* Washington, D.C.: Overseas Development Council, pp. 3-27.

Pearce, Andrew (1979). *Seeds of Plenty, Seeds of Want.* London: Oxford University Press.

Petras, James (1984). "Toward a Theory of Industrial Development in the Third World." *Journal of Contemporary Asia,* XIV, No. 2, pp. 182-203.

Prescott-Allen, Robert and Christine Prescott-Allen (1982). "The Case for in situ Conservation of Crop Genetic Resources." *Nature and Resources,* XVIII, No. 1, January-March, pp. 15-20.

Reichert, Walt (1982). "Agriculture's Diminishing Diversity." *Environment,* XXIV, No. 9, November, pp. 7-11, 39-43.

Rodale Press (1981). *Empty Breadbasket?* Emmaus, Penn.: The Cornucopia Project of Rodale Press.

Robinson, Joan (1979). *Aspects of Development and Underdevelopment.* Cambridge: Cambridge University Press.

Semmel, Bernard (1970). *The Rise of Free Trade Imperialism.* Cambridge: Cambridge University Press.

Shanin, Theodor (1984). *Late Marx and the Russian Road: Marx and the "Peripheries of Capitalism."* New York: Monthly Review Press.

Sideri, S. (1970). *Trade and Power: Informal Colonialism in Anglo-Portuguese Relations.* Rotterdam: Rotterdam University Press.

Swaminathan, M.S. (1984). "Rice." *Scientific American,* CCL, No. 1, January, pp. 81-93.

United Nations (1982). *Statistical Yearbook.* New York: United Nations.

Wilson, Barry (1985). "International Setting for Seed Bank Struggle." *Western Producer,* November 14, p. 30.

World Bank (1984; 1983). *World Development Report.* Washington, D.C.: World Bank.

Yapa, Lakshman S. (1979). "Ecopolitical Economy of the Green Revolution." *Professional Geographer,* XXXI, No. 4, November, pp. 371-376.

Index

"Think Tanks," 45
Third World countries: *see* Underdeveloped
   countries
Thirlwell, A.P., 142
Thomas, Clive Y., 256, 273, 274
Tokyo Round, of trade negotiations, 139
Tonkin, 123
Torres, Camillo, 51
Total-factor productivity, 59
Toten, Suzanne C., 50
Townsend, Peter, 15
Trainer, F.E., 23
Transnational food corporations (TNCs),
   134, 143
Transnational Institute, 52
Treaty of Alcacovas, 107
Treaty of Nanking, 121
Treaty of Shimonoseki, 121
Trevelyan, Sir Charles, xiii
Triangular Trade, 91, 95
Tribe, D.E., 160, 239
"Trickle down" approach to economic
   development, 255
Trinidad/Tobago, undernourishment in, 10
Troughton, Michael, 130
Tunisia, food riots in, ix
Turner, Frederick Jackson, 67
"Two bourgeois rights," 280
Tyler, William G., 264

Underdeveloped countries
   alternate strategies, 312
   balance of payment problems, 303
   and commodity production, 134
   dependency on external trade, 311
   high rate of population growth, 310
   large service sector, 310
   and "late development," 311
   and plantation system, 133
   as producers of luxury foods, 143
   and slave labour under colonialism, 133
   state repression, 312
   underemployment in agriculture, 310
Undernutrition
   and anemia, 3-4, 8
   effects on children, 415
   genetic adaptation approach, 11
   and goitre, 3
   and immune system, 4
   individual adaptability model, 11
   measured by All-India Institute of Medical
      Sciences, 8-9
   measured by Harvard Reference Standard,
      8
   measured by Indian Council of Medical
      Research Standard, 8
   measured by U.S. National Center for
      Health Statistics, 8
   most evident in urban areas, 10

and persistence of poverty and inequality,
   13-15
and productivity, 4
UNICEF survey of Sri Lankan nutrition,
   254
United East India Company (VOC), 113-14
United Kingdom
   agricultural activity important for
      industrialization, 65
   capital investment in farming, 63
   colonial profits, 65
   Corn Laws, 63
   crop failures, 61
   Deanston system of drainage, 63-64
   drop in labour force, 62
   enclosures, 62, 64
   free trade, 66
   high labour productivity, 62
   Industrial Revolution, 60-61
   innovations in agriculture, 62
   landlord class, 63
   Norfolk four-field rotation, 62
   pauperization, 64
   prohibition of Indian cottons, 66
   poverty, 61
   proletarianization, 64
   slave trade as a source of capital, 63
   sources of capital for first
      industrialization, 65
   see also British, the
United National Party (UNP), 251
United Nations Conference on Trade and
   Development (UNCTAD), 264
United Nations Environment Programme
   (UNEP), 37, 166
United Nations Fund for World Population
   Activities, 210
United Nations World Food Conference
   (1974), 5, 29, 49, 215
United Nations Conference on
   Desertification, 190, 193, 199
Universal Soil Loss Equation (USLE), 187
United States, the
   aid to Taiwan, 262
   and Cuba, 288
   challenge to British industrial
      predominance, 98
   destruction in North Korea, 282
   and Nicaragua, 291-92
   relations with South Korea, 258
   seizes Philippines, 123
   support to Chinese Nationalists, 275
U.S. agriculture, 66-69
   British Navigation Act, 67
   climate, 66
   ecological conditions, 66
   "end of the frontier," 67
   human costs, 69
   labour force in agriculture, 66